John Timbs

School-Days of Eminent Men

From the London Edition

John Timbs

School-Days of Eminent Men
From the London Edition

ISBN/EAN: 9783337190170

Printed in Europe, USA, Canada, Australia, Japan

Cover: Foto ©ninafisch / pixelio.de

More available books at **www.hansebooks.com**

SCHOOL-DAYS

OF

EMINENT MEN.

I.

SKETCHES OF THE PROGRESS OF EDUCATION IN ENGLAND, FROM THE REIGN OF KING ALFRED TO THAT OF QUEEN VICTORIA.

II.

EARLY LIVES OF CELEBRATED BRITISH AUTHORS, PHILOSOPHERS AND POETS, INVENTORS AND DISCOVERERS, DIVINES, HEROES, STATESMEN AND LEGISLATORS.

BY

JOHN TIMBS, F.S.A.,

AUTHOR OF "CURIOSITIES OF LONDON," "THINGS NOT GENERALLY KNOWN," ETC.

FROM THE LONDON EDITION.

COLUMBUS:
FOLLETT, FOSTER AND COMPANY.
M DCCC LX.

*Printers, Stereotypers, Binders
and Publishers,*
COLUMBUS, OHIO.

TO THE READER.

To our admiration of true greatness naturally succeeds some curiosity as to the means by which such distinction has been attained. The subject of "the School-days of Eminent Persons," therefore, promises an abundance of striking incident, in the early buddings of genius, and formation of character, through which may be gained glimpses of many of the hidden thoughts and secret springs by which master-minds have moved the world.

The design of the present volume may be considered an ambitious one to be attempted within so limited a compass; but I felt the incontestible facility of producing a book brimful of noble examples of human action and well-directed energy, more especially as I proposed to gather my materials from among the records of a country whose cultivated people have advanced civilization far beyond the triumphs of any nation, ancient or modern. In other words, I resolved to restrict my design to BRITISH WORTHIES.

I had no sooner sketched the outline of my plan than the materials crowded upon me with an excess "whose very indices are not to be read over in an age." I then resolved to condense and select from the long line of Educated Worthies, rather than attempt to crowd the legion into a few hundred pages. Thus additional interest was gained; for the smaller the charmed circle of light, the more intensely will it point upon the reader.

The present volume is divided into two Sections. The first is historical as well as biographical: it sketches the PROGRESS OF EDUCATION, commencing with the dark age of our history, when knowledge was wrapt in the gloom and mysticism of the Druidical grove; and thence the narrative travels onward and upward to the universal teachings of the present time. In this section are portrayed the *Education of each Sovereign*, his early habits and tastes, which often exercised powerful influence upon the people. In each reign I have described the foundation of the great Schools, and sketched the Educational customs of the period. The teaching of its illustrious men is also incidentally recorded; and wherever such men have proved benefactors by the proposition or establishment of special Schools or Systems of Education, their lives and plans are narrated with fuller

To the Reader.

detail. How fraught with pious memories and hallowed associations are those great institutions of this great country—her Public Schools! How consecrated are their localities—how illuminated by the bright lights of centuries—whether around an ancient college nestling at the hill-foot—fit home for the tender young—as at Winchester; whether amid picturesque spires and towers, as in "the watery glade" of Eton; or in the kindred regal munificence of Christ's Hospital and Westminster—in the olden cloister and cell peopled with busy sons of learning, and earnest expounders of the Reformed Faith; or where citizenship and philanthropy have kept pace with kingly dispensation, raising within many a city, town, and hamlet, homes for the orphan and friendless—where the good seed might be sown, and the tiny child trained up in the way he should go.

Each of these foundations has its history, relics of its celebrated sons, and fond memorials of their worth. For centuries after the victory of Agincourt, were shown the rooms in which was reared Henry V. at Oxford; to this day, Dryden's autograph in wood is preserved at Westminster; and with each returning summer is renewed the leafy shade beneath which Addison loved to meditate at Magdalene.

Among the incidental varieties of this Section are the descriptions of the changes in manners and customs, the old usages and quaint forms, ceremonies and observances, of a more picturesque age than the present.

Nor, in journeying through these bye-ways of local history have I passed by those ancient seats of learning where the solemn church, the stately hall, and the embellished depositories of the wisdom of past ages, have been reared with pious feeling, and endowed by the gratitude of those who became, walking in the paths of duty and honor, rich in this world's wealth. How much of England's greatness has been nurtured in these magnificent seats of academic glory, and matured amidst the congenial repose of their groves and gardens!

The Second Section of the work is devoted to ANECDOTE BIOGRAPHIES, or sketches of the early lives—the School and College Days—of Eminent Men who, by their genius, learning, and character, have shed luster upon their name and country. In these brief memoirs I have recorded the incidents of their birth, boyhood, and education, until they have entered upon the world-wide field of action.

That by narrating the circumstances under which these Eminent Men have severally reached their excellence—that the number and variety of suggestive points in this volume may exercise a beneficial influence, and not only interest the reader, but induce him to emulate their examples,— is the sincere wish of   THE AUTHOR.

CONTENTS.

PROGRESS OF EDUCATION.

	PAGE
Education of the Early Britons	1
Schools of the Druids	2
The Roman-British Schools	3
Introduction of Writing	3
Education of the Clergy	4
Canterbury and other Monastic Schools in the Seventh Century	5
Rise of Anglo-Saxon Schools	6
The Schools of Alfred	7
St. Dunstan, the Scholar of Glastonbury	10
King Canute a Poet	11
The Earliest Books	11
The Saxon Language.—Formation of the English Language	12
Education of William the Conqueror	15
Lanfranc.—Ingulphus and the Schools of Croyland	15
William II.—Henry I.—Stephen	18
Henry II.—His love of Letters.—Sports of the London Scholars	19
Rise of Anglo-Norman Schools	21
Richard I., the Poet King	22
Church Schools.—Benefit of Clergy	22
Rise of Universities	23
Troubled Reign of King John	25
Henry III.—Settlement of the English Language	26
Roger Bacon an Educational Reformer	26
Edward II.—Schools in his Reign	27
Edward III.—His Accomplishments	28
Schools in the Age of Chaucer	29
Scholarship of Edward the Black Prince	30
Winchester College founded by William of Wykeham	31
Wickliffe Translates the Bible	33
Education of Richard II.—His Patronage of Gower	35
Henry IV.—His Accomplishments	36
Henry V. at Queen's College, Oxford	36
Early Parochial Schools.—Schools in Churches	38
Education at Home.—Music	39
Childhood and Youth of Henry VI	41
Henry VI. founds Eton College, and King's College, Cambridge	42
John Carpenter and the City of London School	47
Mercer's School.—The First Grammar School	48
Saint Paul's School founded	48
Edward IV. and his Tutors	50
Costliness of Manuscript Books	51

Contents.

	PAGE
Edward V. in Ludlow Castle	52
Introduction of Printing	53
Early Printed Books	53
Childhood and Education of Richard III	54
Troubled Boyhood of Henry VII	56
An Eminent Grammarian and Poet Laureate	59
Early Life and Character of Henry VIII	60
Ill-educated Nobility	61
The School of Sir Thomas More	62
Wolsey, Latimer, and Cranmer	64
Boyhood and Learning of Edward VI	65
Edward VI. founds Christ's Hospital	68
King Edward's Schools at Birmingham, Lichfield, Tunbridge and Bedford	72
Education and Reign of Queen Mary	75
Education of Queen Elizabeth	76
Roger Ascham—His "Schoolmaster"	77
Lady Jane Grey and her Schoolmaster	78
Sir Anthony Cook and his four Learned Daughters	79
A Truant punished in the 16th Century	80
Flogging in Schools	81
Westminster College School founded	81
A Poor Westminster Scholar	85
Merchant Taylors' School founded	86
Gresham College founded	88
Statesmen, Poets, and Dramatists of Elizabeth's Reign	88
Rugby School founded	90
Harrow School founded	93
Education of James I	95
Education of Prince Henry	97
Literature of the Reign of James I	99
Burton and Selden	100
Thomas Fuller's "Schoolmaster"	101
Charter-house School founded	102
Education of Charles I	104
Literature and Learning at the Accession of Charles I	106
A Good Education in the Seventeenth Century	108
Sir Matthew Hale's Plan of Instruction	109
Newspapers Introduced	110
Milton's System of Instruction	111
Locke's System of Education	113
Grammar-Schools in the Seventeenth Century	115
Influence of the Writings of Lord Bacon	115
The First Scientific Treatises in English	117
Invention of Logarithms.—Napier's Bones—Gunter's Scale	117
The Sciences at Oxford and Cambridge	118
Boyhood and Education of Oliver Cromwell	120
Charles II.—His Patronage of Letters	121
Nonconformist Schools at Islington and Newington Green	123
Boyhood of James II	124
Literature of the Seventeenth Century	125
Rise of Free Schools or Charity-Schools	126
Education of William III	130
The Reign of Queen Anne—The Augustan Age of Literature	132
Reigns of George I. and George II	134

Contents.

	PAGE
Education of George III	135
Sunday Schools established	138
The Monitorial System of Bell and Lancaster	139
The Primer and the Hornbook	140
Progress of Education in the Reigns of George IV. and William IV	144

ANECDOTE BIOGRAPHIES.

Early Fortunes of William of Wykeham	149
William Caxton, the First English Printer	150
Boyhood and Rise of Sir Thomas More	151
The Poets Wyatt and Surrey	152
Lord Burleigh at Cambridge	153
Camden's Schools	155
Sir Edward Coke's Legal Studies	156
Spenser at Cambridge	157
Richard Hooker at Heavitree	157
Sir Philip Sidney—" the English Petrarch "	158
Boyhood of Lord Bacon	160
The Admirable Crichton	161
How George Abbot, the Clothweaver's son, became Archbishop of Canterbury	163
Shakspeare at Stratford-on-Avon	164
Lord Herbert of Cherbury, in Shropshire	165
Admiral Blake at Bridgwater	166
Waller's Dullness	166
Dr. Busby, head-master of Westminster School	167
Lord Clarendon's Studies	169
Sir Matthew Hale's Early Life	170
Samuel Butler at Worcester	171
Jeremy Taylor at Cambridge	172
Cowley at Westminster	172
John Evelyn at Eton and Oxford	173
Marvell's Scholarship	175
John Aubrey in Wiltshire	175
The Hon. Robert Boyle, a true Patron and Cultivator of Science	176
John Bunyan, author of "The Pilgrim's Progress"	177
Isaac Barrow at the Charter-house	179
Dryden at Westminster and Oxford	180
Philip Henry at Westminster	182
Sir Christopher Wren at Westminster and Oxford	182
Dr. South at Westminster	184
Bishop Ken at Winchester	185
Sir Dudley North—How he made up for his Dullness at School	188
Newton at Grantham and Cambridge	190
William Penn at Oxford	192
The Great Duke of Marlborough at St. Paul's School	194
Matthew Prior at Westminster	195
Addison at Lichfield, Charter-house, and Oxford	196
Dr. Isaac Watts—His Schools and Educational Works	197
Pope's Schools and Self-tuition	198
John Gay at Barnstaple	202
How Edmund Stone taught himself Mathematics	202
John Wesley at the Charter-house and Oxford	203
Lord Mansfield at Westminster	206

Contents.

	PAGE
Lord Chatham at Eton and Oxford	207
Dr. Johnson at Lichfield, Stourbridge, and Oxford	207
How James Ferguson taught himself the Classics and Astronomy	212
Lord Camden at Eton and Cambridge	213
Shenstone's "Schoolmistress"	213
Gray at Eton and Cambridge	215
How Brindley taught himself the Rudiments of Mathematics	217
William Collins at Winchester and Oxford	218
Lord Clive—His Daring Boyhood	220
Captain Cook's Education on board Ship	221
John Hunter's Want of Education	222
Edmund Burke at Ballitore and Dublin	223
Cowper at Market-street and Westminster	226
Warren Hastings at Westminster	228
Gibbon, the Historian—His Schools and Plan of Study	229
Archdeacon Paley at Cambridge	230
Sir Joseph Banks at Eton	231
Sir William Jones at Harrow	232
How Dr. Parr became a Parson instead of a Surgeon	234
Lords Eldon and Stowell at Newcastle and Oxford	236
The Two Brothers Milner	238
How William Gifford became a Scholar and Critic	239
Lord Nelson's Schools in Norfolk	240
Robert Burns, "the Ayrshire Plowman"	243
Richard Porson, " the Norfolk Boy," at Happesburgh, Eton, and Cambridge	246
The Marquis Wellesley at Eton and Oxford	250
Lord Chief-Justice Tenterden at Canterbury and Oxford	252
How Robert Bloomfield wrote his " Farmer's Boy" in the heart of London	253
Precocity of Sir Thomas Lawrence	254
The Duke of Wellington's Schools	256
George Canning at Eton and Oxford	260
Sir Walter Scott—His Schools and Readings	262
Lord Hill, the Waterloo Hero	267
Coleridge at Christ's Hospital and Cambridge	269
Robert Southey at his Schools, and at Oxford	271
Charles Lamb at Christ's Hospital	274
Sir Humphry Davy at Penzance—His Schools and Self-education	277
George Stephenson, the Railway Engineer — His Schoolmasters and Self-tuition	281
(Note—James Watt)	283
Boyhood and Early Death of Henry Kirke White	285
Sir Robert Peel at Harrow and Oxford	288
Lord Byron at Aberdeen, Harrow, and Cambridge	290
Dr. Thomas Arnold at Winchester and Oxford	293
Sir Henry Havelock at the Charter-house	295
APPENDIX: University Honors — Tripos	301, 302
St. Paul's School founded	302

SCHOOL-DAYS OF EMINENT MEN.

Progress of Education.

EDUCATION OF THE EARLY BRITONS.

TO trace the modes of teaching which were practiced among a rude people inhabiting caves, or at best, houses built of stakes and wattles, in forest glades, has been an inquiry attended with slight results. Such a people inhabited Britain; and all that we can gather amid the glimmerings of the earliest history of its aborigines is, that skill in certain field sports, healthful pastimes, and domestic amusements, formed the only approach to education which the youth received from their parents. They knew not how to read—indeed, they held it dishonorable to learn—but they sung and danced to music, and learned hymns by heart.

The early British games consisted in lifting up great weights, running, leaping, swimming, wrestling, and riding; and it is supposed, charioteering, or the skillful driving and management of carriages. The other pastimes were playing with the sword, and buckler, and spear; coursing, fishing, and fowling; poetical composition; playing on, and singing to, the harp, etc.

Herodian mentions iron girdles as used by the Britons for keeping the bellies of the youth within its size: this they were also to effect by fasting, running, riding, and swimming; all which Giraldus mentions of the Welsh and Irish. We discover no traces of the use of letters among the Britons previous to their subjugation by the Romans, and their subsequent intercourse with that extraordinary people; for although alphabets have been produced and attributed to them, yet the display of these alphabets has been neither accompanied, nor their existence confirmed, by the exhibition of a single manuscript.

SCHOOLS OF THE DRUIDS.

The native place and stronghold of Druidism was Britain. The Druids were the Priests of the Ancient Britons; and the picture which Cæsar has drawn of the Druidical sacrifices of burning men alive in huge images of wickerwork, leaves upon childhood a terrific impression of their cruelties; whilst the existence of Stonehenge and other worship-temples attributed to the Druids, indicates the vast power of these "ministers of sacred things." But this was a power founded in the exclusive possession of knowledge. Accordingly, they were the depositories of whatever learning existed in the country; and they are stated to have had numerous schools, where they taught "many things respecting the stars and their motion, respecting the extent of the world and of our earth, respecting the nature of things, and respecting the power and the majesty of the immortal gods." These doctrines were supposed to have originated in Britain; and in Cæsar's time those Gauls who wished to study them, visited our island for that purpose.

The leading maxim which the Druids gave to *the people* was well calculated to maintain their power; for they taught that the fertility of the fields depended upon the riches of themselves. Amongst other rites, they cut the mistletoe, with a sickle of pure gold, upon the sixth day of the moon; and, in all probability, this is the origin of hanging the mistletoe in our houses at Christmas. The oak is also said to have been venerated amongst the Druids, and it is the figurative as well as the real monarch of our forests to this day; but, beyond a few particulars preserved by Greek and Roman writers, we know little or nothing concerning the tenets of the Druids. "Their doctrines," says Sir F. Palgrave, "were not reduced into writing, but preserved by oral tradition; and when the Druidical priesthood was extinguished, their lore was lost, excepting the few passages which may be collected from the compositions of the British Bards, and the proverbial *triads* (hymns) of the Cymri."

<small>The Druids were the only physicians, and blended some knowledge of natural medicines with the general superstitions by which they were characterized. Certain herbs formed the chief of their medicines. Their famous Mistletoe, or *all-heal*, was considered as a certain cure in many diseases, an antidote to poison, and a sure remedy against infection. (A nostrum called *Heal-all* is compounded at this day.) Another plant, called Samoclus, or Marchwort, which grew in damp places, was believed to preserve the health of swine and oxen, when it had been bruised and put in their water-troughs. But it was required to be gathered fasting, with the left hand, without looking back when it was being plucked. A kind of hedge hyssop called Selago, was esteemed to be a general charm and preservation from sudden accidents and misfortunes; and it was to be gathered with nearly the same ceremonies as the mistletoe. To these might be added Vervain, the herb Britannica, which was either the great water-dock or scurvy grass; and several other plants; the virtues of which, however, were greatly augmented by the rites in plucking them: superstitions not entirely out of use whilst the old herbals were regarded as books of medicine.</small>

THE ROMAN-BRITISH SCHOOLS.

The records of the state of Britain during the occupation of a portion of the country by the Romans for nearly four centuries and a half, afford but few glimpses of the education of the people. That the Romans erected schools and academies in our island, there can be little doubt. The remains of the engineering labors of this mighty people consist of massive walls and other military works, and frequently upon their roads we lay the railway of our times; we also find traces of curious art in the pavements of baths, the floors of mansions, and the fragments of temples rich in the false glories of Pagan worship: there is abundant evidence of luxury, and the iron hand of military rule; but the most speculative archæologist will search in vain for the remains of a Roman school. Yet, the Roman language was that of administration, and most probably that of judicial proceedings also; whilst all natives, or persons of mixed blood, who were allowed to aspire to any civil employment, must have learned the Roman language and laws. Agricola, in his second campaign, A.D. 79, overran the whole country, and induced many of the chiefs to allow their sons to receive a Roman education; so that they who had lately scorned to learn the language of their conquerors became fond of acquiring the Roman eloquence; but Tacitus says: "all this innovation was by the inexperienced styled politeness and humanity, when it was indeed part of their bondage." To the above period also belongs the first introduction of Christianity by St. Augustine, which necessarily was accompanied with a knowledge of the Greek language.

INTRODUCTION OF WRITING.

Writing is supposed to have been very little practiced in England before the mission of St. Augustine, A.D. 595; but after that time many Saxon manuscripts, chiefly on religious subjects, were executed on parchment, stained with rich colors, written in golden characters, and decorated with gilding and illuminations. Saxon Writing was of the five following kinds: 1. *Roman Saxon*, with *uncial* or initial letters, interspersed with smaller. 2. *Set Saxon*, with square or cornered capitals in the titles of books, and the first letters often in the shape of men and animals. 3. *Running-hand Saxon*, with numerous contractions, which render them difficult to be read. 4. *Mixed Saxon*, partly Roman, Lombardic, and Saxon. 5. *Elegant Saxon*, more beautiful than the contemporary writing of either France, Italy, or

Germany: it lasted until the Norman invasion, and was entirely disused before the twelfth century.

The Writing introduced by William I. is commonly called Norman, though the characters are nearly Lombard; and they were used in charters till the reign of Edward III., with very little variation. The hand called modern Gothic was introduced into England in the twelfth century, though it had been practiced in Germany about the close of the ninth. The Normans also brought into England the custom of using seals, bearing the impress of a knight on horseback; instead of the Anglo-Saxon custom of signing a deed.

EDUCATION OF THE CLERGY.

Reading and Writing (says Sir F. Palgrave), though no longer mysteries, as in the Pagan age, were still acquirements almost wholly confined to the clergy. Hence the word "Clericus," or "Clerk," became synonymous with penman, the sense in which it is still most usually employed. If a man could write or even read, his knowledge was considered as proof presumptive that he was in holy orders. If kings and great men had occasion to authenticate any document, they subscribed the *sign* of the Cross opposite to the place where the "Clerk" had written their name. Hence we say, to *sign* a deed or a letter. Illiterate people still make their signs or *marks*, in this manner (just as Offa used to do, by drawing a X), by the side whereof the lawyer's clerk adds their Christian and surnames.

The laity, or people who were not clerks, did not feel any urgent necessity for the use of letters. Commerce was carried on principally by truck or barter, or by payments in ready money; and sums were cast up, as among the Romans, upon an abacus, or accounting-table, the amount being denoted by *counters* or similar tokens. From the difficulty of communicating between place and place, common people had seldom any opportunity of conveying intelligence to absent friends. Many important transactions, which now require writing, could then be effected by word of mouth, or, as lawyers say, by *parole*. At the present day, if you wish to buy a horse, it is sufficient for you to pay the money to the owner: he delivers the horse to you, you ride him to the stable, and the bargain is completed. But if you wish to buy a field, a huge deed must be drawn by a solicitor, and engrossed upon a parchment, which is stamped— money being paid to Government for the same. This is called a *conveyance*. Now, in early times, the horse and the field might be *conveyed* with equal simplicity, and without any writing whatever. When land was sold, the owner cut a turf from the greensward, and cast it in the lap of the purchaser, as a token that the possession of the earth was transferred; or he tore off the branch of a tree, and put it in the hand of the grantee, to show that the latter was to be entitled to all the products of the soil. And when the purchaser of a house received *seizin*, or possession, the key of the door, or a bundle of thatch plucked from the roof, signified that the dwelling had been yielded up to him; the intent of these symbols being to supply the place of writing, by impressing the transaction upon the recollection of the witnesses who were called together upon the occasion.*

CANTERBURY AND OTHER MONASTIC SCHOOLS IN THE SEVENTH CENTURY.

One of the oldest schools of which anything is known, is the school of Canterbury, which is stated to have been probably established by St. Augustine. About a quarter of a century afterward, Sigebert, King of the East-Angles, is stated by Bede to have founded an institution for the instruction of youth of his dominions similar to those he had seen in France. At Canterbury, St. Augustine was succeeded by Archbishop Theodore, who, with his learned friend Adrian, delivered instructions to crowds of pupils, not only in divinity, but also in astronomy, medicine, arithmetic, and the Greek and Latin languages. This school certainly existed for a long time, and there is a record of a suit before the Archbishop of Canterbury, in 1321, between the rector of the grammar-schools of the city (supposed to be Theodore's school, or its representative) and the rector of St. Martin's, who kept a school in right of the church. This school, probably, existed till the Reformation; at least, the present King's School of Canterbury was established by Henry VIII., and probably on the ruins of the old school.

Schools now began to multiply in other parts, and were generally to be found in all the monasteries and at the bishops' seats. Of these episcopal and monastic schools, that founded by Bishop Benedict in his abbey at Wearmouth, where Bede was educated, and that which Archbishop Egbert established at York, where Alcuin studied, were the most famous. Alcuin, in a poem wherein he describes his own education at York, enumerates the studies there to have been, besides grammar, rhetoric, and poetry, "the harmony of the sky, the labor of the sun and moon, the five zones, the seven wandering planets; the laws, risings, and settings of the stars, and the aërial motions of the

* Sir F. Palgrave's History of England. Anglo-Saxon Period.

sea; earthquakes; the nature of man, cattle, birds, and wild beasts, with their various kind and forms; and the sacred Scriptures."

RISE OF ANGLO-SAXON SCHOOLS.

The Latinity which Agricola had so established in this island, as to make it rather a Roman than a British nation, had become almost extinct before the time of Alfred. Some native rays of intellectual light had, however, been shed upon Britain even before this dark period; and the literature of the Anglo-Saxons must be dated from their conversion to Christianity. When St. Augustine came into England, the Pope sent him several books, some of which are even now extant; and in the seventh century, a desire for learning began to inspire the Anglo-Saxons, when the King of East Anglia established in his dominions a school for the instruction of youth. The venerable Bede, "the Wise Saxon," who flourished in the eighth century, represents many persons as reading and studying the Scriptures. Egbert, Archbishop of York, in 712, had a library of the Fathers, and several of the ancient and later classics. What the value of such a collection must have been may be gathered from the fact, that many years afterward a Countess of Anjou gave 200 sheep, and a large parcel of rich furs, for a volume of Homilies. Egbert's library was burnt in 1067; but the catalogue was preserved by his pupil, Alcuinus. The wit and learning of the archbishop induced the Emperor Charlemagne (*who really could not write his own name*) to invite him to his court; and in one of his letters to this prince, Egbert solicits him to send the noble youth of France and Germany to be educated in the excellent schools of Britain.

For many centuries knowledge was confined to the clergy; although under this denomination were comprehended many who did not exercise the office of religious ministry. Among the Anglo-Saxons, we find children learning the psalms and some books by heart; and brought up religiously at home under their parents or masters, either in monasteries, or under bishops, who either made of them monks or clerks, or sent them, when young men, armed, to the King; and so minute are the accounts, that figs, grapes, nuts, almonds, apples, pears and money are specified as the school rewards.

Needle-work was at this early period an important branch of female education; and the English work was celebrated abroad for its excellence. An Anglo-Saxon lady usually embroidered upon a curtain some famous action of her husband's life. Maidservants used to work with their mistresses; and needle-work was practiced by men. The patterns of work were drawn in books, which, being cut to pieces, were used by women to work upon and transfer to their samplers. The working of flowers was particularly specified; and we find one kind practiced "in the manner of a vineyard."

THE SCHOOLS OF ALFRED.

Such was the state of knowledge in the reign of Alfred the Great—deemed in his time the wisest man in England. Although the son of a king, he was wholly uninstructed until he had reached the age of twelve years, when he was taught in hunting, building, and psalmody. Though he could not read, however, he listened day and night to the verses which were recited by minstrels and glee-men, the masters of Anglo-Saxon song; and a volume of Anglo-Saxon poetry shown to him by his mother, and which became his own as soon as he could read it, so encouraged his love of poetry that he contrived to compose verses at intervals throughout his busy life. The second volume which Alfred obtained was a selection of psalms and daily prayers according to the ancient usage of the church.

Alfred was born at Wantage, on the borders of the Vale of the White Horse, in Berkshire, in 849. As a royal seat, Wantage was, probably, a place of some consequence in the Saxon times; it is conjectured to have been a Roman station, and upon the site of a vallum of this period, the palace in which Alfred was born is supposed to have stood. The event of his birth has been commemorated in a manner worthy of its interest. Wantage had its grammar-school founded in the reign of Elizabeth: it fell into decay, but has been re-founded under the following circumstances. On the 8th of September, 1849, the thousandth anniversary of the birth of Alfred, that event was celebrated in the place of his birth. After divine service in Wantage Church, there were addresses and music in the Town-hall; a procession to "King Alfred's Well;" distribution of food to the poor of Wantage; an ox was roasted whole by the aid of the steam-engine; and a medal (believed to be the only one ever struck in honor of Alfred) was struck for this "Anglo-Saxon Jubilee." The commemoration took a more permanent form in the following year, 1850, when a fund having been raised in augmentation of the limited sum appropriated for the grammar-school since the reign of Elizabeth, there was laid the first stone of a new school building which has been completed. It is in the Pointed style of the thirteenth century, and accommodates seventy scholars, of which number thirty are boarders. Thus have the Governors of the Wantage Town Lands revived their grammar-school, and provided for the middle classes of their neighborhood a cheap and efficient course of instruction, embracing not only a rudimental acquaintance with the Latin language, but the addition of a sound modern education.

Alfred is related to have never been without a book in his bosom, in which volume he entered any memorable passage which occurred in conversation, until it was entirely full, after which a new book was made, by the advice of Asser, his tutor, and filled with diversified extracts on all subjects; this the King called his Hand-book. Asser wrote the life of Alfred, wherein is a passage which has given rise to a dispute as to the superior antiquity of the schools of Oxford and Cambridge. The authentic proofs of the latter do not extend beyond the seventh century; whilst the evidence of Asser shows that there were public schools at Oxford at least in the fifth or sixth century; but this evidence is questionable.

The harp at this period was a badge of rank, for, by the British law, a slave might not use it; and no one was esteemed a gentleman unless he possessed a harp, and could play upon it. Alfred's skill in this art led to one of his most brilliant victories. At Eddington, near Hungerford, in Berkshire, in the disguise of a harper, in 878, he visited the Danish camp, and obtained information which enabled him to surprise and entirely defeat the enemy.

We next find Alfred actively engaged in "the diffusion of knowledge" among his people. No Council or Board of Education in our time can have exceeded the zeal of our Anglo-Saxon sovereign of ten centuries since. Alfred addressed to the bishops a circular letter earnestly recommending the translation of "useful books into the language which we all understood; so that *all the youth of England*, but more especially those who are of gentle kind, and at ease in their circumstances, may be grounded in letters—for they cannot profit in any pursuit until they are well able to read English." Yet, gross was the ignorance of those days. "When I took the kingdom," says Alfred, "very few on this side of the Humber, very few beyond, not one that I could recollect south of the Thames, could understand their prayers in English, or could translate a letter from Latin into English." To supply this deficiency, Alfred employed such scholars as the time afforded; he himself acquired sufficient knowlege of Latin in his thirty-eighth year to translate the only book of Saxon history then extant; he translated other works of great learning, and attempted a complete version of the Bible, the finishing of which was prevented by his early death. He even enforced education by refusing to promote the uneducated, as well as by his own example. He insisted that the "ministers," or the persons whom he employed, should qualify themselves for their office; and in case of non-compliance he rejected them. Aldermen, and mayors, and governors, were compelled to go to school for this late instruction, to them a grievous penance, rather than give up their emoluments and office; and at an advanced period of his reign, Alfred, "the truth-teller," thanked God that those who sat in the chair of the instructor were then capable of teaching.

Alfred is believed to have re-established many of the old monastic and episcopal schools. Asser expressly states that he founded a seminary for sons of the nobility, to the support of which he devoted one-eighth part of his whole revenue. Hither even some noblemen repaired who had far outgrown their youth, but scarcely or not at all begun their acquaintance with books. This school was attended not only by the sons of almost all the nobility of the realm, but also by many of the inferior classes. It was provided with several masters; and this seminary is maintained by many antiquaries to have been the foundation of the University of Oxford.

Alfred's Schools were intended from the first for every person of rank or substance, who, either from age or want of capacity, was unable to learn or read himself, and who was compelled to send to school either his son or a kinsman, or if he had neither, a servant, that he might at least be read to by some one; for, that rank was no guarantee of learning, we have already seen; and Anglo-Saxon charters exist, which, instead of the names of kings, exhibit their marks, used, as it is frankly explained, in consequence of their ignorance of letters.

The means by which this patriotic King thus benefited his people are preserved to us. He usually divided his time into three equal portions: one was passed in sleep and recruiting his body by diet and exercise; another in the dispatch of business; a third in study and devotion; and that he might the more exactly measure the hours, he employed burning tapers of equal length; for, at this time, we must recollect clocks and watches were unknown. And by such a regular distribution of his time, though he suffered much by illness, Alfred, who fought in person fifty-six battles by sea and land, was able, during a life of no extraordinary length, to acquire more knowledge, and even to compose more books, than studious men, who, in more fortunate ages, have made literature their uninterrupted study. Translations of the Bible were multiplied through Alfred's assiduity; and from this, or the Anglo-Saxon age, down to that of Wickliffe (or, for nearly five centuries), we in England can show such a succession of versions of the Bible in metre, and in prose, as are not to be equaled amongst any other nation in Europe. Alfred is believed to have given a large estate for a single book on a learned subject; a bargain which may have given rise to the saying, "Learning is better than house and land."

Alfred's children, six in number, were taught Anglo-Saxon prose, poetry and psalms. Æthelweard, Alfred's youngest son, received a sort of public education: he was committed to proper teachers, with almost all the noble children of the province, and with many of inferior rank; they were all instructed in Latin and Saxon, and writing; and when their matured age gave the requisite strength, in gymnastics and archery,* as auxiliary to

---

* Roger Ascham (in his *Toxophilus*) supposes the English to have learned Archery from the Saxons; hence, by the ancient English laws, there is a more severe penalty for hurting the finger, which is necessary for letting the arrow fly, than for the maiming of any of the others. Barrington traces *Bow* to the German word *bogen*, and *Arrow* to the

warlike habits. Nor was Alfred's example lost upon his successors. Wolstan says of Ethelwold—"It was always delightful to him to teach children and youth, and to construe Latin books to them in English, and explain to them the rules of grammar and Latin versification."

ST. DUNSTAN, THE SCHOLAR OF GLASTONBURY.

About six miles from the ancient city of Wells, in Somersetshire, are the picturesque ruins of Glastonbury Abbey, once the richest abbey in the kingdom, and the most magnificent pile of Anglo-Norman ecclesiastical architecture. In the village hard by was born St. Dunstan, A.D. 925. His earliest instruction in the learning of his time he received in the monastery. The place was not then conventually regulated; and thither came chiefly from Ireland many illustrious men versed in sacred and secular science, and there opened schools, admitting the children of the nobility. Among these scholars was St. Dunstan. He applied himself to "the sciences of the philosophers" with uncommon ardor: thus he learned arithmetic, geometry, astronomy, and music. Like the prophet David, he would sometimes seize his psaltery, strike the harp, swell the organ, or touch the cymbal.

Upon quitting school, he passed a few years at the court of King Athelstan, when upon some affront, he returned to Glastonbury, and having in early youth received the tonsure there, he built himself a cell or hermitage, with an oratory, and in the intervals of his devotional austerities, employed himself in such manual arts as were useful to the service of the church—in the formation of crosses, vials, censers, vestments, etc.: he could paint, write a beautiful hand, carve figures, and work in gold, silver, brass, or iron; and after Alfred, the liberal arts were much indebted to his zeal: he was altogether one of the most memorable men of his time.

Apart from its interest as an ancient seat of learning, Glastonbury is one of the most hallowed spots in the kingdom; and as the wind sighs through its lone arches and hoary stones, you reflect that here lie the bodies of Joseph of Arimathea, King Edgar, and King Arthur; and numberless martyrs and bishops, and other men of mark. The building which now serves as the George Inn was in the monastic times an hospital for pilgrims to the shrine of St. Joseph. His chapel, and the monastery kitchen, remain.

Saxon *arepe*. Archery in war seems to have been disused immediately after the Norman Conquest, and to have been revived by the Crusaders: they had, doubtless, felt the effects of it from the Saracens, (who had probably derived it from the Parthians)—Edward I. was wounded by one of their arrows; and in this King's reign was formed a society called the Archers of Finsbury. The same society, having laid aside the bow and a.row, became subsequently the Artillery Company of the City of London.

KING CANUTE A POET.

Under the Danish dynasty, little seems to have been done for the promotion of letters, if we except the brilliant example of Canute. He was successful in war; and in peace, humane, gentle, and religious. He was a liberal patron of men of letters: he afforded the amplest encouragement to Scandinavian poetry, and Olenes names eight Danish poets who flourished at his Court. Sir Bulwer Lytton has an ingenious speculation upon the great influence which the poetry of the Danes has had upon our early national muse; and he has little doubt but that to its source may be traced the minstrelsy of our borders, and the Scottish Lowlands; while even in the central counties, the example and exertions of Canute must have had considerable effect upon the taste and spirit of our Scopec. Canute himself, too, was the author of a popular ballad, which long after his death remained a favorite with the people.

The verse that has been preserved of this song composed by Canute as he was one day rowing on the Nen, while the holy music came floating on the air, and along the water from the neighboring minster of Ely—a song which, we are told by the historian, continued to his day, after the lapse of a century and a half, to be a universally popular favorite—is very nearly such English as was written in the fourteenth century. This fragment is as follows:

> Merie sungen the munneches binnen Ely
> Tha Cnut Ching rew there by;
> Roweth, cnihtes, noer the land,
> And here we thes muneches saeng.

That is literally:

> Merrily (sweetly) sung the monks within Ely
> (When) that Canute king rowed thereby:
> Row, Knights, near the land,
> And hear we these monks' song.

Being in verse and in rhyme, it is probable that the words are reported in their original form; they cannot, at any rate, be much altered.—*Literature and Learning of England*. By G. L. Craik, M.A.

The Danes were, in general, the destroyers of learning at this period; nearly all the monasteries and schools connected with them throughout the kingdom being either actually laid in ashes by these Northern invaders, or deserted in the general terror and destruction occasioned by their attacks. Under Canute, who was a wise as well as a powerful sovereign, the schools destroyed during the Danish wars, no doubt, rose again and flourished.

THE EARLIEST BOOKS.

Staves, or rods of wood, appear to have preceded the introduction of school-books; for the Egyptian papyrus was rarely to be obtained in Europe, and parchment or vellum was too costly for ordinary use; so that a painstaking clerk could find it worth his while to erase the writing of an old manuscript in order to use the blank vellum for another writing. The only learned works were written in Latin, which was used in all documents relating to church affairs, but could only be acquired with great difficulty by the people. Copious dictionaries were then unknown; although there might have been a meager vocabulary, of which perhaps three or four copies existed in a whole kingdom; but a stock of words could only be acquired from a teacher, and by memory.

The studies of this period must have been greatly impeded by the scarcity and high price of books; although their multiplication went on much more rapidly than formerly. Few of the monasteries were without libraries of greater or less extent. A convent without a library, it used to be proverbially said, was like a castle without an armory. When the monastery of Croydon was burnt, in 1091, its library, according to Ingulphus, consisted of 900 volumes, of which 300 were very large. To these instances may be added that the founder of the Abbey of Wearmouth, about the end of the seventh century, collected a considerable library, at the cost not only of much money, but also of great exertion, he having made five journeys to Rome for the purchase of books and other items for the establishment. Bede records that the founder sold one of his volumes, a work on cosmography, to his sovereign, Alfred of Northumberland, for eight hides of land.

In every great abbey there was an apartment called the *Scriptorium*, where many writers were constantly buried in transcribing not only the service-books for the choir, but books for the library. "The Scriptorium of St. Alban's Abbey was built by Abbot Paulin, a Norman, who ordered many volumes to be written there, about the year 1009. Archbishop Lanfranc furnished the copies. Estates were often granted for the support of the Scriptorium. . . . . Some of the classics were written in the English monasteries very early. Henry, a Benedictine monk of Hyde Abbey, near Winchester, transcribed in the year 1178, Terence, Boethius, Suetonius, and Claudian. Of these he formed one book, illuminating the initials, and forming the brazen bosses of the cover with his own hands." The monks were accustomed both to illuminate and to bind books, as well as to transcribe them. "The scarcity of parchment undoubtedly prevented the transcription of many other books in these societies. About the year 1120, one Master Hugh, being appointed to the convent of St. Edmondsbury, in Suffolk, to write and illuminate a grand copy of the Bible for their library, could procure no parchment for this purpose in England." (*Warton's Introduction of Learning into England.*) Mr. Hallam supposes the deficiency to have been of skins beautiful enough for the purpose: it cannot be meant that there was no parchment for legal instruments. Paper made of cotton, however, was certainly in common use in the twelfth century, though no evidence exists that that manufactured from linen rags was known till about the middle of the thirteenth.

THE SAXON LANGUAGE.—FORMATION OF THE ENGLISH LANGUAGE.

The primitive character of the population of Britain having been effaced by its Roman occupation, its great masters were eventually overrun and conquered by the Teutons, whose three distinct tribes of the Low Germans—the Angles, the Saxons, and the Jutes—made themselves masters of our island. They naturally brought with them a change of language: the Teutonic superseded the Latin, one cause of which was that the population of Britain had been continually and largely increased by the immigration of German settlers, so that the German spirit was far more powerful than the Roman. The three different branches of Low Germans could understand one another with not much more difficulty than at the present day a Lancashire peasant would discourse with a Yorkshireman. There was, doubtless, a strong difference of dialect between the languages spoken by the Angles, the Saxons, and the Jutes, and these divisions were the foundation of the great classes of the modern dialects of England.

The Jutes, represented chiefly by the people of Kent, were the least numerous, and exercised no permanent literary influence upon the great Anglo-Saxon confederacy. It was the Angles, numerically by far the most powerful of the Teutonic settlers, who first took the lead in intelligence and in literature. To them chiefly belong the earliest literary productions of the Anglo-Saxons, and the oldest Anglo-Saxon traditions known; and their influence over the rest was so great, that not only did they accept from them the general title of *English*, but even the nations of the Continent who had generally preserved the Roman language, generally agreed in giving to the Teutonic population of Britain the name of *Angli*. Thus we derive from this one branch of the triple composition of our race, the national name of which we are proud, that of Englishmen, and it is from them that our language is called ENGLISH.

Nevertheless, the Anglian division of the race fell in the course of the eighth century under the superior influence of the Saxons, and Wessex, or the kingdom of the West Saxons, not only gave us finally our line of Kings, but furnished us with the model of our language and literature. The written English of the present day is founded upon that dialect in which King Alfred wrote; and with this change in the predominance of race, the term *Saxon* came into more frequent use to designate the Teutonic population of this island; and as there continued to be Saxons on the Continent as well as in England, it has become the practice to call our own ancestors, by way of distinction and not as indicating an amalgamation of race, the ANGLO-SAXONS, that is, the Saxons of England. Still, it must be borne in mind that our knowledge of the Anglo-Saxon language is, after all, imperfect; for our nomenclature is made up from written documents of a partial description, and there no doubt existed a great number of words in the Anglo-Saxon language which are now entirely lost. No doubt, many words now found in the English language, and especially in the provincial dialects, of which the origin is unknown, had their equivalents in pure Anglo-Saxon. This language was not influenced by the Danes; and that which our forefathers spoke in the middle of the eleventh century was the same Low German dialect which they had brought with them into the island, with certain changes of time and circumstances. At this period, the Norman Conquest brought a new language, French, as it was then talked and written in Normandy; and the resulting dialect, Anglo-Norman, continued during two centuries to be exclusively the language of the aristocracy of England. Meanwhile, the Anglo-Saxon, or as we must henceforward call it, the English tongue, was not abandoned or disused; for the Anglo-Saxon grammar of the Latin language by Alfric, continued to be used in the English schools till late in the twelfth century. To the first half of this century is ascribed a manuscript of Alfric's grammar, with an interlinear gloss of some of the Saxon words in Anglo-Norman. Hicks, the Anglo-Saxon scholar, had in his possession the above manuscript; and Sir Thomas Phillipps found among the archives of Worcester cathedral some leaves of a copy of Alfric's grammar, written in the degraded form of the Anglo-Saxon language which prevailed in the middle and latter half of the twelfth century. From various literary remains it is evident that the use of the English language, during the twelfth century, and the first half of the thirteenth, was by no means confined to the lower classes of society, but it prevailed generally among the middle and educated classes, among the clergy and in the monastic houses, at least those devoted to females.*

The English Language consists of about 38,000 words. This includes, of course, not only radical words, but all derivatives, except the preterites and participles of verbs; to which must be added some few terms, which, though set down in the dictionaries, are either obsolete, or have never ceased to be considered foreign. Of these, about 23,000, or nearly five-eighths, are of Anglo-Saxon origin.† The majority of the rest, in what proportions we cannot say, are Latin and Greek: Latin, however, has the larger share.

---

* Abridged from a very able Lecture on the History of the English Language, delivered before the Historic Society of Lancashire, by Thomas Wright, Esq., M.A., F.S.A., etc. See Transactions of the Historic Society, Vol. ix.
† Dr. Bosworth, the eminent Anglo-Saxon scholar, has published a work by King Alfred in the original Anglo Saxon and in an English version. The text is from two existing manuscript copies: the subject is a description of Europe, Asia, and Africa, with the voyages of Ohthere and Wulfstan.

EDUCATION OF WILLIAM THE CONQUEROR.

In the curious old town of Falaise, in Normandy, is shown a small house-front which exhibits a bust of WILLIAM THE CONQUEROR, whose name the house bears. But "the cradle of the Conqueror" is a small chamber in the thickness of the wall of the Norman ducal palace or castle at Falaise. "It was in this narrow room," says Miss Costello, "once said to have been adorned with gold and vermillion, and other gay hues, that a child was born in secresy and mystery, and that by the imperfect light his beautiful mother looked upon the features of the future hero of Normandy." That good fortune which never deserted William in after-life, shone upon his infancy. He soon became a favorite with his father, and was carefully nurtured and brought up in the castle, where princely attendance was lavished upon him, and up to his ninth year his father bestowed the utmost care upon his education. He was early inured to military exercise: at the age of five he is said to have commanded a battalion of children, at the head of which he went through the usual evolutions. At the age of nine he could already read and explain Cæsar's Commentaries: he was removed by his father to the French court, where his education was carefully completed with the aid of the first masters. At Paris, he was brought up with the young French princes, where he received instruction in the military schools; and he was surpassed by none of his youthful comrades in the varied accomplishments of feudal nobility, or in extensive reading and sound study of the military art. The intervals between his studies he spent either in field-sports, especially hawking and hunting, or in evolutions with the troops, of which he was remarkably fond. Sometimes also he would attend the envoys of the French King in their missions to surrounding courts and states, and thus became instructed in diplomacy. Meanwhile, he was temperate and active, and assiduously eager in the acquisition of fresh knowledge. Of William's genius there is ample record: the Norman writers praise him as a wise and pious King; the Chronicle of the Sea Kings of Norway describes him as "a very wise man, but not considered a man to be trusted;" and even the Saxon Chronicler, who had lived some time in his Court, says, "he was wise and rich, mild to good men, but beyond all measure severe to those who withstood his will."

LANFRANC—INGULPHUS AND THE SCHOOLS OF CROYLAND.

William the Conqueror patronized and loved letters. Many of the Norman prelates preferred in England by him were polite scholars. Herman, a bishop of Salisbury, founded a noble library in his cathedral. Godfrey, prior of St. Swithin's, at Winchester, was an elegant epigrammatist, and wrote with the smartness and ease of Martial. Geoffrey, another learned Norman, established a school at Dunstable, where he composed a play, which was acted by his scholars, dressed in character in copes borrowed from the neighboring abbey of St. Alban's.

One of the most learned men of this age was Lanfranc, a native of Lombardy, and born of a noble family. Having obtained the best education that the universities of Italy could afford, he practiced as a lawyer in his native city of Pavia. He next quitted the bar, passed the Alps, and settling in Normandy, opened a school in Avranches. He suddenly disappeared, and in three years was discovered in the small and poor monastery of Bec, where he had become a monk, and had risen to the office of prior. He then opened a school there, was quickly surrounded with scholars, while his fame as a teacher enriched the monastery. His natural arrogance and deep policy was shown in an incident which occurred on a visit made him by Bishop Herfast, with a numerous company of Duke William's courtiers. When they appeared in his lecture-room, he had the audacity to hand the bishop a spelling-book. This insult was resented: complaint was made to William, the farm of the monastery was burned, and Lanfranc was ordered to fly from Normandy. He mounted on a poor lame horse, rode to the Court, and told the Duke he was most willing to obey his orders, but that it was plain he could not with the animal on which he was mounted, and begged the favor of a good horse. William laughed heartily, took him into favor, and made him Abbot of St. Stephen, at Caen, where he established an academy. He accompanied William to England, and four years after the Conquest he was called to the See of Canterbury. It is reasonable to suppose that Lanfranc, who had done so much for Normandy, and whose literary fame was commensurate with Europe, established schools in England, and revived the love of letters; for we are told that, by incessant labors, "he roused the rude minds of many to good, rubbed away the rust of viciousness, extirpated the seeds of evil, and planted those of virtue." Speaking of the monks of his own time, the historian of Malmesbury says: "Their minds are still formed on the model of Lanfranc; his memory is dear to them; a warm devotion to God, to strangers a pleasing affability, still remain; nor shall ages see extinguished what in him was a benevolence of heart, comprising the human race, and felt by each one that approached him."

One of Lanfranc's admirers was Ingulphus, the Abbot of Croyland: he is remarkable as the first upon record who, having laid the foundation of his learning at Westminster, proceeded for its further cultivation to Oxford. He was born of English parents, and a native of the city of London. Whilst a school-boy at Westminster, he was so fortunate as to interest in his behalf Egitha, the daughter of Earl Godwin, and queen of Edward the Confessor—a young person of great beauty and learning, modest, and of a sweet disposition. "I have often seen her in my childhood," says the Abbot Ingulphus, "when I went to visit my father, who was employed in the King's palace. If she met me on my return from school, she interrogated me upon my grammar, poetry, or even logic, in which she was well versed; and when she had entangled me in the meshes of some subtle argument, she never failed to bestow upon me three or four crowns, by her servant, and to send me to have refreshment in the buttery." Egitha was mild and kind to all who approached her; those who disliked the somewhat savage pride of her father and brother, praised her for not resembling them, as is poetically expressed in a Latin verse, then much esteemed: "*Sicut spina rosam, genuit Godwinus Editham.*"—"As the thorn produces the rose, Godwin produces Editha."

"It is possible" (says the Rev. Mr. Tyler, in his *Henry of Monmouth*) "that many of our fair countrywomen, in the highest ranks now, are not aware that, more than 800 years ago, their fair and noble predecessors could play with a Westminster scholar in grammar, verses, and logic." Ingulphus tells how he made proficiency beyond many of his equals in mastering the doctrines of Aristotle, and covered himself to the very ankles in Cicero's Rhetoric!

In his History of the Abbey of Croyland, which he governed, he minutely describes its buildings, its various fortunes, possessions, and immunities, its treasures, its monks, its occupations, and its statutes. No distinct period seems to have been allotted to study; though it is related that, on one occasion, a present of forty large original volumes of divers doctrines, and of more than one hundred smaller copies of books of various subjects, was made to the common library. Sometimes also the names are mentioned of men said to have been "deeply versed in every branch of literature." In the story of the abbot Turketul, we read that as the convent was rich, he relieved the indigent, solaced the unhappy, and provided succor for all in distress. In the neighborhood, such children were educated as were designed for the monastic life. These the abbot visited once every day, watching, with parental solicitude, their progress in their several tasks; rewarding their diligence with such little presents (which a servant carried with him) as children love; and animating all by exhortation, or, when necessary, compelling them by chastisement, to the discharge of their duties.

Of Croyland Abbey, standing upon the south border of Lincolnshire, there remain considerable portions of its church, of Norman, Early English, and Perpendicular architecture; and, as the lover of our national antiquities stands upon the adjoining triangular bridge of the 14th century (supposed to have been designed as a symbol of the Holy Trinity), he may reflect that within the hallowed convent walls dwelt some of the earliest promoters of education; and as from these picturesque ruins over the neighboring fens the eye ranges, it may rest upon some nobly built churches, yet it would not unwillingly exchange the view of the monastic ruins for many an uninjured abiding home of the Reformed faith.

WILLIAM II.—HENRY I.—STEPHEN.

Of the education of WILLIAM II., the third son, and the successor of the Conqueror, we have few details. He was born about 1060, and was placed by his father under Lanfranc, who superintended his education, and conferred on the prince the honor of knighthood, agreeably to the manners of the time.

HENRY I., born in 1068, at Selby, in Yorkshire, the only son of the Conqueror who was an Englishman by birth, was surnamed *Beauclerc,* or the scholar, having received a more literary education than was then usually given either to the sons of kings or to laymen of any rank: this advantage was seconded by natural abilities of a superior order; and in his after-life, in the midst of his profligacy and unscrupulous ambition, Henry cherished a love of letters, and in his leisure was fond of the society of learned men.

The early years of instruction Henry passed in liberal arts, and so thoroughly imbibed the sweets of learning, that no warlike commotions, no pressure of business, could ever erase them from his noble mind; although he neither read much openly, nor displayed his attainments except sparingly. His learning, however, to speak the truth, though obtained by snatches, assisted him much in the science of governing; according to that saying of Plato, "Happy would be the commonwealth, if philosophers governed, or kings would be philosophers." Not slightly tinctured by philosophy, then, by degrees, in process of time, he learned how to restrain the people with lenity; nor did he ever suffer his soldiers to engage but where he saw a pressing emergency. In this manner, by learning, he trained his early years to the hope of the kingdom; and often in his father's hearing made use of the proverb, that "An illiterate king is a crowned ass." They relate, too, that his father, observing his disposition, never omitted any means of cherishing his lively prudence; and that once when he had been ill-used by one of his brothers, and was in tears, he spirited him up, by saying, "Weep not, my boy; you too will be a king."—*William of Malmesbury.*

Henry was sent by his father to the abbey of Abingdon, where he was initiated in the sciences under the care of the Abbot

Grymbald, and Farice, a physician of Oxford. Robert d'Oilly, constable of Oxford Castle, was ordered to pay for the board of the young prince in the convent, which the Conqueror himself frequently visited. Henry was also well educated in France: his talents were great, and under such a prince, pre-eminently entitled to be styled *Beauclerc*, the arts of peace prospered; the seminaries of learning were protected; teachers abounded; the convents furnished an undisturbed retreat to the studious; and, in short, letters were generally patronized and cultivated.

STEPHEN, born about 1096, was brought up at the court of his uncle, Henry I., and received many benefits from him.

HENRY THE SECOND, HIS LOVE OF LETTERS—SPORTS OF THE LONDON SCHOLARS.

Henry II., born at Mans, in Maine, in 1133, was brought to England in his tenth year, by his uncle, Robert Earl of Gloucester, who being distinguished for his scholarship and love of letters, superintended the education of the young prince, while he remained for five years shut up for safety in the strong castle of Bristol. From his excellent uncle Henry imbibed a greater degree of literary culture than was then usual among princes: his faculties received a learned training, and to the end of his days he preserved an attachment to literature and to the conversation of scholars, and he drew around him many of the chief lights of the time. His reign has, however, according to a very common but incorrect mode of speaking, been called a *Dark Age*; for an age cannot possibly be dark which had such men living in it as John of Salisbury, Peter of Blois, Thomas à Becket, and many others, especially historians, whose writings show the great extent of their reading and intellectual power. John was well acquainted with the Latin and Greek writers; he had some knowledge of Hebrew; he was skilled in the mathematics, natural philosophy, theology, and morals; he was an elegant orator and an eminent poet; and he was amiable and cheerful, innocent and good. His letters are delightful reading: his style was best adapted to this species of composition, and his correspondents were among the first personages of the age. Peter of Blois was invited by Henry into England, became his secretary, and enjoyed high ecclesiastical dignities: his writings are chiefly theological, but his letters are now alone read: like the letters of John of Salisbury they abound in quotations from Scripture, and from ecclesiastical and profane writers, but Peter's own writing is encumbered by forced antitheses and a constant play upon words. Thomas à Becket was born in London, and educated at Oxford, but was sent to France, while young, to lose the English accent, the hateful vulgarity of which would have rendered his association with respectable people impossible. He returned from his travels fully accomplished. Theobald, archbishop of Canterbury, made him his deacon, and the King made him his chancellor; he was also intrusted with the education of the King's eldest son, and he subsequently became archbishop of Canterbury.

From Fitzstephen's life-like description of London in this reign we obtain a picture of the hardy sports which then formed an important portion of the education of the people, as it did of the early Britons. To the north of the City were pasture-lands, with mill-streams; and beyond was an immense forest, with dense thickets, where stags, fallow-deer, and wild bulls had their coverts; and through this district the citizens, by the Charter of Henry I., had liberty to hunt. This great hunting-ground is now a surburb of the metropolis; and as the Londoner strolls over the picturesque locality of "Hamstead Heath," he may encounter many an aged thorn—the lingering indications of a forest—and in the beautiful domain of Caen Wood, he may carry his mind's-eye back to these Anglo-Norman sports of seven centuries since. Hawking was also among their free recreations. Football was their favorite game; the boys of the schools, and the various guilds of craftmen, having each their ball. In summer the youths exercised themselves in leaping, archery, wrestling, stone-throwing, slinging javelins, and fighting with bucklers. In winter, when "the great fen or moor" which washed the city walls on the north was frozen over, sliding, sledging, and skating were the sports of crowds, who had also their sham fights on the ice, which latter had their advantages; for, as Fitzstephen says, "Youth is an age eager for glory and desirous of victory, and so young men engage in counterfeit battles, that they may conduct themselves more valiantly in real ones." We are even told how the young Londoners, by placing the leg-bones of animals under their feet, and tying them around their ankles, by aid of an iron-shod pole, pushed themselves forward with great velocity along the ice of the frozen moor; and one of these *bone-skates*, found in digging Moorfields, may now be seen in the British Museum.

The Latinity of the writers during this reign was more pure than in many of the following ones. It has been presumed that the monks of these times were ignorant of classical learning, from Caxton speaking in one of his prefaces of Virgil's Æneis as a story then hardly known, and without any commendation of the poetry; but it appears by Fitzstephen that in the schools of his time, the scholars daily *torquent enthymemata*, an expression which shows that he was well versed in Juvenal. John of Salisbury was as well versed and as ready in citing the Latin classics as the men who have been most eminent for this knowledge in modern times. The Saxons also seem to have made a distinction between the Latin which was spoken by some of the clergy, and what was to be found in classical books.

RISE OF ANGLO-NORMAN SCHOOLS.

Schools and other seminaries of learning were zealously established in connection with the cathedrals and monasteries in all parts of the kingdom. In 1179 was ordered by the council of Lateran, that in every cathedral should be maintained a head teacher, or *sholastic*, as was the title given to him, who, besides keeping a school of his own, should have authority over all the other schoolmasters of the diocese, and the sole right of granting licences, without which no one would be entitled to teach ; and this office was filled in many cases by the most learned persons of the time. Besides the cathedral schools, there were others established in the religious houses ; and it is reckoned that of religious houses of all kinds there were found no fewer than five hundred and fifty-seven, between the Conquest and the death of King John: and besides these there still existed many others that had been found in the Saxon times. All these schools, however, appear to have been intended exclusively for the instruction of persons proposing to make the church their profession ; but mention is made of others established in many of the principal cities, and even in villages, which would seem to have been open to the community at large ; for the laity, though generally excluded from the benefits of learning, it is presumed were not left wholly without elementary education.

Fitzstephen has left the following animated picture of the disputations of the schools of London at this period :

On festival days, the masters assemble their pupils at those churches where the feast of the patron is solemnized, and there the scholars dispute, some in the demonstrative way, and others logically; some again write enthymemes, while others use the most perfect syllogism. Some, to show their abilities, engage in such disputation as is practiced among persons contending for victory alone; others dispute upon a truth, which is the grace of perfection. The sophisters, who argue upon feigned topics, are deemed clever according to their fluency of speech and command of language. Others endeavor to impose by false conclusions. Sometimes certain orators in their rhetorical harangues employ all the powers of persuasion, taking care to observe the precepts of the art, and to omit nothing opposite to the subject. The boys of the different schools wrangle with each other in verse, and contend about the principles of grammar, or the rules of the perfect and future tenses. There are some who in epigrams, rhymes, and verses, use that trivial raillery so much practiced amongst the ancients, frequently attacking their companions with Fescenine* license, but suppressing the names, discharging their scoffs and sarcasms against them, touching with Socratic wit the feelings of their school-fellows, or perhaps of greater personages, or biting them more freely with a Theonine† tooth. The audience,

Well disposed to laugh,
With curling nose double the quivering peals.‡

---

* Fescennina carmina, (derived from Fescenina, a town of Etruria,) rude jesting dialogue, in extempore verse, full of good-tempered raillery and coarse humor. — *Maclean's Notes on Horace.*

† From Theon, a malignant wit, and a poor freedman of Rome, in Horace's time.

‡ The last line is imitated from one of the Satires of Persius:
  " Ingeminant tremulos naso crispante cachinnos."—Sat. iii. v. 87.

The practice of school-training thus vividly described by Fitz-stephen in the twelfth century continued to the end of the sixteenth.

RICHARD I., THE POET KING.

Richard I., third son of Henry II, born at Oxford in 1157, lived much in the court of the princes of Provence, learned their language, and practiced their poetry, then called the *gaye science*, and the standard politeness of that age; it is recorded of him, that "he could skillfully make poetry on the eye of fair ladies."

<small>A new era of Anglo-Norman literature opens with the reign of Richard I. The lion-hearted king prided himself on his poetic talents; and he was the patron of jongleurs and trouveres, who were not properly minstrels; they did not recite their own works, but committed them to writing, which is the cause of their being preserved in early manuscripts. They were monks, and some of them appear to have embraced the monastic life after having been professed poets, and to have made atonements for the profane productions of their earlier years, by dedicating their talents to sacred subjects.—*Wright's Biographia Britannica Literaria*.</small>

Richard, the earliest recorded writer of French verse—although nothing of his poetry remains except the fame, preserved in the writing of another Trouvère of the next age—was sent by his father to be educated at Bayeux; and his taste for poetry is said to have been first awakened by the songs of the land of his ancestors. According to Ritson, Richard is never known to have uttered a single English word, unless when he said of the King of Cyprus, "O dole, this is a fole Breton." Many great nobles of this century were utterly ignorant of the English language: even Longchamp, Bishop of Ely, chancellor and prime minister to Richard I., according to a contemporary letter, did not know a word of English.

CHURCH SCHOOLS.—BENEFIT OF CLERGY.

At the close of Richard's reign, about the year 1198, there was founded at Bury St. Edmund's a school for forty poor boys, by Sampson, Abbot of St. Edmund's, a man of great force of character, who had risen from the people to wear a miter and be a Peer of Parliament; and in his greatness he did not forget his lowly origin, for he is recorded to have said to one suing him for a benefice, "Thy father was master of the schools, and at the time when I was a poor clerk, he granted me freely and in charity an entrance to his school and the means of learning; now I, for the sake of God, do grant to thee what thou dost ask."

The same good work which Abbot Sampson accomplished at Bury was being accomplished throughout the land for several centuries before him, and several centuries after him, so that knowledge became the special inheritance, not of the high-born and the rich, but of those of low estate. It is true that for the most part those who were educated in the chantries and schools attached to cathedrals and monasteries were the recruits whom the Church was preparing for her militant service. But they were taken from the people, and they lived amongst the people, keeping alive in the hearts of the community the humanizing influences of letters and of religion. Few of the laity, rich or poor, could read; but the poor saw their children winning the rewards of learning without favor or affection; and the light of truth, though mingled with error, spread from the altar to the meanest hovel, and kept our fathers from barbarism. The old law called *Benefit of Clergy* shows how gradually the ability to read extended to the clergy. In the early times clergymen claimed the privilege of being exempt in certain cases from criminal punishment by secular judges. They appeared in clerical habit, and claimed the *privilegium clericale.* At length, the *ability to read* was considered sufficient to establish the privilege, and all offenders who claimed their " clergy " had to read a passage from the Psalms, which came to be humorously called " the neck verse." This was no merely theoretical privilege, for the *ability to read,* absurd as it may appear, saved an offender in the first instance from the full penalty of his crime. In the *Paston Letters* it is recorded that in 1464, Thomas Gurney employed his man to slay "my Lord of Norwich's cousin." They were both tried and convicted of the crime. Thomas Gurney pleaded his clergy, and was admitted to mercy as " clerk convict;" the less guilty servant, being unable to read, was hanged. But the rank of Thomas Gurney gave no assurance that he possessed any knowledge of letters.

RISE OF UNIVERSITIES.

The twelfth century was the age of the institution of what we now call Universities in Europe, which had, however, long before existed as schools, or *studia.* Oxford and Cambridge had undoubtedly been seats of learning long before this time; but there is no evidence that either had at an earlier date become anything more than a great school, or held any assigned rank or privilege above the other great schools of the kingdom.

Since the Conquest, OXFORD, ill treated by William, and disregarded by his son Rufus, under Beauclerc again became the object of royal favor, and numbers flocked to her academic groves. The predilection of Beauclerc for the muses made him partial to the neighborhood; and he granted some privileges to the place. In his time, Robert Pulleyn, who had studied in Paris, gave lectures in theology at Oxford; and by his exertions the love of science was greatly revived, and the number of students increased. Here the study of the civil law began at this period. Oxford continued, throughout the reign of Henry II., to follow the line of studies which the fashion of the age recommended; and her pupils were second to none in fortune and fame. Thomas à Becket, who had studied at Bologna, disdained not to receive academical honors at Oxford, as honors were then conferred; and after his promotion to the highest dignities in church and state, he attested, on all occasions, his kind remembrance of the favors which he had received. Richard I., who was born at Oxford, is stated to have patronized and fostered the University. To this statement, however, Berington demurs, and asks: "Because Richard's father often resided at Woodstock, and sometimes visited the monks at Abingdon, can it be thought that the love of letters attracted him to the spot, as on grounds not more substantial it is said of Beauclerc, who was probably impelled by the joys of the chase to the woods of Cumner and Bagley?"

CAMBRIDGE, which, from the ravages of the Danes, and the insults of the first Normans, had long lain in obscurity and neglect, revived about the year 1109, when Joffrid, Abbot of Croyland, intending to rebuild his monastery, which had been lately destroyed by fire, sent Master Gislebert, with three other monks, to his manor of Cottenham, whence they went every day to Cambridge, where, having *hired a barn*, they gave public lectures, and soon collected a great concourse of scholars; for in the second year after their arrival, the number of their scholars from the town and country increased so much that there was no house, barn, nor church capable of containing them. They accordingly dispersed over different quarters of the town: brother Odo read grammar early in the morning, to the boys and younger students; at one o'clock, brother Terricus read Aristotle's Logic to the elder class; at three, brother William gave lectures on Tully's Rhetoric and Quintilian's Institution; while Master Gislebert, not understanding English, but very ready in the Latin and French languages, preached in the several churches to the people on Sundays and holidays. "Thus, from this small source, which has swollen into a great river, we now behold the city of God made glad, and all England rendered fruitful by many teachers and doctors issuing from Cambridge as from a most holy paradise." But a few years after this was written, during the war between King John and his barons, this paradise was entered and plundered by both parties.

Antony à Wood has preserved a few Latin verses by an English student at Paris, written in 1170, which well describe the spirit of display and love of expense for which his countrymen were already noted. The translation is as follows:

> Of noble manners, gracious look and speech,
> Strong sense, with genius brightened, shines in each.
> Their free hand still rains largess; when they dine,
> Course follows course, in rivers flows the wine.

The erection of Colleges in the Universities for the residence of their members, as separate communities, may be dated from about the middle of the thirteenth century.

University College is the *foundation* of King Alfred; but the present building is not of a date earlier than Charles I. The right of the crown to the visitation of the college rests, however, on the ground that it is a royal foundation through Alfred; a claim which was preferred in favor of the royal prerogative in the Court of King's Bench, so lately as the year 1726. The University of Oxford is not much indebted to the kings of England for their munificence and benefations, if we except Alfred.

From the Roll of the Household Expenses of Swinfield, Bishop of Hereford, in 1289, we find that the expenses of two students who were maintained by the Bishop at the University of Oxford, and their incidental charges, amounted to half a mark a week—a considerable sum, if valued by the comparative value of money in these times. "Six shillings and eightpence weekly for two scholars was a sum probably not far short of three hundred pounds a year of our own times. It is pleasant to know, from this record, that the great men of those days had an affectionate regard for youths of promise, and by giving them the best education opened their way to positions of public usefulness."—*Knight's Popular History of England.*

TROUBLED REIGN OF KING JOHN.

John, the youngest son of Henry II., was born at Oxford in 1166; but of his education we have no record of interest.

John has had no historian; so that we possess but little information of his personal character. He appears to have shown little taste for letters or for any other refined pursuits. But, however hated by other classes, John seems to have been attached to, and a personal favorite with, the seafaring people, much of his time in each year being ordinarily spent on the coast, as appears from the Close and Patent Rolls: hence, probably, arose the story by Matthew Paris, now known to be incorrect, that John, immediately after the granting of Magna Charta, retired to the Isle of Wight, and there passed his time in familiar association with mariners and fishermen.

Under this troubled reign, Latin poetry flourished most: it became extremely popular, and continued to exist in its original vigor long after the style of the most serious Latin poets became hopelessly debased. Very little Latin prose that is tolerable, was written after the middle of the thirteenth century.

HENRY III.—SETTLEMENT OF THE ENGLISH LANGUAGE.

Henry III., surnamed of Winchester, from the place of his birth, was the eldest son of King John, and was born in 1206: he succeeded to the throne in his tenth year, his education being, in all probability, superintended by his guardian, William, Earl of Pembroke, who acted as Protector of the Kingdom.

With the thirteenth century, the English language began to be cultivated; and about the commencement of the fourteenth century, our language had undergone the great change through the introduction of Norman words. Many French and Latin words have, indeed, been introduced in later ages, but by learning or caprice, rather than by the convenience of familiar intercourse.

An able critic in the *North British Review* thus describes this important epoch in the literature of our country:

An immense distance continued to exist between the Normans and the English people even so late as the early part of the fourteenth century. A Poitevin, who was prime minister in the time of Henry III., being asked to observe the great charter and the laws of the land, answered—"I am no *Englishman* that I should know these charters and these laws." Robert Grosse-tete, bishop of Lincoln, principal chaplain to the army of the barons, then reckoned only two languages in England, Latin for men of letters, and French for the uneducated, in which language he himself in his old age wrote pious books for the use of the laity, making no account of the English language, or of those who spoke it. The poets, even those of English birth, composed their verses in French; but there was a class of ballad-makers and romance-writers who employed either pure Saxon, which was now revived, or a dialect mixed up of Saxon and French, which served for the habitual communication between the higher and lower classes. This was the origin of our present language, which arose out of the necessities of society. In order to be understood by the people, the Normans *Saxonized* their speech as well as they could; and on the other hand, in order to be understood by the upper classes, the people *Normanized* theirs. This intermediate idiom first became current in the cities, where the population of the two races had become more intermingled, and where the inequality of conditions was less marked than in the rural districts.*

About the middle of the fourteenth century, a great many poetical and imaginative works appeared in this new language. At length, the French language was entirely laid aside, not only in the courts of justice but also in the high court of Parliament, as well as by all the writers who addressed themselves to the middle classes and the lower populations. We still indeed retain a venerable relic of the old Norman, in the custom of giving the royal assent in that language: the formula is—*Le Roy le veult—le Roy s'avisera*—not even, we believe, modernizing the orthography.

ROGER BACON, AN EDUCATIONAL REFORMER.

At this early period (about the middle of the thirteenth century), there appeared a sagacious advocate of reform in education, reading, and reasoning, in Roger Bacon, who was born at Ilchester, in Somersetshire, near the year 1214. Till nearly the middle of the last century, the vulgar notion of him was that of the learned monk searching for the philosopher's stone in his laboratory, aided only by infernal spirits. He was accused of practicing witchcraft, thrown into prison, and nearly starved; and, according to some, he stood a chance of being burned as

* This differs from the view taken by another able writer, quoted at pp. 12-14.

a magician. He was educated at Oxford, and next proceeded to Paris, then the first university in the world. Returning to Oxford, he applied himself closely to the study of languages and experimental philosophy; but the lectures which he gave in the University were soon prohibited, and he was accused of magic, a charge then frequently brought against those who studied the sciences, and particularly chemistry. The following detached passages of his *Opus Majus* no doubt contains opinions which its author was in the habit of expressing:

Most students have no worthy exercise for their heads, and therefore languish and stupefy upon bad translations, which lose them both time and money. Appearances alone rule them, and they care not what they know, but what they are thought to know by a senseless multitude. There are four principal stumbling blocks in the way of arriving at knowledge—authority, habit, appearances as they present themselves to the vulgar eye, and concealment of ignorance combined with ostentation of knowledge. Even if the first three could be got over by some great effort of reason, the fourth remains ready.—Men presume to teach before they have learnt, and fall into so many errors, that the idle think themselves happy in comparison—and hence, both in science and in common life, we see a thousand falsehoods for one truth.—And this being the case, we must not stick to what we heard read, but must examine most strictly the opinions of our ancestors, that we may add what is lacking, and correct what is erroneous, but with all modesty and allowance.—We must, with all our strength, prefer reason to custom, and the opinions of the wise and good to the perceptions of the vulgar; and we must not use the triple argument: that is to say, this has been laid down, this has been usual, this has been common, therefore it is to be held by. For the very opposite conclusion does much better follow than the premises. And though the whole world be possessed by the causes of error, let us freely bear opinions contrary to established usage.

The *Opus Majus* begins with a book on the necessity of advancing knowledge, and a dissertation on the use of philosophy in theology. It is followed by books on the utility of grammar and mathematics;* in the latter of which the author runs through the various sciences of astronomy, chronology, geography, and music. Bacon was also long reputed to have been acquainted with gunpowder and the telescope; but the former is proved to have been known centuries before his time; and though he discovered optic lenses, he was not acquainted with the principle of the telescope.

EDWARD II.—SCHOLARS IN HIS REIGN.

Edward II., the eldest surviving son of Edward I., born at Carnarvon, in 1284, at the age of seven years lost his excellent mother, Eleanor of Castile, who would probably have guided his education better than his less stern father. He was of a kindly nature, of impulsive character and passionate will, though not wanting in courage; for at seventeen he led a battalion against the Scots.

* Bacon said of those who applied themselves to the study of mathematics in his time, most stopped at the fifth proposition of Euclid. Hence this proposition used to be called the *Pons Assininus*, or *Asinorum*, or *Asses' Bridge*, a name by which it is still known.

Among the most distinguished names in literature and science that belong to the reign of Edward I., is Duns Scotus, a Franciscan friar, educated in a convent of that Order at Newcastle. He became a Fellow of Merton College, Oxford, and professor of theology in the University, his great fame causing incredible numbers to attend his lectures. Although he died at the early age of forty-three, "he wrote so many books that one man is hardly able to read them." In his day he was accounted "the Subtle Doctor;" but his learning was only in the Divinity of Schoolmen, far removed from the sound and useful learning which enables the scholar to discover the truth, and to impart the knowledge of it to others. Scotus having dared to controvert some positions of Thomas Aquinas, who was deemed the oracle of the Schools, he became the founder of a new sect in philosopy, and revived, with inextinguishable ardor, the old disputes between the *Realists* and the *Nominalists*. The Greeks and Persians, it has been observed, never fought against each other with more fury and rancor than these two discordant sects. Oxford was a grand theater of their contests. Though much poetry now began to be written, the name of only one English poet has descended to posterity: Adam Davy or Davie, the author of various poems of a religious cast, which have never been printed. There is still extant a curious Latin poem on the battle of Bannockburn, written in rhyming hexameters, by Robert Baston, a Carmelite friar, whom Edward carried along with him to celebrate his anticipated victory; but who being taken prisoner, was compelled by the Scotch to sing the defeat of his countrymen in this jingling effusion. Bale speaks of this Baston as a writer of tragedies and comedies, some English; but none of them are now known to exist.

EDWARD III.—HIS ACCOMPLISHMENTS.

Edward III., the eldest son of Edward II., was born at Windsor in 1312. Joshua Barnes, in his Life of this renowned king, a closely-printed folio volume of 900 pages, gives the following "small taste" of his character:

From his Birth he was carefully bred up to all things that seemed necessary or proper for Princes to excel in; so that, through the Vigor of his Parts, being rendered very apt to imbibe the best Principles, he made a speedy and extraordinary improvement in all Noble Qualities;for he was of a very piercing Judgment, Sweet Nature and Good Discretion, and considering the many weighty affairs that employed his whole Life, not only kind to the Muses, but much befriended by them, as appears by those Learned Writings of which *Pitsons* says he was the Author. When he was capable of receiving more ingenious Education, a Man of Great Reading, Erudition and Honor, was provided from Oxford to be his Tutor, who though commonly called *Richard Bury*,[*] from the place of his Birth, was indeed Son to one *S. Richard Aungervile*, Knight, but was afterward by this his Royal Pupil, made Privy Seal and Treasurer of England, then Dean of *Wells*, Lord Chancellor of *England* and Bishop of *Durham*.

* From a passage in Richard of Bury it might be inferred that about 1343, none but ecclesiastics could read at all. He deprecates the putting of books into the hands of

Edward was proclaimed king when in his fifteenth year, and in a few months marched at the head of a large army against the Scotch; so that his boyhood presented few opportunities for his intellectual culture; but the glories of his reign of fifty years gave "a more vigorous activity to the faculties of England." This was the golden age of chivalry, of architecture, and of costume; and in literature the age of Chaucer—his tales being read alike in the baronial hall and the student's chamber. The universities were filled with scholars. From the Anglo-Norman had finally been involved that noble tongue upon which our literature has been built, though many books perfectly intelligible to us were written before this reign. In 1307, Sir John Mandeville wrote a narrative of his Travels in English, as well as in French and Latin; and Wickliffe, the great Reformer, delivered his earliest appeals to the people on questions of religion in English.

SCHOOLS IN THE AGE OF CHAUCER.

Chaucer, traditionally born in 1328, of a wealthy and respectable family, received the education of a gentleman; he is believed to have studied both at Cambridge and Oxford; he was well acquainted with divinity and philosophy, and the scholastic learning of his age, and displays in numerous passages an intimate knowledge of astronomy, and most of the sciences as far as they were then known or cultivated. " Chaucer's language," says Mr. Bell, " is that of the good society in which he lived, and into which a large accession of Norman blood, usages, and idioms, had been infused."* Heretofore, Norman-French had been the language of education, of the court, and of legal documents; and when the Normanized Anglo-Saxon was employed by literary men, it was for the special purpose, as they were usually very careful to mention, of conveying instruction to the common people. But now the distinction between the conquering Normans and subjected Anglo-Saxons was nearly lost in a new and fraternal national feeling, which recognized the country under the name of *England*, and the people and language under the simple appellation of *English*. Scriveners at this time were chiefly employed in copying books. Chaucer thus addresses his scrivener:

 Adam Scrivener, yf ever it the befalle
 Boice or Troilos for to write newe,
 Under thy long locks thou mayst have the scalle,

---

laici (laymen), who do not know one side from another; and in several places, it seems that he thought books were meant for the " tonsured alone." But a great change took place in the ensuing half century; and he can be scarcely construed strictly even as to his own time.

* Annotated Edition of the English Poets: Life of Chaucer.

But after my making thou write more true;
So after a day I more thy werke renewe,
It to correcte, and eke to rubbe and scrape,
And al is thorow thy negligence and rape.

Such was the affectation for speaking French in this reign, that it became a proverb — "Jack would be a gentleman, if he could speak French." It was, however, often very corrupt, in allusion to which Chaucer says in the *Prologue to the Prioress's Tale*:

"And French she spak ful fayre and fety saly
After the schoole of Stratford at the Bow,
For French ol Paris was to her unknowe."

It was, nevertheless, so necessary, that Robert of Eglesfield, who founded Queen's College in Oxford, directed by his statutes that the scholars should speak either French or Latin.

Female education at this period consisted in needle-work (especially) and reading. Boccacio describes a wife as "young and beautiful in her person; mistress of her needle; no man-servant waiting better at her master's table; skilled in horsemanship and the management of a hawk; no merchant better versed in accounts." Chaucer mentions reading and singing as the education of little children.

SCHOLARSHIP OF EDWARD THE BLACK PRINCE.

Edward the Black Prince, the eldest son of Edward III., was born at Woodstock in 1330:

Nursed at the bosom of his mother (Queen Phillippa), he ho received health and strength from the same pure blood that had given him existence; the gentle impress of her own sweet mind fixed upon her child, dur ng his early education, those kindly virtues which tempered in his nature the fierceness of his father's courage. Never, perhaps, in the world's history, do we find so strong an example of the qualities possessed by both parents being blended in the child, as in the case of the Black Prince, in whose heart the generous and feeling nature of Phillippa elevated rather than depressed the indomitable valor and keen sagacity of Edward III.—*James's Life of the Black Prince.*

Holinshed tells us that Phillippa herself selected for the Prince's tutor a person of whose talents and virtues she had possessed the opportunity of judging; this was Doctor Walter Burleigh, a well-known scholar of Merton College, Oxford, who had been appointed almoner to the Queen, and had remained from that time attached to her household. Simon Burleigh, "a near kinsman of the Doctor's (says Barnes), was admitted, with other young gentlemen, to be school-fellows with this noble Prince." Before the Prince was seven years of age he was girded by his father with a sword, and saluted the first English Duke; and immediately, in exercise of his new dignity, he dubbed twenty knights. In his thirteenth year he entered upon the chivalrous training of the time, which, by inuring the body to fatigue, and the limbs to the continual use of arms, gave skill and great power of endurance to his active and robust figure. In 1343, he was created Prince of Wales, upon which the knightly feast of the Round Table was appointed to be held in an ample theater near Windsor Castle; at the age of sixteen, the Black Prince led an army to the field of battle, and in a few years grew to be "the flower of all chivalry in the world."

WINCHESTER COLLEGE FOUNDED BY WILLIAM OF WYKEHAM.

In the reign of Edward III. lived the celebrated William of Wykeham, who was born at the village of Wykeham, in Hampshire, in 1324. By the liberality of Sir Nicholas Uvedale, governor of Winchester Castle, the boy Wykeham was sent to "the Great Grammar-school in Winchester," originally an institution for education founded before the Conquest. Uvedale next presented Wykeham to Edward III. for his skill in architecture. In the short space of four years he was promoted through civil and ecclesiastical grades, to be Bishop of Winchester and Lord High Chancellor of these realms. He had already commenced the building of New College at Oxford; and in the following year, with the view of taking the early education of youth out of the hands of the monks, "it was his admirable thought to raise a nursery school preparatory to his coöperating with a higher course in his college; and thus to raise the standard of education in the country, to that stamp and character which has ever since (through his institution and the copies which were drawn from it) distinguished the English gentlemen amongst the families of Europe."* Thus arose Winchester College, the scholars of which are designated to this day *Wykehamists*. The novelty and merit of the plan were imitated by Chicheley, at All Souls, Oxford; Henry VI. at Cambridge; and Waynflete at Magdalene. "Twenty years before his hives were built (1373), Wykeham had gathered his swarming bees under temporary roofs, with masters and statutes: which with parental solicitude he watched, altered, and amended from time to time, by his daily experience. So long before his colleges were built was his institution effective." Wykeham died in 1404, at the age of eighty years, with the respect and admiration and gratitude of all; and like the spirit which he had ever sought throughout his amiable life, "length of days were in his right hand, and in his left riches and honor." He is buried in Winchester Cathedral: "beneath the spot where the school-boy prayed, the honored prelate sleeps."—*Walcott.*

* C. R. Cockerell, R.A.—Chicheley was a Wykehamist: as was apparently Waynflete, who certainly was master of Wykeham's school in 1429.

Wykeham's College buildings stand immediately adjoining the main street of Winchester, a city of kindred quiet. The Middle Gate Tower has under three canopied niches, the Angelic Salutation, and the Founder in prayer. The gateway leads to a truly noble quadrangle of Wykeham's architecture. On the left side is the dining-hall, with an oaken roof finely carved with the busts of kings and prelates; and in the center is a louver, through which the smoke ascended in olden times, when the scholars gathered round the hearth to sing and listen to the tales of the chroniclers. Here also plays were acted in the days of the Tudors; the boy-bishop custom was observed as at Eton; and monarchs, prelates, and nobles have been feasted. On the south side of the quadrangle is the chapel, with an oaken roof of fan tracery; the large window, forty feet in height, is filled with painted glass, as are also the side windows. Next are the cloisters, surrounding an area, in the centre of which is the former chapel, now the library. Beyond is the Public School; it was built in 1687, chiefly by subscription among the Wykehamists, and is the noblest structure of the kind in the kingdom. Upon the walls are inscribed in Latin the admonitions and rules for the government of the scholars; on the west wall are painted upon a large tablet, a miter and crozier, the rewards of clerical learning; a pen and inkhorn and a sword, the ensigns of the civil and military professions; and a Winton rod, the dullard's quickener; beneath each symbol is its apt legend: "Aut disce," "Aut discede," "Manet sors tertia cædi."—" Either learn;" "or depart;" "or in the third place be flogged;" underneath is the flogging-place. On the east wall is a corresponding tablet, bearing the School laws, in Latin. The Chamber walls are carved with the names of many an illustrious Wykehamist; but, the most interesting memorial is the Seventh Chamber and the adjoining passage. This "was the ancient school wherein Waynflete taught, and was called by the founder, '*Magna illa domus:*' the stone 'books' in the embayed windows still remain; it could accommodate scarcely more than ninety boys." At present, the foundation scholars at Winchester are limited to 70; and the commoners are in general about 130. The College and its Grammar School differ little in management from Eton. Among its characteristic customs is the chanting of the Latin song " Dulce Domum," to which justice cannot be done in any English translation. It is sung in College Hall on the six last Saturdays of the "long half" before "evening bells;" and at the July festival:

> Nations, and thrones, and reverend laws, have melted like a dream,
> Yet Wykeham's works are green and fresh beside the crystal stream;
> Four hundred years and fifty their rolling course have sped,
> Since the first surge-clad scholar to Wykeham's feet was led:

And still his seventy faithful boys, in these presumptuous days,
Learn the old truth, speak the old words, tread in the ancient ways;
Still for their daily orisons resounds the matin chime—
Still linked in bands of brotherhood, St. Catherine's steep they climb;
Still to their Sabbath worship they troop by Wykeham's tomb—
Still in the summer twilight sing their sweet song of home.
Roundell Palmer's Anniversary Ballad.

Another eminent Wykehamist, the Rev. Mackenzie Walcott, M.A., has commemorated in his *William of Wykeham and his Colleges,* the glories of Winchester, with an earnest eloquence, and affection for this school of near five centuries, which accompanies the reader through every page of Mr. Walcott's volume. It is delightful to see with what pride the author contemplates

"the success of a school, which in its earliest days produced Chichcley and Waynflete, the founders of the two grandest colleges in our ancient universities; the gentle Warham; Grocyn, the reviver of the Greek language; the philosophic Shaftesbury and profound Harris; the moralist, Browne; among poets—some of them distinguished ornaments of the Augustan age—Otway, Young, Collins, Somerville, Phillips, Crowe; the learned Bilson, Burgess, Lowth, and meek Ken; the graceful Wotton; among judges, Erle and Cranworth; among speakers, Onslow, Cornwall, Sidmouth, and Lefevre; among seamen, Keats and Warren; among soldiers, Lord Guildford, Seaton, Daltiac, Myers, and their gallant companions in the hard-fought fields of the last war. . . . . . It has never failed in contributing its share of faithful men to serve the country in Church and State; it has well sustained the reputation which should attach to the only ancient institution not founded by a sovereign which boasts itself to be a royal college."—*Preface to William of Wykeham and his Colleges.*

WICKLIFFE TRANSLATES THE BIBLE.

As Chaucer was the Morning Star of our poetry in the reign of Edward III., so Wickliffe, who first translated the Scriptures into English, has been called the Morning Star of the Reformation; whilst his works being written in English, and dispersed among the people, greatly contributed to the progress of the English tongue. John Wickliffe was born in 1324, in a little village in Yorkshire, was educated at Oxford, and was one of the students who attended the lectures of the pious Bradwardine at Merton College.* At that time he was in the flower of his age, and produced a great sensation in the university. He was elected in 1364 warden of Balliol, and in 1365 warden of Canterbury College also. His biblical and philosophical studies, his knowledge of theology, and his penetrating mind, were extraordinary. We have only space to speak of his translation of the Scriptures, the work of his latter years:

Scholasticism had banished the Scriptures into a mysterious obscurity. It is true that Bede had translated the Gospel of St. John; that the learned men at Alfred's court had translated the four evangelists; that Elfric in the reign of Ethelred had translated some books of the Old Testament; that an Anglo-Norman priest had paraphrased the Gospels and the Acts; that Richard Rolle, "the hermit of Hampole," and some pious clerks in the fourteenth century, had produced a version of the Psalms, the Gospels, and

---

* Bradwardine was also one of the greatest geniuses of his time, and occupies the first rank among astronomers, philosophers, and mathematicians. His Arithmetic and Geometry have been published; but we are not aware if his Astronomical Tables have enjoyed this advantage.

the Epistles: but these rare volumes were hidden, like theological curiosities, in the libraries of a few convents, ... The time appeared ripe for the publication of a Bible. The increase of population, the attention the English were beginning to devote to their own language, the development which the representative system of government had received, the awakening of the human mind—all these circumstances favored the Reformer's design.

Wickliffe was ignorant indeed of Greek and Hebrew; but was it nothing to shake off the dust which for ages had covered the Latin Bible, and translate it into English? He was a good Latin scholar, of sound understanding and great penetration; but above al', he loved the Bible, he understood it, and desired to communicate this treasure to others. Let us imagine him in his quiet study: On his table is the Vulgate text corrected after the best manuscripts; and, lying open around him are the commentaries of the doctors of the Church, especially those of St. Jerome and Nicholas Syrensis. Between ten and fifteen years he steadily prosecuted his task; learned men aided him with their advice, and one of them, Nicholas Hereford, appears to have translated a few chapters for him. At last, in 1380, it was completed.—*D'Aubigne's History of the Reformation.*

The translation being finished, the labor of the copyists began, and the Bible was ere long widely circulated either wholly or in portions. It was welcomed by citizens, soldiers, and the lower classes; the high-born curiously examined the unknown book; and even Anne of Luxemburg, wife of Richard II., having learnt English, began to read the Gospels. She did more than this; she made them known to Arundel, Archbishop of York, Chancellor, who, struck at the sight of a foreign lady—of a queen, humbly devoting her leisure to the study of *such a virtuous book*, commenced reading them himself, and rebuked the prelates who neglected this holy pursuit. "You could not meet two persons on the highway," says a cotemporary writer, "but one of them was Wickliffe's disciple." Yet, all in England did not equally rejoice: the lower clergy opposed the enthusiasm. The Reformer was violently attacked, yet the clamors did not alarm him; he did not stand alone : in the palace, as in the cottage, and even in parliament, the rights of the Holy Scriptures found defenders. A motion having been made in the Upper House (1390) to seize all the copies of the Bible, the Duke of Lancaster (who had been Wickliffe's firm friend throughout the great work, and was the friend of Chaucer and of Gower) exclaimed: "Are we then the very dregs of humanity, that we cannot possess the laws of our religion in our own tongue?" The texts of the Bible were now in every mouth, as they were re-echoed in the sermons of preachers, in churches, and open places. The poor treasured up the words of comfort for all earthly afflictions. The rich and great meditated upon the inspired sentences which so clearly pointed out a more certain road to salvation than could be found through indulgences and pilgrimages. Wickliffe died in peace, in his rectory at Lutterworth, in 1384, but the effect of his preaching still lives. In the vestry of Lutterworth church they show to this day the chair in which sat "the great English Reformer."

EDUCATION OF RICHARD II.—HIS PATRONAGE OF GOWER.

This distinction of literature extended through the reign of Edward's successor, Richard, the son of Edward the Black Prince, born at Bordeaux, in 1366, and who succeeded to the throne when only in his twelfth year. His government and education were committed to Simon Burleigh, a school-fellow of the Black Prince, who had by him been made Knight of the Garter.

In a manuscript of the year 1385, we read that English began to be the language into which school-boys construed their lessons in the reign of Richárd the Second; as in the following extract:

"oon is (sc. reason) for children in scholes agenst the usage and manner of all other nations, beeth compelled for to leave hire own language, and for to construe hire lessons, and here things in Frenche, and so they haveth sethe Normans come first into Eng londe; also gentilmen children beeth taught to sj eke Frensche, from the time that they beeth rockked in here cradel. . . . And uplondiche men will likne hymself to gentyl men, and sondeth with gret besynesse for to speak Frensche for to be told of."

One of the bright lights of this reign, Gower, was patronized by Richard. Gower the poet was born a few years later than Chaucer, though he is believed to have been his college friend. Gower studied law; he possessed considerable landed property in the counties of Nottingham and Suffolk. He wrote his principal work, the *Confessio Amantis*, in consequence of Richard II. meeting him in his state barge on the Thames, and asking him to "book some new thing;" his gravity led to his being called "the moral Gower." He stands half way between the minstrel of Normandy and the English poet, and he seems to have transferred the faults of a declining literature into the language of one newly arisen. "Gower prepared for his bones a resting in the monastery of St. Mary Overie, where, somewhat after the old fashion he lieth, right sumptuously buried, with a garland on his head, in token that he in his life-daies flourished freshly in literature and science."

Richard, during childhood and youth, was committed in succession to the charge of several guardians; and, like children (says an historian) whose nurses have been often changed, he thrived none the better for it. He did good or evil according to the influence of those around him, and had no decided inclination, except for ostentation and licentiousness. In his reign, laymen, among whom Chaucer and Gower are illustrious examples, received occasionally a learned education; and indeed the great number of gentlemen who studied in the inns of court is a conclusive proof that they were not generally illiterate. The common law required some knowledge of two languages. Upon the whole, we are inclined to think, that in the year 1400, or at the accession of Henry IV., the average instruction of an English gentleman of the first class would comprehend common reading and writing, a tolerable familiarity with French, and a slight tincture of Latin; the latter attained, or not, according to his circumstances, as school learning is at present.

HENRY IV.—HIS ACCOMPLISHMENTS.

Of Henry IV. of Bolingbroke, eldest son of John of Gaunt, and born in the ancient castle of Bolingbroke, in Lincolnshire, in 1366, few early traits are recorded; and as his father was a subject, nothing of material interest was at the time associated with his appearance in the world. Blanche, his mother, survived the birth of Bolingbroke not more than three years; he thus early lost the benefit of maternal care, which, with his father's subsequent life of profligacy, may account for the excesses of Prince Henry. Richard II. presented him, on his father's second marriage, with a costly ring. Froissart reports that Henry Bolingbroke was a handsome young man; and we read that he excelled in music. It was his custom every year, on the Feast of the Lord's Supper—that is, on the Thursday before Easter—to clothe as many poor persons as equaled the number of years he had completed on the preceding birthday. Henry was a gallant young knight, often distinguishing himself at jousts and tournaments, and in the Pell Rolls of 1401 is recorded the payment of 10*l*. "to Bartolf Vanderlurey, who fenced with the present lord the King, with the long sword, and was hurt in the neck by the said lord the King." Henry was of an active, ardent, and enterprising spirit; but we have no ground for believing that he devoted much of his time and thought to the education of his children. In this reign was built a library in Durham College (now Trinity College), Oxford, for the large collection of books of Richard of Bury, said to consist of more volumes than all the bishops of England had then in their possession.

_{Richard of Bury had bestowed certain portions of his valuable library upon a company of scholars residing in a Hall at Oxford; and he drew up "A provident arrangement by which books may be lent to strangers," meaning students of Oxford not belonging to that Hall. The custody of the books was deputed to five of the scholars, of which three, and in no case fewer, could lend any books for inspection and use only; but for copying and transcribing, he did not allow any book to pass without the walls of the house. And when any scholar, whether secular or religious, was qualified for the favor, and demanded the loan of a book, the keepers, provided they had a duplicate of the book, might lend it to him, taking a security exceeding in value the book lent. The reader may smile at the caution; but we have known some possessors of books in our own day adopt similar rules.}

HENRY V. AT QUEEN'S COLLEGE, OXFORD.

Of Henry V. of Monmouth, the childhood and youth are chronicled more nearly cotemporarily than those of his predecessor. Henry was born in 1387, in the castle of Monmouth, of which

Progress of Education.

the crumbling ruins are now a few vine-clad walls, washed by the Monmow. From this castle, tradition says, that being a sickly child, Henry was sent to Cornfield, six or seven miles distant, to be nursed there; and the cradle in which he was rocked was shown there some thirty years since. In the Wardrobe Accounts of Henry's father we find an entry of a charge for a "long gown" for the young Lord Henry; and we further learn that very shortly after he ascended the throne, he settled an annuity of 20l. upon his nurse, Johanna Waring, "in consideration of what was done to him in former days." In the records of the Duchy of Lancaster, in the year 1397, is the charge of 8d. paid "for harp-strings purchased for the harp of the young Lord Henry;" 12d. "for a new scabbard of a sword;" and "1s. 6d. for three-fourths of an ounce of tissue of black silk for a sword of young Lord Henry." In 1396, we find a charge of "4s. for seven books of grammar contained in one volume, and bought at London for the young Lord Henry." There is reason to believe that so early as 1399, Henry was placed in Queen's College, Oxford, under the superintendence of his half-uncle, Henry Beaufort, then Chancellor of the University; so that even the above volume of grammar may have been first learned under the direction of the future Cardinal.

In the old building of Queen's College, a chamber used to be pointed out by successive generations as Henry the Fifth's.* It stood over the gate-way opposite to St. Edmund's Hall. A portrait of him in painted glass, commemorative of his residence there, was seen in the window, with an inscription (as it should seem of comparatively recent date) in Latin:

To record the fact forever,
The Emperor of Britain,
The Triumphant Lord of France,
The Conqueror of his enemies and of himself,
Henry V.
Of this little chamber,
Once the great Inhabitant.

The tender age of Henry at this period does not render the tradition improbable; for many then became members of the University at the time they would now be sent to school. Those who were designed for the military profession were compelled to bear arms, and go to the field at the age of fifteen; consequently, the little education they received was confined to their boyhood. Hence it may be inferred that Henry (though perhaps without himself being enrolled among the regular academics) lived with his uncle, then chancellor, and studied under his superintendence. It is nearly certain that before the October term, 1398, Henry had been removed to King Richard's palace, carefully watched; whilst in 1399 he accompanied that monarch in his expedition

* Fuller, in his *Church History*, informs us that Henry's chamber over the College gate was then inhabited by the historian's friend, Thomas Barlow, and adds, "his picture remaineth there to this day in *brass*.

to Ireland. Shortly after his return, on his father's accession, he was created Prince of Wales; and had he subsequently become a student of the University, its archives would have furnished evidence of the fact; but, as the boy of the Earl of Derby, or the Duke of Hereford, living with his uncle, the omission of his name is not remarkable. In all probability his uncle superintended his general education, intrusting the details to others more competent to instruct him in the various branches of literature. Among his college associates was John Carpenter, of Oriel; and Thomas Rockman, an eminent astronomer and learned divine, of Merton. Among other pious and learned persons much esteemed by Henry was Robert Mascall, a Carmelite friar, confessor to his father; and Stephen Partington, a popular preacher, whom some of the nobility invited to court. It is impossible to read Henry's letters, and reflect on what is authentically recorded of him, without being impressed by a conviction that he had imbibed a very considerable knowledge of Holy Scripture, even beyond the young men of his day; whilst chroniclers bear testimony that "he held in great veneration such as surpassed in learning and virtue." Here we take leave of Henry, since an event in the autumn of 1398 turned the whole stream of his life into an entirely new channel, and led him by a very brief course to the inheritance of the throne of England.*

Prior to the reign of Henry V., specimens of English correspondence are rare; letters previously to that time, were usually written in French or Latin, and were the the productions chiefly of the great or the learned. The letters of learned men were verbose treatises, mostly on express subjects; those of the great, who employed scribes, resembled, from their formality, legal instruments. We have nothing earlier than the 15th century which can be termed a *familiar letter*. The material, too, upon which these letters were written, up to the same period, was usually vellum; very few instances, indeed, occurring, of more ancient date, of letters written on common paper. The earliest royal signature known in this country is the signature of Richard III.—*Ellis's Original Letters*, 1st series, p. 9.

EARLY PAROCHIAL SCHOOLS—SCHOOLS IN CHURCHES.

Plain Education dates from the fourteenth century; reading and writing were the chief branches, but children were also taught grammar. Parochial grammar-schools occur in the fifteenth century; but so few were they, and so low was the grammar-learning taught in them, that in 1477, several clergymen of London petitioned Parliament for leave to set up schools in their respective churches, not only to check schools conducted by illiterate men, but also to provide for the great demand for tuition,

* Selected and abridged from *Henry of Monmouth*. By J. Endell Tyler, B.D. It is a curious fact, not generally known (says Mr. Tyler), that Henry IV. in the *first* year of his reign took possession of all the property of the Provost and Fellows of Queen's College (on the ground of mismanagement), and appointed the Chancellor, the Chief Justice, the Master of the Rolls, and others, guardians of the College. This is, we think, scarcely consistent with the supposition of his son being resident there at the time, or of his selecting that college for him afterward.

in consequence of the law which made it illegal to put children to private teachers, enacted to prevent the spread of Wicklivism, or the doctrines of Wickliffe. This church school was held in a room at or over the porch called *parvise*.* The custom is alluded to by Shakspeare; and we find it as late as the seventeenth century, for John Evelyn, the son of a gentleman of fortune, and born at Wotton, in 1620, states in his Diary that he was not initiated into any rudiments till he was four years old, and then one Frier taught him at the church porch.

EDUCATION AT HOME—MUSIC.

Education, in all the early stages, was very rarely conducted at home, but at courts, or in the houses of nobles, etc. The period of infancy and boyhood was intrusted to women, and at the age of eleven years, tuition was commenced in earnest. In royal houses, the parents selected some veteran and able soldier of noble family, under whose roof their son was placed, and in whose castle, commencing his services as a page, he received instructions in the exercises and accomplishments befitting his condition. Thus, Edward the Black Prince delivered his son Richard, afterward Richard II., to Sir Guiscard d'Aigle, as his military tutor. Henry IV. intrusted the education of his son Henry, afterward the valorous Henry V., to Sir Thomas Percy, a brave and veteran warrior; and James I. of Scotland being taken prisoner, and confined in the Tower of London and Windsor Castle, received there an excellent education through Henry IV. of England, who placed him under the care of Sir John de Pelham, constable of Pevensey Castle, a man of note, both as a statesman and a warrior.

James, during his captivity in the Round Tower of Windsor Castle, composed "The King's Quair,"—that is, the King's *quire*, or *book*. It is a serious poem, of nearly 1400 lines, arranged in seven-line stanzas; the style in great part allegorical; the subject, the love of the royal poet for the Lady Joanna Beaufort, whom he eventually married, and whom he is said to have first beheld walking in the garden below from the window of his prison. In the concluding stanza James makes grateful mention of his—

    Ministers dear,
  Gower and Chaucer, that on the steppes sate
   Of rhetorick while they were live and here,
  Superlative as poets laureate,
   Of morality and eloquence ornate;

and he is evidently an imitator of the great Father of English poetry. The poem, too, must be regarded as written in English rather than in Scotch, though the difference between the two dialects was not so great at this early date as it afterward became; and although James, who was in his eleventh year when he was carried away to England in 1405, by Henry IV., may not have altogether avoided the peculiarities of his native idiom.—*G. L. Craik, M.A.*

* The Sergeant-at-law in Chaucer's *Canterbury Pilgrims* had been at *parvise*. The choristers of Norwich Cathedral were formerly taught in the *parvise*, i. e., the porch The chamber over a porch in some churches may have been the school m ant—as at Doncaster Church, and at Sherborne Abbey Church. "Responsions," or the preliminary examinations at Oxford, are said to be held *in parvise*, i. e. in the porch, or antecnamber before the schools. Wotton Church porch has not a room.

The King's Quair contains poetry superior to any except that of Chaucer, produced in England before the reign of Elizabeth. Two other poems of considerable length, in a humorous style, have also been attributed to James I.—"Peebles to the Play," and Christ's Kirk on the Green"— both in the Scottish dialect; but they are more probably the productions of his equally gifted and equally unfortunate descendant, James V., slain at Flodden, in 1513. Chalmers, however, assigns the former to James I.

Among the elegant accomplishments which were blended with the early tuition of both sexes, we should not omit to notice music, which was intended to render the learner a delightful companion in the hall at home, as his skill in warlike exercises was calculated to make him a formidable enemy in the field. The science of music, both instrumental and vocal; the composition and recitation of ballads, roundelayes, and other minor pieces of poetry; and an acquaintance with the romances and popular poems of the times, were all essential branches in the system of education which was adopted in every castle in the fourteenth and fifteenth centuries. The brave and accomplished military leader, Sir John Chandos, sang sweetly, and solaced his master, Edward III. on a voyage, by his ballads; and the Count de Foix, a celebrated hero, frequently requested his secretaries, in the intervals of severer occupation, to recreate themselves by chanting songs and roundelayes. Again, Churchmen studied music by profession; and the law students at the Inns of Court learned singing, and all kinds of music. A few of our early sovereigns were skilled in music: Richard II. is known to have assisted at divine service, and to have chanted a collect-prayer; Henry IV. is described as of shining talents in music; and Stow tells us that Henry V. "delighted in songs, meters, and musical instruments."

We obtain an interesting glimpse of Female Education from a curious book of *Advice to Ladies*, written in the year 1371. At this time, in the upper ranks, the education of females was generally conducted in the monasteries, or in the family of some relative or friend, if possible, of superior rank; the latter from its being thought that abroad daughters would be more likely to form advantageous connections than at home. Under all these forms, however, the character of the education seems to have been nearly the same. It consisted of needle-work, confectionery (or the art of preserving fruits, etc.), surgery (or a knowledge of the healing art,) and the rudiments of church music; to which, in an education at a monastery, was generally added the art of reading; The prejudices of the times, and particularly of the male sex, were opposed to any higher degree of cultivation of the mind: arising, probably, from a suspicion, that it might render women an overmatch for their admirers. Nor is it certain that the reading of the time was beneficial. "Instead of reading bokes of wisdom and science," says the author of the *Advice*, "they studye in nought but the bokes that speak of love's fables, and other worldlie vanities;" he also considers writing as dangerous and unnecessary, and thinks it better "if women can nought of it." He appears to have set two priests and two clerks to select a book of "ensamples," or extracts from the Bible, the acts of Kings, the chronicles of France, Greece, and England. In speaking of female manners, one of the first faults which he corrects, and which was natural to ignorant and uneducated girls, was that of levity. Among other points, he fixes on their conduct at mass, at which the grossest irreverence and disorder are known to have prevailed. The church, during the celebration of the service, seems to have been an established scene of gossip and flirtation. The men came with their hawks and dogs, walking to and fro to converse with their friends, to make bargains and appointments, and to show their splendid coats.

CHILDHOOD AND YOUTH OF HENRY THE SIXTH.

It has been shrewdly observed that there are few instances of kings who ascend the throne at a very early age answering the expectations of their people. In our own history Richard II. and Henry VI. are striking instances of this remark; for which there seems to be an obvious reason, viz, that a minor king received generally a worse education than he who is only destined to a throne.

Henry VI., called of Windsor, from having been born there in 1421, was not quite nine months old when the death of his father, Henry V., left him King of England. Fabian relates this extraordinary instance of the adulation paid to this minor sovereign: "Henry VI., when but eight months old, sat in his mother's lap in the parliament chamber; and the speaker made a famous *præposition*, in which he said much of the providence of God, who had endowed the realm with the presence of *so toward a prince and sovereign governor*." His childhood was passed at Windsor Castle. In accordance with the will of his dying father, the boy Henry, when six years old, was placed under the tutelage of Richard de Beauchamp, Earl of Warwick, the companion in arms of Henry V. This appointment was made under the authority of the Council: Warwick was to instruct his pupil in all things worthy to be known, nurturing him in the love and fear of his Creator, and in hatred of all vice. The Earl held this office till the King was sixteen : his discipline was very strict; for the pupil was not to be spoken to, unless in the presence of Warwick, or of the four knights appointed to be about his person; "as," says the entry in the Rolls of Parliament, "the King, by the speech of others in private, has been stirred by some from his learning, and spoken to of divers matters not behoveful." The Earl appears to have complained to the Council of the King's misconduct, for they promised to assist him in chastising his royal pupil for his defaults. Warwick applied for this aid as protection against the young Henry's displeasure and indignation, "as the King is grown in years, in stature of his person, and in conceit of his high authority." Severe corporal punishment was, it appears, considered the most efficient instrument of good education at this period; and Warwick, doubtless, *belashed* the young King.

How much of the fire of the Platnagenets was trodden out of Henry VI. by the severities of his early discipline cannot now be estimated. He was born to a most unhappy position; but it is satisfactory to believe that his hard lot was solaced by that religious trust which lightens the burthens of the wretched, whether on a throne or in a dungeon. The Earl of Warwick, who, like many other leaders of chivalry, was an enthusiastic in the efficiency of vows and pilgrimages, may have injured his pupil by that strong feeling of ceremonial devotion which caused him long to be regarded as a saint. To a right direction of that

piety, we owe, however, the noble foundations of Eton and King's College, Cambridge.—
worthy monuments which still call upon us to respect the memory of the most meek and
most unfortunate of king's.—*Knight s Popular History of England.*

Meanwhile, the scholastic training of the young King was intrusted to his great uncle, the Bishop of Winchester, better known as Cardinal Beaufort; and under his tuition, Henry became an accomplished scholar in all the learning of the age; as well as "the truest Christian gentleman that ever sat upon a throne."

The statutes of St. Mary's College, Oxford, in this reign, show how great must have been the inconveniences and impediments to study in those days from the scarcity of books: "Let no scholar occupy a book in the library over one hour, or two hours at most, so that others shall be hindered from the use of the same." Still there was a great number of books at an early period of the Church, when one book was given out by the librarian to each of a religious fraternity at the beginning of Lent, to be read diligently during the year, and to be returned the following Lent. Books were first kept in chests, and next chained to the desks, lest their rarity and value might tempt those who used them; and it was a very common thing to write in the first leaf of a book, "Cursed be he who shall steal or tear out the leaves, or in any way injure this book;" an anathema which, in a modified form, we have seen written in books of the present day.

HENRY THE SIXTH FOUNDS ETON COLLEGE, AND KING'S COLLEGE, CAMBRIDGE.

Hall, the chronicler, when speaking of the causes which led Henry VI. to found Eton College, and King's College, Cambridge, says of him: "he was of a most liberal mind, and especially to such as loved good learning; and those whom he saw profiting in any virtuous science, he heartily forwarded and embraced." An ingenious writer of our own time has, however, more correctly characterized the young King's motive: "still stronger in Henry's mind was the desire of marking his gratitude to God by founding and endowing some place of pious instruction and Christian worship."* Henry seems principally to have followed the magnificent foundations of William of Wykeham at Winchester and Oxford; resolving that the school which he founded should be connected with a college in one of the Universities, whither the best of the foundation scholars of his school should proceed to complete their education, and where a permanent provision should be made for them. Standing upon the north terrace of Windsor Castle, near Wykeham's tower, and

* Memoirs of Eminent Etonians. By E. S. Creasy, M.A.

looking toward the village of Eton, upon the opposite bank of the silver-winding Thames, we can imagine the association to have first prompted the devout King's design—in the words of the Charter, "to found, erect, and establish, to endure in all future time,

A College consisting of and of the number of one provost and ten priests, four clerks and six chorister boys, who are to serve daily there in the celebration of divine worship, and of twenty-five poor and indigent scholars who are to learn grammar; and also of twenty-five poor and infirm men, whose duty it shall be to pray there continually for our health and welfare so long as we live, and for our soul when we shall have departed this life, and for the souls of the illustrious Prince, Henry our father, late King of England and France ; also of the Lady Katherine of most noble memory, late his wife, our mother ; and for the souls of all our ancestors and of all the faithful who are dead: (consisting) also of one master or teacher in grammar, whose duty it shall be to instruct in the rudiments of grammar the said indigent scholars and all others whatsoever who may come together from any part of our Kingdom of England to the said College, gratuitously and without the exaction of money or any other thing."

The works were commenced in 1441, with the chapel of the College ; and to expedite the building, workmen were "pressed" from every part of the realm. The freemasons received 3s. a week each, the stone-masons and carpenters 3s. ; plumbers, sawyers, tilers, etc., 6d. a day, and common laborers 4d. The grant of arms expresses this right royal sentiment : "If men are ennobled on account of ancient hereditary wealth, much more is he to be preferred and styled truly noble, who is rich in the treasures of the sciences and wisdom, and is also found diligent in his duty towards God." Henry appointed Waynflete first provost, who, with five fellows of Winchester, and thirty-five of the scholars of that College, became the primitive body of Etonians, in 1443. The works of the Chapel were not completed for many years ; and the other parts of the College were unfinished until the commencement of Henry the Eighth's reign.

Eton, in its founder's time, was resorted to as a place of education by the youth of the higher orders, as well as by the class for whose immediate advantage the benefits of the foundation were primarily designed. Those students not on the foundation were lodged at their relations' expense in the town (*oppidum*) of Eton, and thence called *Oppidans*. The scholars on the foundation (since called Colle-gers) were lodged and boarded in the College-buildings, and at the College expense. There are two quadrangles, built chiefly of red brick : in one are the school and the chapel, with the lodgings for the scholars ; the other contains the library, the provost's house, and apartments for the Fellows. The chapel is a stately stone structure, and externally very handsome. The architecture is Late Perpendicular, and a good specimen of the style of Henry the Seventh's reign. In the center of the first quadrangle is a bronze statue of Henry VI. ; and in the chapel another statue, of marble, by John Bacon. The foundation scholars seem to have been first placed in two large chambers on the ground floor, three of the upper boys in each; they had authority over the others, and were responsible for good conduct being maintained in the dormitory. Subsequently was added "the Long Chamber" as the common dormitory of all the scholars. Dinner and supper were provided daily for all the members of the College; and every scholar received yearly a stated quantity of coarse cloth, probably first made up into clothing, but it has long ceased to be so used.

The King's Scholars or Collegers are distinguished from oppidans by a black cloth gown. The boys dined at eleven, and supped at seven; there being only two usual meals.

King Henry is recorded to have expressed much anxiety for his young incipient Alumni. One of his chaplains relates that—

When King Henry met some of the students in Windsor Castle, whither they sometimes used to go to visit the King's servants, whom they knew, on ascertaining who they were, he admonished them to follow the path of virtue, and besides his words, would give them money to win over their good-will, saying, "Be good boys; be gentle and docile, and servants of the Lord." (Sitis boni pueri, mites et docibiles, et servi Domini.

The progress of the buildings was greatly checked by the troubles toward the close of the reign of Henry VI.; and his successor, Edward IV., not only deprived Eton of large portions of its endowments, but obtained a bull from Pope Pius II. for disposing of the College, and merging it in the College of St. George at Windsor; but Provost Westbury publicly and solemnly protested against this injustice, the bull was revoked, and many of the endowments were restored, though the College suffered severely. The number on the foundation consisted of a provost and a vice-provost, 6 fellows, 2 chaplains, 10 choristers, the upper and lower master, and the 70 scholars. The buildings were continued during the reign of Henry VII., and the early years of Henry the Eighth, whose death saved Parliament from extinguishing Eton, which was then confirmed to Edward VI.

Among the Paston Letters is one written in 1467, by "Master Willam Paston at Eton, to his Worshipful Brother, John Paston, acknowledging the receipt of 8d in a letter, to buy a pair of slippers; 13s. 4d. to pay for his board, and thanking him for 12lb. of Figgs and 8lb. of Raisins which he was expecting by the first barge; he then narrates how he had fallen in love with a young gentlewoman to whom he had been introduced by his hostess, or dame; and he concludes with a specimen of his skill in Latin versification.

A MS document in Corpus Christi College, Cambridge, shows the general system of the school, the discipline kept up, and the books read in the various forms, about the year 1560. The holidays and customs are also enumerated; great encouragement was then shown to Latin versification (always the pride of Eton), and occasionally to English, among the students; care was taken to teach the younger boys to write a good hand. The boys rose at five to the loud call of "Surgite;" they repeated a prayer in alternate verses, as they dressed themselves, and made their beds, and each swept the part of the chamber close to his bed. They then went in a row to wash, and then to school, where the under-master read prayers at six; then the præpositor noted absentees, and one examined the students' faces and hands, and reported any boys that came unwashed. At seven, the tuition began: great attention was paid to Latin composition in prose and verse, and the boys conversed in Latin. Friday seems to have been flogging day. Among the books read by the boys in the two highest forms are mentioned Cæsar's Commentaries, Cicero De Officiis and De Amicitia, Virgil, Lucian, and, what is remarkable, *the Greek Grammar;* a knowledge of Greek at this period being a rare accomplishment even at our universities. Its study was, however, gaining ground in Elizabeth's reign; and in a book published in 1586, it is stated that at Eton, Winchester, and Westminster, boys were then "well entered in the Latin and Greek tongues and rules of versifying." Throughout this MS. record is shown the antiquity of making the upper boys responsible for the good conduct of the lower, which has ever been the ruling principle at Eton—in the schools, at meal-times, in the chapel, in the playing-fields, and in the dormitory; and there was a præpositor to look after dirty and slovenly boys.*

Of scholars' expenses at Eton early in the reign of Elizabeth, we find a record in the accounts of the sons of Sir William Cavendish, of Chatsworth. Among the items, a breast of mutton is charged tenpence; a small chicken, fourpence; a week's board five shillings each, besides the wood burned in their chamber; to an old woman for sweeping and cleaning the chamber, twopence; mending a shoe, one penny; three candles, ninepence; a book, Esop's Fables, fourpence; two pair of shoes, sixteenpence; two bunches of wax-lights, one penny; the sum total of the payments, including board paid to the bursars of Eton College, living expenses for the two boys and their man, clothes, books, washing, etc., amount to 12*l.* 12*s.* 7*d.* The expense of a scholar at the University in 1514 was but five pounds annually, affording as much accommodation as would now cost sixty pounds, though the accommodation would be far short of that now customary. At Eton, in 1857, the number of sholars exceeded 700.

The College buildings have been from time to time re-edified and enlarged. The Library, besides a curious and valuable collection of books, is rich in Oriental and Egyptian manuscripts, and beautifully illustrated missals. The Upper School Room in the principal court, with its stone arcade beneath, and the apartments attached to it, were built by Sir Christopher Wren, at the expense of Dr. Allstree, provost in the reign of Charles II.

The College Hall interior has been almost entirely rebuilt through the munificence of the Rev. John Wilder, one of the Fellows, and was reopened in October, 1857: these improvements include a new open-timber roof, a louver, windows east and west, a gothic oak canopy, and a carved oak gallery over the space dividing the hall from the buttery. The oak paneling around the room is cut all over with the names of Etonians of several generations.

Among the Eton festivals was the *Montem,* formerly celebrated every third year on Whit-Tuesday, and believed to have been a corruption of the Popish ceremony of the Boy Bishop. It consisted of a theatrical procession of pupils wearing costumes of various periods, for the purpose of collecting money, or "salt," for the captain of Eton, about to retire to King's College, Cambridge. To each contributor was given a small portion of salt, at an eminence named therefrom Salt-Hill; the ceremony concluding with the waving of a flag upon this hill or *Montem.*† Boating and cricket are the leading recreations at Eton: the

---

* Condensed from Mr. Creasy's Memoirs of Eminent Etonians.
† The last Montem was celebrated at Whitsuntide, 1844. The abolition of the custom had long been pressed upon the College authorities, and they at length yielded to the growing condemnation of the ceremony as an exhibition unworthy of the present enlightened age. A memorial of the last celebration is preserved in that picturesque chronicle of events, the Illustrated London News, June 1, 1844.

College walks or playing-fields, extend to the banks of the Thames, and the whole scene is celebrated by Gray, the accomplished Etonian, in his well-known *Ode on a Distant Prospect of Eton College*, commencing—

"Ye distant spires, ye antique towers
That crown the watery glade."

Waynflete was the first provost of Eton. Among the eminent scholars are Archbishop Rotherham, and Bishop West; Croke, the celebrated Hellenist, one of the first who taught the Greek language publicly in any university north of the Alps; Bishop Aldrich, the friend of Erasmus; Hall, the chronicler; Bishop Foxe; Thomas Sutton, founder of the Charter-house; Sir Thomas Smith, and Sir Henry Savile, provosts; Admiral Sir Humphrey Gilbert; Oughtred, the mathematician; Tusser, the useful old rhymer; Phineas and Giles Fletcher, the poets; the martyrs, Fuller. Glover, Saunders, and Hullier; Sir Henry Wotton, provost;* Robert Devereux, third Earl of Essex; Waller, the poet; Robert Boyle; Henry More, the Platonist; Bishops Pearson and Sherlock; the ever-memorable John Hales, "the Walking Library;" Bishops Barrow and Fleetwood; Lord Camden; the poets Gray, Broome, and West; Fielding, the novelist; Dr. Arne, the musical composer; Horace Walpole; the Marquis of Granby; Sir William Draper; Sir Joseph Banks; Marquis Cornwallis; Lord Lowe; Richard Porson, the Greek Emperor; the poets Shelley, Praed, and Milman; Hallam, the historian; and W. E. Gladstone, the statesman.

The Premiers of England during the last century and a half were mostly educated at Eton. Thus, Lord Bolingbroke, Sir William Wyndham, Sir Robert Walpole, Lord Townshend, Lord Lyttleton, Lord Chatham, the elder Fox, Lord North, Charles James Fox, Mr. Wyndham, the Marquis Wellesley, Lord Grenville, Canning, the Duke of Wellington, Lord Grey, and the Earl of Derby—were all Etonians.

Among the celebrities of the College should not be forgotten the periodical work entitled *The Etonian*, the contributors to which were Eton scholars, and the author-publisher was the Etonian Charles Knight—a name long to be remembered in the commonwealth of English literature.

King's College, which Henry founded in 1441, at Cambridge, to be recruited from Eton, is the richest endowed collegiate foundation in that University. The Statutes declare that there shall be a provost and 70 poor scholars.† The Reformation and the changes brought about by three centuries, have, however, rendered obedience to the Statutes impossible, and they are now virtually the Statutes of William of Wykeham, which he had framed for New College. The Civil Wars of the Houses of York and Lancaster, and the violent death of the royal founder, left the College buildings unfinished; while Edward IV. impoverished its revenues, and even dissolved the College. Henry VII., in whose reign the College petitioned Parliament, on account of its straitened resources, contributed to the completion of the

---

* Wotton is described as "a person that was not only a fine gentleman himself, but very skilled in the art of making others so."

† Unquestionably Colleges were eleemosynary foundations, but their sole object was not, like that of an almshouse, to relieve indigence. They were intended, no doubt, to maintain scholars who were poor; and in an age when learning was regarded as ignoble by the great, and when nearly all but the great were poor, persons willing to enter the University as students could hardly be found, except among the poor. If, in modern days, those who impart or seek education in the Universities are not indigent, it must not be thought, therefore, that the poor have been robbed of their birthright. Rather the Universities, among other agencies, have so raised the condition of society, and mental cultivation is now so differently regarded, that persons intended for the learned professions are at present found only among the comparatively wealthy. Such persons, if elected for their merit to Fellowships and Scholarships, would faithfully fulfil the main objects of founders, namely, the promotion of religion and learning.—*Report of the Oxford University Commission*, pp. 39-40.

chapel. The style is Late Perpendicular, but very rich. The interior, with the stained glass windows, was completed by Henry VIII., under the direction of Bishop Foxe.

JOHN CARPENTER AND THE CITY OF LONDON SCHOOL.

Toward the close of the long reign of Edward III. there was born in London a good citizen named John Carpenter, who being styled in the documents of his time *clericus* (clerk), was an educated man, and is supposed to have studied at one of the Inns of Court for the profession of the law. He became Town Clerk of the City; and compiled a large volume in Latin of the civic laws, customs, privileges, and usages, a book of great value and authority. He was at the expense of painting the celebrated "Dance of Death" in St. Paul's cloister, being an encourager of the arts, and he was a personal acquaintance of Lidgate, the monk of Bury. He was 20 years Secretary and Town Clerk, sat in parliament for the City, and was Governor of St. Anthony's Hospital, in Threadneedle-street. At his death he bequeathed certain property in the City "for the finding and bringing up of foure poore men's children with meate, drink, apparell, learning at the schooles in the universities, etc., until they be preferred, and then others in their places for ever." In 1633, however, this property yielded only 29*l*. 13*s*. 4*d*. per annum, At this time the boys wore "coats of London russet" with buttons; and they had periodically to show their copy books to the Chamberlain, in proof of the application of the charity. During the lapse of nearly four centuries, the value of Carpenter's estates had augmented from 19*l*. 10*s*. to nearly 900*l*., or nearly five and forty fold. In t 1835, he funds were greatly increased by subscription, and a large and handsome school built by the city upon the site of Honey-lane market, north of Cheapside, at a cost of 12,000*l*., to accommodate 400 scholars. The citizens have, in gratitude, erected upon the great staircase of the school a portrait statue of Carpenter, in the costume of his age: he bears in his left hand his *Liber Albus*, a collection of the City laws, customs, and privileges. The statue is placed upon a pedestal, inscribed with a compendious history of the founder, and his many benevolent acts.

Such has been the goodly increase of Carpenter's charity. It is not unreasonable to suppose that he may have been prompted to the bequest by the celebrity of the schools of St. Anthony's Hospital, of which he was master. In the scholastic disputations amongst the grammar-schools, it commonly presented the best scholars. Out of this school sprung the great Sir Thomas More; Dr. Heath, Archbishop of York and Lord Chancellor;

Archbishop Whitgift; and the celebrated Dean Colet, the founder of St. Paul's School.

MERCERS' SCHOOL.—THE FIRST GRAMMAR SCHOOL.

In the twenty-fifth year of the reign of Henry VI.—1447—there was presented to Parliament a petition by four clergymen setting forth the lack of grammar-schools and good teachers in the City of London; and praying leave (which was granted to them) to establish schools, and appoint competent masters in their respective parishes. "It were expedyent," say they, "that in London were a sufficient number of scholes, and good enfourmers in gramer; and not for the singular avail of two or three persons grevously to hurt the multitude of yong peple of al this land. For wher there is grete nombre of lerners and few techers, and to noon others, the maistres waxen rid of monie, and the lerners poucrer in connyng, as experyence openlic shewith, agenst all vertue and ordre of well publik."

This is generally considered to have been the origin of Free Grammar Schools, properly so called; but the only one of the schools established immediately in consequence of this petition which has survived to the present time is the Mercers' School, which was originally founded at St. Thomas de Acons (the site of Mercers' Hall, in Cheapside),* for 70 scholars of any age or place, subject to the management of the Mercers' Company. Among the early scholars were Dean Colet, Bishop Thomas, and Bishop Wren. The site of the school-house was changed four times; and it is now on College-hill, on the site of Whittington's Alms-houses, "God's House, or Hospital," which have been rebuilt at Highgate. It is at this day a strange location for a seat of learning, surrounded by hives of merchandise, and close to one of the oldest sites of commerce in the city, its turmoil grates harshly upon the quiet so desirable for a youth of study.

ST. PAUL'S SCHOOL FOUNDED.

In the reign of Edward IV., in 1466, there was born in the parish of St. Antholin, in the city of London, one John Colet, the eldest son of Sir Henry Colet, Knight, twice Lord Mayor, who had, besides him, twenty-one children. In 1483, John Colet was sent to Magdalen College, Oxford, where he passed seven years, and took the usual degrees in arts. Here he studied Latin, with some of the Greek authors through a Latin medium, and mathematics. Having thus laid a good foundation for learn-

* In the porch of Mercer's Chapel, in Cheapside, Guy (founder of Guy's Hospital) was apprenticed to a bookseller in 1660; the house was rebuilt after the Great Fire, and was rented by Guy, then a master bookseller.

ing at home, he traveled in France and Italy from 1493 to 1497; he had previously been preferred to the rectory of Dennington, in Suffolk, being then in acolyth's orders. At Paris, Colet became acquainted with the scholar Budæus, and was afterward introduced to Erasmus. In Italy he contracted a friendship with Grocyn, Linacre, Lilly, and Latimer, all of whom were studying the Greek language, then but little known in England. Whilst abroad, he devoted himself to divinity, and the study of the civil and canon law. Colet returned to England in 1497, and subsequently rose through various degrees of preferment to be Dean of St. Paul's. By his lectures and other means, he greatly assisted the spirit of inquiry into the Holy Scriptures which eventually produced the Reformation. He had, however, many difficulties to contend with; and tired with trouble and persecution, he withdrew from the world, resolving in the midst of life and health, to consecrate his fortune to some lasting benefaction, which he performed in the foundation of St. Paul's School, at the east end of St. Paul's churchyard, in 1512; and, "it is hard to say whether he left better lands for the maintenance of his school, or wiser laws for the government thereof."—*Fuller.*

The original school-house, built 1508–12, was destroyed in the Great Fire of 1666, but was rebuilt by Wren. This second school was taken down in 1824, and the present school built of stone from the designs of George Smith: it has a handsome central portico upon a rusticated base, projecting over the street pavement. The original endowment and for several years the only endowment of the school, was 55*l*. 14*s*. 10½*d*., the annual rents of estates in Buckinghamshire, which now produce 1858*l*. 16*s*. 10½*d*. a-year; and, with other property, make the present income of the school upward of 5000*l*. Lilly, the eminent grammarian, the friend of Erasmus and Sir Thomas More, was the first master of St. Paul's, and "Lilly's Grammar" is used to this day in the school; the English rudiments were written by Colet, the preface to the first edition probably by Cardinal Wolsey; the Latin syntax chiefly by Erasmus, and the remainder by Lilly: thus, the book may have been the joint production of four of the greatest scholars of the age. Colet directed that the children should not use tallow, but wax candles in the school; fourpence entrance-money was to be given to the poor scholar who swept the school; and the masters were to have livery gowns, "delivered in clothe."

Colet died in his 53d year, in 1519. He wrote several works in Latin; the grammar which he composed for his school was called "Paul's Accidence." The original Statutes of the school, signed by Dean Colet, were many years since accidentally picked up at a bookseller's, and by the finder presented to the British Museum. The school is for 153 boys "of every nation, country and class;" the 153 alluding to the number of fishes taken by St. Peter (*John* xxi. 2). The education is entirely classical; the presentations to the school are in the gift of the Master of the Mercers' Company; and scholars are admitted at fifteen, but eligible at any age after that. Their only expense is for books and wax tapers. There are several valuable exhibitions, decided at the Apposition, held in the first three days of the fourth week after Easter, when a commemorative oration is delivered by the senior boy, and prizes are presented from the governors. In the time of the founder, the "Apposition dinner" was "an assembly and a litell dinner, ordaynod by the surveyor, not exceedynge the pryce of four nobles."

In the list of eminent Paulines (as the scholars are called) are, Sir Anthony Denny and Sir William Paget, privy counselors, to Henry VIII.; John Leland, the antiquary; John Milton, our Great epic poet; Samuel Pepys, the diarist; John Strype, the ecclesiastical historian; Dr. Calamy, the High Churchman; the Great Duke of Marlborough; R. W. Elliston, the comedian; Sir C. Mansfield Clarke, Bart.; Lord Chancellor Truro, etc. Among the annual prizes contended for is a prize for a copy of Latin Lyrics, given by the parent of a former student named Thurston, the High Master to apply a portion of the endowment to keeping up the youth's gravestone in the Highgate Cemetery.

EDWARD THE FOURTH AND HIS TUTORS.

Edward IV., born at Rouen, in 1441, has little if any claim to be recorded as a promoter of education. We have seen how he impoverished the two royal Colleges of his predecessor, Henry VI., at Eton and Cambridge, by seizing upon their endowments, and endeavoring to divert the streams of their munificence. The whole life of Edward was divided between the perils of civil war, and unrestrained sensual indulgence. Nevertheless, Edward drew up for the observance of his offspring, a set of regulations, which so closely corresponded with those made by his mother, that it may be fairly inferred he followed the same plans which had been strictly enforced in the education and conduct of himself and his brothers in their own youth in Ludlow Castle.* Though the discipline was constant and severe, the noble children expressed with familiarity their childish wishes to their father and communicated to him their imaginary grievances. This is instanced in a letter preserved in the Cottonian MSS. from

---

* In this celebrated fortress, now a mass of picturesque ruins, Milton produced his masque of Comus; and in a room over the gateway, Butler wrote *Hudibras*.

Edward to his father, written when he was a mere stripling, petitioning for some "fyne bonnets" for himself and his brother; and complaining of the severity of "the odious rule and demeaning" of one Richard Crofte and his brother, apparently their tutors.

In another letter, one of the earliest specimens extant of domestic and familiar English correspondence—it being written in 1454, when Edward the Earl of March was twelve, and the Earl of Rutland eleven, years of age — addressing their father as "Right high and mighty Prince, our most worshipful and greatly redoubted lord and father," they say:

> And if it please your highness so know of our welfare at the making of this letter, we were in good health of body, thanked be God; beseeching your good and gracious fatherhood of your daily blessing. And where you command us by your said letters to attend specially to our learning in our young age, that should cause us to grow to honor and worship in our old age, please it your highness to wit, that we have attended our learning since we came hither, and shall hereafter, by the which we trust to God your gracious lordship and good fatherhood shall be pleased.

Yet, Edward's attachment in his maturer years to his tutor Crofte, of whom he complains above, was evinced by the emoluments which he bestowed upon him after his accession to the crown. Sir Richard Crofte espoused the lady governess of the young Plantagenets: he lived to a great age, and was one of the most distinguished soldiers of his time; he survived every member of the family in whose service he had been engaged, and had to mourn the premature and violent deaths of the whole of his princely pupils. — *Retrospective Review*, 2d S. vol. i.

Edward has, perhaps, a better title to be considered a legislator than any other King of England, as he actually presided in the courts of justice, according to Daniel, who states that in the second year of his reign Edward sat three days together, during Michaelmas term, in the Court of King's Bench, in order to understand the law; and he likewise, in the 17th year, presided at the trials of many criminals.

COSTLINESS OF MANUSCRIPT BOOKS.

The books that were to be found in the palaces of the great at this period, were for the most part highly illuminated manuscripts, bound in the most expensive style. In the wardrobe accounts of King Edward IV., we find that Piers Baudwyn is paid for "binding, gilding, and dressing" of two books, twenty shillings each, and of four books sixteen shillings each. Now, twenty shillings in those days would have bought an ox. But the cost of this binding and garnishing does not stop here: for there were delivered to the binder six yards of velvet, six yards of silk, laces, tassels, copper and gilt clasps, and gilt nails. The price of velvet and silk in those days was enormous. We may reasonably conclude that these royal books were as much for show as use. One of these books thus garnished by Edward the Fourth's binder, is called "Le Bible Historiaux" (the Historical Bible), and there are several copies of the same book in manuscript in the British Museum.

Edward was, however, a reader. In his Wardrobe Accounts are entries for binding his Titus Livius, his Froissart, his Josephus, and his Bibles, as well as for the cost of fastening chests to remove his books from London to Eltham; and the King and his court lent a willing ear to the great discovery of Printing, which was to make knowledge a common property, causing, as Caxton says Earl Rivers did, in translating three works for his press, "books to be imprinted and so multiplied to go abroad among the people."

A letter of Sir John Paston, written to his mother in 1474, shows how scarce money was in those days for the purchase of luxuries like books. He says: "As for the books that were Sir James's (the Priest's), if it like you that I may have them, I am not able to buy them, but somewhat would I give, and the remainder, with a good devout heart, by my troth, I will pray for his soul. . . . If any of them are claimed hereafter, in faith I will restore it." The custom of borrowing books, and not returning them, is as old as the days of the Red and White Roses. John Paston left an inventory of his books, eleven in number. One of the items in this catalogue is "A Book of Troilus, which William B—— hath had near ten years, and lent to Dame Wingfield, and there I saw it."

EDWARD V. IN LUDLOW CASTLE.

Edward, the eldest son of Edward IV., was born in the sanctuary at Westminster, in 1470. At the death of his father he was twelve years old, keeping a mimic court at Ludlow Castle, with a council. Ordinances for the regulation of the prince's daily conduct were drawn up by his father shortly before his death, which prescribe his morning attendance at mass, his occupation "at school," his meals, and his sports. No man is to sit at his board but such as Earl Rivers shall allow: and at this hour of meat it is ordered "that there be read before him noble stories, as behoveth a prince to understand; and that the communication at all times, in his presence, be of virtue, honour, cuning (knowledge), wisdom, and deeds of worship, and nothing that shall move him to vice."—(*MS. in British Museum.*) The Bishop of Worcester, John Alcock, the president of the council, was the prince's preceptor. On the death of his father, in 1483,

Edward was called to the throne; but after a mere nominal possession of less than three months, he and his brother, Richard Duke of York, both disappeared, and nothing is known as to their fate; but the prophetic words of the dying Edward IV. were fulfilled: "If you among yourselves in a child's reign fall at debate, many a good man shall perish, and haply he too, and ye too, ere this land shall find peace again."

INTRODUCTION OF PRINTING.

The reign of Edward IV. is illustrious as being that in which Printing was introduced into England. From the weald of Kent came William Caxton to London to be apprenticed to a mercer or merchant. By skill and industry he arose to be appointed agent for the Mercers' Company in the Low Countries. Leaving, however, his mercantile employment, he was absent for two years in Germany, when the art of Printing from movable types was the wonder of the country. By this art books could be produced at a tenth of the price of manuscripts. Caxton learned the mystery, and brought Printing into England, and thus rendered Bibles and other books alike the property of the great and the mean. In the Almonry of the abbey church at Westminster, Caxton set up the first printing-press ever known in England; the first book printed here being *The Game and Play of the Chesse*, 1474, folio; and the very house in which this great work was done remained until the year 1845, or 371 years from the date of the first book printed in England. This book was intended by Caxton for the diffusion of knowledge amongst all ranks of people: it contains authorities, sayings, and stories, "applied unto the morality of the public weal, as well as of the nobles and of the common people, after the game and play of chess;" and Caxton trusts that "other, of what estate or degree he or they stand in, may see in this little book that they may govern themselves as they ought to do."

EARLY PRINTED BOOKS.

The greater part of the works which were issued from the press during the first century of printing, both in England and on the continent of Europe, were such as had been written in the previous ages, and had long existed in manuscript. The first printers were always booksellers, and sold their own impressions. The two occupations were not divided till early in the sixteenth century.

Ames and Herbert have recorded the titles of nearly 10,000 distinct works, published in Great Britain, between 1471 and 1600, equaling, on an average, seventy-six works each year.

Many of these works, however, were single sheets; but, on the other hand, there were, doubtless, many which have not been recorded. The number of readers in Great Britain during this period was comparatively small; and the average number of each book printed is not supposed to have been more than 200.

We believe that the books which have been written in the languages of western Europe, during the last two hundred and fifty years, translations from the ancient languages, of course, included, are of greater value than all the books which at the beginning of that period were extant in the world.

CHILDHOOD AND EDUCATION OF RICHARD THE THIRD.

All that remains of the town of Fotheringhay, one of the famous historic sites of Northamptonshire, is a small village, with a noble collegiate church of the fifteenth century. Here, amidst the ancient gilding of a shield of arms, has been traced "a boar, for the honour of Windsor," possessed by Richard III.:

> The bristled boar, in infant gore,
> Wallows beneath the thorny shade.—*Gray.*

The device reminds one that in the castle of Fotheringhay, which was the principal seat of the Plantagenets, was born in 1452, Richard Plantagenet, usually designated as Richard the Third, the youngest son of Richard Duke of York, who fell at the battle of Wakefield. His duchess Cecily, "the Rose of Raby," chose for the instruction of her numerous family, a lady governess of rank, from whom, in the absence of their natural parents, the young Plantagenets received an education very superior to that which was then ordinarily bestowed even upon high-born youth. In the household of the Duchess, religious and moral sentiments were strictly inculcated: even at "dynner tyme," she had "a lecture of holy matter, either 'Hilton, of Contemplative and Active Life,' or other spiritual and instructive works;" and "in the tyme of supper," she "recyted the lecture that was had at dynner to those that were in her presence."*

Notwithstanding the idle tales of monkish chroniclers relative to the birth of Richard—which Shakspeare has adopted from the narratives of prejudiced historians—no authentic record is extant of Richard's birth, beyond the time and place. W. Hut-

---

* In the document preserved at the Board of Green Cloth, whence the above details are quoted, are the following *Rules of the House:*
Upon eating days. At dinner by eleven of the clocke.
Upon fasting days. At dinner by twelve of the clocke.
At supper upon eating dayes ; for the officers at four of the clocke.
My lady and the household at five of the clocke at supper.
Livery of fires and candles, from the feast of All-hallows, unto Good Friday—then expireth the time of fire and candles.

ton, who devoted eighteen years to the traditions connected with this prince, asserts, after minute inquiries among the localities of his childhood, that "his infancy was spent in his father's house, where he cuekt his ball and shot his taw with the same delight as other lads." But, Richard's parents lived in royal state in Fotheringhay castle; and cotemporary annals record that their young children were at times surprised and seized in their retirement, and had to fly in all haste from the enemy; when the infant Richard was peculiarly watched by the Lady Cecily; and Richard, despite of Lancastrian prejudices, is proved to have testified through life the most respectful deference for his affectionate mother. He was little more than seven years of age when he was made prisoner with her at the sacking of Ludlow castle; and escaping to London, instead of taking up their abode in Baynard's castle, they privately sought an asylum at the law chambers of Sir John Paston, in the Temple;* and after the defeat and death of their father at Sendal, near Wakefield, the widowed Duchess had her children conveyed to Holland, where, under the protection of Philip Duke of Burgundy, at Utrecht they had princely and liberal 'education; the Low Countries being, at this crisis, the seat of chivalry, and distinguished by its patronage of learning and the fine arts. Hence the exiled children were brought to England by order of their brother, Edward IV., to be instructed in the practice of arms preparatory to knighthood, when Richard was created Duke of Gloucester and Admiral of the Sea.

<small>The Chivalrous Education of this period was very severe. The infant aspirant for knighthood, whether prince or peer, remained until the age of seven under the tutelage of his mother or female relatives; while he was carefully instructed in religious and moral and domestic duties, and taught the limited scholastic acquirements of that period. At the age of seven, he was removed into the family of some renowned feudal lord, who initiated him into the mysteries and hardships of a martial and chivalrous career; there he remained as a page until the age of fourteen, when invested with the first degree of squire he exchanged the short dagger for the sword, and thus became qualified to follow his gallant leader to the field of battle, to the joust or tournament; to lead his war-steed, or buckle on his armor; to furnish him with fresh horses and weapons; and himself to strive and win the spurs of knighthood. At the age of twenty-one he was knighted with great solemnity, impressive rites and ceremonies, the initiation being hallowed by the Church; and thus he became the warrior knight of the Middle Ages.—*Abridged from Miss Halstead's Richard III.*</small>

As Sir George Buck states that the King, when he called home his two brothers, entered them into the practice of arms, it is most probable that Gloucester passed the next seven years in the abode of some powerful baron, there to be well tutored in chivalrous accomplishments; and an exchequer-roll records that money was "paid to Edward Earl of Warwick ('the Kingmaker') for costs and expenses incurred by him on behalf of the Duke of

---

* Sir John Paston was knighted by Edward IV. at his coronation, probably in requital for this faithful service.

Gloucester, the King's brother." Thus was founded the military fame of Richard's after years—highly extolled even by his enemies. He is thought to have passed his youth at the castle of Middleham, in Yorkshire, associated with the flower of English chivalry, practicing manly exercises, bold and athletic, or sportive, with "hawk and hound, seasoned with lady's smiles," and forming early friendships which lasted through life.* At the early age of fourteen, Richard was created a Knight of the Garter, which is sufficient evidence of the progress he must then have made in military accomplishments and princely and gallant deportment. Richard's public career may be said to date from this period: his first act being, by appointment of the King, to transport the remains of his father for interment in the church at Fotheringhay; and Richard is thought to have finished the building of this church, from the carved boar, his crest, being on each side of the supporters of the royal arms, already mentioned. There are undoubted memorials that Gloucester was a prince of powerful mind, with shrewdness and discretion far beyond his years, and "in wit and courage equal to either of his brothers, though in body and prowess far beneath them both" (*Sir Thomas More*), nature having compensated him by strength of mind for inferiority in personal appearance. Lastly, he was "a high-spirited youth, whom all were praising and applauding;" yet none have been more grievously misrepresented in after life, as is proved by the Public Statutes of his reign. He bestowed alms on various religious bodies, and was a benefactor to a college in each University. And we learn from Rymer that Richard had in his service an Italian whose name was Titus Livius, and who was both Poet and Orator to the Duke.

<small>Yet how perversely has the character of Richard been vilified. The magic powers and Lancastrian partialities of Shakspeare, based on Sir Thomas More, have fixed this calumny in the public mind: in the reign of James I. the middle classes referred to Shakspeare for English history; and the Great Duke of Marlborough, Lord Chatham, and Southey, the poet, acknowledge their principal acquaintance with English history to have been derived from Shakspeare's historical dramas.</small>

TROUBLED BOYHOOD OF HENRY VII.

Henry VII., the son of Edmund Tudor, Earl of Richmond,

<small>* One of Richard's most devoted associates at Middleham was the young Lord Lovell, whose attachment to Gloucester in after times led him into many tragical vicissitudes: he accompanied the prince in most of his military campaigns; during the protectorate he held the lucrative office of chief butler of England; wore one of the swords of justice, and walked on the king's left hand, at his coronation; and after attending him to the battle of Bosworth, he is supposed to have been starved to death at his own seat, Minster Lovell, in Oxfordshire; the skeleton of a man seated in a chair, with his head reclining upon a table, being accidentally discovered there in a chamber underground, towards the close of the 17th century. The Lord Lovell probably took refuge in this place of concealment after his defeat at the battle of Stoke, a large reward being offered for his apprehension; and his melancholy end is supposed to have occurred from neglect on the part of those who were intrusted with his secret.—*Lingard*, vol. v. p. 290.</small>

and Margaret Beaufort, his countess, was born in the castle of Pembroke, in 1456. The small apartment in which Henry was born is represented to be near the chapel in the castle; but Leland, who lived near that time, states that the monarch first saw the light in one of the handsome rooms of the great gateway : " In the latter ward I saw the chambre where King Henry the Seventh was borne, in knowledge whereof a chymmeney is now made with the armes and badges of King Henry VII." His father dying in the following year, left his infant son Henry to the care of his brother, Jasper Earl of Pembroke. His mother was twice remarried : she was rich, pious, charitable, and generous; and to her bounty Christ's College, Cambridge, and St. John's College, Cambridge, owe their existence. The Countess also established a Professorship of Divinity in each university, the holders of which are called Lady Margaret's Professors : she likewise appointed a public preacher at Cambridge, whose duties are now confined to the delivery of one Latin sermon yearly.

Henry was cradled in adversity, but found a protector in his uncle, the Earl of Pembroke, till the earl was attainted, and fled; when his castle and earldom were granted to Baron William Herbert, who coming to take possession, and finding there Margaret and her son Henry, then in his fifth year, he was carried by that nobleman to his residence, Raglan Castle, Monmouthshire, now an ivied ruin. Long afterward, Henry told the French historian, Comines, that he had either been in prison, or in strict surveillance, from the time he was five years of age.

Sir William's family of four sons and six daughters afforded Henry companions in his own sphere of life, and gave him opportunities to acquire accomplishments and practice exercises that would have been wholly unattainable on account of the retired habits of the Countess of Richmond. Yet, Henry grew up sad, serious and circumspect; full of thought and secret observation; peaceable in disposition, just and merciful in action. From the old Flemish historians, and his biographer Lord Bacon, it further appears that Henry "was fair and well spoken, with singular sweetness and blandishment of words, rather studious than learned, with a devotional cast of countenance; for he was marvellously religious both in affection and observance."—(*Life of Henry VII.*) He appears to have excited no common degree of interest in the hearts of his guardians in Pembroke Castle, and to have continued to win upon their love and affection, as he advanced in years, as it is asserted that by the Lady Herbert he was well and carefully educated, and that Sir William desired to see him wedded to his favorite daughter Maud.

After the battle of Banbury, in which Sir Richard Herbert

was taken prisoner, and beheaded, the youthful Earl of Richmond, though strictly watched, and considered in the light of a captive, in Pembroke Castle, was most courteously treated, and honorably brought up by the Lady Herbert. Andreas Scott, a priest of Oxford, is said to have been his preceptor; and Henry's cotemporary biographer, Sandford, in recording this fact, mentions also the eulogiums bestowed by Scott on his great capacity and aptitude for study. Nevertheless, as he was now fourteen years of age, his uncle, Jasper Tudor, took him from Wales, and carried him to London, where, after being presented to Henry VI., he was placed as a scholar at Eton. Such is the statement of Miss Halstead, quoting Sandford as her authority. Lord Bacon relates, that Henry VI. washing his hands at a great feast, at his newly-founded College at Eton, turned toward the boy Henry and said: "This is the lad which shall possess quietly that that we now strive for;" which vaticination has been thus beautifully rendered by Shakspeare:

> *K. Henry.*—"My Lord of Somerset, what youth is that,
>   Of whom you seem to have so tender care?"
> *Som.*—"My liege, it is young Henry, Earl of Richmond."
> *K. Henry.*—"Come hither, England's hope. If secret powers
>   Suggest but truth to my divining thoughts,
>   This pretty lad will prove our country's bliss.
>   His looks are full of peaceful majesty;
>   His head by nature fram'd to wear a crown;
>   His hand to wield a sceptre, and himself
>   Likely, in our time, to bless a royal throne.
>   Make much of him, my lords; for this is he,
>   Must help you more, than you are hurt by me."
>   *Henry VI., Scene VI., Act IV.*

This is a favorite tradition; but the only printed authority for it is that of Sandford, who, in his Genealogical History, says that "while he (Henry VII.) was a child *and a scholar in Eton College*, he was there by King Henry the Sixth, prophetically entitled the Decider of the then difference between that prince and King Edward the Fourth." Hall, the chronicler, himself an Etonian, does not, however, record among its students the sagacious founder of the dynasty of the Tudors; and Mr. Creasy has searched in vain the archives of the College for evidence.

Miss Halstead relates, however (but without the authority), that the young Earl was subsequently withdrawn from Eton by his uncle, Jasper Tudor, and sent again, for greater security, to Pembroke Castle, where his mother continued to sojourn. After the battle of Tewkesbury, Henry was sent back to Raglan Castle, whence he was secretly carried off by his uncle to his own castle of Pembroke; whence they escaped the search of King Edward, and taking to sea, were driven on the coast of Britanny, where they long remained in a position between guests and prisoners.

Progress of Education. 59

As Henry grew to manhood, his personal character for ability and courage caused him to be recognized, without any hereditary claim, as the head of the Lancastrian exiles.

<small>Philip de Comines, who knew Henry well, testifies that he was perfect in that courtly breeding, which so conciliates favor in princes who are ready of access, and plausible in speech. He had become master of the French language during his exile; and though, in consequence of his long imprisonment, and the trials which had saddened his early life, he was singularly cautious and timid, he had, nevertheless, gained wisdom from the same school of adversity—a wisdom that enabled him to profit by any favoring circumstance that might lead to more prosperous days.—*Miss Halstead's Life of Margaret Beaufort*, p. 101.</small>

Henry VII., though he was called "the Solomon of England," did little for the spread of education beyond his works at Eton College. The sayings recorded of him show more weariness and cunning than knowledge of literature; and though he possessed great penetration, his mind was narrow. Arthur, son of Henry VII., we are told, was well instructed in grammar, poetry, oratory, and history. In this reign the purity of the Latin tongue was revived, the study of antiquity became fashionable, and the esteem for literature gradually propagated itself throughout Europe. The newly introduced art of Printing facilitated the progress of this amelioration; though some years elapsed before its beneficial effects were felt to any considerable extent.

A custom of this date shows the zeal of the London scholars. Upon the eve of St. Bartholomew (September 5), they held disputations; and Stow tells us that the scholars of divers grammar-schools disputed beneath the trees in the churchyard of the priory of St. Bartholomew, in West Smithfield. These disputations ceased with the suppression of the priory, but were revived *one* year under Edward VI., when the best scholar is stated to have received a silver arrow for his prize; but in some cases, the prize was a silver pen.

AN EMINENT GRAMMARIAN, AND POET LAUREATE.

Early in the sixteenth century flourished Robert Whittington, the author of several grammatical treatises which were long used in the schools. He was born at Lichfield, about the year 1480, and was educated by the eminent grammarian John Stanbridge, in the school then attached to Magdalene College, Oxford; and having taken priest's orders, he set up a grammar-school of his own, about 1501, possibly in London. Besides school-books, he wrote also Latin verse with very superior elegance; and he is remembered in modern times principally as the last person who was made poet laureate (*poeta laureatus*) at Oxford. This honor he obtained in 1513, on his petition to the congregation of regents of the University, setting forth that he had spent fourteen years in studying, and twelve in teaching the art of grammar, (which was understood to include rhetoric and poetry, or versification), and praying that he might be laureated or graduated in the said art. These academical graduations in grammar, on occasion of which, as Warton states, a "wreath of laurel was presented to the new graduate, who was afterward styled *poeta laureatus*," are supposed to have given rise to the appellation as applied to the King's poet, or versifier, who seems to have been merely a graduated grammarian or rhetorician employed in the service of the King.

EARLY LIFE AND CHARACTER OF HENRY VIII.

Henry VIII., the second son of Henry VII. and Elizabeth of York, was born in 1491, at his palace in his "manor of Pleazaunce," at Greenwich.

Henry was from the first destined to the Archbishopric of Canterbury; "that prudent King, his father," observes Lord Herbert (in the History of his Life and Reign), "choosing this as the most cheap and glorious way of disposing of a younger son." He received, accordingly, a learned education; "so that," continues this writer, "besides his being an able Latinist, philosopher, and divine, he was (which one might wonder at in a King) a curious musician, as two entire masses, composed by him, and often sung in his chapel, did abundantly witness." But the death of Henry's elder brother Arthur, in 1502, made him heir to the crown before he had completed his eleventh year, and his clerical education was not further proceeded with. However, he was initiated into the learning of the ancients, and though he was so unfortunate as to be led into the study of the barren controversies of the schools, which was then fashionable, he still discovered, says Hume, "a capacity fitted for more useful and entertaining knowledge." He founded Trinity College, at Cambridge, and amply endowed it; and the countenance given to letters by the King and his ministers rendered learning fashionable. The Venetian Ambassador to England, Sebastian Giustinian, describes Henry at this period (1515), as "so gifted and adorned with mental accomplishments of every sort that we believe him to have few equals in the world. He speaks English, French, and Latin; understands Italian well; plays almost on every instrument; sings and composes fairly."

One of the means which Cardinal Wolsey employed to please the capricious Henry was to converse with him on favorite topics of literature. Cavendish, who was gentleman-usher to Wolsey, and who wrote his life, tells us that "his sentences and witty persuasions in the council-chamber were always so pithy, that they, as occasion moved them, continually assigned him for his filed tongue and excellent eloquence to be expositor unto the King in all their proceedings."

Education had done much for Henry; and of his intellectual ability we need not trust the suspicious panegyrics of his cotemporaries. His state papers and letters are as clear and powerful as those of Wolsey or of Cromwell. In addition to this, Henry had a fine musical taste, carefully cultivated; he spoke and wrote in four languages; and he possessed a knowledge of a multitude of subjects. He was among the first physicians of his age; he was his own engineer, inventing improvements in artillery, and new constructions in ship-building. His reading was vast, especially in theology, which could not have been acquired by a boy of twelve years of age, for he was no more when he became Prince of Wales. He must have studied theology with the full maturity of his understanding. In private he was good-humored and good-natured. But, like all princes of the Plantagenet blood, he was a person of most intense and imperious will. His impulses, in general nobly directed, had never known contradiction; and late in life, when his character was formed, he was forced into collision with difficulties with which the experience of discipline had not fitted him to contend.*

ILL-EDUCATED NOBILITY.

Some amongst the highest in rank affected to despise knowledge, especially when the invention of Printing had rendered the ability to read more common than in the days of precious manuscripts. Even as late as the first year of Edward VI. (1547), it was not only assumed that a Peer of the Realm might be convicted of felony, but that he might lack the ability to read, so as to claim Benefit of Clergy; for it is directed that any Lord of the Parliament claiming the benefit of this Act (1st Edward VI.), "*though he cannot read*, without any burning in the hand, loss of inheritance, or corruption of his blood, shall be judged, taken, and used, for the first time only, to all intents, constructions, and purposes, as a clerk convict."

That the nobility were unfitted, through ignorance, for the discharge of high offices in the State, at the time of the Reformation, is shown by a remarkable passage in Latimer's "Sermon of the Plow," preached in 1548:

Why are not the noblemen and young gentlemen of England so brought up in the knowledge of God, and in learning, that they may be able to execute offices in the commonweal? . . . If the nobility be well trained in godly learning, the people would follow the same train; for truly such as the noblemen be, such will the people be. . . . Therefore for the love of God appoint teachers and schoolmasters, you that have charge of youth, and give the teachers stipends worthy their pains.

---

* Abridged from Froude's History of England.

Honest old Latimer thus demanded that "the young gentlemen" of England should be educated, and be "well brought up in the learning and knowledge of God," so that "they would not, when they came to age, so much give themselves to other vanities."

THE SCHOOL OF MORE.

Among the most eminent men of this remarkable period was Sir Thomas More, the records of whose early life and private history throw considerable light upon the state of education in his time. The interesting traits of More's boyhood—his school-days at St. Anthony's in Threadneedle-street (one of the four grammar-schools founded by Henry VI.); his removal into the household of Cardinal Morton; and his college days at Oxford; will be found sketched elsewhere in this volume. We here follow More into his domestic retirement at Chelsea.

More hath built near London (says Erasmus), upon the Thames, such a commodious house, and is neither mean, nor subject to envy, yet magnificent enough. There he converseth affably with his family, his wife, his son and daughter, his three daughters and their husbands; with eleven grand-children. . . . . You would say that there were in that place Plato's academy; but I do the house injury in comparing it to Plato's academy, wherein were only disputations of numbers and geometrical figures, and sometimes of moral virtues. I would rather call his house a school or university of Christian religion; for there is none therein but readeth or studieth the liberal sciences; their special care is piety and virtue; there is no quarreling or intemperate words heard; none seem idle; which household discipline that worthy gentleman doth not govern by proud and lofty words, but with all kind and courteous benevolence. Everybody performeth his duty, yet is there always alacrity, neither is sober mirth anything wanting.

In the intervals of business, the education of his children formed More's greatest pleasure. His opinions respecting female education differed very widely from what the comparative rudeness of the age might have led us to expect. By nothing, he justly thought, is female virtue so much endangered as by idleness, and the fancied necessity of amusement; and against these is there any safeguard so effectual as an attachment to literature? Some security is indeed afforded by a diligent application to various sorts of female employments; yet these, while they employ the hands, give only partial occupation to the mind. But well-chosen books at once engage the thoughts, refine the taste, strengthen the understanding, and confirm the morals. Female virtue, informed by the knowledge which they impart, is placed on the most secure foundations, while all the milder affections of the heart, partaking in the improvement of the taste and fancy, are refined and matured. More was no convert to the notion, that the possession of knowledge renders women less pliant; nothing, in his opinion, was so untractable as ignorance. Although to manage with skill the feeding and clothing of a family is an essential portion in the duties of a wife and a mother, yet to secure the affections of a husband, he judged it no less indispensable to possess the qualities of an intelligent and agreeable companion. Nor ought a husband, if he regards his own happiness, neglect to endeavor to remove the casual defects of female education. Never can he hope to be so truly beloved, esteemed, and respected, as when the wife confides in him as her friend, and looks up to him as her instructor. Such were the opinions, with regard to female education, which More maintained in discourse, and supported by practice. His daughters, rendered proficients in music, and other elegant accomplishments proper for their sex, were also instructed in Latin, in which language they read, wrote and conversed with the facility and correctness of their father. The results of this assiduous attention soon became conspicuous, and *the School of More*, as it was termed, attracted general admiration. In the meantime the stepmother of the daughters, a notable economist, by distributing tasks, of which she required a punctual performance, took care that they should not remain unacquainted with female works, and with the management of a family. For all these employments, which together appear so far beyond the ordinary industry of women, their time was found sufficient, because no part of it was wasted in idleness or trifling amusements. If any of More's servants discovered a taste for reading, or an ear for music, he allowed them to cultivate their favorite pursuit. To preclude all improper conversation before children and servants at table, a domestic was accustomed to read aloud certain passages, so selected as to amuse for the time, and to afford matter for much entertaining conversation.

Margaret Roper, the first-born of More's children, was as celebrated for her learning as beloved for her tender affection to her father in his hour of suffering. Erasmus called her *the ornament of Britain, and the flower of the learned matrons of England*, at a time when education consisted only of the revived study of ancient learning. She composed a touching account of the last hours of her father.

With a few words upon Sir Thomas More's views on Public Education we conclude. That he conceived *the education of all classes* to be most conducive to happiness, is evident from the following passage in his *Utopia*, professedly written to describe "the best state of a public weal," or in more familiar words, a sort of model nation. More says: "though there be not many in every city which be exempt and discharged of all other labors, and appointed only to learning — that is to say, such in whom, even from their very childhood, they have perceived a singular towardness, a fine wit, and a mind apt to good learning—*yet all* in their childhood be instructed in learning. And the better part of the people, both men and women, throughout all their whole life do bestow in learning those spare hours which we said they have *vacant from their bodily labors.*" This was written nearly three centuries and a half since ; the people of England have not yet reached this condition, although they are tending toward it by efforts at affording *elementary instruction for all children,* and inducing *the habit of self-culture in all adults.*

WOLSEY, LATIMER, AND CRANMER.

The boyhood of three great men of this period shows the means of education then obtainable by the middle classes. WOLSEY, who was the son of "an honest poor man," not a butcher's son, as commonly supposed,* was sent when a boy to the Free Grammar-school at Ipswich; thence he was removed to Magdalene College, Oxford, and was subsequently appointed master of a grammar-school dependent on that college. Part of his ill-acquired wealth, Wolsey, late in life, expended in the advancement of learning. At Oxford, he founded the college of Christchurch; but before his magnificent design was completed, Wolsey had lost the favor of his sovereign, and the King having, immediately on the Cardinal's fall, taken possession of the revenues intended for the support of the college, the design had well nigh fallen to the ground; when Wolsey, in the midst of all his troubles, among his last petitions to the King, urgently requested that "His Majesty would suffer his college at Oxford to go on." This the King did, but transferred the credit of the measure to himself. Meanwhile, Wolsey had founded at Ipswich, in 1527, a school, as a nursery for his intended college at Oxford; and this school is said for a time to have rivaled the colleges of Eton and Winchester.

HUGH LATIMER, the son of a Leicestershire farmer, born in or about 1472, was first sent to a grammar-school, and afterward to Cambridge. Of his family circumstances, Latimer has left us this interesting record : "My father," he writes, "was a yeoman, and had no lands of his own ; only he had a farm of three or four pounds by the year at the uttermost, and hereupon he tilled so much as kept half-a-dozen men. He had walk for a hundred sheep, and my mother milked thirty kine. He was able, and did find the king a harness with himself and his horse. I remember that I buckled on his harness when he went to

---

* Wolsey was not born in Ipswich, as generally stated ; but at Long Melford, near Ipswich. (See *Curiosities of History,* p. 225.) He is said to have written the preface to "Lilly's Grammar ;" but this is doubtful. In this preface the truest principles of tuition are ably laid down ; and the necessity of making a scholar learn thoroughly what he is taught step by step is fully stated and enforced.

Blackheath field. *He kept me to school, or else I had not been able to have preached before the king's majesty now.* He married my sisters with five pounds, or twenty nobles, each, having brought them up in godliness and fear of God. He kept hospitality for his poor neighbors, and some alms he gave to the poor; and all this he did of the said farm."

THOMAS CRANMER was born at Aslacton, Notts, in 1489, of a family who had been settled in that county for some generations. His first instruction was received from the parish-clerk. at the village school, from which he was removed by his mother, now become a widow, who placed him in 1503 at Jesus College, Cambridge, amongst "the better sort of students," where Greek, Hebrew, and theology were the principal objects of his industry.

BOYHOOD AND LEARNING OF KING EDWARD THE SIXTH.

The most munificent patron of education who ever sat upon the British throne was Edward VI., the only son of Henry VIII. who survived him. He was born at Hampton Court in 1537, on the 12th of October, which being the vigil of St. Edward, he received his Christian appellation in commemoration of the canonized king. His mother, Queen Jane Seymour, died on the twelfth day after giving him birth. The child had three stepmothers in succession after this; but he was probably not much an object of attention with either of them. Sir John Hayward, who has written the history of his life and reign with great fullness, says that " he was brought up among nurses until he arrived at the age of six years. He was then committed to the care of Dr. (afterward Sir Anthony) Cook, and Mr. (afterward Sir John) Cheke, the former of whom appears to have undertaken the prince's instruction in philosophy and divinity, the latter in Greek and Latin." He succeeded to the throne when little more than nine years of age. The conduct of the young prince toward his instructors was uniformly courteous; and his generous disposition won for him the highest esteem. In common with the children of the rich and great, he was from his cradle surrounded with means of amusement. It is related that at the age of five years, a splendid present was made to him by his godfather, Archbishop Cranmer; the gift was a costly service of silver, consisting of dishes, plates, spoons, etc. The child was overjoyed with the present, when the prince's valet, seeking to impress on his mind its value, observed: " Your highness will be pleased to remember that although this beautiful present is yours, it must be kept entirely to yourself; for if others are permitted to touch it, it will be entirely spoiled." "My good Hinbrook," replied the prince mildly, "if no one can touch these valuables without spoiling them, how do you then suppose they would ever have been given to me?" Next day, Edward invited a party of young friends to a feast, which was served upon the present of plate; and upon the departure of the young guests, he gave to each of them an article of the service, as a mark of regard.

Cranmer, to encourage Edward in his studies, was in the habit of corresponding with him once a week, and requiring of him an account of what he had done during that time. The prince also complied with the request of his venerable godfather, by keeping a journal, for which purpose he divided a sheet of paper into five columns, and under that arrangement recorded his progress in mythology, history, geography, mathematics, and philosophy.

At the age of fifteen, Edward is said to have possessed a critical knowledge of the Greek and Latin languages; and to have conversed fluently in French, Spanish, and Italian. A manuscript is still preserved in the British Museum, containing a collection of his exercises in Greek and Latin; several of his letters, in French and Latin, written with singular accuracy of diction, are also extant; as well as a French tract, composed before he was twelve years old, against the abuses of Popery. In the Ashmolean and Cottonian collections are other papers in his handwriting; some of which relate to state affairs, and evince an intimate knowlege of the domestic and foreign policy of his government, and his anxious concern for the welfare of his people. But the most striking of his existing productions are "King Edward the Sixth's own Arguments against the Pope's Supremacy;" and "A Translation into French of several passages of Scripture, which forbid idolatry, or the worshipping of false gods." There are also some "Metrical Stanzas on the Eucharist," which Fox has printed in his Martyrology, and characterizes as highly creditable to the young prince; and when to his other accomplishments it is added that he was well versed in natural philosophy, astronomy, and logic, his acquirements will be allowed to have been extraordinary. "This child," says Carden, the celebrated physician, who had frequently conversed with Edward, "was so bred, had such parts, was of such expectation, that he looked like a miracle of a man; and in *him* was such an attempt of Nature, that not only England, but the world, had reason to lament his being so early snatched away."

In a register kept for the purpose, Edward noted down the characters of public men; and all the important events of his reign, together with the proceedings in council, were recorded in a private journal, which he never allowed to pass out of his possession. The original of this Journal * still remains; and a soundness of judgment is displayed in the various entries, and the reflections with which they are accompanied, far beyond Edward's years. "It gave hopes," said Lord Orford, " of his proving a good king, as in so green an age he seemed resolved to be acquainted with his subjects and his kingdom." He was quite familiar with the value of money, and the principles of finance; and the mercantile and military affairs of the country. He was inflexibly just both in public and private; and his attention to his social duties was no less remarkable than his strict discharge of the regal functions. In disposition he was meek, affable, and benevolent; dignified, yet courteous in conversation; and sincere and disinterested in his friendship. " If ye knew the towardness of that young prince," observes one that was about his person, " your hearts would melt to hear him named; the beautifullest creature that liveth under the sun, the wittiest, the most amiable, and the gentlest thing of all the world." His compassion for the poor and the distressed was enlarged, yet unostentatious; and the distribution of his charities was rendered doubly valuable by the promptitude and considerate delicacy with which they were conferred.

Perhaps, however, the most prominent features in the character of the young king were his sincere piety and zeal in the cause of religion. He showed this strength of feeling even in his infancy. One of his companions having stepped upon a large Bible for the purpose of obtaining a toy which was out of his reach, he rebuked him severely for so doing, and left the play in which they were engaged. At his coronation, when the swords of the three kingdoms were carried before him, he observed that one was still wanting, and called for the Bible. " *That*," said he, " is the sword of the Spirit, and ought in all right to govern us, who use them for the people's safety, by God's appointment. Without that sword we can do nothing: from that, we are what we are this day. Under that we ought to live, to fight, to govern the people, and to perform all our affairs. From that alone we obtain all power, virtue, grace, salvation, and whatever we have of divine strength." Such indeed was Edward's regard for religion, and for everything connected with it, that it was usual to compare him to Josiah; and he had also acquired the characteristic appellation of " Edward the Saint." It was his custom to take notes of the sermons which he heard; particularly of those which seemed to bear any immediate relation to his own duties

---

* This is preserved, with some other Remains of the young King in the British Museum, and printed, though imperfectly, in the collection of Records, forming vol. ii. part ii., of Burnet's History of the Reformation.

and difficulties; and the attention which he paid to the precepts inculcated in the discourses of the eminent divines who preached before him, frequently produced a visible and permanent effect upon his conduct, as will be seen presently.

EDWARD VI. FOUNDS CHRIST'S HOSPITAL.

Few events in the history of Christian benevolence are so minutely recorded as the foundation of this the noblest institution in the world. At the same time, Edward founded St. Thomas's and Bridewell Hospitals; the three foundations forming part of a comprehensive scene of charity, resulting from a sermon preached before the King by the pious Bishop Ridley, at Westminster, in 1552. The Bishop, discoursing on the excellence of charity, "made a fruitful and goodly exhortation to the rich to be merciful unto the poor, and also to move such as were in authority, to travail by some charitable ways and means, to comfort and relieve them." Edward's heart was touched by the earnestness of the appeal, and "understanding that a great number of poor people did swarm in this realm, and chiefly in the city of London, and that no good order was taken of them," he sent the Bishop a message when the sermon was ended desiring him not to depart till he had spoken with him. As soon as he was at leisure, he took him aside into a private gallery, where he made him sit down and be covered; and giving him hearty thanks for his sermon, entered into conversation on several points, which, according to his usual practice, he had noted down for special consideration. Of this interview, the venerable Ridley remarked: "Truly, truly, I could never have thought that excellency to have been in his grace, but that I beheld and heard it in him."

Adverting, at length, to the Bishop's exhortation in behalf of the poor, Edward greatly commended it, and it had evidently made a powerful impression upon his mind. He then acknowledged the application of Ridley's exhortation to himself, and prayed the Bishop to say his mind as to what ways were best to be taken. Ridley hesitated for a moment to reply. At length, he observed that the city of London, as well on account of the extreme poverty which prevailed there on the one hand, and of the wise and charitable disposition of its more wealthy inhabitants on the other, would afford a favorable opening for the exercise of the royal bounty; and advised that letters should be forthwith directed to the Lord Mayor, requiring him, with such assistants as he might think meet, to consult upon the matter. Edward wrote the letter upon the instant, and charged Ridley to deliver it himself; and his delight was manifested in the zeal with which he undertook the commission, for the King's letter and message were delivered on the same evening. On the following day Ridley dined with the Lord Mayor, who, with two Aldermen and six Commoners, took the King's proposal into consideration; other counselors were added, and at length the plan recommended to his Majesty was to provide Christ's Hospital for the education of poor children; St. Thomas's, for the relief of the sick and diseased; and Bridewell, for the correction and amendment of the idle and the vagabond.

For Christ's Hospital was granted the monastery of the Grey Friars; the King also presenting the foundation with a considerable stock of linen, which the commissioners, who had lately been appointed to inspect the churches in and about the metropolis, had deemed superfluous for the performance of divine service, as celebrated since the Reformation. For the second hospital, an almonry was fitted up; and for the third hospital, Edward granted his royal palace of Bridewell. He then bestowed certain lands for the support of these foundations; and having signed the instrument, ejaculated in the hearing of his Council— "Lord, I yield thee most hearty thanks, that thou hast given me life this long, to finish this work to the glory of thy name."

A large picture (attributed to Holbein), which hangs in the Great Hall of Christ's Hospital, portrays this interesting scene. The young monarch sits on an elevated throne, in a scarlet and ermined robe, holding the sceptre in his left hand, and presenting with the other the Charter to the kneeling Lord Mayor. By his side stands the Chancellor holding the seals, and next to him are other officers of State. Bishop Ridley kneels before him with uplifted hands, as if supplicating a blessing on the event; whilst the Aldermen, etc., with the Lord Mayor, kneel on both sides, occupying the middle ground of the picture, and lastly, in front, are a double row of boys on one side, and girls on the other, from the master and matron down to the boy and girl who have stepped forward from their respective rows, and kneel with raised hands before the King.

Edward lived about a month after signing the Charter of Incorporation of the Royal Hospitals: in the spring of 1552 he had been seized with the small-pox, when he had scarcely recovered from the measles; a consumptive cough came on; his medical advisers were dismissed, and his cure intrusted to the ignorant empiricisms of an old nurse; this disorder was greatly aggravated, and he died in the arms of Sir Henry Sidney, on the 6th July, 1553, in the sixteenth year of his age, praying God to receive his spirit, and to defend the realm from papistry.

The old Grey Friars buildings adjoining Newgate-street were now repaired by aid of the citizens' benefactions, and in November, 1552, there were admitted 340 "poore fatherlesse children" within the ancient monastery walls. "On Christmas-day," says Stow, "while the Lord Maior and Aldermen rode to Paul's, the children of Christ's Hospitall stood from St. Lawrence-lane end in Cheape towards Paul's, all in one livery of russet cotton, 340 in number; and at Easter next they were in *blue*, at the Spittle, and so have continued ever since." Hence the popular name of the Hospital, "the Blue-Coat School."

Since this period, the income of the institution has known much fluctuation; and, consequently, the number of inmates. The 340 children with which the Hospital opened had dwindled in 1580 to 150. The object of the institution has also, in the lapse of time, become materially changed, which may in a great measure be attributed to the influence of the Governors, or benefactors, its chief supporters.

The Hospital, with the church of the monastery, was destroyed by the Great Fire, but was soon rebuilt. Later was added the Mathematical School, founded by Charles II., in 1672, for 40 boys, to be instructed in navigation; they are called "King's Boys," and wear a badge on the right shoulder; and there was subsequently added, by the legacy of a Governor, a subordinate Mathematical School of 12 boys ("The Twelves"), who wear a badge on the left shoulder; and, lastly, to these have been added "The Twos."

This was the first considerable extension of the system of education at the Hospital, which originally consisted of a grammar-school for boys, and a separate school for girls; the latter being taught to read, sew, and mark. A book is preserved containing the records of the Hospital from its foundation, and the anthem sung by the first children.

Of the school buildings, there remains the Writing School, a large edifice built by Sir Christopher Wren, in 1694, at the expense of Sir John Moore, of whom a marble statue is placed in the façade. Of the ancient Friary—portions of the cloisters only remain. The great Dining Hall was commenced in 1825, and is built partly on the ancient wall of London, and partly on the foundation of the refectory of the monastery. It is a vast edifice in the Tudor style, by Shaw, the principal front facing Newgate-street, with the inclosed play-ground; the Hall, with its lobby and organ gallery, is 178 feet long; it is lit by nine large windows, and is, next to Westminster Hall, the noblest room in the metropolis. Here, besides the large Charter picture already described, is a painting by Verrio, of James II. on his throne, receiving "the Mathematical Boys," in the same form as at their annual presentation to this day; though in Verrio's picture are girls as well as boys.

In this Hall are held the "Suppings in Public," on the seven Sunday evenings preceding Easter Sunday, and on that evening, to which visitors are admitted by tickets. The tables are laid with cheese in wooden bowls; beer in wooden piggins, poured from leathern jacks; and bread brought in huge baskets. The official company then enter, the Lord Mayor or President taking his seat in a chair made of oak from old St. Katherine's Church; a hymn is sung, accompanied by the organ; a Grecian reads the evening service from the pulpit silence being enforced by three strokes of a hammer. After prayers, the meal commences, the visitors walking between the tables At its close, the " trade boys " take up the piggins and jacks, baskets, bowls, and candlesticks, and pass in procession before the authorities, bowing to them; the entire 800 boys thus passing out.

The Spital (or Hospital) Sermons are preached in Christchurch, Newgate-street, on Easter Monday and Tuesday. On Monday, the children proceed to the Mansion House, and return in procession to Christchurch with the Lord Mayor and City authorities to hear the sermon. On Tuesday, the children again go to the Mansion House, and pass through the Egyptian Hall before the Lord Mayor, each boy receiving a glass of wine, two buns, and a shilling; the monitors half-a-crown each, and the Grecians a guinea. They then return to Christchurch, as on Monday.

At the first Drawing-room of the year, forty "Mathematical Boys" are presented to the Sovereign, who gives them 8*l*. 8*s*. as a gratuity. To this, other members of the Royal Family formerly added smaller sums, and the whole was divided among the ten boys who left the school in the year. On the illness of King George III. these presentations were discontinued; but the Governors of the Hospital continued to pay 1*l*. 3*s*., the amount ordinarily received by each, to every boy on quitting. The practice of receiving the children was revived by William IV.

Each of the "Mathematical Boys" having passed his Trinity-House examination, and received testimonials of his good conduct, is presented with a watch, worth from 9*l*. to 13*l*., in addition to an outfit of clothes, books, mathematical instruments, a Gunter's scale, a quadrant, and sea-chest. On St. Matthew's Day (Sept. 21), "the Grecians" deliver orations, this being a relic of the scholars' disputations in the cloisters.

The dress of the Blue-Coat Boys is the costume of the citizens of London at the time of the foundation of the Hospital, when blue coats were the common habit of the apprentices and serving-men, and yellow stockings were generally worn. This dress is the nearest approach to the monkish costume now worn; the dark-blue coat, with a closely-fitting body and loose sleeves, being the ancient tunic, and the under-coat, or "yellow," the sleeveless under-tunic of the monastery. The red leathern girdle corresponds to the hempen cord of the friar. Yellow worsted stockings, a flat black woolen cap (scarcely larger than a saucer), and a clerical neckband, complete the dress.

The education of the boys consists of reading, writing, and arithmetic, French, the classics, and the mathematics. There are sixteen Exhibitions for scholars at the Universities of Oxford and Cambridge, etc. There are also separate trusts held by the Governors of the Hospital, which are distributed to poor widows, to the blind, and in apprenticing boys, etc. The annual income of the Hospital is about 50,000*l*.; its ordinary disbursements 48,000*l*.

Among the eminent *Blues* are Leigh Hunt; Thomas Barnes, many years editor of the *Times* newspaper; Thomas Mitchell, the translator of Aristophanes; S. T. Coleridge, the poet, and

Charles Lamb, his cotemporary; Middleton, Bishop of Calcutta; Jeremiah Markland, the best scholar and critic of the last century; Samuel Richardson, the novelist; Joshua Barnes, the scholiast; Bishop Stillingfleet; Camden, "the nourrice of antiquitie;" and Campion, the learned Jesuit of the age of Elizabeth. Coleridge, Charles Lamb, and Leigh Hunt have published many interesting reminiscences of their cotemporaries in the school.

The subordinate establishment is at Hertford, to which the younger boys are sent preparatory to their entering on the foundation in London. At Hertford there is likewise accommodation for 80 girls.

Besides the Lord Mayor, Court of Aldermen, and twelve members of the Common Council, who are Governors *ex officio*, there are between 400 and 500 other Governors, at the head of whom are the Queen and Prince Albert, with the Prince of Wales and Prince Alfred. The Duke of Cambridge is President. The qualification for Governor is a donation of 500*l.*; an Alderman may nominate a Governor for election at half-price. There are from 1400 to 1500 children on the foundation, including those at the branch establishment at Hertford. About 200 boys are admitted annually (at the age of from seven to ten years), by presentations of the Governors; the Queen, the Lord Mayor (two presentations), and the Court of Aldermen, presenting annually, and the other Governors in rotation, so that the privilege occurs about once in three or four years. A list of the Governors having presentations is published annually in March, and is to be had at the counting-house of the Hospital. "Grecians" and "King's Boys" remain in the school after they are fifteen years old; but the other boys leave at that age.

KING EDWARD'S SCHOOLS AT BIRMINGHAM, LICHFIELD, TUNBRIDGE, AND BEDFORD.

We have seen in the foregoing narrative that Endowments for Education are, probably, nearly as old as endowments for the support of the church. The monasteries had schools attached to them in many instances. Still, it must often have happened (thickly scattered though the monasteries were) that the child lived at an inconvenient distance from any one of them, and, probably, little was learned there after all. Before the Reformation, schools were also connected with chantries, and it was the duty of the priest to teach the children grammar and singing. Of this connection between schools and religious foundations, the keeping of them in the church, or in a building which was part of it, is an indication. (*See page* 38.) There are many schools still in existence which were founded before the Reformation, but a very great number was founded immediately after that event; and one object of Edward VI. in dissolving the chantries and other religious foundations then existing, was for the purpose of establishing Grammar Schools. But Strype assures us that the law for this purpose was grossly abused; for "though the public good was intended, yet private men had most of the benefit, and the king and the commonwealth, the state of learning and the condition of the poor, were left as they were before, or worse." King Edward's Schools were founded out of tithes that formerly belonged to religious houses or chantry lands;

and many of these schools, owing to the improved value of their property, are now among the richest foundations of the kind in England. There is no doubt, it should be added, that the desire to give complete ascendancy to the doctrines of the Reformed Church weighed strongly with the founders of these schools; and the clergy were enjoined by proclamation " to exhort the people to teach their children the Lord's Prayer, the Creed, and the Ten Commandments in English;" the service of the church having been previously performed in Latin.

"The King's School" at Sherborne is said to have been the first of King Edward's foundation, in all probability owing this rank to the Protector Somerset, who at that time held the estates of Sherborne Castle. The school premises, which are a fine specimen of olden architecture, were arranged by Bishop Jewel; and the foundation takes a high position among the leading schools of England.

Birmingham Free Grammar School is one of the richest foundations of the kind, Edward having endowed it with the property of suppressed religious houses. The Guild of the Holy Cross yielded it lands of the yearly value of 21*l*.; and the Governors were to nominate and appoint "a pedagogue and sub-pedagogue," with statutes and ordinances for the government of the school, "for the instruction of boys and youths in the learned languages." The value of the endowment had increased, in 1829, to upward of 3000*l*. a-year; and, in 1831, the Governors were empowered by law to build a new school for teaching modern languages, the arts and sciences; besides eight other schools for the elementary education of the poorer inhabitants of the town. The endowed income of this noble foundation is now 8000*l*.; it has ten university exhibitions; and the number of scholars in the Grammar School is nearly 500. The school-house is a handsome stone structure, in the Tudor style; designed by Barry, the architect of the new Houses of Parliament.

Lichfield Free Grammar School was also founded in this reign. Here were educated Elias Ashmole, the antiquary; Gregory King, the herald; George Smalridge, Bishop of Bristol; Dr. Wollaston, author of the *Religion of Nature;* Addison, who was the son of a Dean of Lichfield; Lord Chief-Justices Willes and Wilmot; Lord Chief Baron Parker; Judges Noel and Lloyd; Dr. Samuel Johnson, who was born at Lichfield; David Garrick; and Henry Salt, the traveler in Abyssinia. As early as the reign of Henry III., the bishop of the diocese founded a religious establishment, but it subsequently went under the name of "The Hospital School;" in 1740 it merged into the Grammar School.

Tunbridge School, in Kent, is another of our richly-endowed grammar-schools, the benefits of which have been vastly extended. This school was founded by Sir Andrew Judd, Knight, a native of the town of Tunbridge. He acquired a large fortune in London by trade in furs, and he served as Lord Mayor in 1550, when, says Holinshed, "he erected one notable Free School at Tunbridge, in Kent, wherein he brought up and nourished in learning grite store of youth, as well bred in that shire as brought up in other counties adjoining. A noble act, and corresponding to others that have been done by like worshipful men, and others in old time, in the same cittie of London." Sir Andrew Judd obtained a charter from Edward VI., in 1553, which empowered him to buy land within a limited sum for the endowment of his school. After his death, this property was conveyed to the Skinners' Company for the same uses; Sir Andrew, by his will, executed in 1558, devising to the Company certain lands and houses "for the perpetual maintenance of the school that he had erected at Tunbridge." Judd Place, east and west, Tunbridge Place, Burton Crescent, Mabledon Place, Judd, Bidborough, Hadlow, Speldhurst and Leigh Streets, in London, and others in Pancras parish, are situated on this property. There is also property in Gracechurch Street, Cornhill, Bishopsgate, and other places in the city of London.

For a long time the produce of these estates was little more than sufficient to defray all the expenses with which the school had been charged by the founder; until the building leases granted on the property in Pancras parish, and the improvement in Leadenhall market, raised the revenues to some thousands per annum; and at the expiration of all the present leases, it is stated that the endowment of Tunbridge School will be the most valuable in the kingdom. In this school, all whose parents live within ten miles, in Kent, are foundationers; there are several exhibitions, a fellowship at St. John's College, Oxford, etc. The instruction is according to the doctrines of the Church of England; whereas, at the Birmingham School a boy may be excused all examination "in the fundamental principles and doctrines of the Christian religion," though examiners are appointed for this purpose.*

The Grammar School of the Bedford Charity is likewise of King Edward's foundation, in 1552. There is, perhaps, no English town of similar extent equal to Bedford in the variety and magnitude of its charitable and educational establishments. But

---

* This is a very singular provision to introduce among the rules of one of King Edward's foundations, and its effect is to destroy one of the chief objects which the King had in view in establishing these schools.—*On Grammar Schools, by George Long.*

the principal benefactor was Sir William Harpur, alderman of London, who endowed the above free-school for the instruction of the children of the town "in grammar and good manners;" conveying to the corporation 13 acres of land in the parish of St. Andrew, Holborn, for the support of the school, and for portioning poor maidens of the town; the overplus, if any, to be given in alms to the poor. There have been built upon the land Lamb's Conduit Street, Harpur Street, Theobald's Road, Bedford Street, Bedford Row, New North Street, and some smaller streets; and thus the property has gradually risen in value from below 150*l* a-year, a quarter of a century since, to upward of 13,500*l*.! The income of the Grammar School is under 3000*l*. a-year; there are about 160 scholars, and 8 exhibitions. The Warden and Fellows of New College, Oxford, are the visitors.

REIGN OF QUEEN MARY.

King Edward's aids to education were cut short by his early death. His successor, Queen Mary, was brought up from her infancy to the Roman Catholic religion; and during her brief reign, she was too much occupied with the sanguinary persecutions of the adherents to the Reformed doctrines, to attend to the business of public education; little is recorded of her girlhood, though she is said to have possessed a share of the distinguished vigor and ability of her family.

Mary, the only child of Henry VIII. and Katherine of Arragon who survived her parents, was born at Greenwich, in 1516. She was brought up from infancy under the care of her mother, and Margaret, Countess of Salisbury, the effect of whose instructions was not impaired by the subsequent lessons of the learned Ludovicus Vives, who, though somewhat inclined to the English religion, was appointed by Henry to be her Latin tutor. In her tenth year a separate establishment was formed for her, and she was sent to reside at Ludlow, with a household of 300 persons, and with the Lady Salisbury for her governess. The time she passed there was probably the happiest of her days, for her life was early embittered by the controversy regarding her parents' marriage. Mary was brought up in a profound veneration for the see of Rome, by her mother, with whom she naturally sided; and thus she gave deep offense to her imperious father. Entries in her Privy Purse Account from 1536 to 1544, published by Sir Frederic Madden, show Mary's active benevolence toward the poor, compassion for prisoners, friendly regard and liberality to her servants; and also indicate elegant pursuits and domestic virtues, for which in general she does not receive credit.

EDUCATION OF QUEEN ELIZABETH.

Elizabeth, the only surviving child of Henry VIII. by Anne Boleyn, was born at Greenwich, in 1533. She is considered by Ascham, one of her teachers, as having attained the lead of the lettered ladies of England at this period. Camden describes her as "of a modest gravity, excellent wit, royal soul, happy memory, and indefatigably given to the study of learning; insomuch as before she was seventeen years of age she well understood the Latin, French, and Italian tongues, and had an indifferent knowledge of the Greek. Neither did she neglect music, so far as it became a princess, being able to sing sweetly, and play handsomely on the lute. With Roger Ascham, who was her tutor, she read over Melancthon's Common Places, all Tully, a great part of the histories of Titus Livius, certain select orations of Isocrates (whereof two she turned into Latin), Sophocles' Tragedies, and the New Testament in Greek, by which means she framed her tongue to a pure and elegant way of speaking," etc. Ascham tells us in his *Schoolmaster,* that Elizabeth continued her Greek studies subsequent to her accession to the throne. "After dinner" (at Windsor Castle, 10th December, 1563), he says, "I went up to read with the Queen's Majestie: we read there together in the Greek tongue, as I well remember, that noble oration of Demosthenes against Æschines for his false dealing in his embassage to Philip of Macedonia." Elizabeth was for some time imprisoned by her sister, Queen Mary, at Woodstock. A New Testament is still preserved, which bears the initials of the captive princess, in her own beautiful handwriting, with the following mixed allusion to her religious consolations and solitary life : " I walk many times into pleasant fields of Holy Scriptures, where I pluck up goodly sentences by pruning, eat them by reading, chew them by musing, and lay them up at length in the high seat of memory; that, having tasted their sweetness, I may the less perceive the bitterness of this miserable life."

Of Elizabeth's compositions (a few of which are in verse), her speeches to the parliament afford evidence of superior ability. She, like her royal predecessor, King Alfred, completed an English translation of Bœthius's Consolations of Philosophy, which translation, partly in her Majesty's handwriting, and partly in that of her Secretary, was discovered about the year 1830, in the State Paper Office.

Mary, Queen of Scots, merits mention among the learned women of this age. She was sent by her mother, in her fifth year, to a convent in France, where she made such rapid progress in the literature and accomplishments of the time, that when visiting her in 1550, her mother, Mary of Guise, with her Scottish attendants, burst into tears of joy. Upon her removal to the French court, Mary became the envy of her sex, surpassing the most accomplished in the elegance and fluency of her language, the grace and loveliness of her movements, and the charm of her whole manner and behavior. She wrote with elegance in the Latin and French languages; and many of her compositions have been preserved, consisting of poems, letters, and a discourse of royal advice to her son. Like Queen Elizabeth, she greatly excelled in music, especially on the virginal, an instrument in use among our ancestors prior to the invention of the spinnet and harpsichord: many compositions which were written for Elizabeth, are known in the musical world at the present day; and the identical virginal upon which the queen played is in existence in Worcestershire.

ROGER ASCHAM—HIS "SCHOOLMASTER."

One of the most remarkable men of this period was Roger Ascham, who attained such proficiency in Greek, that, when a boy, he read lectures in it to other boys who were desirous of instruction; he also learned to play on musical instruments, and was one of the few who then excelled in the mechanical art of writing. He took the degree of M.A. at St. John's College, Cambridge; he commenced tutor when 20 years of age, and was one of those who restored the pronunciation of Greek to our own modern mode of utterance. His favorite amusement was archery, upon which he wrote a treatise, entitled *Toxophilus*, in 1544, which he dedicated to King Henry VIII., who rewarded him with a pension of 10*l.* a-year. He taught the Lady Elizabeth to write a fair hand, and for two years he instructed her in the learned languages: he informs us that Elizabeth understood Greek better than the clergy of Windsor. He was next appointed Latin Secretary to King Edward: upon one occasion, he is stated to have composed and transcribed, with his usual elegance, in three days, 47 letters to princes and personages, of whom cardinals were the lowest. On the accession of Queen Elizabeth he was reappointed her Latin secretary and tutor, and read some hours with the Queen every day. In 1563, upon the invitation of Sir Richard Sackville, he began to write the *Schoolmaster*, a treatise on Education, considered by Dr. Johnson to contain the best advice that was ever given for the study of languages. Ascham died in 1568, lamented as a scholar and a man; when Queen Elizabeth heard of his death, she exclaimed, "she would rather have thrown ten thousand pounds into the sea, than have lost her Ascham." His great benefit to literature was his introduction of an easy and natural style into English writing, instead of the pedantic taste of his day; he adopted, he tells us, the counsel of an ancient writer, "to speak as the common people do, to think as wise men do." One of Ascham's tracts (on the Affairs of Germany) is described by Dr. Johnson as written "in a style which to the ears of that age was undoubtedly mellifluous, and which is now a very valuable specimen of genuine English."

LADY JANE GREY AND HER SCHOOLMASTER.

Foremost among the learned women of this time was the beauteous Lady Jane Grey, who was born at Bradgate, on the border of Charnwood Forest, four miles from Leicester, and educated by Aylmer, her father's chaplain. The story of her "almost infancy" would be incredible were it not well authenticated. Burton calls her "that most noble and admired Princess Lady Jane Grey; who being but young, at the age of seventeen years, as John Bale writeth, attained to such excellent learning, in the Hebrew, Greek, and Latin tongues, and also in the study of divinity, by the instruction of Mr. Aylmer, as appeareth by her many writings, letters, etc., that, as Mr. Fox saith of her, had her fortune been answerable to her bringing up, undoubtedly she might have been compared to the house of Vespasian, Sempronius, and Cornelia, mother of the Gracchi in Rome, and, in these days, the chiefest men of the universities." At Bradgate Roger Ascham paid the Lady Jane a visit, which he thus describes in his *Schoolmaster:*

"Before I went into Germanie, I came to Brodegate, in Leicestershire, to take my leave of that noble Lady Jane Grey, to whom I was exceeding much beholding. Her parentes, the Duke and the Dutchesse, with all the householde, Gentlemen and Gentlewcemen, were hunting in the Parke : I found her in her chamber, reading Phædon Platonis in Greeke, and that with as much delite, as some gentleman would read a merry tale in Bocase. After salutation and dutie done, with some other talke, I asked her why shee should leese such pastime in the Parke. Smiling she answered me: I wisse, all their sport in the Parke, is but a shadow to that pleasure, that I finde in Plato: Alas good folke, they never felt what true pleasure ment. And how came you, Madame, quoth I, to this deepe knowledge of pleasure, and what did chiefly allure you vnto it, seeing not many women, but very fewe men have attained thereunto ? I will tell you, quoth shee, and tell you a troth, which perchance ye will marvel at. One of the greatest benefits that ever God gaure me, is, that hee sente so sharp and seuere parentes, and so gentle a schoolmaster. For when I am in presence of either father or mother, whether I speake, keepe silence, sit, stand, or go, eate, drinke, be merry, or sad, bee swoing, playing, dancing, or any thing els, I must doe it, as it were, in such weight, measure, and number, euen so perfectly, as God made the world, or ells, I am so sharply taunted, so cruelly threatened, yea presently sometimes, with pinches, nippes, and bobbes, and other wayes, which I will not name, for the honor I beare them, so without measure misordered, that I thiuk myself in hell, till time come, that I must go to Mr. Elmer, who teaches me so gently, so pleasantly, with such faire allurements to learning, that I thinke all the time nothing, while I am with him. And when I am called from him, I fall on weeping, because, whatever I do els but learning, is full of greefe, trouble, feare, and whole misliking vnto mee ; and thus my booke hath been so much my pleasure and more, that in respect to it, all other pleasure, in very deede, bee but trifles and troubles vnto mee.—I remember this talke gladly, both because it is so worthy of memory, and because also it was the last talke that ever I had, and the last time that ever I saw that noble and worthy lady." *

---

* Scholemaster, fol. edit. 1671.

On the morning of her execution, the Lady Jane wrote a letter in Greek to her sister on the blank leaf of a Testament in the same language, and in her note-book three sentences in Greek, Latin, and English, of which the last is as follows: " If my faults deserved punishment, my youth, at least, and my imprudence, were worthy of excuse. God and posterity will show me favour."

Fuller says of Jane: " She had the innocence of childhood, the beautie of youth, the soliditie of middle, the gravitie of old age, and all at eighteen: the bust of a princesse, the learning of a clerk, the life of a saint, yet the death of a malefactor, for her parents' offences."

SIR ANTHONY COOK AND HIS FOUR LEARNED DAUGHTERS.

In the reign of Elizabeth, ladies generally understood Italian, French, the lute, often some Latin, and sometimes the use of the globes, and astronomy. The plan of the education of females which the example of Sir Thomas More had rendered popular, continued to be pursued among the superior classes of the community. The learned languages, which, in the earlier part of Elizabeth's reign, contained everything elegant in literature, still formed a requisite of fashionable education; and many young ladies could not only translate the authors of Greece and Rome, but compose in their languages with considerable elegance.

Sir Anthony Cook, whom we have already mentioned as tutor to Edward VI., bestowed the most careful education on his four daughters; and they severally rewarded his exertions, by becoming not only proficients in literature, but distinguished for their excellent conduct as mothers of families. Their classical acquirements made them conspicuous even among the women of fashion of that age. Katherine, who became Lady Killigrew, wrote Latin Hexameters and Pentameters, which would appear with credit in the *Musæ Etonenses*. Mildred, the wife of Lord Burleigh, is described by Roger Ascham as the best Greek scholar among the young women of England, Lady Jane Grey always excepted. Anne, the mother of Francis Bacon, was distinguished both as a linguist and as a theologian. She corresponded in Greek with Bishop Jewell, and translated his *Apologiæ* from the Latin so correctly that neither he nor Archbishop Parker could suggest a single alteration. She also translated a series of sermons on fate and free-will, from the Tuscan.

Yet, Lord Macaulay considers the highly-educated ladies of this period, and their pursuits, to have been unfairly extolled at the expense of the women of our time, through one very obvious and very important circumstance being overlooked. " In the time of our Henry VIII. and Edward VI.," says our historian, "a person who did not read Greek and Latin could read nothing, or next to nothing. The Italian was the only modern language which presented anything that could be called a literature. All the valuable books extant in all the vernacular dialects of Europe would hardly have filled a single shelf. England did not yet possess Shakspeare's Plays and the Fairy Queen, nor France Montaigne's Essays, nor Spain Don Quixote. In looking round a well-furnished library, how many English or French books can we find which were extant when Lady Jane Grey and Queen Elizabeth received their education? Chaucer, Gower, Froissart, Rabelais, nearly complete the list. It was, therefore, absolutely necessary that a woman should be uneducated, or classically educated. Latin was then the language of courts, as well as of the schools; of diplomacy, and of theological and political controversy. This is no longer the case: the ancient tongues are supplanted by the modern languages of Europe, with which English women are at least as well acquainted as English men. When, therefore, we compare the acquirements of Lady Jane Grey with those of an accomplished young woman of our own time, we have no hesitation in awarding the superiority to the latter."

A TRUANT PUNISHED IN THE SIXTEENTH CENTURY.

Sir Peter Carew, born of a distinguished family in Devonshire, in 1514, after a turbulent youth, took an active part in the Continental wars of that period. He was at the battle of Pavia, subsequently became a favorite of Henry VIII., and lived through a part of the reign of Queen Elizabeth. His life was written by a cotemporary (John Vowell, alias Hooker, of Exeter), and describes Peter, "in his prime days, as very pert and forward, wherefore his father

brought him, being about the age of twelve years, to Exeter, to school, and lodged him with one Thomas Hunt, a draper and alderman of that city, and did put him to school to one Freers, then master of the Grammar School there; and whether it were that he was in fear of the said Freers, for he was counted to be a very hard and cruel master, or whether it were for that he had no affection to his learning, true it is he would never keep his school, but was a daily truant, and always ranging; whereof the schoolmaster misliking did oftentimes complain unto the foresaid Thomas Hunt, his host; upon which complaint, so made, the said Thomas would go, and send, abroad to seek out the said Peter. And, among many times thus seeking him, it happened that he found him about the walls of the said city, and, he running to take him, the boy climbed up upon the top of one of the highest garrets of a turret of the said wall, and would not, for any request, come down, saying moreover to his host that, if he did press too fast upon him, he would surely cast himself down headlong over the wall; and then, said he, 'I shall break my neck, and thou shalt be hanged, because thou makest me to leap down.' His host, being afraid of the boy, departed, and left some to watch him, and so to take him, as soon as he came down. But forthwith he sent to ir William Carew, and did advertise him of this, and of sundry other shrewed parts of his son Peter, who, at his next coming then to Exeter, called his son before him, tied him in a line, and delivered him to one of his servants to be carried about the town, as one of his hounds, and they led him home to Mohun's ottery, like a dog. And after that, he being come to Mohun's ottery, he coupled him to one of his hounds, and so continued him for a time."

The discipline at Oxford was about this time very rigid; for we read that Samuel Parker, the Puritan, who was educated at Wadham College, " did," says Anthony à Wood, " according to his former breeding, lead a strict and religious life, fasted, prayed, with other students, weekly together, and for their refection, feeding on thin broth, made of oatmeal and water only, they were commonly called *gruellers.*"

FLOGGING IN SCHOOLS.

In the Middle Ages, we read of, besides stationary, itinerant schoolmasters, and teachers of reading. In the wood-cuts of a work printed by Caxton, the schoolmaster holds a rod in his hand, and the boy kneels before him. The practice of flogging is sometimes engraved upon the seals of public schools: thus, the seal of St. Olave's School, dated 1576, represents the Master sitting in a high-backed chair at his desk, on which is a book, and the rod is conspicuously displayed to the terror of five scholars standing before him; and the seal of St. Saviour's School, 1573, represents the Master seated in a chair, with a group of thickly-trussed pupils before him. Dr. Busby, who was 50 years head-master of Westminster School, is said to have boasted his rod to be the sieve to prove good scholars; but his severity is traditional. The practice of flogging in Winchester is illustrated upon the walls of the great School, as already described.

WESTMINSTER COLLEGE SCHOOL FOUNDED.

It is one of the unfading glories of ancient Westminster that it has been a seat of learning since the time when it was a "thorny island," and at least eight centuries since was rebuilt the Abbey Church " to the honour of God and St. Peter." The queen of the Confessor is related to have played with a Westminster scholar in grammar, verses, and logic, as she met him in his way from the monastery school to the palace, as related by the chronicler with all the circumstantial minuteness of the account of a royal visit of yesterday. Equally direct is the evidence that, from the latter part of the reign of Edward III., down to the dissolution of the Abbey, a salary was paid to a schoolmaster, styled " *Magister Scholarium pro eruditione puerorum grammaticorum,*" who was distinguished from the person who taught the children of the choir to sing.

The earliest school was thus an appurtenance of the monastery; and is included in the draft (in the archives of the Chapter) of the new establishment for the See of Westminster.

During the reign of Queen Mary, Cardinal Pole appears to

have suffered the school to languish wholly unsupported. Her successor enforced the right of election to studentships, restored the revenues, and the foundation of an Upper and Lower Master and forty scholars, and gave the present statutes, whence Elizabeth has received the honorable title of Foundress. This Queen added an important statute to regulate the mode of election of novitiates into St. Peter's College. Evelyn has recorded one of these examinations:

> In 1661, May 13, I heard and saw such exercises at the election of scholars at Westminster School to be sent to the University, in Latin, Greek, Hebrew, and Arabic, in themes and extemporary verses, with such readiness and will as wonderfully astonished me in such youths.

Dean Goodman was the next benefactor, in obtaining a perpetual grant of his prebend of Chiswick, to be a place of refuge for the members of the Chapter and College whenever pestilence might be desolating Westminster. During this Deanship, the scholars were lodged in one spacious chamber, their commons were regulated, and the apartments of the Masters received an increase of comfort and accommodation. Among the earliest grants is a perpetual annuity of twenty marks, made in 1594, by Cecil, Lord High Treasurer, to be presented as gifts to scholars elected to either of the Universities.

Before the middle of the reign of Elizabeth, the rudiments of the Greek language were taught to boys at Westminster School; and Harrison, in his preface to Holinshed, about 1586, states that the boys of the three great collegiate schools (Winchester, Eton, and Westminster) were "well entered in the knowledge of the Latin and Greek tongues and rules of versifying."

> Dean Goodman had for his successor that man of prayer and "most rare preacher," Dr. Launcelot Andrewes, who would often supply the place of the Masters for a week together. It was one of his simple pleasures, "with a sweetness and compliance with the recreations of youth," always to be attended, in his little retirements to the cheerful village of Chiswick, by two of his scholars; and often thrice in the week, it is said, he assembled about him in his study those of the Upper Form; and the earnest little circle frequently, through the whole evening, with reverential attention, heard his exposition of the Sacred Text; while he also pointed out to them those sources of knowledge in Greek and Latin, from which he had gathered his own stores of varied learning.—Walcott's *Memorials of Westminster.*

Once more evil days fell upon the rising school. The Abbey was desecrated, and the families of the scholars were threatened or assailed by the horrors of the Great Rebellion, when Parliament, having for about four years exercised power over the School through a Committee, in 1649 assumed a protectorate, intrusting the management of the School to a government of fifty members established in the Deanery. The fee or inheritance of many of the Abbey estates was sold; old rents only being reserved to the College. This control lasted until the Restoration in 1660, since which period the scholars have been maintained by the common revenues of the Collegiate Church, at a cost of about 1200*l*. a-year.

The Queen's Scholars wear caps and gowns; and there are four "Bishop's Boys" educated free, who wear purple gowns, and have 60*l*. annually amongst them. Besides this *foundation*, a great number of sons of the nobility and gentry are educated here. Of the Queen's Scholars an examination takes place in Rogation week, when four are elected to Trinity College, Cambridge, and four to Christchurch, Oxford; scholarships of about 60*l*. a-year.

The scholars from the fourth, fifth, and Shell Forms "stand out" in Latin, Greek, and grammatical questionings, on the Wednesday before Ascension Day, in the presence of the Head Master, who presides as umpire, when the successful competitors being chosen to fill the vacancies, "the Captain of the Election" is chaired round Dean's Yard, or the school court. On Rogation Tuesday, a dinner is given to the electors, and all persons connected with the School, by the Dean and Chapter; and any old Westminster scholar of sufficient rank or standing is entitled to attend it. After dinner, epigrams are spoken by a large proportion of the Queen's Scholars. There are several funds available to needy scholars; and the whole foundation and school is managed by the Dean and Chapter of Westminster.

The school buildings are in part ancient. You enter the School court from the Broad Sanctuary, through an archway in a block of houses of mediæval architecture. The porch of the School is stated to have been designed by Inigo Jones. On the north front is the racket-court, formed against part of the west wall of the dormitory. The venerable School itself, once the dormitory of the monks, ranges behind the eastern cloister of the Abbey. It is a long and spacious building, with a semicircular recess at one end, the Head Master's table standing in front of it; four tiers of forms, one above the other, are ranged along the eastern and western walls; and the room has a massive open-timber roof of chestnut. The Upper and Lower Schools are divided by a bar, which formerly bore a curtain: over this bar on Shrove Tuesday, at eleven o'clock, the College cook, attended by a verger, having made his obeisance to the Masters, proceeds to toss a pancake into the Upper School, once a warning to proceed to dinner in the Hall.

<small>An interesting tradition is attached to the bar at the time it bore a curtain. Two boys at play, by chance made a grievous rent in the pendent drapery; and one of the delinquents suffered his generous companion to bear the penalty of the offence — a severe flogging. Long years went by; the Civil War had parted chief friends; and the boys had grown up to manhood, unknown to each other. One of them, now become a Judge and sturdy Republican, was presiding at the trial of some captive cavaliers, and was ready to upbraid and sentence them, when he recognized in the worn features of one gray-haired veteran,</small>

the well-remembered look of the gallant boy who had once borne punishment for him. By certain answers, which in the examination he elicited, his suspicions were confirmed ; and with an immediate resolve, he posted to London, where, by his influence with Oliver Cromwell, he succeeded in preserving his early friend from the scaffold.—Walcott's *Memoria's of Westminster.*

The School is fraught with pious memories. Here "that sweet singer of the Temple, George Herbert," was reared ; and that love of choral music, which "was his heaven upon earth," was, no doubt, implanted here, while he went up to pray in the glorious Abbey. And it was here that South, in his loyal childhood, reader of the Latin prayers for the morning, publicly prayed for Charles I. by name, "but an hour or two at most before his sacred head was struck off." Nor can we forget among the ushers, the melody of whose Latin poems had led him to be called "Sweet Vinny Bourne;" or the mastership of Busby, who boasted his rod to be the sieve to prove good scholars, and walked with covered head before Charles II.; then humbly at the gate assured his Majesty that it was necessary for his dignity before his boys to be the greatest man there, even though a king were present. How successfully, too, is Busby commemorated in the whole-length portrait of the great schoolmaster standing beside his favorite pupil, Spratt. Upon the walls are inscribed many great names; and in the library is preserved part of the form on which Dryden once sat, and on which his autograph is cut.

In the *Census Alumnorum*, or list of *foundation* scholars, are Bishops Overall and Ravis, translators of the Bible ; Hakluyt, collector of Voyages ; Gunter, inventor of the Scale ; "Master George Herbert;" the poets Cowley and Dryden ; South ; Locke ; Bishops Atterbury, Spratt, and Pearce ; the poet Prior, and Stepney the statesman ; Rowe and "Sweet Vinny Bourne," the poets ; Churchill, the satirist ; Warren Hastings ; Everard Home, surgeon ; Dr. Drury, of Harrow School, etc. Among the other eminent persons educated here are Lord Burleigh ; Ben Jonson ; Nat Lee ; Sir Christopher Wren ; Jasper Mayne, the poet; Barton Booth, the actor ; Blackmore, Browne, Dyer, Hammond, Aaron Hill, Cowper, and Southey, the poets ; Horne Tooke ; Gibbon, the historian ; Cumberland, the dramatist ; Colman the Younger ; Sir Francis Burdett ; Harcourt, Archbishop of York ; the Marquis of Lansdowne ; Lord John Russell ; the Marquis of Anglesey ; Sir John Cam Hobhouse (Lord Broughton) ; George Bidder, of calculating fame, now the eminent civil engineer.

Among the eminent Masters are Camden, "the Pausanias of England," who had Ben Jonson for a scholar ; and Dr. Busby, who had Dryden, and who, out of the bench of bishops, taught sixteen.

The College Hall, originally the Abbot's refectory, was built by Abbot Litlington, *temp.* Edward III.: the floor is paved with chequered Turkish marble; at the south end is a musician's gallery, now used as a pantry, and behind are butteries and hatches; at the north side, upon a dais, is the high table; those below, of chestnut-wood, are said to have been formed out of the wreck of the Armada. The roof-timbers spring from carved corbels, with angels bearing shields of the Confessor's and Abbot's arms; and a small louver rises above the central hearth, upon which in winter a wood and charcoal fire used to burn until the year 1850.*
The Library is a modern Italian room, and contains several memorials of the attachment of "Westminsters." The old dormitory, built in 1380, was the granary of the monastery; and was replaced by the present dormitory in 1722, from the designs of the Earl of Burlington: its walls are thickly inscribed with names. Here Latin plays are represented upon the second Thursday in December, and the Monday before and after that day. These performances superseded the old Mysteries and Moralities in the reign of Queen Mary, when the boy actors were chiefly the acolytes, who served at mass. Warton mentions that this "liberal exercise is yet preserved, and in the spirit of true classical purity, at the College of Westminster." Garrick designed scenery for these pieces; but the modern dresses formerly used were not exchanged for Greek costume until 1839. The plays acted of late years have been the *Andria, Phormio, Eunuchus,* and *Adelphi,* of Terence, with Latin prologue and epilogue pleasantly reflecting in their humor events of the day. Two new scenes were drawn for the theatre, in 1857, by Professor Cockerell, R.A.

Boating is a favorite amusement of the Westminsters, who have often contested the championship of the Thames with Eton. On May 4, 1837, the Westminsters won a match at Eton; when, by desire of William IV., the victors visited Windsor Castle, and were there received by the good-natured king.

A POOR WESTMINSTER SCHOLAR.

Dr. Stubbe, the eminent physician, one of the most learned men of his time, was born in 1631, near Spilsby, in Lincolnshire, whence his father, an Anabaptist minister, removed to Ireland; but when the Rebellion broke out in that country in 1641, his mother fled with him to London, walking thither on foot from

---

* Fires continued to be made on a hearth in the middle of the hall called the reredos, in many college halls in Oxford and Cambridge, until about the year 1820.

Liverpool. She maintained herself in the metropolis by her needle, and sent her son, then about ten years old, to Westminster School. Here he frequently obtained pecuniary relief from his school-fellows, as a remuneration for writing their exercises. Busby was struck by Stubbe's rare talents and assiduity, and introduced him to Sir Henry Vane, who happened one day to come into the school; when Sir Henry relieved the immediate wants of the lad, and remained for ever afterward his steady friend; assisting him at his election to Oxford, where he became of considerable consequence; his reputation for learning increased daily, and he used to converse fluently in Greek in the public schools.

MERCHANT TAYLORS' SCHOOL FOUNDED.

The royal example of Edward VI. was nobly followed by one of the great City companies founding, in the succeeding reign, a grammar-school in the metropolis, principally through the personal benevolence of its members. In the year 1561, the Merchant Taylors' Company, chiefly by the gift of 500*l*., and other subscriptions of members of the Court of Assistants, raised a fund for this great educational object. Among the contributors was Sir Thomas White, some time master of the Company, and who had recently founded St. John's College, Oxford. With the above fund, the generous band of citizens purchased a certain property lying between Cannon-street and the Thames, part of "the Manor of the Rose," a palace originally built by Sir John Poultney, Knt., five times Lord Mayor of London, in the reign of Edward III. In these premises, consisting principally of a gate-house and court-yard, the Company established their school. The Great Fire, however, destroyed the ancient buildings; and in 1675, the present school and the head-master's residence were erected: it includes a library (on the site of an ancient chapel), which contains a fair collection of theological and classical works. The school now consists of about 260 boys, who are charged 10*l*. per annum each: they are admitted at any age, on the nomination of the members of the Court of the Company in rotation: and the scholars may remain until the Monday after St. John the Baptist's Day preceding their nineteenth birthday. Hebrew, Greek, and Latin have been taught since the foundation of the school; mathematics, writing, and arithmetic were added in 1829, and French and modern history in 1846. There is no property belonging to the school except the buildings: it is supported by the Merchant Taylors' Company out of their several "funds," without any specific fund being set apart for that object; it has, therefore, been exempt from the inquiry of the Charity Commissioners; but, like Winchester, Eton, and Westminister, it has a college almost appropriated to its scholars. Thirty-seven out of the fifty fellowships of St. John's College, Oxford, and other exhibitions at Oxford and Cambridge, are attached to it; the election to which takes place annually on St. Barnabas's Day (June 11), when the school prizes are distributed; there is another speech day (Doctors' Day) in December. Plays were formerly acted by the boys of this school, as at Westminster: the earliest instance known was in 1665, when the scholars performed, in the old Hall of the Merchant Taylors' Company, Beaumont and Fletcher's comedy of "Love's Pilgrimage," but under order that this "should bee noe precident for the future." Garrick, who was a personal friend of the head-master in his time, took great interest in these performances. They have been continued to our day, in a noble crypt, which is all that remains of the manorial mansion of the Rose. The School Feasts and Anniversary Feasts of the old scholars have, however, long been held in the Company's Hall. The School has ever been famed for the classical attainments and sound Protestant principles of her sons, whence the boys have been called "Loyalty's Bull-dogs." When James II. recommended a person suspected of Popery to be head-master of the School, the Company prevailed on the King to recall his recommendation; and in 1796, great was the scandal to the foundation when two mischievous scholars hoisted a tri-colored flag on the ramparts of the Tower, an act which was indignantly repudiated by their school-fellows, and by one of the under-masters chronicling the affair in a song which became very popular.

Amongst the eminent scholars educated at Merchant Taylors' were, Bishops Andrewes, Dove, and Tomson, three of the translators of the Bible; Archbishop Juxon, who attended Charles I. to the scaffold; Bishop Hopkins (of Londonderry); Archbishops Sir William Dawes, Gilbert, and Boulter; Bishop Van Mildert, and eleven other prelates; Titus Oates, who contrived the "Popish Plot;" Sir James Whitelocke, Justice of the King's Bench; Bulstrode Whitelocke, who wrote his "Memorials;" Shirley, the dramatic poet, cotemporary with Massinger; Charles Wheatly, the ritualist; Neale, the historian of the Puritans; Edmund Calamy, and his grandson Edmund, the Nonconformists—the former died in 1666, from seeing London in ashes after the Great Fire; the great Lord Clive; Dr. Vicesimus Knox, subsequently celebrated as the head-master of Tunbridge School; Dr. William Lowth, the learned classic and theologian; Nicholas Amhurst, associated with Bolingbroke and Pulteney in the *Craftsman;* Charles Mathews the elder, comedian; Lieut. Col. Denham, the explorer of Central Africa; and J. L. Adolphus, the barrister, who wrote a *History of the Reign of George III.* Also, Sir John Dodson, Queen's Advocate; Sir Henry Ellis, and Samuel Birch, of the British Museum; John Gough Nichols, F.S.A., etc.

GRESHAM COLLEGE FOUNDED.

In the middle of the reign of Elizabeth, one of her merchant-princes — *Flos Mercatorum*, as he was deservedly styled — evinced his love of the higher branches of knowledge by the foundation and endowment of a College which considerably assisted the promotion of science in England in the early part of the seventeenth century. The founder was Sir Thomas Gresham, the originator of the Royal Exchange, the rents arising from which, together with his mansion, on the death of Lady Gresham, in 1597, to be vested in the Corporation of London and the Mercers' Company. They were conjointly to nominate seven professors, to lecture successively, one on each day of the week, their salaries being 50*l.* per annum: a more liberal remuneration than Henry VIII. had appointed for the Regius Professors of Divinity at Oxford and Cambridge, and equivalent to 400*l.* or 500*l.* at the present day. The Lectures commenced June, 1597, in Gresham's mansion, which, with alms-houses and gardens, extended from Bishopsgate-street westward into Broad-street. Here the Royal Society originated in 1645, and met (with interruptions) until 1710. The buildings were then neglected, and in 1768 were taken down, the Excise Office being built upon their site; and the reading of the Lectures was transferred to a room on the south-east side of the Royal Exchange; the lecturers' salaries being raised to 100*l.* each, as an equivalent for the lodging they had in the old College, of which there is a view, by Vertue, in Ward's *Lives of the Gresham Professors*, 1740. On the rebuilding of the Royal Exchange, the Gresham Committee provided for the College, in Basinghall-street, at the corner of Catcaton-street, a handsome stone edifice, in the enriched Roman style, with a Corinthian entrance-portico. It contains a large library, and professors' rooms; and a lecture-room, or theatre, capable of holding 500 persons. The Lectures, on Astronomy, Physic, Law, Divinity, Rhetoric, Geometry, and Music, are here read to the public gratis, during "Term Time," daily, except Sundays, in Latin and English.

STATESMEN, POETS, AND DRAMATISTS OF ELIZABETH'S REIGN.

We now approach a galaxy of bright stars of the Elizabethan age, that it may be convenient here to group together; although many incidents of their boyhood and school-days will be related elsewhere in this volume.

At the grammar school were taught the illustrious men of this brilliant period of our history. The great Lord Burleigh, who was upward of 50 years prime minister of England, was placed successively at the grammar schools of Grantham and Stamford; at the age of 15 he was removed to St. John's College, Cambridge; at 16 he delivered a lecture on the logic of the schools, and in three years afterward another on the Greek language; and in later life, books, and the superintendence of his garden at Theobalds, formed his chief amusements in his few hours of leisure.

Two of the most acccomplished men of this age were "the Admirable Crichton," and Sir Philip Sidney, both born in the same year, 1561. Crichton was educated at St. Andrews, then the most celebrated seminary in Scotland: at fourteen he took his degree of Master of Arts. Sidney was born at Penshurst, in Kent, and was sent at an early age to the Royal Free Grammar School at Shrewsbury, which had then been founded but ten years. This school is free to sons of ancient burgess freemen of Shrewsbury: it has an income from endowment of 3100*l*. per annum, and several exhibitions.

Among the learned ladies of the above period was Mary Sidney, Countess of Pembroke, "Sidney's sister, and Pembroke's mother:" for her amusement Sir Philip Sidney wrote his heroic romance, entitled *The Countess of Pembroke's Arcadia*.

Michael Drayton, stated to have been born in Warwickshire about 1563, and the son of a butcher, discovered in his earliest years such proofs of a superior mind, that he was made page to a person of quality,—a situation which was not in that age thought too humble for the sons of gentlemen. He is said to have studied at Oxford, and in early life was warmly patronized by persons of consequence. His *Polyolbion*, a poetical description of England, is so accurate in its information as to be quoted as an authority by antiquaries: Drayton was poet-laureate in 1626.

Beaumont and Fletcher may be described as born and bred "fine gentlemen," educated in all the conventionalities and artificial manners of their time. Massinger, the son of one of the Earl of Pembroke's retainers (employed as an official messenger to Queen Elizabeth), was born at Salisbury, and was sent early to Oxford by the Earl of Pembroke, the patron of logic and philosophy; but the young Massinger passed much of his college time in reading poetry and romances.

Of Sir Walter Raleigh's school-days we have scanty record;

but it is stated that about 1568, he became a commoner of Oriel College, Oxford, and Fuller adds, of Christchurch also. At Oriel, he proved "the ornament of the junior fry," and was a proficient in oratory and philosophy. His *History of the World* is one of the noblest works of a noble mind; and his Counsels to his Son is a treasure of great value.

Neither have we any particulars of Spenser's education, until we find him, in 1659, entered a sizar (one of the humblest class of students) of Pembroke College, Cambridge, where he continued to attend seven years, taking his degree of M.A. in 1576.

Ben Jonson was born in Hartshorne-lane, Strand, in 1574; he was sent early to "a private school in St. Martin's Church;" and next to Westminster School, under Camden, then junior master. He traveled with the son of Sir Walter Raleigh on the Continent, and on his return went to Cambridge. Jonson is said to have worked with his father-in-law, a bricklayer, in building the garden wall of Lincoln's Inn, when, as Fuller says, "having a trowel in his hand, he had a book in his pocket;" and there is no reason to doubt this statement.

We now come to the most illustrious cotemporary of Ben Jonson, born ten years earlier, in 1564, William Shakspeare, who was educated at the Grammar School of Stratford-upon-Avon, of which we shall speak more at length hereafter.

William Harvey, the author of the true theory of the circulation of the blood (and, perhaps, the only man who ever lived to see his own discovery established in his lifetime), was born at Folkestone, in 1578, and at ten years of age was sent to the Grammar School at Canterbury; and having there laid the foundation of Classical learning, he was removed to Cambridge in 1593. In five years he left the University, and went abroad for the acquisition of medical knowledge, and fixed himself in his 23d year at Padua University, where he took his doctor's degree in 1602, being then only 24 years old.

RUGBY SCHOOL FOUNDED.

Our narrative has now reached that "critical epoch in the advance of civilization, when the discovery of a new world had opened space to the expanding intellect of the old one, which had just then been awakened from the long slumber of the dark ages by the restoration of classical literature; and a new life was thus infused into the sacred cause of education. Luther had taught the laity the weapon with which they could wrest from the papal clergy the monopoly of knowledge; and the dissolution of monasteries had thrown into the market lands hitherto locked up in mortmain, with which far-sighted benefactors were enabled to endow their new foundations.*

One of the first to seize this prevalent spirit was Lawrence Sheriff, a native of Rugby, who had accumulated a large fortune in dealing with the fruits and spices of the West Indies. He was warden of the Grocers' Company in 1566; and in Fox's Book of Martyrs he is spoken of as "servant to the Lady Elizabeth, and sworn unto her Grace," which seems to imply that he was "grocer to the Queen:" he kept shop "near to Newgate Market." Sheriff died in 1567, and by his last will, made seven weeks previously, bequeathed a third of his Middlesex estate to the foundation of "a fair and convenient school-house, and to the maintaining of an honest, discreet, and learned man to teach grammar;" the rents of that third, which then amounted to 8*l.* annually, had swelled in 1825 to above 5500*l.* The estate in Lamb's Conduit Fields (originally Close) adjoins the Foundling Hospital, and comprises Lamb's Conduit, Milman, New and Great Ormond, and other adjacent streets.

Immediately upon the founder's death, the school was commenced in a building in the rear of the house assigned for the master; it consisted of one large room, having no playground attached. The first page of the school register, commencing in 1675, shows that of the 26 entrances in that year, 12 were boys not upon the foundation, and one of them came even from Cumberland. The school now took a higher stamp; and early in the list we find the Earls of Stamford and Peterborough, the Lords Craven, Griffin, Stawell, and Ward, the younger sons of the houses of Cecil and Greville, and many of the baronets of the adjacent counties.

The school buildings were from time to time enlarged; until the improved value of the endowment enabled the trustees to commence, in 1809, the present structure, designed by Hakewill, in the Elizabethan style, and built nearly upon the same spot as the first humble dwelling. The buildings consist of cloisters on three sides of a court; the Great School, and the French and Writing Schools; the dining hall, and the chapel; and the master's house, where and in the town the boys are lodged. The group of buildings cost 35,000*l.*, but are of "poor sham Gothic." A library has since been added. The only former playground was the churchyard; but Rugby has now its bowling-green close, with its tall spiral elms; and its playground, where cricket and foot-ball are followed out-of-doors with no less zest and delight than literature is pursued within.

* Quarterly Review, No. 204.

Foot-ball is *the* game, *par excellence*, of Rugby, as cricket is of Eton. The fascination of this gentle pastime is its mimic war, and it is waged with the individual prowess of the Homeric conflicts, and with the personal valor of the Orlandos of mediæval chivalry, before villainous saltpetre had reduced the Knigh-errant to the ranks. The play is played out by boys with that dogged determination to win, that endurance of pain, that bravery of combative spirit, by which the adult is trained to face the cannon-ball with equal alacrity.—*Quarterly Review*, No. 204.

The instruction at Rugby retains the leading characteristics of the old school, being based on a thoroughly grounded study of Greek and Latin. But the treatment has been much improved: formerly the boys were ill-used, half imprisoned, and put on the smallest rations, a plentiful allowance of rod excepted; and a grim tower is pointed out in which a late pedagogue, Dr. Wooll, was accustomed to inflict the birch unsparingly. Nevertheless, in Wooll's time were added six exhibitions to the eight already instituted; books were first given as prizes for composition; and the successful candidates recited their poems before the trustees, thus establishing the Speeches.

To Dr. Wooll * succeeded Dr. Thomas Arnold, the second and moral founder of Rugby. Of the great change which he introduced in the face of education here, we can speak but in brief. Soon after he had entered upon his office, he made this memorable declaration upon the expulsion of some incorrigible pupils: " It is *not* necessary that this should be a school of three hundred, or one hundred, or of fifty boys; but it *is* necessary that it should be a school of Christian gentlemen."

The three ends at which Arnold aimed were — first, to inculcate religious and moral principle, then gentlemanly conduct, and lastly, intellectual ability. One of his principal holds was in his boy sermons — that is, in sermons to which the young congregation could and did listen, and of which he was the absolute inventor. The feelings of love, reverence, and confidence which he inspired, led his pupils to place implicit trust on his decision, and to esteem his approbation as their highest reward. His government of the school was no reign of terror; he resorted to reasoning and talking as his first step, which failing, he applied the rod as his *ultima ratio*, and this for misdemeanors inevitable to youth — lying, for instance — and best cured by birch. He was not opposed to *fagging*, which boys accept as part and parcel of the institution of schools, and as the servitude of their feudal system; all he aimed to do was to regulate, and, as it were, to legalize the exercise of it. The keystone of his government was in the Sixth Form, which he held to be an intermediate power between the master and masses of the school; the

---

* Dr. Wooll was small in stature, but powerful in stripes; and under his head-mastership Lord Lyttleton suggested for the grim closet in which the rods are kept, the witty motto: " *Great Cry and Little Wool.*"—*See the Book of Rugby School, its History and Daily Life.* 1856.

value of which internal police he had learned from the Prefects at Winchester. But he carefully watched over this delegated authority, and put down any abuse of its power. The Præpositors themselves were no less benefited. "By appealing to their honor, by fostering their self-respect, and calling out their powers of governing their inferiors, he ripened their manhood, and they early learnt habits of command; and this system, found to work so well, is continued, and with many of its excellent principles, is now acted on in most of the chief public schools of England."*
Dr. Arnold died in 1841, on the day preceding his forty-seventh birth-day, having presided over the school for fourteen years: in the chapel at Rugby he rests from his labors, surrounded by those of his pupils who have been prematurely cut off. "Yet," touchingly says the Rugbeian writer in the *Quarterly Review*, "if they have known few of the pleasures of this world, they at least have not, like him, felt many of its sorrows, and death has not separated those who in life were united."

Dr. Arnold procured from the Crown a high mark of royal favor — her Majesty having founded an annual prize of a Gold Medal, to which several other prizes have been added. Dr. Arnold was succeeded in the head-mastership by the Rev. Dr. Tait, who retired on his appointment to the Deanery of Carlisle, in 1849; and who, in 1856, was preferred to the bishopric of London.

In the list of eminent Rugbeians are the Rev. John Parkhurst, the Greek and Hebrew lexicographer; Sir Ralph Abercrombie, the hero of Alexandria; William Bray, F.S.A., the historian of Surrey; Dr. Legge, Bishop of Oxford; Sir Henry Halford, Bart., President of the College of Physicians; Dr. Butler, editor of Æschylus, etc.

HARROW SCHOOL FOUNDED.

At the village of Harrow-on-the-Hill, ten miles north-west of London — where Lanfranc built a church, Thomas à Becket resided, and Wolsey was rector — in the reign of Elizabeth there lived a substantial yeoman named John Lyon. For many years previous to his death he had appropriated 20 marks annually to the instruction of poor children; and in 1571, he procured letters patent and a royal charter from the Queen, recognizing the foundation of a Free Grammar School, for the government of which, in 1592, he drew up the orders, statutes, and rules. The head-master is directed to be, "on no account, below the degree of Master of Arts;" or the usher "under that of a Bachelor of Arts." They are always to be "single men, unmarried." The stipends of the masters are settled; the forms specified; the

* Quarterly Review. No. 204. Review of *Tom Brown's School-days*, a real picture drawn at Rugby of a boy of his class, at the moment when Dr. Arnold was working out his great educational experiment.

books and exercises for each form marked out; the mode of correction described; the hours of attending school, the vacations and play-days appointed; and the scholars' amusements directed to be confined to " driving a top, tossing a hand-ball, running and shooting;" and for the last mentioned diversion all parents were required to furnish their children with " bow-strings, shafts, and braces to exercise shooting." In addition to scholars to be educated freely, the schoolmaster is to receive the children of parishioners as well as "foreigners;" from the latter " he may take such stipends and wages as he can get, except that they be of the kindred of John Lyon the founder." The sum of 20*l.* was allotted for four exhibitions—two in Gonville and Caius College, Cambridge; the others in any college at Oxford — which scholarships have been increased. The revenues of the School estates which Lyon left are now very considerable; so that one portion of the property, which 70 years ago produced only 100*l.* a-year, now returns 4000*l.*

The school was built about three years after Lyon's decease; * the school-room, fifty feet in length, has large, square, heavy-framed windows, and is partly wainscoted with oak, which is covered with the carved names of many generations of Harrovians. The plastered walls above the wainscot were formerly filled with names and dates, but they have been obliterated with whitewash. Boards have since been put up on which the names are neatly carved, in regular order and of uniform size.

<small>Among these inscriptions are the names of Parr; Sheridan (only the initials R. B. S.); W. Jones (Sir William); Bennett (Bishop of Cloyne); Ryder (Bishop of Lichfield and Coventry); Murray (Bishop of Rochester); Dymock (the Champion); Ryder (Lord Harrowby); Temple (Lord Palmerston); Lord Byron; and Peel (Sir Robert; between the two last letters of the latter name is the name of Percival, as cut by the lamented statesman.</small>

Above the school-room is the Monitors' Library. Here is a portrait of Dr. Parr; a portrait and bust of Lord Byron, and a sword worn by him when in Greece; and a superb fancy archery dress, worn on the day of shooting for the silver arrow, about the year 1766. Here, also, is a quarto volume of " Speech Bills."

<small>* John Lyon is buried in Harrow Church : the brass of his tomb states, " who hath founded a free grammar-school in this parish to have continuance for ever; and for maintenance thereof, and for releyffe of the poore, and of some poore schollars in the universityes, repairing of highwayes and other good and charitable uses, hath made conveyance of lands of good value to a corporation granted for that purpose. Prayse be to the Author of all goodness, who makes us myndful to follow his good example." Over the tomb is a marble monument erected by Old Harrovians in 1813; the Latin inscription written by Dr. Parr; above, the sculptor, Flaxman, has represented a master and three pupils, said to be Dr. Butler, the then head-master, and the three Percevals, the sons of the Minister.
In the church also is a monument by Westmacott, to Dr. Drury, with a bass-relief of two boys contemplating the bust of their master; the likenesses of the boys are appropriated to Sir Robert Peel and Lord Byron. Here likewise is a mural monument to Dr. Sumner, head-master, with a Latin inscription by Dr. Parr. In the churchyard lies another head-master. Dr. Thackeray, who introduced the Eton system of Education at Harrow, which, with few modifications, has continued in use ever since.</small>

Near the School is the Speech Room, built by old Harrovians: the windows are filled with painted glass, and here is a painting of Cicero pleading against Catiline, painted by Gavin Hamilton. There is a Chapel for the accommodation of the scholars only; to which was added, in 1856, a "Memorial Chapel," in honor of those officers who fell in the Crimean war, who had been educated at Harrow School.* The head-master's house is in the street of Harrow, and with the school buildings and chapel, is in the Elizabethan style. The device of the school is a lion, rampant, the armorial bearings of the founder, and a rebus of his name (motto, *Stet Fortuna Domus*), to which have been added two crossed arrows, denoting the ancient practice of archery enjoined by Lyon; and on the Anniversary, six or twelve boys shot for a silver arrow, the competitors wearing fancy dresses of spangled satin. The last arrow was contended for in 1771: the butts were set up on a picturesqued spot, "worthy of a Roman amphitheatre," at the entrance to the village.

Beyond the court-yard are courts for racket, a favorite game at Harrow. There is likewise a cricket-ground, and a bathing-place, formerly known as the Duck Puddle."

The scholars, chiefly the sons of noblemen and gentlemen, number about 400.

Among the eminent Harrovians are William Baxter, the antiquary and philologist; John Dennis, the poet and critic; Bruce, the traveler in Abyssinia; Sir William Jones, the Oriental scholar; the Rev. Dr. Parr; the heroic Lord Rodney; Richard Brinsley Sheridan; Viscount Palmerston; the Marquis Wellesley; Mr. Malthus, the political economist; Spencer Perceval; Earl Spencer, who collected the magnificent library at Althorp; the Earl of Aberdeen; W. B. Proctor (Barry Cornwall), the poet; Lord Elgin, who collected the "Marbles" from the Parthenon; Lord Chancellor Cottenham; the Earl of Shaftesbury; and Lord Byron and Sir Robert Peel, both born in the same year, 1788.

EDUCATION OF JAMES I.

Prince James, only son of Mary Queen of Scots by Henry Lord Darnley, her second husband, was born in Edinburgh Castle, in 1566; and in consequence of the dethronement of his mother, was proclaimed King of Scotland by the title of James VI. in the following year, principally through the preponderance of the chiefs of the Presbyterian party over the Roman Catholic leaders. The direction of James's childhood was intrusted to the Earl of Mar, governor of Stirling Castle. To imbue the mind of the prince as early and as deeply as possible with the principles which placed him upon the throne, was naturally regarded as an object of high importance; it was also considered that he should be early and thoroughly grounded in classical learning;

---

* In the Chapel, the Church, and the School, there is no distinction of seats for the sons of noblemen. It was for this reason that Rufus King, the American Ambassador, sent his sons to Harrow, as the only school where no distinction was shown to rank.—*Smith's Handbook*.

for which purpose the celebrated George Buchanan was appointed to the office of preceptor. Buchanan was sixty years older than the King of Scots: his faculties had, however, suffered nothing by age, for his great work, the *History of Scotland*, was the product of a still later period of his life. But his original faults of temper appear to have been aggravated into habitual moroseness; "that contempt also for the artificial distinctions of rank and fortune, so natural to men conscious of having elevated themselves from obscurity by the unaided force of native genius, was in Buchanan degenerated into a species of republican cynicism which often impelled him to trample on the pride of kings with greater pride than their own." It is said that he once took upon him to severely whip the young monarch, for disturbing him at his studies; and his general treatment of James may be collected from a speech used by him concerning a person in high place about him in England, "that he ever trembled at his approach, he minded him so of his pedagogue." The tutor, on his part, confessed a failure when, being reproached for making the King a pedant, he replied, that it was the best he could make of him. James, nevertheless, under the guidance of so able a master, accumulated a mass of erudition which formed through life his pride and boast; but his judgment was feeble, and his temperament cold. The most accomplished Latin poet and scholar of the age was unable to refine or elevate his taste; to inspire him with due respect for the public will, or warm his bosom with the sentiments of a patriot King; although with the latter view Buchanan wrote for James, then in his fourteenth year, a learned Latin dialogue concerning the Constitution of Scotland. Notwithstanding Buchanan addressed this to his pupil as a testimony of his affection, he must have made himself rather an object of awe than of love; or he (James) would have preserved so much respect for one of the first literary characters in Europe, and the founder of his own erudition, as neither to have suffered him to die in penury, nor to receive interment at the cost of the city of Edinburgh, which charged itself with this honorable burthen.

During the civil wars which agitated Scotland under the successive regencies of the Earls of Murray, Lenox, Mar, and Morton, the royal minor James remained tranquil and secluded in Stirling Castle; but in 1577, the Earls of Athol and Argyle succeeded in depriving Morton of the regency, and, gaining access to the young king, they persuaded him, then in his twelfth year, to take into his own hands the administration of the country. Morton shortly after repossessed himself of Stirling Castle, and of the custody of James's person; yet a parliament assembled in 1578, had the absurdity to confirm the king's premature assumption of manhood. Here the interest of James's educational tutelage may be said to cease. He had been altogether carefully instructed by Buchanan; and he wrote several works, both in prose and poetry, which, though now censured as pedantic, show him to have possessed a cultivated mind, and a style quite equal to the generality of writers of his time. He also aspired to theological learning; for before he was twenty years of age, he wrote a Latin commentary on the Apocalypse; and he founded a seminary for champions in the Romish controversy upon the site of the present Chelsea Hospital. His amusements, however, were of the coarsest description; cock-fighting, bull, bear, and lion baiting, and the more ordinary field sports, occupying his time to the utter neglect of public affairs. But, he was a patron of learning; and it ought not to be forgotten that the authorized translation of the Bible was commenced and completed under his auspices. Shortly after he had succeeded to the English throne, at a conference of divines held at Hampton Court, in 1603, James expressed a strong opinion on the imperfections of the existing translations of the Scriptures. "I wish," said he, "some special pains were taken for a uniform translation, which should be done by the best learned in both universities, then revised by the bishops, presented to the privy council, and lastly ratified by royal authority, to be read in the whole church, and no other." Out of this speech of the king's arose the present English Bible, which has now for nearly 250 years been the only Bible read in the English church, and is also the Bible universally used in dissenting communities.

EDUCATION OF PRINCE HENRY.

James I. married, in 1590, Anne of Denmark, by whom he had a family of seven children. Prince Henry Frederic, the eldest son, was born at Stirling Castle in 1594. His father committed his infancy to the joint care of the Earl of Mar and the Countess his mother, who had been the king's own nurse: both were persons of merit, and were loved by their young charge, although the countess is said to have been far from over-indulgent. Neither James nor his queen desired that their children should receive education under their own eyes, or be domesticated beneath the same roof with themselves. In consequence, the younger children were *boarded out* in the families of different noblemen; whilst for the heir-apparent a separate establishment was formed, almost immediately on his quitting his nurse. His principal attendants were the Earl of Mar as governor, and Sir David Murray as gentleman of the bedchamber. At five or six years of age, the prince was placed under the tuition of Adam Newton, a good scholar, who afterward translated into Latin the King's discourse against Vorstius. About the same time James composed his *Basilicon Doron*, a collection of precepts and maxims in religion, in morals, and in the arts of government, addressed to Prince Henry, nominally for his instruction, but more truly for displaying James's skill in common-places, and uttering to the world his maxims of state. Upon the little prince arriving in England, the king created him a Knight of the Garter, at nine years of age, and settled him in one of the royal palaces, his household consisting of seventy servants, which the King doubled next year; and in 1610, the establishment of the prince had increased to 426 persons, besides artificers under the management of Inigo Jones, comptroller of the works.*

Different factions now strove to gain the ear and heart of the young prince. A Scotch officer being directed to procure for his highness a suit of armor, expressed his hopes that he would follow the footsteps of Edward the Black Prince, and added, "I shall bring with me also the book of Froissart, who will show your grace how the wars were led in those days; and what just title and right your grace's father has beyond the seas." The queen told him she hoped one day to see him conquer France, like another Henry V. To learning the prince does not appear to have been greatly inclined, but he remained true to the Protestant faith; and the martial spirit thus fostered in him had the effect of rendering him a warm admirer of Henry IV. of France, and by degrees of drawing him strongly within the influence of this distinguished prince and warrior.

"None of his pleasures," writes M. Broderie, in 1606, "savour in the least of a child. He is a particular lover of horses, and what belongs to them; but is not fond of hunting. He is fond of playing at tennis, and at another Scotch diversion very like mall; but always with persons elder than himself, as if he despised those of his own age. He studies two hours in the day, and employs the rest of his time in tossing the pike, or leaping, or shooting with the bow, or throwing the bar, or vaulting, or some other exercise of that kind; and he is never idle."—*Birch's Life*.

* No. 17, Fleet-street, is a reputed residence of Prince Henry, but not mentioned as such by his biographers. The first-floor front-room has, however, an enriched plaster ceiling, inscribed P. (triple plume) H., which, with part of the carved wainscoting, denote the house to be of the time of James I. Here Mrs. Salmon exhibited her wax-work, and she was, probably, the first who styled the place "once the Palace of Henry Prince of Wales, son of King James I.;" a statement, perhaps, as authentic as the present inscription on the house—"Formerly the Palace of Henry VIII. and Cardinal Wolsey." The size of the dwelling does not correspond with the magnificent household of Prince Henry; it is more probable that the ceiling was decorated with the royal plume and initials by one of the Prince's retainers, which courtly compliment was formerly not rare.

Near Leicester-fields, upon the site of Gerrard-street, Soho, was formerly a piece of ground walled in by Prince Henry, for the exercise of arms; here were an armory and a well-furnished library of books relating to feats of arms, chivalry, military affairs, encamping, fortification, in all languages, and kept by a learned librarian. It was called the Artillery Ground; and after the Restoration of Charles II. it was bought by Lord Gerard, and let for building, about 1677.—*Curiosities of London*.

Henry patronized that excellent man and preacher, Joseph Hall, afterward Bishop of Norwich. Having heard two of the sermons, the prince, then in his fourteenth year, appointed him one of his chaplains. Henry was early impressed with a strong sense of religion; and besides exhibiting strict religious observance in his own conduct, his youthful zeal ordered boxes to be kept at his three houses, to receive the penalties on profane swearing, which he commanded to be strictly levied on his household; and he is stated to have once declared that "all the pleasure in the world is not worth an oath." He took early interest in naval matters; frequently visited the dockyards; took great delight in a model ship which was constructed for him, and received Phineas Pett, the builder, into his special favor and protection. He greatly admired the genius of Sir Walter Raleigh, and more than once exclaimed that "no king but his father would keep such a bird in a cage." Henry died in his nineteenth year: the grief of the people was unbounded: the young and adventurous bewailed a prince supposed to resemble Henry V., that favorite of English story, equally in his outward form and in the nobler qualities of his mind; and the zealous party in religion mourned a stanch defender of the Protestant church. The two universities produced sermons, Latin orations, and collections of verses, in honor of the lamented Prince Henry. Most of the cotemporary poets, with the very remarkable exception of Ben Jonson — the court poet, though not yet the laureate — hastened to scatter their voluntary offerings round the tomb of Henry. Chapman, the translator of Homer, bewailed in the prince his "most dear and heroical patron." Webster and Heywood each produced an elegy. William Browne, who published in the following year *Britannia's Pastorals*, first exercised his muse on the loss of Henry; and Dr. Donne, known chiefly by his satires, in a tender elegy commemorated the virtue of this lamented prince. His handsome person and knightly figure are vividly portrayed in the print engraved by Crispin Pass.

LITERATURE OF THE REIGN OF JAMES THE FIRST.

The best learning of this age was derived from the study of the ancients; which, however, tended to introduce the pedantry and forced conceits and sentiments so prevalent in the writing of the time. The English language, after having been improved by Spenser and Sir Philip Sidney, and rendered almost perfect by Richard Hooker, in his immortal books of the Ecclesiastical Polity, had begun, after the middle of the reign of Elizabeth, to lose some of its native vigor, being molded by every writer according to his own fancy. The introduction of the Latin idiom, which had caused many innovations in the last reign, greatly increased under James I., who was himself infected with the bad taste of his time. The prose composition has been considered to be more imperfect than the verse; the purest language spoken in the Courts of Elizabeth and James I. is thought to have differed but little from the best of modern times; wherefore the unpolished and Latinized prose of the seventeenth century has been attributed to the station in society of the authors. But the English tongue could boast of Shakspeare, Ben Jonson, and Edward Fairfax, the translator of Tasso; Sir John Harrington, who rendered Ariosto into British verse; Dr. Donne, whose wit and deep feeling, thrown into his lines, are almost entirely obscured by an uncommonly harsh and uncouth expression; Dr. Joseph Hall, Bishop of Exeter, the first author of satires in English; Sir Walter Raleigh; Beaumont and Fletcher; Owen Feltham and Lord Bacon. The last was one of the greatest glories of the literature of this period. He wrote more in Latin than in English, and perhaps had more strength than elegance in either; but he is rendered famous by the great variety of his talents as a public speaker, a statesman, a wit, a courtier, an author, a philosopher, and a companion.

In this reign, in 1608, the great Lord Clarendon, Chancellor to Charles II., was born at Dinton, near Salisbury, where he was first instructed by the clergyman of the parish, who was also a schoolmaster, and afterward at Magdalen College, Oxford, where he entered at the age of thirteen: we obtain a glimpse of the manners of the students at the University at that period from Clarendon's quitting Oxford "in consequence of the habit of hard drinking which then prevailed there."

In the same year, 1608, was born John Milton; and in 1612, Samuel Butler; of whose school-days some account will be given in a future page.

BURTON AND SELDEN.

To the scholars of this period belongs Robert Burton, who wrote the *Anatomy of Melancholy*, the favorite of the learned and witty, and beyond all other English authors, largely dealing in apt and original quotations. Burton was born at Lindley, in Leicestershire, in 1576, and was sent early to the free grammar-school of Sutton Coldfield, in Warwickshire, as he mentions in his *Anatomy*—in his will, he also states Nuneaton; probably he may have been at both schools. At the age of 17, he was admitted a commoner at Brazen Nose College, Oxford, where he made considerable progress in logic and philosophy; in 1599, he was elected student of Christchurch; and about 1628, he became rector of Segrave, Wood describes him as—

"'an exact mathematician, a curious calculator of nativities, a general-read scholar, a thorough-paced philologist, and one that understood the surveying of lands well. As he was by many accounted a severe student, a devourer of authors, a melancholy and humorous person, so by others who knew him well, a person of great honesty, plain dealing, and charity. I have heard some of the antients of Christchurch often say that his memory was very merry, facete, and juvenile; and no man in his time did surpass him for his ready and dexterous interlarding his common discourses among them with verses from the poets, or sentences from classical authors; which, being then all the fashion in the University, made his company more acceptable."

We gather from Burton's account of himself, that he aimed at a smattering in all; that he had read many good books, but to little purpose, for want of a good method; that all his treasure was in Minerva's tower; that he lived a collegiate student, as Democritus in his garden, and led a monastic life, sequestered from the tumults and troubles of the world, but now and then walking abroad, to see the fashions, and look into the world. He was an inordinate reader, and was liberally supplied with books from the Bodleian Library, to which and Christchurch Library he bequeathed his own books.

John Selden, described as "an English gentleman of most extensive knowledge and prodigious learning," was born at Salvington, in Sussex, in 1584: he was sent early to the prebendal free school at Chichester, which had been refounded by Bishop Edward Story, about 1470; but the school is believed to be coeval with the cathedral. From Chichester, Selden was sent to Oxford. Antony à Wood says: "he was an exact critic and philologist, an excellent Grecian, Latinist, and historian, and, above all, a profound antiquary."

By his works Selden acquired the esteem and friendship of Camden, Spelman, Sir Robert Cotton, Ben Jonson, Browne, and also of Drayton, to whose *Polyolbion* he furnished notes. By Milton he is spoken of as "the chief of learned men reputed in this land." "He was of so stupendous a learning," says Lord Clarendon, "in all kinds and in all languages (as may appear in his excellent writings), that a man would have thought he had been entirely conversant among books, and had never spent an hour but in reading and writing; yet his humanity, affability, and courtesy were such, that he would have been thought to have been bred in the best courts, but that his good nature, charity, and delight in doing good exceeded that breeding." His amanuensis for twenty years enjoyed the opportunity of hearing his employer's discourse, and was in the habit of faithfully committing "the excellent things that usually fell from him;" which were subsequently published as Selden's *Table Talk*.

THOMAS FULLER'S "SCHOOLMASTER."

The witty Thomas Fuller, one of the most original writers in our language, was born in 1608, at Aldwinckle, in Northamptonshire; his father being rector of St. Peter's, in that village. His early education was conducted chiefly under the paternal roof, and so successfully, that at twelve years of age he was sent to Queen's College, Cambridge. At the age of sixteen he took his degree of B.A., and that of M.A. in 1628.* He soon became an extremely popular preacher, and preferment came rapidly. Among his numerous works, Fuller has portrayed "The Good Schoolmaster," of whose office he says: "There is scarce any profession in the commonwealth more necessary, which is so slightly performed. The reasons whereof I conceive to be these: First, young scholars make this calling their refuge; yea, perchance, before they have taken any degree in the University, commence schoolmasters in the country; as if nothing else were required to set up this profession, but only a rod and a ferula. Secondly, others, who are able, use it only as a passage to better preferment; to patch the rents in their present fortune, till they can provide a new one, and betake themselves to some more gainful calling. Thirdly, they are disheartened from doing their best, with the miserable reward which in some places they receive, being masters to the children, and slaves to their parents. Fourthly, being grown rich, they grow negligent; and scorn to touch the school, but by the proxy of an usher.

"Some men had as lieve be school-boys as school-masters — to be tied to the school, as Cooper's *Dictionary* and Scapula's *Lexicon* are *chained to the desk* therein; and though great scholars, and skillful in other arts, are bunglers in this.

"But *a good schoolmaster studieth his scholars' natures as carefully as they their books*, and ranks their dispositions into several forms. He refuseth cockering mothers who proffer him money to purchase their sons' exemption from his rod, and scorns the late custom in some places of commuting whipping into money, and ransoming boys from the rod at a set price." These are interesting glimpses of schoolmasters' practice and the state of common education in the seventeenth century.

THE CHARTER-HOUSE SCHOOL FOUNDED.

In one of the secluded corners of the City of London, and

* Fuller's power of memory was very great. It is said that he could "repeat five hundred strange words after once hearing them, and could make use of a sermon *verbatim*, under the like circumstances." Still further, it is said that he undertook, in passing from Temple Bar to the extremity of Cheapside, to tell, at his return, every sign as it stood in order on both sides of the way (repeating them either backward or forward), and that he performed the task exactly. This is pretty well, considering that in that day every shop had its sign. Of his method of composition, it is said that he was in "the habit of writing the first words of every line near the margin down to the foot of the paper, and, that then beginning again, he filled up the vacuities exactly, without spaces, interlineations, or contractions; and that he "would so connect the ends and beginnings that the sense would appear as complete as if it had been written in a continued series, after the ordinary manner."

not far from Smithfield, which was once the Town Green, was founded by the chivalrous Sir Walter Manny, in the 14th century, a monastery of Carthusians, in which the founder was buried the year after its completion. Here Sir Thomas More gave himself to devotion and prayer for about four years. The monastery, after the surrender, had several noble owners; and in 1611 was sold to Thomas Sutton, the wealthy merchant, who endowed it as "the Hospital of King James; though it is now known as the Charter-house, corrupted from Chartreux, the place where the order of Carthusians was originally instituted. Sutton designed the foundation as a collegiate asylum for the aged; a school-house for the young; and a chapel; but he died before he had perfected his good work, "the greatest gift in England, either in protestant or catholic times, ever bestowed by any individual." The foundation was, however, soon after completed. Few portions of the monastery buildings remain; but the wooden gates are those over which the mangled body of the last prior was placed by the spoilers at the Dissolution.

Upon the foundation are maintained 80 pensioners, or poor brethren, who "live together in collegiate style," and are nominated in the same manner as the 40 foundation scholars, "Gown Boys," by the Governors, who present in rotation. The foundation scholars receive their board, education, and clothing free of expense, and enjoy the right of election to an unlimited number of exhibitions, of from 80*l*. to 100*l*. a-year, at either university. Others receive donations toward placing them out in life. The foundation scholars also enjoy the preference over the Scholars of presentation to valuable church preferment in the gift of the Governors. The number of scholars is about 180.

For the establishment of a school for forty boys, the sum of 5000*l*. was bequeathed expressly; and a sum of 40*l*. was limited to be paid with every boy, either to advance him in college, or as an apprentice fee in trade. It is rather significant of the inadequacy of that sum for the purpose, and of the greatly reduced value of money, that we find the exhibitions to college enlarged by the governors to more than 40*l*. a-year for four years; and also that the amount of 40*l*. as an apprentice premium was wholly useless and insufficient : so much so, that those premiums have been discontinued, no youth having been apprenticed from the school since John P. Kemble was bound apprentice to his uncle, the comedian, to learn the histrionic art! In truth, the 40*l*. in 1611, as compared to the same nominal amount of our currency, may be estimated at 400*l*., or ten times the sum. This calculation ought to be borne out in all the details, for most assuredly the value of the estates has increased tenfold; and yet the gross rental, which was, in the year 1691, 5391*l*., averaged for the last six years less than 21,000*l*., representing an increase little exceeding *three times* that amount!—*The Builder*, No. 631.

The Great Hall, built about the middle of the sixteenth century, has for its west wall part of the conventual edifice. It has a screen, music gallery, sculptured chimney-piece, and lantern in the roof; and here hangs a noble portrait of the founder, Sutton. In this apartment is celebrated the anniversary of the foundation, on December 12; when is always sung the old Carthusian melody, with this chorus:

> "Then blessed be the memory
> Of good old *Thomas Sutton;*
> Who gave us lodging — learning.
> And he gave us beef and mutton."

The present school-house is a modern brick building (1803); the large central door is surrounded by stones bearing the names of former Carthusians. There are two play-greens,—for the "Uppers" and "Unders;" and by the wall of the ancient monastery is a gravel walk upon the site of a range of cloisters. The Master has his flower-garden, with its fountain; there are courts for tennis, a favorite game among Carthusians; a "wilderness" of fine trees, intersected by grass and gravel walks; the cloisters, where football and hookey are played; the old school, its ceiling charged with armorial shields; the great kitchen, probably the banqueting-hall of the old priory; the chapel where Sutton lies, beneath a sumptuous tomb; and lastly, the burial-ground for the poor brethren. There are besides solitary courts, remains of cloisters and cells, and old doorways and window-cases, which assert the antiquity of the place; and the governors have wisely extended the great object of the founder by the grant of a piece of ground, where a church and schools for the poorer classes have been built.

Among the eminent Schoolmasters of Charter-house is the Rev. Andrew Tooke, author of "The Pantheon." Among the eminent Scholars: Richard Crashaw, the poet, author of "Steps to the Temple;" Isaac Barrow, the divine — he was celebrated at school for his love of fighting; Sir William Blackstone, author of the *Commentaries;* Joseph Addison and Richard Steele, scholars at the same time; John Wesley, the founder of the Wesleyans;* Lord Chief-Justice Ellenborough; Lord Liverpool, the Prime Minister; Bishop Monk; W. M. Thackeray; Sir C. L. Eastlake, P.R.A. The two eminent historians of Greece, Bishop Thirlwall and George Grote, Esq., were both together, in the same form, under Dr. Raine.—*Abridged from Cunningham's Handbook of London.*

To the list will surely be added "Old Phlos." The pet name will be remembered by Carthusians, whose memories can go back some forty years or more. They will not have forgotten the gentle and thoughtful lad who used to stand looking on while others played, and whose general meditative manner procured for him the name of "Philosopher," subsequently diminished to "Phlos," and occasionally applied as "Old Phlos." That young and popular philosopher is the soldier at whose name the hearts of Englishmen beat with honest pride. "Old Phlos" of the Charter-house is Havelock, the hero of Cawnpore.—*Athenæum.*

Among the *Poor Brethren:* Elkanah Settle, the rival and antagonist of Dryden; John Bagford, the antiquary, who left a large collection of materials for the history of Printing; Isaac de Groot, by several descents the nephew of Hugo Grotius — he was admitted at the earnest intercession of Dr. Johnson; and Alexander Maclean, Johnson's assistant in his Dictionary.

EDUCATION OF CHARLES I.

Little is recorded of the early life of this ill-fated prince. He was the second son of James VI. of Scotland, by Anne of Denmark, his queen, and was born at the royal castle of Dun-

* Wesley imputed his after-health and long life to the strict obedience with which he performed an injunction of his father's, that he should run round the Charter-house playing-green three times every morning.

fermline, in Scotland, in 1600. At three years of age he was committed to the care of the lady of Sir George Cary, and under her management the weakly constitution of the young prince improved; it became firm and vigorous when he had attained to manhood, and he is said to have shown great activity in his field sports and exercises; his stature, however, remained below the middle size, and the deformity of his childhood was never entirely corrected.* Another natural defect under which he labored was an impediment in utterance, which through life generally manifested itself whenever Charles became earnest in discourse, and which had, doubtless, a great share in producing the taciturnity for which he was remarkable. On completing his fourth year, Charles was brought to England; on Twelfth Day, 1605, he was created a Knight of the Bath, with twelve companions, and afterward solemnly invested with the dignity of Duke of York.

Miss Aikin searched in vain among cotemporary letters and memoirs for early anecdotes of this prince. His habits were sedentary and studious, and were much ridiculed by his elder brother Henry, whose death rendered Charles heir-apparent to the British crown; but he appears still to have lived in seclusion. An encomiastic biographer attributes his supposed obstinacy and suspected perverseness to the above natural defects. An old Scottish lady, his nurse, used to affirm that he was of a very evil nature in his infancy, and the lady who afterward took charge of him stated that he was "beyond measure willful and unthankful." These faults of temper were, however; checked as Charles grew up. His reserve saved him from excesses: he was moderate in his expenses, prudent in his conduct, and regular at his devotions; he was industrious, and his pursuits and tastes were of an elegant turn. King James sought to inspire his son with his own love of learning. At the premature age of ten, Charles was made to go through the form of holding a public disputation in theology, and he actually became acquainted with the polemics of the time. His own inclinations, however, led him to the study of mechanics and the fine arts. An attached adherent has thus described the young prince's accomplishments:

With any artist or good mechanic, traveler, or scholar, he would discourse freely; and as he was commonly improved by them, so he often gave light to them in their own art or knowledge. For there were few gentlemen in the world that knew more of useful or necessary learning than this prince did; and yet his proportion of books was but small, having, like Francis the First of France, learned more by the ear than by study. . . . . . His exertions were manly; for he rid the great horse very well; and on the little saddle he was

* In the fine equestrian portrait of Charles I., by Vandyke, now at Hampton Court, a curvature at the knee is distinctly visible.

not only adroit, but a laborious hunter or fieldsman, and they were wont to say of him, that he never failed to do any of his exercises artificially, but not very gracefully.

A collection of antiques (says Miss Aikin), and other objects of curiosity bequeathed to him by Prince Henry, appears first to have directed his attention toward painting and sculpture; the taste was afterward fostered in him by the Duke of Buckingham, and his merits as a connoisseur and patron of art and artists were unquestionably great.

At the age of sixteen, Charles was solemnly created Prince of Wales; and his household was formed, almost all the officers being Scotch. Mr. Murray, his tutor, who had been about him from his sixth year, was also a Scotsman and a Presbyterian. These circumstances led to many fears and jealousies, and being represented to the king, he appointed Dr. Hakewill, an eminent divine, of Oxford, as Charles's religious instructor; who, endeavoring to dissuade the prince from his marriage with the Spanish Infanta, a Catholic princess, was imprisoned, deprived of his office about Charles, and for ever debarred of further preferment: but the provostship of Eton was afterward conferred upon him in recompense for his long service.

<small>The prince's "exercises of religion were most exemplary: for every morning early, and evening not very late, singly and alone, he spent some time in private meditation, and he never failed, before he sat down to dinner, to have part of the liturgy read to him and his servants; and when any young nobleman or gentleman who was going to travel, came to kiss his hand, he cheerfully would give him some good counsel leading to moral virtue, especially a good conversation."</small>

Charles was certainly one of the most elegant and forcible English writers of his time, and a great friend to the fine arts; and to him we owe the first formation of the royal collection of pictures now in the palaces. Charles's works consist chiefly of letters, and a few state papers, and of the famous *Eikon Basilike*, which first appeared immediately after the death of the king:* his claim to the authorship was much disputed; but Dr. Ch. Wordsworth, in an octavo volume of patient research, is considered to have proved the book to have been the production of Charles; Dr. Wordsworth states that Hooker, the divine Herbert, and Spenser were the king's favorite reading; and, "the closet companion of his solitudes, William Shakspeare."

LITERATURE AND LEARNING AT THE ACCESSION OF CHARLES I.

At the period of Charles's accession, the cumbrous erudition

<small>* A curious piece of evidence of the publication of this work is recorded in an Historical Account of Mr. John Toland, 1722, who, at an auction of books at Button's Coffee-house, in Russell-street, Covent Garden, bought Mr. Toland's *Amyntor;* or, *A Defence of Milton's Life,* in page 120 whereof was written by one Dr. Thompson the following memorandum; "Mr. John Wilson, barrister-at-law, author of the *Vindication of Icon Basilike,* against Milton, told me in person that he bought the *Icon Basilike,* Jan. 31, 1648, for ten shillings, the very next day after the king was beheaded! Fra. Thompson, D.D.</small>

of scolarship began to be laid aside, and general information was more prized than what is technically called learning. Books of voyages and travels were printed in considerable numbers, and read with avidity. Hakluyt published his collection of voyages; he was appointed lecturer on geography at Oxford, and was the first to introduce maps, globes, and spheres into the common schools. Purchas published his Pilgrimage; George Sandys, his Travels and Researches on Classical Antiquities; Knowles, his History of the Turks; Camden, his Annals of Queen Elizabeth; Speed, his Chronicle; Lord Herbert of Cherbury, his Life of Henry VIII.; and Lord Bacon, his Life of Henry VII.

Among the earliest results of the intellectual progress of the age was an extension of the established plan of education, as far, at least, as regarded youths of family and fortune. Peacham's "Complete Gentleman," addressed to his pupil, Thomas Howard, fourth son of the Earl of Arundel, presents us with a summary of the requirements at this time necessary to a man of rank. He stigmatises the class of schoolmasters, so often ignorant and incompetent, and generally rough and even barbarous to their pupils, who were "pulled by the ears, lashed over the face, beaten about the head with the great end of the rod, smitten upon the lips for every slight offence, with the ferula," etc. Domestic tutors he represents to have been still worse; ignorant and mean-spirited men, engaged by sordid persons at a pitiful salary, and encouraged to expect their reward in some family living, to be bestowed as the meed of their servility and false indulgence. Peacham blames parents for sending to the universities "young things of twelve, thirteen, or fourteen, that have no more care than to expect the carrier, and where to sup on Fridays and fasting nights; no further thought of study than to trim up their studies with pictures, and to place the fairest books in open view, which, poor lads, they scarce ever open, or understand not." . . . "Other fathers, if they perceive any wildness or unstayedness in their children," hastily despairing of their "ever proving scholars or fit for anything else, to mend the matter, send them either to the court to serve as pages, or into France and Italy to see fashions and mend their manners, where they become ten times worse." We gather from Peacham's work, that geography, with the elements of astronomy, geometry, and mechanics; the study of antiquities, comprising mythology and the knowledge of medals, and the theory and practice of the arts of design, — were parts of learning now almost for the first time enumerated amongst the becoming accomplishments of an English gentleman.

Lord Herbert of Cherbury has sketched a plan of education still more extensive, being modeled apparently on his own acquirements. He advises that after mastering the grammar, the pupil should proceed with Greek, in preference to Latin, on account of the excellence of the writers of that language "in all learning." Geography and the state and manners of nations he would have thoroughly learned, and the use of the celestial globe; judicial astrology for general predictions only, as having no power to foreshow particular events; arithmetic and geometry "in some good bold measure;" and rhetoric and oratory. Like Bacon, he seems much addicted to medical empiricism, and enjoins the study of drugs and antidotaries. He speaks of botany as a pursuit highly becoming a gentleman, and judiciously recommends anatomy as a remedy against atheism.* He recommends riding the great horse and fencing; but disapproves of "riding running horses, because there is much cheating in that kind, and hunting takes up too much time." "Dicing and carding" he condemns.

Female education, in the higher class, shared in the advancement. In classical learning, the reign of James supplied no rivals to the daughters of Sir Anthony Cooke, to Lady Jane Grey, or Queen Elizabeth; but Lady Anne Clifford received instructions from Daniel in history, poetry, and general literature; Lucy Harrington, afterward Countess of Bedford, was a medalist and Latin scholar; Lady Wroth, born a Sidney, was both herself a writer and a patroness of the learned. Mrs. Hutchinson, whose admirable Memoirs of her husband bespeak a highly cultivated mind, informs us that at about the age of seven, she "had at one time eight tutors in several qualities — languages, music, drawing, writing, and needle-work." †

A GOOD EDUCATION IN THE SEVENTEENTH CENTURY.

"To learn to read and write" appears to have been the sum of good Education two centuries and a half since. Dekker, a dramatist at the beginning of the seventeenth century, however, makes a man of substance who is asked, "Can you read and write, then?" reply, "As most of your gentlemen do — my bond has been taken with my mark at it." Public records of the days of Elizabeth and James I. show that some of the men in authority — worshipful burgesses and aldermen — as commonly made their marks as others signed their names in fair Italian or German hands. There must be a general reason for this, besides

* Memoirs of the Court of King Charles the First. By Lucy Aikin.
† Ibid

the particular aptitude, or the particular unfitness, of the individual for acquiring the rudiments of learning. The reason is tolerably obvious. The endowed Grammar-schools which survived the Reformation were few in number, and were not established upon any broad principles of diffusing education throughout the land. Where they were established by Royal charter, or by the zeal of individuals, they did their work of keeping the sources of knowledge open to a portion of the people; some of the children of the middle classes availed themselves of their advantages, and could write a Latin letter as well as make a fair ledger entry; others, and there was no consequent derogation from their respectability, kept their accounts by the score and the tally, and left the Latin to the curate. The learning of the middle classes was then won by them as a prize in a lottery.

Now, at the end of two centuries, we find the same inequality still prevailing amongst what we term the lower classes. The old test of the spread of the rudiments of knowledge, in the exhibition of the ability to write, existed to our time. The Report of the Registrar-General for the year 1846 says: "Persons when they are married, are required to sign the marriage register; if they cannot write their names, they sign with a mark: the result has hitherto been, that nearly one man in three, and one woman in two married, sign with marks."

SIR MATTHEW HALE'S PLAN OF INSTRUCTION.

The great lawyer of this and the succeeding reign, Sir Matthew Hale, in his "Advice to his Grandchildren," and "Counsels of a Father," has left the following course of instruction for sons: Till eight, English reading only. From eight to sixteen, the grammar-school. Latin to be thoroughly learned, Greek more slightly. From sixteen to seventeen at the university, or under a tutor: more Latin, but chiefly arithmetic, geometry, and geodesy. From seventeen to nineteen or twenty, "logic, natural philosophy, and metaphysics, according to the ordinary discipline of the university;" but after "some systems or late topical or philosophical tracts," the pupil to be chiefly exercised in Aristotle. Afterward, should he follow no profession, yet to gain some knowledge of divinity, law, and physics, especially anatomy. Also of "husbandry, planting, and ordering of a country farm." For recreations, he advises "reading of history, mathematics, experimental philosophy, nature of trees, plants, or insects, mathematical observations, measuring land; nay, the more cleanly exercise of smithery, watchmaking, carpentry, joinery work of all kinds."

NEWSPAPERS INTRODUCED.

The Newspaper, which has now existed in England for nearly two centuries and a quarter, has from the first proved an active element of civilization, instruction, and popular enlightenment; until it has finally been elevated into a "Fourth Estate." In former times, much of the intelligence conveyed in newspapers was crude and ill-told: but so gigantic have been the improvements in the newspaper of the present century, that it is not too much to regard it as a powerful adjunct, if not a direct agent, in the education of the people. Its origin, therefore, should be noticed in the present work.

Until lately it was believed that the three numbers of "The English Mercurie," preserved in the British Museum, and professing to record the attack of the Spanish Armada, were the first newspapers printed in England; upon the credit of which the invention was given to Lord Burleigh. In 1840, however, this "Mercurie" was proved to be a clumsy forgery.* Pamphlets containing foreign news began to be occasionally published during the reign of James I. The first of these news-pamphlets, published at regular intervals, appears to have been "The News of the Present Week," edited by Nathaniel Butter, which was started in 1622, in the early days of the Thirty Years' War, and was continued, in conformity with its title, as a weekly publication.

But the English newspaper, properly so called, at least that containing domestic intelligence, commences with the Long Parliament. The earliest discovered is a few leaves, entitled "The Diurnal Occurrences, or Daily Proceedings of Both Houses, in this great and happy Parliament, from the 3d of November, 1640, to the 3d of November, 1641." More than a hundred newspapers, with different titles, appear to have been published between this date and the death of Charles I.; and upward of 80 others between that event and the Restoration.

Where our modern newspapers begin, the series of our chroniclers closes, with Sir Richard Baker's "Chronicles of the Kings of England,"—first published in 1641. It was several times reprinted, and was a great favorite with our ancestors for two or three succeeding generations; but it has now lost all its interest, except for a few passages relating to the author's own time; and Sir Richard and his Chronicle are now popularly remembered principally as the great historical authorities of

---

* For the details of this discovery, see Popular Errors Explained and Illustrated, pp. 61-63.

Addison's Sir Roger de Coverly.—(See *Spectator*, No. 329.)*

To conclude — the educational effect of Newspapers has resulted from the perusal of them encouraging and keeping alive *the habit of reading;* for a newspaper is to the general reader far more attractive than a book — in fact, a man can read a newspaper when he cannot read anything else. He often finds, however, that fully to understand the news of the day, he must have recourse to books — so difficult is it for educated persons, who now write in newspapers, to write with sufficient simplicity to be invariably understood by the uneducated, or rather the imperfectly educated. It is, moreover, in chronicling the progress of our educational institutions — from the university to the ragged-school — and in the fearless advocacy of the great cause of public instruction and political rights — that the newspaper must be regarded as the most powerful aid to education.

MILTON'S SYSTEM OF INSTRUCTION.

Of the educational movements of this period, the above was the most remarkable, inasmuch as it was grounded upon active experience. The education of John Milton, one of the great lights of this period, and himself "an actual schoolmaster," was conducted with great care. He was born Dec. 9, 1608, in Bread-street, Cheapside, where his father was a scrivener, living at the sign of the Spread Eagle, the armorial ensign of his family. The poet was baptized in the adjoining church of Allhallows, where the register of his baptism is still preserved. He was first placed under a person of Puritan opinions, named Young, who was master of Jesus College, Cambridge, during the Protectorate. At fifteen he was sent, even then an accomplished scholar, to St. Paul's School, London, under Alexander Gill. From St. Paul's he proceeded to Christ's College, Cambridge, where, as the college register informs us, he was admitted, Feb. 12, 1624. At the university he was distinguished for the peculiar excellence of his Latin verses, and, according to his own statement, he met with "more than ordinary favor and respect" during the seven years of his stay here. Dr. Johnson, however, "is ashamed to relate what he fears is true, that Milton was one of the last students in either university that suffered the public indignity of corporal correction," or flogging; but there appears

---

* During the time that Sidney Godolphin filled the office of Lord High Treasurer, between the years 1701 and 1710, he occasionally visited his seat in Cornwall. No conveyances then proceeded regularly onward further west than Exeter; but when certain masses of letters had accumulated, the whole were usually forwarded together by what was called "the Post." But the Lord High Treasurer engaged a weekly messenger from Exeter to bring his letters, dispatches, and the newspaper: and on the fixed day of the messenger's arrival, the gentlemen assembled at Godolphin House, from many miles round, to hear the newspaper read in the Great Hall.

small reason to believe the fact. Milton was designed for the church, but he preferred a "blameless silence" to what he considered "servitude and forswearing." At this time, in his twenty-first year, he had written his grand *Hymn on the Nativity*, any one verse of which was sufficient to show that a new and great light was about to rise on English poetry. In 1632 he retired from the university, having taken his degree of M.A., and went to his father's house at Horton, Bucks: here, during a residence of five years, he read over all the Greek and Latin classics, and here he wrote his *Arcades, Comus*, and *Lycidas*. In 1637, on the death of his mother, Milton traveled into Italy, during which journey he was introduced to Grotius, to Galileo, and to Tasso's patron, Manso. On Milton's return to England, he devoted himself to the education of his nephews, John and Edward Phillips, at his house in Aldersgate-street, which was then "freer from noise than any other in London." Of Milton's system of teaching, we gather, from his letter to Mr. Hartlib, that the knowledge of words is best obtained in union with the knowledge of things; that "language is but the instrument conveying to us things useful to be known." He looked upon the reading of good books as the best and only means of obtaining a knowledge of language, wherefore he protests against "the preposterous exaction of forcing the empty wits of children to compose themes, verses, and orations," as a way to obtain a knowledge of the language; for he regards them as "the acts of ripest judgment, and the final work of a head filled by long reading and observing, with elegant maxims, and copious invention." He preferred physical studies to humane or moral studies; but like Bacon, he protests against that method which starts from abstractions and conclusions of the intellect; and he maintains that all true method must begin from the objects of sense. Possibly his protests against making logic and metaphysics the introduction to knowledge in the universities, when they ought to be the climax of knowledge, were more appropriate to his own day, when boys went to Cambridge or Oxford at 15 or 12, than to the present time.

Milton wished his college to be both school and university: the studies, therefore, proceed in an ascending scale, from the elements of grammar to the highest science, as well as to the most practical pursuits. The younger boys are to be especially trained to a clear and distinct pronunciation, "as like as may be to the Italian." Books are to be given them like Cebes or Plutarch, which will "win them early to the love of virtue and true labor." In some hour of the day they are to be taught the rules of arithmetic and the elements of geometry. The evenings are to be taken up "with the easy grounds of religion, and the study of Scripture." In the next stage they begin to study books on agriculture, Cato, Varro, and Columella. These books will make them gradually masters of ordinary Latin prose, and will be at the same time "occasions of inciting and enabling them hereafter to improve the tillage of their country." The use of maps and globes is to be learnt from modern authors; but Greek is to be studied as soon as the grammar is learnt, in the "historical physiology of Aristotle and Theophrastus." Latin and Greek authors together are to teach the principles of arithmetic, geometry, astronomy, and geography. Instruction in architecture, fortification, and engineering follows. In natural philosophy, we ascend through the history of meteors, minerals, plants and living creatures, to anatomy. Anatomy leads on to the study of medicine. Milton would have us always conversant with facts rather than with names. He aims at the useful as directly as the most professed utilitarian. The pupils are to have "the helpful experiences of hunters, fowlers, fishermen, shepherds, gardeners, and apothecaries" to assist them in their natural studies. These studies are to increase their interest in Hesiod, in Lucretius, and in the Georgics of Virgil.

In other words, the tendency of Milton's scheme was not so much to supply the then existing deficiency of instruction in the knowledge of nature, or to substitute some other treatise on such matters for the works of Aristotle, but to exchange, as quietly as possible, and at the same time as decidedly, the merely formal routine of classical teaching for one in which the books that were read might arouse thought as well as exercise memory. His list comprises almost all the technical treatises extant in Latin and Greek, but excludes history and almost all the better known books of poetry, probably because he only intended it for children, and postponed such subjects for the instruction or amusement of riper years. His aims were not those of a mathematician or the philosopher of nature ; the state, not science, was in his view, and his object was to make, not good members of a university, but well-informed citizens. To this tend his eulogy of manly exercises and his plans for a common table, which could have had little importance in the eyes of a student. But the ends of Milton's system were as noble and as practicable as those of any that was ever conceived.

LOCKE'S SYSTEM OF EDUCATION.

Equally illustrative of the important business of Education are the writings of John Locke, one of the wisest and sincerest of Englishmen. He was born at Wrington, near Bristol, in 1632.

He was the eldest of two sons, and was educated with great care by his father, of whom he always spoke with the highest respect and affection. In the early part of his life, his father exacted the utmost deference from his son, but gradually treated him with less and less reserve, and when grown up, lived with him on terms of the most entire friendship; so much so, that Locke mentioned the fact of his father having expressed his regret for giving way to his anger, and striking him once in his childhood when he did not deserve it. In a letter to a friend, written in the latter part of his life, Locke thus expresses himself on the conduct of a father toward his son:

"That which I have often blamed as an indiscreet and dangerous practice in many fathers, viz, to be very indulgent to their children whilst they are little, and as they come to ripe years to lay great restraint upon them and live with greater reserve toward them, which usually produces an ill understanding between father and son, which cannot but be of bad consequences; and I think fathers would generally do better, as their sons grow up, to take them into a nearer familiarity, and live with them with as much freedom and friendship as their age and temper will allow."

Locke was next placed at Westminster School, from which he was elected, in 1651, to Christchurch, Oxford. Here he applied himself diligently to the study of classical literature; and by the private reading of the works of Bacon and Descartes, he sought to nourish that philosophical spirit which he did not find in the philosophy of Aristotle, as taught in the school at Oxford. Though the writings of Descartes may have contributed, by their precision and scientific method, to the formation of Locke's philosophical style, it was the principle of the Baconian method of observation which gave to the mind of Locke that taste for experimental studies which forms the basis of his own system, and probably determined his choice of a profession. He adopted that of medicine, which, however, the weakness of his constitution prevented him from practicing.

Of the writings of Locke, it must suffice for us to mention his great work, *An Essay concerning Human Understanding*, in which, setting aside the whole doctrine of innate notions and principles, the author traces all ideas to two sources, sensation and reflection; treats at large of the nature of ideas, simple and complex; of the operation of the human understanding in forming, distinguishing, compounding, and associating them; of the manner in which words are applied as the representatives of ideas; of the difficulties and obstructions in the search after truth, which arise from the imperfection of these signs; and of the nature, reality, kinds, degrees, casual hindrances, and necessary limits of human knowledge. The influence of this work, written in a plain, clear, expressive style, upon the aims and habits of philosophical inquirers, as well as upon the minds of educated men in general, has been extremely beneficial. Locke also wrote *Thoughts upon Education*, to which Rousseau is largely indebted for his *Emile*. The following passage on the importance of Moral Education is very striking:

"Under whose care soever a child is put to be taught during the tender and flexible years of his life, this is certain, it should be one who thinks Latin and languages the least part of education; one who, knowing how much virtue and a well-tempered soul is to be preferred to any sort of learning or language, makes it his chief business to form the mind of his scholars, and give that a right disposition; which, if once got, though all the rest should be neglected, would in due time produce all the rest; and which, if it be not got, and settled so as to keep out ill and vicious habits—languages and sciences, and all the other accomplishments of education, will be to no purpose but to make the worse and more dangerous man."

GRAMMAR-SCHOOLS IN THE SEVENTEENTH CENTURY.

John Aubrey, the Wiltshire antiquary, has left this picture-in-little of the public schools of his time:
"Before the Reformation, youth were generally taught Latin in the monasteries, and young women had their education not at Hackney, as now, 1678, but at nunneries, where they learnt needle-work, confectionary, surgery, physic (apothecaries and surgeons being at that time very rare), writing, drawing, etc. Old Jacquar, now living, has often seen from his house the nuns of St. Mary Kington, in Wilts, coming forth into the Nymph Hay with their rocks and wheels to spin, sometimes to the number of threescore and ten, all whom were not nuns, but young girls sent there for education." . . . . . "The gentry and citizens had little learning of any kind, and their way of breeding up children was suitable to the rest. They were as severe to their children as their schoolmasters, and their schoolmasters as the masters of the House of Correction: the child perfectly loathed the sight of his parents as the slave his torture. Gentlemen of thirty and forty years old were made to stand like mutes and fools bareheaded before their parents; and the daughters (grown women) were to stand at the cupboard-side during the whole time of their proud mother's visits, unless (as the fashion was) leave was desired forsooth that a cushion should be given them to kneel upon, brought them by the serving-man, after they had done penance by standing. The boys had their foreheads turned up and stiffened by spittle."

INFLUENCE OF THE WRITINGS OF LORD BACON.

"Everything relating to the state of the natural sciences at this period," says Dr. Vaughan, "may be found in the writings of Bacon. It was reserved to the genius of that extraordinary man to direct the scientific minds not only of his country but of

Christendom, into the true path of knowledge; to call the attention of men from metaphysical abstraction to the facts of nature; and in this manner to perform the two most important services that could be rendered to the future world of philosophy,—first, by indicating how much it had to unlearn, and how much to acquire; and secondly, by pointing out the method in which the one process and the other might be successfully conducted; and, as this system depended on the most rigid and comprehensive process of experiment, it obtained for its illustrious author the title of 'the Father of Experimental Philosophy.'"

This subject is too vast for a running comment upon the progress of Learning like that which is here attempted. It is by his *Essays* that Bacon is best known to the multitude. The *Novum Organum* and *De Augmentis* are much talked of, but little read. They have, indeed, produced a vast effect upon the opinions of mankind; but they have produced it through the operation of intermediate agents. They have moved the intellects which have moved the world. It is in the *Essays* alone that the mind of Bacon is brought into immediate contact with the minds of ordinary readers. There he opens an exoteric school, and talks to plain men, in language which everybody understands, about things in which everybody is interested. He has thus enabled those who must otherwise have taken his merits on trust, to judge for themselves; and the great body of readers have, during several generations, acknowledged that the man who has treated with such consummate ability questions with which they are familiar, may well be supposed to deserve all the praise bestowed on him by those who have sat in his inner school. The following passage from the *Essays** is in Bacon's early style:

"Crafty men contemn studies; simple men admire them; and wise men use them; for they teach not their own use: that is a wisdom without them, and won by observation. Read not to contradict, nor to believe, but to weigh and consider. Some books are to be tasted, others to be swallowed, and some few to be chewed and digested. Reading maketh a full man, conference a ready man, and writing an exact man. And therefore, if a man write little, he had need have a great memory; if he confer little, have a present wit; and if he read little, have much cunning to seem to know that he doth not. Histories make men wise, poets witty, the mathematics subtle, natural philosophy deep, morals grave, logic and rhetoric able to contend."

Lord Macaulay has well observed: "It will hardly be disputed that this is a passage to be 'chewed and digested.' We do not believe that Thucydides himself has anywhere compressed so much thought into so small a space."

No book ever made so great a revolution in the mode of think-

---

* For educational purposes we recommend attention to the ably edited reprints of the *Essays*, and *The Advancement of Learning*, by Thomas Markey, M.A. Archbishop Whately's annotated edition of the *Essays* is intended for a different class of students.

ing, overthrew so many prejudices, introduced so many new opinions—as the *Novum Organum*. Its nicety of observation has never been surpassed; it blazes with wit, but with wit which is employed only to illustrate and decorate the truth. But what is most to be admired is the vast capacity of that intellect which, without effort, takes in at once all the domains of science—all the past, the present, and the future—all the encouraging signs of the passing times—all the bright hopes of the coming age.

Lord Bacon wrote paraphrases of the Psalms, of which it has been said: the "fine gold of David is so thoroughly melted down with the refined silver of Bacon, that the mixture shows nothing of alloy, but a metal greater in bulk, and differing in show from either of the component elements, yet exhibiting, at the same time, a luster wholly derived from the most precious of them."

THE FIRST SCIENTIFIC TREATISES IN ENGLISH.

Here should be mentioned the founder of the school of English writers, that is to say, to any useful or sensible purpose,—Robert Recorde, the physician, a man whose memory deserves, on several accounts, a much larger portion of fame than it has met with. He was the first who wrote on Arithmetic, and the first who wrote on Geometry in English; the first who introduced Algebra into England; the first who wrote on Astronomy and the doctrine of the Sphere in England; and finally, the first Englishman (in all probability) who adopted the system of Copernicus. Recorde was also the inventor of the present method of extracting the square-root; the inventor of the sign of equality; and the inventor of the method of extracting the square-root of multinomial algebraic quantities. According to Wood, his family was Welsh, and he himself a Fellow of All Souls' College, Oxford, in 1531; he died in 1558 in the King's Bench Prison, where he was confined for debt. Some have said that he was physician to Edward VI. and Mary, to whom his books are mostly dedicated. They are all written in dialogue between master and scholar, in the rude English of the time.

INVENTION OF LOGARITHMS.—GUNTER'S SCALE.

Another great benefactor to science was Baron Napier, of Merchiston, by his great invention of Logarithms, in 1614, which, from his own day to the present hour, has been one of the most active and efficient servants of all the sciences dependent upon calculation; nor could those of them in which the most splendid triumphs have been achieved have been possibly carried to the heights they have without the assistance of Logarithms.

> By reducing to a few days the labor of many months (says Laplace), it doubles, as it were, the life of an astronomer, besides freeing him from the errors and dissent inseparable from long calculations. As an invention it is particularly gratifying to the human mind, emanating as it does exclusively from within itself. Logarithms (says Professor Playfair) have been applied to numberless purposes which were not thought of at the time of their first construction. Even the sagacity of the author did not see the immense fertility of the invention he had discovered:. he calculated his tables merely to facilitate arithmetical and chiefly trigonometrical computation; and little imagined that he was at that time constructing a scale whereon to measure the density of the strata of the atmosphere and the heights of mountains, that he was actually computing the areas and lengths of innumerable curves, and was preparing for a calculus, which was yet to be discovered, to make more clear many of the most refined and most valuable of its resources. Of Napier, therefore, if of any man, it may safely be pronounced, that his name will never be eclipsed by any one more conspicuous, or his invention be superseded by anything more valuable.

Napier's Bones, or Rods, are a contrivance of Napier to facilitate the performance of multiplication and division; and might be used with advantage by young arithmeticians in verification of their work.

Of the same period as their invention is *Gunter's Scale,* the useful wooden logarithmic scale invented by Edmund Gunter, to whom we are also indebted for the sector and the common surveyor's chain, and several printed works: he was also the author of the convenient terms *cosine, cotangent,* etc.—for "sine," "tangent," etc., of the complement. "Whatever, in short," it has been observed, "could be done by a well-informed and ready-witted person to make the new theory of Logarithms more immediately available in practice to those who were not skillful mathematicians, was done by Gunter."

THE SCIENCES AT OXFORD AND CAMBRIDGE.

An acute writer in the *Companion to the Almanac* for 1837 observes:—"The University of Cambridge appears to have acquired no scientific distinction in the Middle Ages. Taking as a test the acquisition of celebrity on the Continent, we find that Bacon, Sacrobosco, Greathead, Eastwood, etc., were all of Oxford. The latter University had its morning of scientific splendor, while Cambridge was comparatively unknown, and (with regard, at least, to definite college foundations) hardly beginning to exist: it had also its noon-day illustrated by the names of such men as Briggs, Wren, Wallis, Halley, and Bradley. The age of science at Cambridge is said to have begun with Francis Bacon; and but that we think much of the difference between him and his celebrated namesake (Roger Bacon), lies more in time and circumstances than in talents or feelings: we would rather date from 1600 with the former, than from 1250 with the latter. Praise or blame on the side of either university is out of the question, seeing that the earlier foundation of Oxford, and its superiority in pecuniary means, rendered all that took place highly probable. We rejoice in the recollections by the production of which we are enabled to show that this country held a conspicuous rank in the philosophy of the Middle Ages; and we cheerfully and gratefully remember that, to the best of our knowledge and belief, we are in a great measure indebted for the liberty of writing our thoughts to the cultivation of the liberalizing sciences at Oxford in the *dark* ages. With regard to the University of Cambridge, for a long time there hardly existed the materials for any proper instruction, even to the extent of pointing out what books should be read by a student desirous of cultivating astronomy. Of this we have a remarkable instance.

Jeremiah Horrocks, who is well known to astronomers as having made a greater step toward the amendment of the lunar theory than any Englishman before Newton, and whose course might be well known to every reader, but that he died at the age of 23, was at Cambridge in 1633—1635. From the age of boyhood he had been wholly given to the desire of making himself an astronomer. But he could find no one who could instruct him, who could help him by joining him in the study—"such was the sloth and languor which had seized all." Horrocks found that books must be used instead of teachers: these he could not obtain in the University; nor could he there even learn to what books he should direct his attention. Nor were the books themselves which Horrocks (having but small means, and desiring the very best) afterward bought, in any one instance that we can discover, printed in England.

A school-book of great popularity may be mentioned here. This is the well-known "Cocker's Arithmetic." The author, born about 1631, was an engraver and a teacher of writing and arithmetic, and the writer of several books of exercises in penmanship, some of them on silver plates. His celebrated "Arithmetic" was not published until after his death, before 1677: in the title-page it is described as "a plain and familiar method, suitable to the meanest capacity, for the full understanding of that incomparable art, as it is now taught by the ablest schoolmasters in City and Country." The first edition appeared in 1677; the fourth in 1682; the thirty-seventh in 1720; there is no copy of either edition in the British Museum, the libraries of the Royal Society, Sion College, or the London Institution: a copy of the edition of 1678 has been sold for 8*l.* 10*s.* Cocker's Arithmetic was the first which entirely excluded all demonstration and reasoning, and confined itself to commercial questions only. This was the secret of its extensive circulation: upon it, nine out of ten of the subsequent Arithmetics have been modeled; and every method since the author's time has been "according to Cocker."

BOYHOOD AND EDUCATION OF OLIVER CROMWELL.

Cromwell, the son of Robert Cromwell, and his wife Elizabeth, was born at Huntingdon, in 1599. It is traditionally related that when an infant, his life was endangered by a great monkey at his grandfather's house taking him out of the cradle, and carrying him upon the leads of the house, to the dreadful alarm of the family (who made beds and blankets ready in the forlorn hope of catching him), but at last brought him safely down. It is better established, Oliver was saved from drowning in his youth by Mr. Johnson, the curate of Cunnington.

Cromwell was educated at the Free Grammar-school of Huntingdon by Dr. Beard, whose severity toward him is said to have been more than what was usual even in that age of barbarous school discipline.* He was a resolute, active boy, fond of engaging in hazardous exploits, and more capable of hard study than inclined to it. His ambition was of a different kind, which discovered itself even in his youth. He is said to have displayed a more than common emotion in playing the part of Tactus, who finds a royal robe and a crown, in the old comedy of Lingua, performed at the Free-school of Huntingdon.† He is said often, in the height of his fortune, to have mentioned a gigantic figure which, when he was a boy, opened the curtains of his bed, and told him he should be the greatest person in the kingdom. It is also related that Cromwell (being at his uncle's house at Hinchinbrook), when the royal family rested there on their way from Scotland, in 1604, was brought to play with Prince Charles, then Duke of York, quarreled with him, beat him, and made his nose bleed profusely,—which was remembered as a bad omen for the King when Cromwell began to distinguish himself in the Civil Wars.

Before Oliver had completed his seventeenth year, he was removed from the school at Huntingdon to Sydney Sussex College, Cambridge. Though his passion for athletic exercises still continued, so much so that he is said to have acquired the name of a royster in the university, it appears certain that he did not misspend his time there, but that he made a respectable

---

* The frontispiece to the Theatre of God's Judgment is said to be a portrait of this severe schoolmaster. It represents him with two scholars standing behind, a rod in his hand, and *As in præsenti* proceeding from his mouth.

† Selected and abridged from Southey.

proficiency in his studies. Within a year of this, his father died, and his mother, to whose care he appears to have been left, removed him from college. It has been affirmed that he was placed at Lincoln's Inn, but that instead of attending to the law, he wasted his time "in a dissolute course of life, and good fellowship and gaming." But Cromwell's name is not to be found in the registers of Lincoln's Inn, though his son Richard's is. It is, however, probable that Oliver was entered at some other of the inns of court. Returning thence to reside upon his paternal property, he is said to have led a low and boisterous life. However this may have been, he offended at this time by his irregularities both his paternal uncle and his maternal one. But, whatever may have been the follies and vices of Cromwell's youth, it is equally certain that he had strength and resolution enough to shake them off.

In after life Cromwell was not insensible to literary merit. Archbishop Usher received a pension from him; Andrew Marvell and Milton were in his service; and the latter always affirmed of him, that he was not so illiterate as was commonly supposed. He gave 100*l*. yearly to the Professor of Divinity at Oxford; and it is said that he intended to have erected at Durham a college for the northern counties of England.

<small>During the Commonwealth, an 1658, appeared that truly excellent work *The Practice of Christian Graces, or, the Whole Duty of Man*, which, not long after its publication, was translated into the Latin, French, and Welsh languages. Bishop Bull, one of the greatest ornaments of our church, was accustomed to read a chapter out of "The Whole Duty of Man," in addition to the performance of family prayers in his house on Sunday evenings, "for the further instruction of his family, particularly of those who had been deprived of going to church by reason of the necessary services of the house." Bishop Sanderson, Isaak Walton tells us, had some prayers read at night to him and to a part of his family out of "The Whole Duty of Man." Dean Stanhope says, "Happy is the man who can form his style in plain practical preaching, upon the rational, instructive, and familiar way of the Whole Duty of Man;" and of its style a writer in the *Edinburgh Review* says, "after a lapse of 170 years, it contains scarcely a word or phrase which has become superannuated." Yet, the real authorship of this work has never yet been settled on strong and decisive evidence. It has been attributed to Bishop Fell, Dr. Allstree, Bishop Chappel, Archbishop Sterne, Lady Pakington, and Dr. Henry Hammond; to Archbishop Frewen, Abraham Woodhead, Obadiah Walker, Mr. Fulman, and Dr. Chaplin. Lady Pakington's claim is founded upon a copy of the work, in her handwriting, being found amongst her papers after her death; but, as this lady was a very devout person, and was much acquainted with the divines of the day, she is very likely to have been favored with a sight of the work before it was printed, and to have been allowed to take a copy of it for her own use. The Editor of the reprint of the work published by Pickering, in 1842, adduces evidence to show that the author was Dr. Sterne, which he considers strong enough to justify belief. Dr. Southey describes "The Whole Duty of Man" as "a good old book, which contains the substance of a course of sermons, addressed in the plainest language to plain people, and setting before them those duties which they are called upon to perform in the ordinary course of life. The author was a person of sound judgment and sober piety, who sought to make his parishioners practical Christians, and not professing ones; and that he was humble-minded there is conclusive proof, for he concealed his name." Until of late years the work was generally to be found among the books of well-regulated households; and we have ever thought better of a family for its possessing a copy of "The Whole Duty of Man."</small>

CHARLES THE SECOND—HIS PATRONAGE OF LETTERS.

Of the childhood and education of Charles II. we find scanty record. He was the eldest son of Charles I. and Henrietta Maria of France, and was born at St. James's in 1630. He was chiefly brought up by his mother until he was twelve years of age. In his ninth year he was created Prince of Wales: when the Civil War broke out, he accompanied his father to the battle of Edgehill; and in 1645, he served with the royal troops in the west with the title of general. Next year, on the ruin of the royal cause, he joined the Queen, his mother, at Paris, and he afterward took up his residence at the Hague. This must have been almost the earliest opportunity that the Prince could have had for study, which must have been of a practical turn. Evelyn describes Charles as "a lover of the sea, and skillful in shipping; not affecting other studies; yet he had a laboratory, and knew of many empirical medicines, and the easier mechanical mathematics; he loved planting and building, and brought in a politer way of living, which passed to luxury, and intolerable expense." But this is the language of a courtier.

Charles's love of the sea led him early in his reign to entertain the suggestions of certain governors of Christ's Hospital for the institution and endowment of the Royal Mathematical School. With Sir Robert Clayton, it is believed, originated this school; and his project being backed by Sir Jonas Moore, then Surveyor-General of the Ordnance, and by Sir Christopher Wren and Samuel Pepys; and having in its favor the mediation of the Duke of York, then Lord High Admiral of England,—a royal charter was granted, and the school was opened for 40 boys, under the auspices of the King, in the year 1673. Beyond the grant of the charter, however, little was done by Charles toward the maintenance of his new foundation. His endowment did not extend beyond an annuity of 1000*l.*, terminating at the expiration of seven years. The King reserved as many of the boys as might be required for his own services; and a grant was obtained from the Government by Pepys to be given as premiums to merchant-masters for taking the other boys. The revenue was also increased by a gift, which it was thought the King would not approve of, but, on being consulted, he replied, that "so far was he from disliking, that he would be glad to see any gentleman graft upon his stock." The school flourished: for several years Pepys constantly attended the examination of the boys; and Sir Jonas Moore, one of the first practical mathematicians of the day, commenced for the master's use a system of mathematics, which was completed by Halley and Flamsteed.

Another service which Charles rendered to the higher class of studies was his incorporation of the Royal Society, by royal charter, in 1663, when the King signed himself in the charter-book as the founder;* and his brother, the Duke of York, signed as Fellow. Charles also presented the Society with a mace.

Another advantage conferred on science in this reign was Charles's foundation, in 1676, of the Royal Observatory at Greenwich, for the benefit of astronomy and navigation; and the appointment of Flamsteed as the first Astronomer Royal.

After the Restoration, the first steam-engine is commonly believed to have been constructed by the Marquis of Worcester, which he, in his Century of Inventions, describes as "an admirable and most forcible way to drive up water by fire." He used a cannon for his boiler, and he describes the water as running "like a constant fountain-stream, 40 feet high; one vessel of water rarified by fire, driveth up 40 of cold water." This engine was seen at work in 1663, at Vauxhall, by Sorbiere, who foretold that the invention would be of greater use than the machine above Somerset House, to supply London with water.

NONCONFORMIST SCHOOLS AT ISLINGTON AND NEWINGTON GREEN.

In the latter part of the seventeenth century, the village of Islington appears to have been a refuge for Nonconformist ministers. Here, after the Act of Uniformity was passed, in 1662, some of the ministers then ejected from the Church of England opened schools. For a time, however, they were prohibited from teaching; but eventually they succeeded in establishing academies in different places. The Rev. Thomas Doolittle, formerly Rector of St. Alphage's, London Wall, had a school at Islington about the year 1682, and prepared several young men for the ministry, among whom were the pious Matthew Henry and Dr. Edmund Calamy; here the Rev. Ralph Button, of Merton College, Oxford, kept school, and had for one of his pupils Sir Joseph Jekyll. Several ministers also opened schools at Newington Green; and at one of them, kept by the Rev. Charles Morton, previously a rector in Cornwall, "some score of young ministers were educated, as well as many other good scholars." Defoe was a pupil of Mr. Morton's: he says of his instructor, that he was a polite and profound scholar, and a master who taught nothing either in politics or science, which was dangerous to monarchical government, or which was improper for a diligent scholar to know. "Defoe was originally

---

* The first charter (in Latin) has ornamented initials, and a finely executed portrait of Charles II. in Indian ink. The charter empowers the president *to wear his hat while in the chair;* and the fellows addressed the president bareheaded, till he made a sign for them to put on their hats; but these customs are now obsolete.

intended for the ministry: he tells us, it was his disaster first to be set apart *for*, and then to be set apart *from*, the honor of that sacred employ. At Newington he had for his school-fellow the father of the celebrated John Wesley. Another Islington notoriety of this period was Robert Ferguson, the Judas of Dryden's great satire, and conspicuous as an unprincipled politician. By birth a Scotsman, he came to England, and being ejected from his living in Kent, got to be master of a school at Islington, which the Dissenters had set up as a rival to the schools of Westminster and the Charterhouse. At length he strayed into politics—was deeply engaged in the Rye House Plot—was the shameless adviser of the Duke of Monmouth in his rebellion—and was deservedly discarded by the sagacious Prince of Orange. His end, no doubt, was miserable." Lord Macaulay, in his *History*, devotes several pages to him.

BOYHOOD OF JAMES II.

The early life of this prince was clouded by the political troubles of the time, which, as they greatly tended to his personal discomfiture, must have materially interfered with his instruction. James was the second surviving son of Charles I., by his queen Henrietta Maria, and was born at St. James's in 1633. He was immediately declared Duke of York, but not formally created to that dignity till 1643. After the surrender of Oxford to Fairfax, in 1646, the duke, with his younger brother, Henry, afterward created Duke of Gloucester, and his sister Elizabeth, was committed by the Parliament to the care of the Earl of Northumberland, and he continued in the custody of that nobleman till the 21st of April, 1648, when he made his escape from St. James's Palace, disguised in female attire, and took refuge with his sister Mary, Princess of Orange. Here he joined a part of the English fleet, which had revolted from the Parliament, and was then lying at Helvoetsluys; but although at first received on board as an admiral, he soon after resigned that post to his brother, the Prince of Wales, on the arrival of the latter from Paris, and returned to the Hague. When Charles, now styled King by his adherents, came to Jersey, in September, 1649, he was accompanied by the duke, who remained with him during his stay of three or four months. He then returned to the Continent, and resided some time with his mother at Paris.

"Never little family" (says Clarendon, who had an interview with him at Breda, in 1650) "was torn into so many pieces and factions. The duke was very young, yet loved intrigues so well that he was too much inclined to hearken to any men who had the confidence to make bold propositions to him. The king had appointed him to remain with the queen, and to obey her in all things, religion only excepted. The Lord Byron was his governor, ordained to be so by his father, and very fit for that province, being a very fine gentleman, well bred both in France and Italy, and perfectly versed in both languages, of great courage and fidelity, and in all subjects qualified for the trust; but his being absent in the king's service when the Duke made his escape out of England, and Sir John Berkley being then put about him, all pains had been taken to lessen his esteem of the Lord Byron; and Sir John Berkley, knowing that he could no longer remain governor, when the Lord Byron came thither, and hearing that he was on his journey, infused into the Duke's mind that it was a great lessening of his dignity at that age (when he was not above fourteen years of age, and backward enough for that age), to be under a governor; and so, partly by disesteeming the person, and partly by reproaching the office, he grew less inclined to the person of that good lord than he should have been."—*Life*, vol. i. p. 284.

A singular circumstance now occurred, which well bespeaks the character of James. Shortly before his meeting with Clarendon, it had been reported that Charles was dead; upon which the duke, looking upon himself as already King, made several journeys to take counsel with his friends; and, upon the falsehood of the intelligence respecting Charles being discovered, James was so childish that he was rather delighted with the journeys he had made, than sensible that he had not entered upon them with reason enough; observing that "they had fortified him with a firm resolution *never to acknowledge that he had committed any error.*" In the end he was obliged to return to his mother at Paris, where he chiefly resided until he had attained his twentieth year. He served with reputation in both the French and Spanish armies; but his great aptitude was for sea affairs, and after his return to England in 1660, he for some time acted as Lord High Admiral. His exertions, assisted by the indefatigable Pepys, the Secretary of the Navy, raised the fleet which afterward won the battle of La Hogue; as his camp at Hounslow was the nursery for the victorious army of Marlborough. James employed part of the leisure of his retirement in writing an account of his own life, the original manuscript of which extends to nine folio volumes. The manuscript was burnt by the person to whom it had been confided; but a digest of the royal autobiography had been long before drawn up by an unknown hand, apparently under the direction either of James or his son; and this digest being preserved among the papers belonging to the Stuart family, which were obtained by George IV., when Regent, has been printed.

LITERATURE OF THE SEVENTEENTH CENTURY.

It is now time to glance at the literary characters of this period, reserving their personal characteristics for another portion of the present volume.

Foremost in the rank is Milton, though he obtained not in his life the reputation he deserved. Edmund Waller was the first refiner of English poetry, or at least of its rhyme. Cowley was more admired during his life than Milton, and more celebrated after his death. Sir John Denham had a loftiness and vigor, which had scarcely been attained by any previous poet that wrote in rhyme. The Oceana of James Harrington was a political romance, well adapted to astonish when the systems of imaginary republics occupied so much attention.

There was also much admirable writing in the English language, both under Charles I. and II.,—by William Chillingworth, in his "Religion of Protestants, a safe way to Salvation;" in Cleveland's noble letter to Cromwell; in the famous histories of Lord Clarendon, and the pious eloquence of Jeremy Taylor; in the abstract philosophy of Dr. Henry More; in the orthodox and learned divinity of Dr. Isaac Barrow; in the Exposition of Bishop Pearson; in the still popular works of Tillotson; in the courtly volumes of Sir William Temple; and even in the wild and perverted philosophy of Thomas Hobbes.

The reign of Charles II. has sometimes been considered the Augustan age of English literature, though more frequently the honor has been adjudged to the eighteenth century, as having still greater purity and simplicity of language. The authors of this period exhibit much fine genius, though corrupted by the bad taste to which they were forced to conform, as may be seen in the eloquent and spirited works of Dryden, the comic talent of Wycherley, and the pathetic powers of Otway. There were other authors of the time, who wrote with good taste, as the Marquis of Halifax, and the Earls of Mulgrave, Dorset, and Roscommon, though their productions are more limited in extent, or slighter in the character of their composition.

The few female autobiographists who have graced the literature of England were confined to the stirring times of the Commonwealth, when the pressure of circumstances, by acting upon the strongest and finest feelings of woman, developed her intellect, and forced her upon active and even perilous existence. The two most brilliant instances of this charming *genre* of egotism are to be found in the memoirs of the fantastic Duchess of Newcastle, and in those of the heroic Mrs. Hutchinson, both admirable illustrations of their respective classes at the epoch in which they flourished: the one of the pure, unmixed aristocracy of England; and the other of its gentry, or highest grade of middle life.

Mrs. Evelyn was one of the most accomplished women of the court of Charles the Second, and one of the few virtuous women who frequented it. She was a celebrated linguist and artist, and her works in oil and miniature are frequently quoted with pride by her husband.—*Lady Morgan.*

RISE OF FREE-SCHOOLS, OR CHARITY SCHOOLS.

We have already shown that the endowed grammar-schools were the natural successors of the schools and charities of the Church before the Reformation. They contemplated none but the most liberal education. Children were to be brought up as scholars, or to be taught nothing. The grammar-schools were the nurseries of the learned professions, and they opened the way for the highest honors of those professions to the humblest in the land.

About the time of the Revolution, the commercial classes, who had grown into wealth and consequent importance, began naturally to think that schools in which nothing was taught but Latin and Greek were not altogether fitted for those who were destined to a mercantile life. Uneducated men who had pushed their way to fortune and honor generously resolved to do something for their own class; and thus we come to see in every town not a free grammar-school, but a free-school, over whose gates was generally set up the effigy of a boy in blue or green, with an inscription betokening that by the last will of Alderman A. B. this school had been founded for 20 poor boys, to be clothed, and taught reading, writing, and arithmetic.

With a comparatively small population, these free-schools were admirable beginnings of the education of the poorer classes. While the grammar-schools were making divines, lawyers and physicians, out of the sons of the professional classes and the wealthier tradesmen, the free-schools were making clever handicraftsmen and thriving burgesses out of the sons of the mechanics and laborers; and many a man who had been a charity boy in his native town, when he had risen to competence, pointed with honor and pride to the institution which had made him what he was, and he often loosened his purse-strings to perpetuate for others the benefits which he had himself enjoyed.

Thus we see that what the grammar-schools had done for the higher and middle classes, the free-schools did for the lower, in a different measure. They were the prizes for the poor boy, who had no ambition, perhaps no talent, for the struggles of the scholar; they taught him what, amongst the wholly untaught, would give him a distinction and a preference in his humble career,—and he was unenvied by the less fortunate, because they knew that there was no absolute bar to their children and their kindred running the same course.

In a few cases, we owe public-schools to some providential deliverance of the founders; as in the instance of Dame Alice Owen, who, in 1613, founded and endowed in St. John-street-road, London, a school for 30 poor scholars, in memory of her having escaped "braining" by a stray arrow upon the site, then called Hermitage Fields; the arrow having passed through Dame Owen's high-crowned hat.

The originator of this charity-school movement is by some stated to have been William Blake, a woolen-draper, "at the sign of the Golden Boy," Maiden-lane, Covent-garden, who founded the Hospital at Highgate,* called the Ladies' Charity

---

* There was already at Highgate a Grammar School, founded by Sir Roger Cholmeley in the reign of Elizabeth; the first statute ordering that the schoolmaster should "teach

School, before 1685, and who purchased Dorchester House for that purpose, expending 5000*l.* in his benevolent project, Blake had for his coadjutor Alderman Cornish, who, in 1685, was tried and executed as having been concerned in the Rye-house plot. It is generally stated that Charity Schools were first erected in the parish of Aldgate, and St. Margaret, Westminster; and a slab in front of the Aldgate school-house, adjoining the Royal Mint, bears an inscription to the purport that it was the first Protestant Charity School, and was erected by voluntary contributions in 1693. Upon this, Blake says: "If it comes to the earliest London school for poor children, perhaps the Catholics take the lead; for we find that it was part of the tactics of the Jesuits, in the reign of James II. to promote their design of subverting the Protestant religion by infusing their Romish tenets into the minds of the children of the poor by providing schools for them in the Savoy and Westminster."* Blake then describes his scheme as a good work, because it would, in some measure, "stop the mouths of the Papists," who were wont to reproach Protestants with the scarcity of their hospitals.

Blake, who styled himself "housekeeper" to the school, wrote *Silver Drops, or Serious Thoughts,* in which he advocated the good cause. This is a rare book, with four engravings (one a view of Dorchester House), which were torn out and used as receipts for subscriptions to the charity. The Prospectus states:

> Being well informed that there is a pious, good, and commendable work for maintaining near 40 poor or fatherless children, born all at or near Highgate, Hornsey, or Hamsted, we, whose names are subscribed, do engage or promise that if the said boys are decently clothed in blew, lined with yellow; constantly fed all alike with good and wholesom diet; taught to read, write, and cast accompts, and so put out to trades, in order to live another day, then we will give, etc.

Blake then pleads for his project by various addresses, which he calls "charity-school sticks," ostensibly the production of the boys, but in reality written by himself. But Blake's appeals failed, and having "fooled away his estate in building," he was thrown into prison for debt; and while there he wrote another work, entitled "The State and Case of a Design for the better Education of Thousands of Parish Children successively in the vast Northern Suburbs of London vindicated, etc." Next, Blake, about 1650, at the funeral of his wife, thus exhorted his

young children their A B C, and other English books, and to write, and also in their gram mar as they should grow up thereto;" but the foundation dwindling to a mere charity school, by the neglect of the governors, the school was restored, and is now in active operation as a Grammar-school under a scheme of the Court of Chancery. The income is about 777*l.*, and the School is free to 40 boys, nominated by Governors from the neighborhood.

* Notes and Queries, No. 210.

friends to subscribe to the school: "I was brought up by my parents to learne Hail Mary, Paternoster, the Belief, and learne to read; and where I served my apprenticeship little more was to be found," and he attributes it to God's grace that he fell a reading the *Practice of Piety*,* etc. Such were the exertions of Blake, the Covent Garden philanthropist, to whom must be conceded the honor of being the pioneer of our Charity Schools. Westminster has, to this day, four of these schools, distinguished by the color of the clothes worn by the scholars. First is St. Margaret's Hospital, established and endowed in 1633: the master's house bears a bust of Charles I. and the royal arms, richly carved, colored and gilt; adjoining the school-house is a quaint old flower-garden; the boys wear a long *green* skirt, and a red leather girdle; hence St. Margaret's is known as the *Green Coat Hospital;* the grace used here, attributed to Bishop Compton, is the same as that said in Christ's Hospital. Then there is the Westminster *Blue Coat School*, instituted 1688; and next *Gray Coat Hospital*, founded in 1698, and reconstructed in 1706, when the school-house was built: the centre bears the royal arms of Queen Anne, with the motto *Semper Eadem*, flanked by a male and female figure in the olden costume of the children—dark gray dresses, the girl's bodice open in front, and corded. In 1686, Sarah, Duchess of Somerset, bequeathed 100*l*. to support six fatherless boys in the school, to be distinguished by wearing *yellow caps*. The fourth and last is Palmer's School,† the boys of which wear *black coats*.

A school was commenced about this period at Kensington, by a bequest in 1645, to establish " a free school for poor men's children to be taught reading and arithmetic ;" which was extended to clothing and instructing boys and girls " in all needful learning and work, and the principles of the Church, and to dispose them to useful trades." Queen Anne and Prince George of Denmark contributed to the fund, and in 1713 a new schoolhouse was built, west of Kensington Church, by Sir John Vanbrugh: this is a fine specimen of brick work; in the front are costumed statuettes of a charity boy with a pen and scroll, inscribed, " I was naked and ye clothed me ;" and a charity girl presenting a prayer-book : in the old school-room is a vellum list of subscribers to the school from 1701 to 1750.

* The Practice of Piety, by Bayly, Bishop of Bangor, a book much read by John Bunyan.
† Founded by the Rev. Edward Palmer, B. D., who also built alms-houses and a chapel. Around these sprung up cottages and small houses, which grew into " Palmer's Village." Thirty years since, here was an old way-side inn (the Prince of Orange); the cottages had gardens, and here was the village green, upon which the May-pole was annually set up; this rurality has now disappeared, and with it, from maps and plans, the name of " Palmer's Village."—*Curiosities of London*, p. 760.

Among the oldest Charity Schools in the metropolis are those of St. Clement Danes, Strand, established in 1700, on the principles then first propagated by the Society for Promoting Christian Knowledge. The School-house is in the neighborhood of Clare Market, formerly Clement's Inn Fields, where theatres and taverns, and other low haunts of dissipation, held out their baits, and for neglect of Christian education lured many a soul to early ruin.

Another of these early institutions is the Ladies' Charity School, which was established in 1702, at King-street, Snow-hill, London, and was there kept 145 years, when it was removed to John-street, Bedford-row. Mrs. Thrale and Dr. Johnson were subscribers to this school; and Johnson drew from it his story of Betty Broom, in the *Idler*. In the school minutes, 1763, the ladies of the committee censure the schoolmistress for listening to the story of the Cock-lane Ghost, and desire her to "keep her belief in the article to herself." The 150th anniversary of this School was celebrated with a public dinner at Stationers' Hall, in 1852.

EDUCATION OF WILLIAM III.

Although William Henry, Prince of Orange Nassau, occupies a prominent place in the history of England and of mankind, his boyhood and education, and subsequent encouragement of letters, may be briefly told. He was born in 1650, and was the posthumous son of William II. of Orange, by Mary, daughter of Charles I., king of England. He was a weak and sickly child; but Lord Macaulay describes him as largely endowed by nature with the qualities of a great ruler, which education developed in no common degree. The historian says:

His attention was, however, confined to those studies which form strenuous and sagacious men of business. From a child he listened with interest when high questions of finance, alliance, and war were discussed. Of geometry he learned as much as was necessary for the construction of a ravelin or a hornwork. Of languages, by the help of a memory singularly powerful, he learned as much as was necessary to enable him to comprehend and answer without assistance everything that was said to him, and every letter which he received. The Dutch was his own tongue. He understood Latin, Italian, and Spanish. He spoke and wrote French, English, and German—inelegantly, it is true, and inexactly, but fluently and intelligently. He was carefully instructed in the Calvanistic divinity, to which his family was attached; and his theological opinions were even more decided than those of his ancestors. The tenet of predestination was the keystone of his religion.

The faculties which are necessary for the conduct of important business ripened in him at a time of life when they have scarcely begun to blossom in ordinary men. Since Octavius, the world had seen no such instance of precocious statesmanship. Skillful diplomatists were surprised to hear the weighty observations which at seventeen the prince made on public affairs, and still more surprised to see the lad, in situations in which he might have been expected to betray strong passion, preserve a composure as imperturbable as their own. At eighteen, he sat among the fathers of the Commonwealth, grave, discreet, and judicious as the oldest of them. At twenty-one, in a day of gloom and terror, he was placed at the head of the administration. At twenty-three, he was renowned throughout Europe as a soldier and a politician.

Meanwhile, he made little proficiency in fashionable or literary accomplishments. His manners were altogether blunt Dutch. He was little interested in letters or science. The discoveries of Newton and Leibnitz, the poems of Dryden and Boileau, were unknown to him. Dramatic performances tired him. He had indeed some talent for sarcasm, and not seldom employed, quite unconsciously, a natural rhetoric, quaint indeed, but vigorous and original.—*Abridged from Macaulay's Hist. of England*, vol. ii.

After William had become King of England, he was to the last a foreigner in speech, tastes, and habits. He spoke our language, but not well; his accent was foreign, his choice of words was inelegant, and his vocabulary seems to have been no larger than was necessary for the transaction of business. Our literature he was incapable of enjoying or understanding. He never once, during his whole reign, showed himself at the theatre. The poets who wrote Pindaric verses in his praise complained that their flights of sublimity were beyond his comprehension; perhaps he did not lose much by his ignorance.*

It is true that his Queen did her best to supply what was wanting. She was English by birth, and English also in her tastes and feelings. She took much pleasure in the lighter kinds of literature, and did something toward bringing books into fashion among ladies of quality. She paid strict attention to her religious duties; and her well-bestowed patronage of Doctor Tillotson proves her to have been a true friend of the church; and even the Jacobite libelers of the time, who respected nothing else, respected her name. Tenison proved himself a friend to public education by founding in St. James's parish, attached to his chapel, a school, with schoolmasters to teach, without charge, 40 poor boys of the parish to read, write, cast accounts, etc. To Tenison also we owe one of the few public Libraries in the metropolis.

Tenison's Library, built by Sir Christopher Wren, is situated in Castle-street, in the rear of the National Gallery. It was founded in 1684 by Dr. Tenison, then Vicar of St. Martin's-in-the-Fields, to supply what he considered a deficiency of "any one shop of a stationer fully furnished with books of various learning within the precinct of the city and liberty of that minster." Evelyn, in his Diary, 15th Feb., 1683-4, records: "He (Tenison) told me there were 30 or 40 young men in Orders in his parish, either governors to young gentlemen, or chaplains to noblemen, who being reproved by him on occasion for frequenting taverns or coffee-houses, told him they would study or employ their time better, if they had books. This put the pious Doctor on his design." The library consists of about 4000 volumes; Lord Bacon's *Note-book*, and various other of his MSS.; and an early Chaucer MS. The collection also contains the rare books bequeathed by Le Courayer, canon and chief librarian of St. Genevieve, and author of the celebrated *Dissertation on the Validity of the Ordinations and the Succession of the Bishops of the Church of England*. The library is open free to "the inhabitants of Westminster and the neighborhood thereof."

The clergy in this reign evinced devotedness for the spread of Christian Education by the establishment of two excellent institutions, which flourish to the present day.

In 1698 was founded "The Society for Promoting Christian

* Prior, who was treated by William with much kindness, and who was very grateful for it, informs us that the king did not understand poetical eulogy. The passage is in a highly curious manuscript, the property of Lord Lansdowne.—*Macaulay's History of England*, vol. ii.

Knowledge," by publishing religious works at a cheap rate, approved of by a committee of members of the Church of England; the profits, together with the legacies and donations to the society's funds, being devoted to the diffusion of Christian knowledge and the general education of the poor; to making gratuitous grants of its publications to parochial and other lending libraries, etc., in England and Wales; and to promoting Christian education abroad by supplying natives and settlers with books, effecting translations, etc. At the close of this reign (in 1701) was incorporated "The Society for the Propagation of the Gospel in Foreign Parts," for the religious instruction of his Majesty's subjects beyond the seas, and for the maintenance of clergymen in the plantations, colonies, and factories of Great Britain. "Among the founders and earliest supporters of this Society were Arbhbishops Tenison, Sharp, Wake, Potter; Bishops Compton, Rocbuck, Burnet, Beveridge; Dean Prideaux, Robert Nelson, William Melmoth, John Evelyn, etc. The Rev. John Wesley was originally a missionary of this Society, and in that character proceeded to America in 1735, returning to England in 1738."

THE REIGN OF QUEEN ANNE.—THE AUGUSTAN AGE.

Anne, the second daughter of James Duke of York, by his wife Anne Hyde, was born at St. James's, in 1665. Her education was intrusted to Dr. Henry Compton (subsequently Bishop of Oxford and of London), and she was by him firmly grounded in the principles of Protestantism.

The reign of Queen Anne (1702 to 1714) was as distinguished for literature as for arms; but, although her administrators numbered among them eminent scholars, her own tastes and opinions had little share in calling forth the literary genius and talent which have led to her reign being styled *the Augustan Era of English Literature*—on account of its supposed resemblance in intellectual opulence to the reign of the Emperor Augustus. This opinion has not been entirely followed or confirmed in the present day. Anne's reign produced Addison, Arbuthnot, Congreve, Pope, Prior, Steele, and Swift—writers of a high degree of excellence in their particular walks, but scarcely to be compared with the great poets of the reign of Elizabeth, or with a few other illustrious names of a succeeding generation, such as Milton and Dryden. Yet, Addison and Steele invented or introduced among us the periodical essay, a species of writing which has never been surpassed, or on the whole equaled, by any one of their many followers. Who can describe the lightness, variety, and urbanity of these delightful papers—the delicate imagination and exquisite humor of Addison, or the vivacity, warm-heartedness, and perfectly generous nature of Steele? This was the age of the *Examiners, Spectators, Tatlers*, and *Guardians*, which gave us the first examples of a style possessing all the best qualities desirable in a vehicle of general amusement and instruction; easy and familiar without coarseness, animated without extravagance, polished without unnatural labor, and from its flexibility adapted to all the varieties of the gay and the serious.

Next to Addison is Arbuthnot, a writer of sound English, pointed wit, and polished humor. Congreve is our most brilliant writer of comedy. Pope wrote the poetry of artificial life with a perfection never since attained; and in the hands of Swift (the most powerful and original prose-writer of the period), satire was carried to its utmost pitch and excellence;[*] whilst Prior, in his graceful and fluent versification, reflected the lively illustration and colloquial humor of his master, Horace. Prior's patron, St. John Lord Bolingbroke (one of Anne's ministry), was so distinguished a scholar, that even his most familiar conversations, it is said, would bear printing without correction; for he was one of the most brilliant orators and talkers of his time. It is lamentable to add, that Bolingbroke from early life had cast off belief in revelation. Fortunately, his works are now but little read.

Harley, Earl of Oxford, the favorite minister of Queen Anne, was not only a great encourager of learning, but the greatest book-collector of his time; and his curious books and manuscripts form the nucleus of the Harleian Library, now one of the richest treasures of the British Museum.

Among the educational events of this reign may be mentioned the establishment of the Clarendon Press at Oxford, in part from the proceeds of the sale of Lord Clarendon's *History of the Rebellion*, presented to the University by his son. The building, by Sir John Vanbrugh, continued to be used according to its original intention until 1830, when additional room being required to supply the increased demand for books, a new building was erected opposite the Radcliffe Observatory.

Among the free schools founded in this reign, one in Aldgate merits special record from its perfect adaptation to the requirements of the times. Such was the school founded by Sir John Cass, Alderman of the ward of Portsoken, in the year 1710. Sir John's father,

---

[*] Arbuthnot, Pope, and Swift, in 1714, engaged to write together a satire on the abuse of human learning in every branch: but the design was not carried out, and great was the loss to polite letters. "Arbuthnot was skilled in everything which related to science; Pope was a master of the fine arts; and Swift excelled in the knowledge of the world. Wit they had all in equal measure; and this so large, that no age perhaps, ever produced three men on whom nature had more bountifully bestowed it, or art had brought it to higher perfection."

Thomas Cass, Esq., of Grove-street, Hackney, had acquired an ample fortune as carpenter to the Royal Ordnance, which, upon his death, descended to his son and only child, who having been educated in the true principles of the Established Church, as he advanced in life was one of those who, in the reign of Anne, distinguished themselves for their zeal in support of her rights by contributing to turn the current of those times, when it became the prevailing fashion to discountenance orthodoxy and uniformity in religious worship, of which Sir John Cass was an exemplary pattern. On the opening of these schools in the year 1710, a sermon was preached in the parish church of St. Botolph, Aldgate, by the Most Rev. Sir William Dawes, Archbishop of York, at which were present no less than sixteen noblemen and forty members of the House of Commons, with the Lord Mayor, Aldermen, Sheriffs, and Common Council, besides many other eminent persons. Some hundreds of children of both sexes have received an excellent education in this establishment, which is, to this day, one of the most flourishing of the City schools.

REIGNS OF GEORGE I. AND GEORGE II.

George I. was born at Hanover, in 1660, on the day before that on which Charles II. made his entry into London, at the Restoration. His education was grossly neglected, notwithstanding that his mother, the Electress Sophia, was the protector of the learned men of her day, and spoke five languages with fluency. The Prince's inattention to study must have been great indeed; for he never acquired even the language of the people (the English) over whom he expected to reign. After his accession to the throne, he established professorships of Modern History in the universities; and he gave the library of the Bishop of Ely, which cost the king 6000 guineas, to the University of Cambridge. He liberally patronized Vertue, the engraver; bestowed the Laureateship upon Nicholas Rowe; and encouraged Dr. Desaguliers in rendering natural philosophy popular, in a course of lectures at Hampton Court. When congratulated by a courtier on his being sovereign of Great Britain and Hanover, "rather," said the King, " congratulate me on having such a subject in one as Newton, and such a subject in the other as Leibnitz."

In this reign were educated Samuel Johnson, and Hume and Robertson, the historians. Of Johnson's boyhood and schooldays we shall speak hereafter.

George II., the only son of George I. and his queen Sophia Dorothea, was born at Hanover, in 1683. He was educated under the direction of his grandmother, but was nowise distinguished for learning, nor in after-life felt or affected the least admiration for art, science, or literature. In his long reign, however, flourished in literature, Sherlock, Hoadley, Secker, Warburton, Leland, Thompson, Akenside, Home, Gray, Johnson, the two Wartons, Robertson, Hume, Fielding and Smollet, not to mention Swift, Pope and Young, the survivors of a former age. Yet, this and the previous reign were a blank half century in the annals of the education of the people.

At the close of the reign of George II. was opened THE

Progress of Education. 135

BRITISH MUSEUM, which may be regarded as one of the educational institutions of the country.

The British Museum has been the growth of a century, between the purchase of Montague House for the collection of 1753, and the completion of the new buildings. The Museum originated in a suggestion in the will of Sir Hans Sloane (d. 1753), offering his collection to parliament for 20,000*l.*, it having cost him 50,000*l.* The offer was accepted; and by an Act (26th George II.) were purchased all Sir Hans Sloane's "library of books, drawings, manuscripts, prints, medals, seals, cameos and intaglios, precious stones, agates, jaspers, vessels of agate and jasper, crystals, mathematical instruments, pictures," etc. By the same Act was bought, for 10,000*l.*, the Harleian Library of MSS (about 7600 volumes of rolls, charters, etc.); to which were added the Cottonian Library of MSS., and the library of Major Arthur Edwards. By the same Act also was raised by lottery 100,000*l.*, out of which the Sloane and Harleian collections were paid for: 10,250*l.* to Lord Halifax for Montague House, and 12,873*l.* for its repairs; a fund being set apart for the payment of taxes and salaries of officers. Trustees were elected from persons of rank, station, and literary attainments; and the institution was named THE BRITISH MUSEUM. To Montague House were removed the Harleian collection of MSS. in 1755; other collections in 1756; and the Museum was opened to the public January 15, 1759.

EDUCATION OF GEORGE III.

How various the fortunes under which the royal youth of England have been reared for her rule and government may be seen by a glance through the preceding pages. The retrospect will be interesting and instructive, in showing the storm and sunshine, the promise and blight, amid which have been reared the princes of

This blessed plot, this earth, this realm, this England,
This nurse, this teeming womb of royal Kings,
Feared by their breed, and famous by their birth.
Shakspeare, Richard II.

As we approach the close of the long line, such violence and trouble as beset the infancy of our earliest sovereigns is no longer to be recorded of the lives of their successors: we have no longer to chronicle how the heir to the crown drew his first lessons, safe only in the strength of the fortress; or how the course of his early studies was broken by shifting from castle to castle, as the only security amidst the fierce contentions of civil war. Such chances of evil have long ceased to beset the infancy of our kings; but they have been succeeded by troubles of a milder kind—though of almost equal ill-promise for the welfare of princes—in the political difficulties which have too often attended their early lives, and beset their training for the kingly office. The boyhood and youth of George III. were clouded with such disadvantages, which, however, the strong natural sense of the prince, in great measure, enabled him to overcome. Whatever may have been the defects of his own training, it must be acknowledged that the King was—what many influential persons of his time were not—" an avowed friend to the diffusion of education, and certainly was not afraid that his subjects should be made either more difficult to govern, or worse in any other respect, by all classes and every individual of them being taught to read and to write." His reign is perhaps to be placed above every other of the same length in modern history, for the accessions to almost every department of knowledge by which it was signalized; and even the latter half of the period, notwithstanding the wars and political confusion by which it was disturbed, was at least as distinguished for the busy and successful cultivation of science and literature, as the quieter time that preceded.

George Willliam Frederick, the eldest son of Frederick Lewis, Prince of Wales, and Augusta, daughter of Frederick II., Duke of Saxe-Gotha, was born in 1738, at Norfolk House, St. James's-square.* The nation were elated at the birth of the heir presumptive to the throne; and on the first anniversary of his birthday, he was congratulated by a company of 60 Lilliputian soldiers, all under twelve years of age, who were received by the infant prince wearing an uniform, hat and feather; and next year he was present at a masque written by Thompson and Mallet, to commemorate the accession of his family to the British throne. At the age of six, the prince was placed under the care of Dr. Francis Ayscough, afterward Bishop of Bristol, who, writing to the pious Dr. Doddridge, says: "I thank God I have one great encouragement to quicken me in my duty, which is the good disposition of the children intrusted to me; as an instance, I must tell you that Prince George (to his honor and my shame) had learnt several pages in your book of verses, without any direction from me."

The Prince of Wales was a liberal patron of men of letters. He paid great attention to the education of his son, for whose use he commissioned Dr. Freeman to write the History of the English Tongue. On the first appearance of the *Rambler*, by Dr. Johnson, he also sought out the author that he might befriend him; the Prince also greatly encouraged Vertue, the engraver; and upon one occasion he sent the poet Glover a bank-note of 500*l.* to console him in his affliction.

To accustom the young Prince and his brothers to rhetoric, plays were got up at Leicester House; when Prince George filled the character of Portius, in Cato, and recited the prologue. The instruction of the young actors was intrusted to Quin, the comedian, who, many years afterward, on hearing of the graceful manner in which George III. delivered his first speech from the throne, said, with delight, "Aye! 'twas I that taught the boy to speak." With Lord Harcourt and Lord Waldegrave successively as governors, and Dr. Hayter, bishop

* The room of the old mansion in the rear of the present Norfolk House is preserved; and the bed in which the prince was born is at Worksop, Notts.

of Norwich, succeeded by Dr. John Thomas, Bishop of Peterborough, as preceptors, and under the more influential superintendence of Lord Bute, the Prince progressed in his studies, but was kept in great privacy by his mother, whose notions were certainly very narrow. One of her complaints against the Bishop of Norwich was that "he insisted upon teaching the Princes logic, which, as she was told, was a very old study for children of their age, not to say of their condition." From Lord Bute the Prince derived his chief knowledge of the constitution; Bute actually drawing his subjects for conversation from the Commentaries of Blackstone, the author permitting him to see that work in manuscript, and even to submit it to be read by the Prince. He grew up to be perfectly master of all the proprieties of his station; and the decorum of his private conduct gave a higher tone to public manners, and made the domestic virtues fashionable even in circles where they were most apt to be treated with neglect. He was well acquainted with the language, habits, and institutions of the English people. "Born and educated in this country," said his majesty, in his opening speech to the Parliament, "I glory in the name of Briton, and I hold the civil and religious rights of my people equally dear with the most valuable prerogative of my crown." And never, throughout the course of a long and anxious reign of sixty years, did his actions as a man or a prince contradict the boast. He was profoundly yet unaffectedly religious; his love of Christianity strongly displaying itself even in his sixteenth year, when he distributed within his own circle one hundred copies of Dr. Leland's View of deistical writers, written in contravention of their pernicious writings. George III. was likewise a lover of music, his favorite composer being Handel, and we have seen in the King's handwriting lengthy programmes of chamber concerts performed in Windsor Castle. He liberally patronized Cook, Byron, and Wallis, the navigators; Herschel, the astronomer; and West, the historical painter; and he took a lively interest in the foundation of the Royal Academy of Arts. He collected a library of 80,000 volumes, the most complete ever formed by a single individual: it is now in the British Museum, and known as "the King's Library." His Majesty collected this library at Buckingham House. Dr. Johnson, by permission of the librarian, frequently consulted books.

"It is curious that the Royal collector (George III.) and his venerable librarian (Mr. Barnard) should have survived almost sixty years after commencing the formation of this, the most complete private library in Europe, steadily appropriating 2000*l*. per annum to this object, and adhering with scrupulous attention to the instructions of Dr. Johnson, contained in the admirable letter printed by order of the House of Commons."—*Quarterly Review*, June, 1826.

To Johnson, Sheridan, Beattie, and Blair, George III. granted pensions; he especially admired Dr. Johnson, who has recorded a long conversation with his majesty; and after the interview, the Doctor observed to the royal librarian, "Sir, they may talk of the King as they will, he is the finest gentleman I have ever seen." He subsequently declared that "the King's manners were those of as fine a gentleman as one might suppose Louis the Fourteenth or Charles the Second to have been."

SUNDAY SCHOOLS ESTABLISHED.

One of the brightest ornaments of our Church has observed, with equal eloquence and truth, " The mainstay of religious education is to be found in our Sunday Schools—the most earnest, the most devoted, the most pious of our several congregations, are accustomed, with meritorious zeal, to dedicate themselves to this great work."* The founder of these invaluable institutions was Mr. Robert Raikes, the proprietor and editor of the *Gloucester Journal.* His attention was first drawn to the wretched state of the prisoners in the bridewell at Gloucester, for want of religious and moral instruction; and for this purpose, whenever he found one among the prisoners that was able to read, he set him to instruct his fellow-prisoners, and rewarded him for his trouble. Mr. Raikes next set to work in other quarters, and in 1783 wrote in his newspaper—" Some of the clergy in different parts of this county, bent upon attempting a reform among the children of the lower class, *are establishing* Sunday Schools for rendering the Lord's Day subservient to the ends of instruction, which has hitherto been prostituted to bad purposes." At this time, the streets were full of noise and disturbance every Sunday; and the churches were unfrequented by the poorer sort of children, and very ill attended by their parents. To them Mr. Raikes proposed that their children should meet him at the early service performed in Gloucester Cathedral on a Sunday morning. The numbers at first were few, but their increase was rapid; and Mr. Raikes soon found himself surrounded by such a set of little ragamuffins as would have disgusted teachers less zealous than the founder of Sunday Schools. The children soon began to look upon him with respect and affection, and were readily drilled into a decent observance of the outward ceremonies of religion. To prevent their running about the streets of the city after and between the services, masters and mistresses were engaged, by means of subscriptions, for a large number of children of both sexes to be educated in the principles of Christianity. From this hour the system of Sunday Schools has gone

* The Rev. Dr. Hook, Vicar of Leeds, in his Letter to the Bishop of St. David's.

on most surely and rapidly developing, until it would be difficult to overrate the positive benefits which have been derived from its extension, until the present (1858) number of scholars has reached two millions and a half.

THE MONITORIAL SYSTEM OF BELL AND LANCASTER.

To each of these philanthropists (as in most similar claims) is attributed, by different authorities, the merit of being founder of the system which bears the name of the latter; but to Lancaster is due the great public attention first bestowed on the subject, and, we think, to Dr. Bell the first adoption of its principles. Whilst superintendent of the Military Orphan Asylum at Madras, in 1791, Dr. Bell one day observed a boy, belonging to a Malabar school, writing in the sand; thinking that method of writing very convenient, both as regards cheapness and facility, he introduced it in the school of the asylum, and as the usher refused to teach by that method, he employed one of the cleverest boys to teach the rest. The experiment was so successful that he extended it to the other branches of instruction, and soon organized the whole school under boy-teachers, who were themselves instructed by the Doctor. On his return to England he published a Report of the Madras Orphan Asylum, in which he particularly pointed out the new mode of school organization, as more efficient than the old.

In the following year, 1798, Dr. Bell introduced the system into the school of St. Botolph, Aldgate,—then at Kendal; and next he attempted, but with small success, to obtain its adoption in Edinburgh. Settling soon after, as rector of Swanage, in Dorsetshire, he was secluded from the world for some years; yet he retained his strong opinion of the value of the new system of education, and had the school at Swanage conducted on that plan.

Meanwhile, Joseph Lancaster, son of a Chelsea pensioner in the Borough-road, London, opened a school in his father's house, in 1798, at the early age of eighteen. He had been usher in schools, and had made certain improvements in tuition; and a pamphlet by Dr. Bell having fallen in his way, Lancaster adopted the Madras system, with alterations. In 1802 he brought his school into a perfect state of organization, and found himself as able to teach 250 boys, with the aid of the senior boys as teachers, as before to teach 80. Lancaster was a member of the Society of Friends, and received much encouragement and assistance from them. His enthusiasm and benevolence led him to conceive the practicability of bringing all the children of the poor under education by the new system. He published pamphlets recommending the plan, and in one of them ascribes the chief merit to Dr. Bell, whom he afterward visited at Swanage. His own school Lancaster made free, and obtained subscriptions from friends of education for its support. At length he was admitted to an interview with George III. at Weymouth, in 1805, and his majesty being charmed with the order and efficiency of his schools, subscribed to the fund 100*l.* a-year, the Queen 50*l.*, and the princesses 25*l.* each, to be employed in the extension of the Lancasterian system, to promote which a Society was formed under the patronage of the King.* Such was the origin of the British and Foreign School Society, originally "the Royal Lancasterian Institution for promoting the Education of the Children of the Poor."†

Dr. Bell's method in process of time was adopted in the Lambeth schools by the Archbishop of Canterbury; and in the Royal Military School at Chelsea; whilst numerous schools sprung into existence under what is known to this day as *the Madras System*. The distinctive features of Bell's National Schools, and Lancaster's British and Foreign School systems were, that the religious instruction in the former was according to the formularies of the Established Church; whilst the latter represented the Dissenting interests, admitting the reception of the Bible as the foundation of all instruction, but without note or comment. This still remains the essential difference between the two societies, and the schools conducted on their principles.

To these systems have since been added Normal and Model Schools; and for the girls in these schools instruction in domestic economy and the duties of servants.

In 1808, Dr. Bell endeavored to induce the Government to establish upon his plans "A National Board" of Education, with schools placed under the management of the parochial clergy. In this he failed; but by aid of friends of the Established Church, and under the patronage of the bishops and clergy, the National Society was eventually formed in 1811.‡

THE PRIMER AND THE HORNBOOK.

The earliest printed book used in the tuition of youth was the Primer (*Primarius*, Latin), a small prayer-book in which chil-

---

* The noble wish of George III.—"that the day might come when every poor child in his dominions would be able to read the Bible"—doubtless greatly assisted by the sanction of Royal Authority this new system of teaching, as well as the Bible Society established in 1804.

† Lancaster resigned his direction of the school in 1808. He died in 1838, having been supported in his latter days solely by an annuity purchased for him by a few old and attached friends.

‡ Dr. Bell died in 1832, leaving the princely sum of 132,000*l.* for the encouragement of literature and the advancement of education.

dren were taught to read—and the Romish book of devotions in the monastic schools. At the Reformation, the Primer was retained, but the requisite changes were made. In 1545, Henry VIII. ordered to be printed an English "form of Public Prayer," entitled the *Primer,* said to be "set furth by the Kinge's majestic and his clergie, to be taught, lerned, and red." A copy of this rare book is extant: it was once the property of Sir John Clark, priest of the chapel of Leedsbridge, and founder of the school. This appears from the following autograph note in the Calendar: "This day I began the schole at Leeds, July 4, 1563."

It would be hard to say when the contents of the Primer were changed from sacred to secular: the change was probably very gradual, more especially as the Primers printed to this day contain occasional prayers—the good seed which cannot be sown too early in the mind of childhood. The accounts of the grammar-schools of the sixteenth century contain much interesting evidence of the value attached to school-books, by the care which is directed to be taken of them. Thus, in the corporation records of Boston, in Lincolnshire, in 1578, it was agreed that "a Dictionarye shall be bought for the scollers of the Free Scoole; and the same boke to be *tyed in a cheque,* and set upon a desk in the scoole, whereunto any scoller may have accesse as occasion shall serve." There are later entries of the Corporation purchasing dictionaries for the use of the school; besides presents of dictionaries, lexicons, grammars, folio English Bibles, etc.—(*Thompson's History of Boston.*)

Another "dumb teacher" was the Hornbook, of which a specimen exists, in black-letter, of the time of Queen Elizabeth. It appears to be at least as ancient as 1570, is mounted on wood, and protected with transparent horn.

"The letters may be read, *through the horn,*
That make the story perfect."—*Ben Jonson.*

There is a large cross, the *criss-cross,* and then the alphabet in large and small letters. The vowels follow next, and their combinations with the consonants; and the whole is concluded with the Lord's Prayer and the *Roman* numerals. The Arabic numerals are not given. Shakspeare thus refers to the cross-row of the Horn-book:

"He hearkens after prophecies and dreams;
And from the cross-row plucks the letter G;
And ·ays, a wizard told him that by G
His issue disinherited should be."—*Richard III.*

Again, in *Love's Labor's Lost,* act v. scene 1, Moth, the page to Armado, says, in describing Holofernes the schoolmaster, "He teaches boys the Hornbook."

Cotgrave has, "*La Croix de par Dieu*, the Christ's-cross-rowe, or *horne-booke*, wherein a child learnes it;" and Florio, ed. 1611, p. 93, " *Centuruola*, a childes horne-booke hanging at his girdle."
In the collection of Sir Thomas Phillipps, at Middlehill, are two genuine Horn-books of the reigns of Charles I. and II. Locke, in his *Thoughts on Education*, speaks of the "ordinary road of the Hornbook and Primer," and directs that "the Lord's Prayer, the Creed, and the Ten Commandments he should learn by heart, not by reading them himself in his Primer, but by somebody's repeating them before he can read."

Shenstone, who was taught to read at a dame-school, near Halesowen, in Shropshire, in his delightfully quaint poem of the *Schoolmistress*, commemorating his venerable preceptress, thus records the use of the Hornbook:

> " Lo; now with state she utters her command;
> Eftsoons the urchins to their tasks repair;
> Their books of stature small they take in hand,
> Which with pellucid horn secured are
> To save from finger wet the letters fair."

Cowper thus describes the Hornbook of his time:

> " Neatly secured from being soiled or torn
> Beneath a pane of thin translucent horn,
> A book (to please us at a tender age
> 'Tis called a book, though but a single page)
> Presents the prayer the Saviour deigned to teach,
> Which children use, and parsons—when they preach."
> *Tirocinium, or a Review of Schools*, 1784.

We have somewhere read a story of a mother tempting her son along the cross-row by giving him an apple for each letter he learnt. This brings us to the gingerbread alphabet of our own time, which appears to have been common a century and a half since:

> " To master John the English maid
> A Hornbook gives of gingerbread;
> And, that the child may learn the better,
> As he can name, he eats the letter."—*Prior.*

An anecdote illustrative of Lord Erskine's readiness is related —that, when asked by a judge if a single sheet could be called a book, he replied, "The common Hornbook, my lord."

Progress of Education. 143

HORNBOOK OF THE EIGHTEENTH CENTURY.

In *Specimens of West Country Dialect,* the use of the Hornbook is thus shown:

"Commether, *Billy Chubb,* an breng the hornen book. Gee ma the vester in tha windor, you *Pal Caine!*—what! be a sleepid—I'll wake ye. Now, *Billy,* there's a good bway! Ston still there, and mind what I da za to ye, an whaur I da point. Now; cris-cross, girt a, little a—b—c—d. That's right, *Billy;* you'll zoon lorn the criss-cross-lain—you'll zoon auvergit Bobby Jiffry—you'll zoon be *a scholard.* A's a pirty chubby bway—Lord love'n!"

John Britton, who was born in the parish of Kington St. Michael's, Wilts, in 1771, tells us, in his *Autobiography,* that he was placed with a schoolmistress: "here," he writes, "I learnt 'the Christ-cross-row' from a Hornbook, on which were the alphabet in large and small letters, and the nine figures in Roman and Arabic numerals. The Hornbook is now a rarity." Such a Hornbook is engraved on the preceding page. It was met with in the year 1850, among the old stock of a bookseller at Peterborough, in Lincolnshire, and is thus described: Its dimensions are 9 by 5 inches. The alphabet, etc., are printed upon white paper, which is laid upon a thin piece of oak, and is covered with a sheet of horn, secured in its place by eight tacks, driven through a border or mounting of brass; the object of this horn-covering being to keep the "book," or rather leaf, unsoiled. The first line is a cross-row; so named, says Johnson, "because a cross is placed at the beginning, to show that the end of learning is piety."

The Hornbook was not always mounted on a board; many were pasted on the back of the horn only, like one used five-and-forty years ago by a friend, when a boy at Bristol.

Such was the rudeness of the "dumb teacher" formerly employed at the dame-school, and elsewhere. It was, in all probability, superseded by Dr. Bell's sand-tray, upon which the children traced their own letters. Next came the "Battledore" and "Reading-made-Easy;" though the Spelling-book is considerably older than either. The Battledore, by the way, reminds us of a strategy of tuition mentioned by Locke: "By pasting the vowels and consonants on the sides of four dice, he has made this a play for his children, whereby his eldest son in coats has played himself into spelling."

PROGRESS OF EDUCATION IN THE REIGNS OF GEORGE IV. AND WILLIAM IV.

There is little to interest the reader in the early personal histories of these sovereigns. George the Fourth, the eldest son of George the Third and Queen Charlotte, was born at Buckingham House, in 1762. At the age of three years he received an address from the Society of Ancient Britons, and was made a Knight of the Garter. In a few months after, he was appointed by a King's letter, addressed to the Lord Mayor, Captain-General of the Honorable Artillery Company of the City of London. He learned his nursery tasks at Kew-house, or the old palace at Kew, where the royal family lived, as Miss Burney says, "running about from one end of the house to the other, without precaution or care." The prince's first governor was the Earl of Holdernesse; Dr. Markham, Bishop of Chester (afterward Archbishop of York), was the prince's preceptor; and Mr. Cyril Jackson, sub-preceptor. These gentlemen, however, suddenly resigned their offices, it is believed from their having found some political works, which they considered objectionable, put into the hands of their pupil by direction of the King. His next preceptor was Dr. Hurd, Bishop of Lichfield and Coventry, afterward of Worcester; with the Rev. William Arnold as sub-preceptor; both these tutors being Cambridge men. The prince was kept by his father in a state of unmitigated pupilage till he was nearly eighteen, soon after which he appeared in public, and fell into dissolute habits, which deeply embittered his after life.

George the Fourth affected patronage of painting and architecture; the results of the latter are best seen in the highly embellished western quarter of London. His encouragement of letters and learned men was narrow and partisan; he was the first patron of the Literary Fund, to which he contributed upward of 5000*l.*; in the Society's armorial bearings is "the Prince of Wales's plume." By his bounty, the Latin manuscript of Milton, discovered in the State Paper Office in 1823, was edited, and a translation published. The King also chartered, in 1826, the Royal Society of Literature, and contributed from the Privy Purse 1100 guineas a-year to its funds; though it should be added, that he was committed to this large annual subscription by a misconception of Dr. Burgess, Bishop of Salisbury, the King intending a donation of 1000 guineas, and an annual subscription of 100 guineas; though his majesty cheerfully acquiesced,* and amused himself with the incident. He also granted the Society the Crown land upon which their house is built in St. Martin's-place; and as if to show that he did not restrict his patronage to the higher aim of letters, there is prominently inscribed upon the exterior façade of the Parochial School of St. Martin's, "built upon the ground the gift of His Majesty King George the Fourth."

In this reign, in 1826, was founded the Society for "the Diffusion of Useful Knowledge," under the chairmanship of Lord Brougham.† This was followed by the founding, in London, of University College and School, in 1828, for affording "literary and scientific education at a moderate expense," divinity not being taught; and in the same year was founded King's College and School, for education in the principles of the Established Church.

William the Fourth, next brother to George the Fourth, was born at St. James's Palace in 1764, and was educated at Kew.

---

* This costly munificence has not been followed by the successors of the sovereign.

† The name and title of the Society was, however, first written in conjunction with the author of the present volume, at Brighton, in the autumn of 1824; and early in 1825, Nicholson's *Operative Mechanic* was published "under the superintendence of the Society for the Diffusion of Useful Knowledge."

When a child at play, his favorite amusement was floating a toy-ship, which one day led him to say, with prophetic boast, "If ever I shall become a king, I will have a house full of ships, and no other King shall dare to take them from me!" The King, his father, encouraged him to enter the naval service; and at the age of fourteen,* he swung his first hammock on board the *Prince George*, 98 guns, under the command of Admiral Digby, where he was furnished as scantily as any youngster of the mess. His entire service at sea extended nearly to eleven years; its most interesting incident was his intimacy with the gallant Nelson, from whom, in the prince's own words, his "mind took its first decided naval turn." This predilection lasted throughout his long life; he was some time Lord High Admiral, and after his accession to the throne was familiarly styled "the Sailor King."

In his reign, in 1833, greatly through the influence of Lord Brougham and his party, upon the report of a Parliamentary Committee, the first annual grant for educational purposes was made by the Government; and in 1836 was formed the Home and Colonial Infant School Society, upon the principle that education must be based on the knowledge of the Holy Scriptures, and as set forth and embodied in the doctrinal articles of the Church of England. In the following year was formed a "Central Society of Education," principally for the collection and publication of facts, and bringing prominently forward the distinction between general and special religious instruction.

Here this historic sketch of the Progress of Education in England may be closed. The history of National Education during the last twenty years scarcely belongs to the object of the present volume. It may, however, be interesting to quote a few of its leading events. In the autumn of 1838, Lord Brougham lamented what he considered as the final and hopeless failure of his life-long efforts in the cause of Popular Education.† But

---

* West painted the prince's portrait at this age, in a family picture now in Hampton Court Palace.

† Lord Brougham received his education at Edinburgh, which, in 1857, he declared in public, he looked upon as a very great benefit conferred on him by Providence. Within a few days of this occasion, at the opening of the University of Edinburgh, Principal Lee, in his introductory address, gave a short account of the school-days of Lord Brougham. "Though descended," he said, "from an ancient English family, he was born in Edinburgh, and his mother was a niece of Principal Robertson. In 1786, when seven years old, he entered the High School, in a class of 164 boys: and he had the advantage of being instructed by Mr. Luke Fraser, who was 40 years a favorite teacher, under whose inspection Sir Walter Scott had commenced his classical studies, along with the late Lord Melville, in the year 1777. The late Lord Jeffrey became a pupil of the same master in 1781. Among the school-fellows of Henry Brougham (amounting, as I have said, to

Progress of Education. 147

early in the subsequent year, a Committee of Council was appointed to dispense the annual Government grant for education, and the amount was increased to 30,000*l*. a year. The next step was the establishment of Normal Schools under Government inspection. This was followed by the foundation of Training Schools and Colleges, for the education and training of Schoolmasters and Schoolmistresses, by apprenticeship as pupil-teachers, and other means. And to provide for the children of the destitute poor, "Ragged Schools" have been established with great success, the scheme commencing with a poor shoemaker at Portsmouth.

Lastly, in June, 1857, was held in London, under the Presidency of the Prince Consort, "A Conference of the Friends of the Education of the Working Classes, on the Early Age at which children are taken from School."

164) were several youths afterward highly eminent, of whom I make special mention of James Abercromby, afterward Speaker of the House of Commons, now Lord Dunfermline; and Joseph Muter, subsequently recognized by the title of Sir Joseph Straton, one of the greatest benefactors of this University. Lord Brougham was 'dux' of the rector's class in 1791. I personally know how pre-eminently conspicuous at this University his attainments were, not in one or two branches of study, but in all to which his attention was directed, and particularly in mathematics and natural philosophy, as well as in law, in metaphysics, and in political science. Some of these shreds of information may not be familiarly known to every one, but I allude no further to a biography which is already, to a great extent, written in our national history." In a later portion of his address, the Principal, who himself entered the University as a pupil in 1794, enumerated the following as having been educated there, cotemporaneously with, or subsequently to, Lord Brougham:—Thomas M'Crie, the historian; George Cranstoun (Lord Corehouse), Mountstuart Elphinstone, Peter Roget, George Birkbeck, Sir David Brewster, Francis Horner, Henry Cockburn, Henry Petty (now Marquis of Lansdowne), John Leyden, Henry Temple (now Lord Palmerston), the Earl of Haddington, Lord Webb Seymour, Lord Dudley, the Earl of Minto, Lord Glenelg, Lord Langdale, and Lord John Russell.

SCHOOL-DAYS OF EMINENT MEN.

Anecdote Biographies.

EARLY FORTUNES OF WILLIAM OF WYKEHAM.

THIS celebrated ecclesiastic, statesman, and architect, was born at Wykeham, or Wickham, in Hampshire, in 1324, of parents who, although poor, were of creditable descent, as well as of respectable character. He was put to school at Winchester, not by his father, who was without the means, but by some wealthy patron, who is traditionally said to have been Nicholas Uvedale, governor of Winchester Castle. The tradition further asserts, that after leaving school, he became Secretary to Uvedale; and that he was Secretary to the Constable of Winchester Castle is stated in a written account compiled in his own time. Afterward he is said to have been recommended by Uvedale to Edyngton, bishop of Winchester, and then by these two friends to have been made known to King Edward III. There seems to be no reason for supposing that he ever studied at Oxford, as has been affirmed. It is evident, indeed, that he had not received a university education, and that he never pretended to any skill in the favorite scholastic learning of his age. He is designated " clericus," or clerk, in 1352. It was, however, by his skill in architecture that Wykeham was, in the short space of 21 years, promoted to be Bishop of Winchester and Lord High Chancellor of these realms. Of the colleges which he built, that at Winchester has been renowned as a seat of learning through nearly five centuries, and its scholars have been known as Wykehamites. And when his growing honors required that Wykeham should adopt a coat of arms, he chose the famous motto:

Manners makyth Man,

which has been written upon the top-beam of our Tudor halls, and has descended as household words from an age of feudalism to our own times of enlightened free-will.

WILLIAM CAXTON, THE FIRST ENGLISH PRINTER.

In the records of the boyhood and after-life of Caxton, which are chiefly to be gathered from his own hand, we obtain some interesting glimpses of the state of our language in the reigns of Henry V. and VI., before a single book had been printed in England. Caxton's birth is stated at about the year 1412, or, as he tells us: "I was born and learned mine English in Kent in the Weald, where I doubt not is spoken as broad and rude English as in any place in England." His father, a proprietor of land, bestowed upon him all the advantages of education which that rude age could furnish; to which he refers with simple gratitude in his *Life of Charles the Great*, printed in 1485, wherein he says:

"I have specially reduced (translated) it after the simple cunning that God hath lent to me, whereof I humbly and with all my heart thank Him, and also am bounden to pray for my father's and mother's souls, that in my youth set me to school, by which, by the sufferance of God, I get my living I hope truly."

Half a century before Caxton's boyhood, the children in the grammar-school were not taught English at all, but French, so as to make the people familiar with Norman-French, the language of their conquerors; and it was the translating, or procuring to be translated, a great number of books from the French into English, as the latter became more employed, as well as the reduction of rude and broad English into the English of his time; and the reconciliation of the varieties of English spoken in different shires, and the simplification of "over curious terms"—which formed Caxton's business in after-life. Of his school-days we have no positive record. He was put apprentice to one Robert Large, a considerable mercer or merchant, of London. Books were now so costly that there was no special trade of bookselling; but the stationers probably executed orders for transcribing books. The mercers or merchants, in their traffic with other lands, were the agents by which valuable manuscripts found their way into England, and books were part of their commerce. Caxton, from his knowledge of business, became a traveling agent or factor in the countries of Brabant, Flanders, Holland, and Zealand; he resided abroad for some years, there translated several works, and in the Low Countries learnt the art of printing, which he brought to England in 1474, and there printed in the Almonry, in Westminster, and subsequently in King-street. All Caxton's works were printed in black letter; the two largest assemblages of the productions of his press now known are those in the British Museum, and in Earl Spencer's library at Althorpe.*

BOYHOOD AND RISE OF SIR THOMAS MORE.

Among the eminent men of one of the most remarkable periods of English history is Sir Thomas More, the records of whose early life throw some light upon the education of the time. More was born in Milk-street, Cheapside, in 1480, five years before the accession of Henry VII. to the throne. He was taught the first rudiments of education at St. Anthony's Free Grammar-school, in Threadneedle-street, one of the four grammar-schools founded by Henry VI., and at that period the most famous in London. Here More soon outstripped all his young companions, and made great proficiency in Latin, to which his studies were confined, Greek not being then taught in schools.

It was the good custom of the age that the sons of the gentry, even of persons of rank, should spend part of their early years in the houses of the nobility, where they might profit by listening to the wisdom of their elders, and become accustomed, by the performance of humble and even menial offices, to stern discipline and implicit obedience. The internal economy of a great man's family, resembling on a smaller scale that of the monarch, was thought to be the proper school for acquiring the manners most conducive to success at court. Persons of good condition were, consequently, eager to place their sons in the families of the great, as the surest road to fortune. In this station it was not accounted degrading to submit even to menial service; while the greatest barons of the realm were proud to officiate as stewards, cup-bearers, and carvers to the monarch, a youth of good family could wait at table, or carry the train of a man of high condition, without any loss of dignity. To profit by such discipline, More, when about fourteen years of age, was removed from school to the palace of Cardinal Morton, archbishop of Canterbury and lord high chancellor. Here he attracted notice among the Cardinal's retinue, and was pointed out by him to the nobility who frequented his house, as a boy of extraordinary promise. "This child waiting at table," he would say, "whosoever shall live to see it, will prove a marvellous man." Listening daily to the conversation, and observing the conduct of such a personage, More naturally acquired more extensive views of men and things than any other course of education could, in that backward age, have supplied. Dean Colet, a visitor at the Cardinal's, used to say, "there is but one wit in England, and that is young Thomas More."

* See Mr. Charles Knight's delightful Biography of Caxton, in *The Old Printer an the Modern Press*. 1854.

At the age of seventeen, More was sent by his patron to Oxford, where he studied Greek, which was then publicly taught in the University, though not without opposition. While at Oxford, More composed the greater number of his English poems, which Ben Jonson speaks of as some of the best in the English language. More retained his love of learning throughout life; and when he had risen to the highest offices, he frequently complained to his friend Erasmus, of being obliged to leave his friends and his books to discharge what were to him disagreeable commissions.

The plan of Education which More adopted in his own family, and his enlightened views on the Education of all Classes, have been already sketched at pp. 62–63 of the present volume.

THE POETS WYATT AND SURREY.

Sir Thomas Wyatt, the poet, was born at Allington Castle, near Maidstone, in 1503. All that is known of his youth is, that at 12 years old he entered St. John's College, Cambridge, and that he took out his degrees of Bachelor and Master in 1518 and 1520. About 1524, Wyatt was introduced at court, where he was received into the King's household; in 1533, he officiated as ewerer for his father at the coronation of Anne Boleyn, upon which occasion his friend Surrey, then about 16 years of age, carried the fourth sword with the scabbard before the King. Wyatt traveled much on the continent; he possessed great conversational powers, and is said to have combined the wit of Sir Thomas More with the wisdom of Sir Thomas Cromwell.* His political knowledge and sound judgment acquired for him a high reputation as a statesman and diplomatist; and his scholarship was in advance of most men of his time. Camden bears testimony to the extent and accuracy of his classical attainments: he spoke French, Italian, and Spanish fluently; excelled in music; and was pre-eminent for skill and dexterity in arms. Surrey has left a portrait of Wyatt, and rarely have so many noble qualities been connected into a single character — virtue, wisdom, beauty, strength, and courage. His letters to his son, written from Spain, exhibit close observation of life; and contain a whole code of maxims for the government of conduct, based on sound religious principles. He co-operated with Surrey in "correcting the ruggedness" of English poetry: it is said that they were devoted friends, and Surrey's lines on the death of Wyatt seem to indicate a close and intimate intercourse.

* One of Wyatt's common sayings was, that there were three things which should always be strictly observed: "Never to play with any man's unhappiness or deformity, for that is inhuman; nor on superiors, for that is saucy and undutiful; nor on holy matters, for that is irreligious."

Henry Howard, Earl of Surrey, exercised great influence on our poetry. "He founded," says Mr. Bell, "a new era in our versification, purified and strengthened our poetical diction, and carefully shunning the vices of his predecessors, set the example of a style in which, for the first time, verbal pedantry and fantastical devices were wholly ignored. He was also the first writer of English blank verse, and the sonnet, and the first poet who understood and exemplified the art of translation." The poet became Earl of Surrey on the accession of his father to the Dukedom of Norfolk in 1524; he is thought to have been born about 1517. He was placed at court, about the person of Henry VIII., at the early age of 15, but it is uncertain whether he studied at college. His boyhood was passed in the society of such men as Lord Berners, the translator of Froissart; Vere, Earl of Oxford; Lord Stafford, Lord Morley, and others equally distinguished by their literary attainments. Surrey, in his childhood, was always sent during the winter months to Hunsdon, one of the estates of his grandfather, the Duke of Norfolk, in Hertfordshire. This seat, about 1536, became the residence of Princess Mary; with her was living the fair Geraldine, with whom Surrey fell in love, and her name is indissolubly united with his in many a legend in prose and verse, wherein he showed "the noblest qualities of chivalry blended with the graces of learning and a cultivated taste." Having traveled into Italy, he became a devoted student of the poets of that country— Dante, Petrarch, Boccaccio, and Ariosto—and formed his own poetical style on theirs.

Surrey, among his general accomplishments, appears to have cultivated the study of heraldry, which helped to bring him to the block; for the chief charge against him by his enemies was his having illegally quartered on his escutcheon the arms of Edward the Confessor, which, however, he was entitled to do. He was beheaded on Tower-hill, January 21, 1547.

LORD BURLEIGH AT CAMBRIDGE.

That truly great statesman, William Cecil, Lord Burleigh, descended from an ancient and respectable family, was born at Bourne, in Lincolnshire, in the year 1520. Both his father and grandfather held honorable appointments under Henry VIII. During his early education, his progress either exhibited nothing remarkable, or has been overlooked by his biographers, amidst the splendor of his succeeding transactions; for we are merely informed that he received the first rudiments of learning at the grammar-school of Grantham and Stamford. But at St. John's College, Cambridge, to which he was removed in the fifteenth year of his age, he gave strong indications of the qualities calculated to raise him to future eminence. Here he was distinguished by the regularity of his conduct, and the intensity of his application. That he might daily devote several hours to study without any hazard of interruption, he made an agreement with the bell-ringer to be called up every morning at four o'clock. Through this extreme application, without proper intervals of exercise, he, however, contracted a painful distemper, which led to his being afflicted with gout in the latter part of his life.

His indefatigable industry at college, and his consequent proficiency, was marked by occasional presents from the Master. He began, at sixteen, to put in practice the method, then usual, of acquiring literary celebrity, by delivering a public lecture. His first topic was the logic of the schools; and three years afterward he ventured to comment on the Greek language. He was subsequently ambitious of excelling as a general scholar; and successively directed his industry to the various branches of literature then cultivated at the university.

At twenty-one he entered Gray's Inn, where he applied himself to the study of the law with the same method and industry as he had observed at Cambridge. He found leisure also for several collateral pursuits: the antiquities of the kingdom, and more especially the pedigrees and fortunes of the most distinguished families, occupied much of his attention; and such was his progress in these pursuits, that no man of his time was accounted a more complete adept in heraldry. This species of information, had he adhered to his destination for the bar, might have been of little utility; but in his career of a statesman, it often proved of essential advantage.

His practice was to record with his pen everything worthy of notice which occurred to him either in reading or observation, arranging this observation in the most methodical manner,—a singular example of diligence, which is authenticated to posterity by collections of his manuscripts, still preserved in many public and private libraries. While from this practice he derived, besides other advantages, an uncommon facility in committing his thoughts to writing, he neglected not to cultivate an accomplishment still more essential to his intended profession—a ready and graceful enunciation. By frequenting various companies, and entering into free discussion, he learned to express himself with ease and confidence; while the extent of his information, and the soundness of his judgment, prevented his fluency from degenerating into declamation.—*Macdiarmid's British Statesmen.*

Such was the educational basis upon which Cecil laid the foundation of his brilliant but sound reputation; and by which means, conjoined with the strong natural gift of sagacity, and a mind tinctured with piety, he acquired the esteem and confidence successively of three sovereigns, and held the situation of prime minister of England for upward of half a century. His sole literary production was a volume of *Precepts or Directions for* the *Well-Ordering and Carriage of a Man's Life,* addressed to his son.

CAMDEN'S SCHOOLS.

Camden, one of the most illustrious of learned Englishmen, was born May 22, 1551, in the Old Bailey, where his father was a painter-stainer. He died when his son was but a child, and left little provision for him. Dr. Smith, in his *Life of Camden,* mentions his early admission into Christ's Hospital as a fact not well authenticated, but very generally believed; and the imperfect state of the records does not admit of its verification. At all events, an attack of the plague caused his removal in 1563; and after his recovery, he was sent to St. Paul's School, and thence to Magdalen College, Oxford, in 1566.—*Trollope's History of Christ's Hospital.*

Wood, in his *Athenæ Oxonienses,* states positively that "when this most eminent person was a child, he received the first knowledge of letters in Christchurch Hospital in London, then newly founded for blue-coated children, where, being fitted for grammar-learning, he was sent to the free school, founded by Dr. Colet, near to St. Paul's Cathedral." Thence he removed to Oxford, where he studied in more than one college. He left the university in 1571, and became an under-master of Westminster School, the duties of which he discharged at the time when he composed the works which have made his name so eminent. The most celebrated of these are his Britannia, a survey of the British Isles; and his Annals of the reign of Elizabeth; both written in pure and elegant Latin. Camden was now looked upon as one of the most distinguished scholars of his age: he is termed "the Pausanias of England." He was made head-master of Westminster School in 1592: he had among his scholars, Ben Jonson; he wrote a small Greek Grammar for the use of the school; and shortly before his death, he founded an historical lecture in the University of Oxford. He died in 1623, and was interred in Westminster Abbey, a great assemblage of the learned and illustrious doing him honor at his funeral.

To Camden, Ben Jonson dedicated his first play, *Every Man in his Humor;* hoping, to use his own words in addressing his Master, "that the confession of my studies might not repent you to have been my instructor; for the profession of my thankfulness, I am sure it will, with good men, find either praise or excuse. Your true lover, Ben Jonson."

The career of Camden strikingly illustrates the benefits of English school foundations. Left a poor orphan, he was one of the first boys admitted into Christ's Hospital, where he sowed the seed of that learning which was matured in the University of Oxford, and employed for the advantage of the next generation in his mastership at Westminster. He left to the Painter-Stainers' Company, of which his father was a member, a silver loving-cup, which is produced on every St. Luke's Day feast.

SIR EDWARD COKE'S LEGAL STUDIES.

This celebrated lord-chief-justice was born in 1551-2, at Mileham, Norfolk, in which county the Cokes had been settled for many generations. His father, who was a bencher of Lincoln's Inn, sent him to the Free Grammar-school at Norwich, whence, in 1567, he removed to Trinity College, Cambridge. After having spent three years at the University, he went to London, to commence his legal education: he became a member of Clifford's Inn, and in 1572 was admitted into the Inner Temple; here he entered into a laborious course of study, which Lord Campbell thus vividly describes:

> Every morning at three, in the winter season lighting his own fire, he read Bracton, Littleton, the Year Books, and the folio Abridgments of the Law, till the Courts met at eight. He then went by water to Westminster, and heard cases argued till twelve, when pleas ceased for dinner. After a short repast in the Inner Temple Hall, he attended "readings" or lectures in the afternoon, and then resumed his private studies till five, or supper-time. This meal being ended, the *moots* took place, when difficult questions of law were proposed and discussed,—if the weather was fine, in the garden by the river side; if it rained, in the covered walks near the Temple Church. Finally, he shut himself up in his chamber, and worked at his common-place book, in which he inserted, under the proper heads, all the legal information he had collected during the day. When nine o'clock struck, he retired to bed, that he might have an equal portion of sleep before and after midnight. The Globe and other theatres were rising into repute, but he would never appear at any of them; nor would he indulge in such unprofitable reading as the poems of Lord Surrey or Spenser. When Shakspeare and Ben Jonson came into such fashion that even "sad apprentices of the law" occasionally assisted in masques and wrote prologues, he most steadily eschewed all such amusements; and it is supposed that in the whole course of his life he never saw a play acted, or read a play, or was in company with a player!

To Coke's merits there cannot be a more direct testimony than that of his great rival, Sir Francis Bacon, who speaks of his great industry and learning in terms of high and deserved commendation; and justly ascribes to him the praise of having preserved the vessel of the common law in a steady and consistent course.

We gather what the fare of the Universities was about this period, from the following description of Cambridge, given at St. Paul's Cross, in the year 1550, by Thomas Lever, soon after made Master of St. John's College:

> "There be divers there at Cambridge which rise daily betwixt four and five of the clock in the morning, and from five until six of the clock use common prayer, with an exhortation of God's word in a common chapel; and from six until ten of the clock use either private study or common lectures. At ten of the clock, they go to dinner; whereas they be content with a penny piece of beef amongst four, having a few pottage made of the broth of the same beef, with salt and oatmeal, and nothing else.

After this slender dinner, they be either teaching or learning until five of the clock in the evening, when they have a supper not much better than their dinner Immediately after the which they go either to reasoning in problems, or into some other study, until it be nine or ten of the clock; and then being without fire, are fain to walk or run up and down half an hour, to get a heat on their feet, when they go to bed.

"These be men not weary of their pains, but very sorry to leave their study; and sure they be not able some of them to continue for lack of necessary exhibition and relief."

SPENSER AT CAMBRIDGE.

Edmund Spenser, one of the great landmarks of English poetry, was born in East Smithfield, near the Tower, about the year 1553; as he sings in his *Prothalamion:*

> Merry London, my most kindly nurse,
> That gave to me this life's first native source,
> Though from another place I take my name,
> An house of ancient fame.

The rank of his parents, or the degree of his affinity with the ancient house of Spenser, is not fully established. Gibbon says: "The nobility of the Spensers has been illustrated and enriched by the trophies of Marlborough; but I exhort them to consider the *Faery Queen* as the most precious jewel in their coronet." The poet was entered a sizar (one of the humblest class of students) of Pembroke College, Cambridge, in 1569, and continued to attend college for seven years. "Of his proficiency during this time," says Johnson, "a favorable opinion may be drawn from the many classical allusions in his works." At Cambridge, he became intimate with Gabriel Harvey, the future astrologer, who induced the poet to repair to London, and there introduced him to Sir Philip Sidney, "one of the very diamonds of her Majesty's court." Of Spenser it has been well said that he and Chaucer are the only poets before Shakspeare who have given to the language anything that in its kind has not been surpassed, and in some sort superseded—Chaucer in his *Canterbury Tales,* and Spenser in his *Faery Queen.* Spenser is thought to have been known as a votary of the Muses among his fellow-students at Cambridge: there are several poems in a *Theatre for Worldlings,* a collection published in the year in which he became a member of the University, which are believed to have come from his pen.

RICHARD HOOKER AT HEAVITREE.

The boyhood of Richard Hooker, the learned and judicious divine, and the earliest and one of the most distinguished prose-writers of his time, presents some interesting traits. He was born at Heavitree, near Exeter, about 1553, of parents "not so remarkable for their extraction or riches, as for their virtue and industry, and God's blessing upon both." When a child, he was grave in manner and expression. By the kindness of his uncle, he obtained a better education at school than his parents could have afforded; and when a school-boy, " he was an early questionist, quietly inquisitive, *Why this was, and that was not, to be remembered? Why this was granted, and that denied?*" Hence his schoolmaster persuaded his parents, who intended him for an apprentice, to continue him at school, the good man assuring them that he would double his diligence in instructing him." "And in the mean time his parents and master laid a foundation for his future happiness, by instilling into his soul the seeds of piety, those conscientious principles of loving and fearing God; of an early belief that he knows the very secrets of our souls; that he punishes our vices, and rewards our innocence; that we should be free from hypocrisy, and appear to men what we are to God, because, first or last, the crafty man is catcht in his own snare." Jewel, bishop of Salisbury, next took Hooker under his care, sent him to Corpus Christi College, Oxford, and contributed to his support. Having entered into holy orders, he was appointed Master of the Temple, London; and the church contains a bust erected by the benchers to his memory. Hooker's most celebrated work is his treatise on " Ecclesiastical Polity," a powerful defense of the Church of England; and the first publication in the English language which presented a train of clear logical reasoning.

SIR PHILIP SIDNEY, "THE ENGLISH PETRARCH."

Sir Philip Sidney—a name which most educated Englishmen have learnt to admire and love—was born in 1554, at Penshurst Place, in Kent, where an oak, planted to commemorate the event, flourishes to this day.

Young Sidney was placed at the Free Grammar-school of Shrewsbury.* While there, his father, Sir Henry Sidney, "a man of great parts," addressed a letter to him, in 1566, full of sterling advice. His biographer and companion, Lord Brooke, states that at this early age, Philip was distinguished for intelligence, and for a gravity beyond his years. In 1569, he was entered at Christchurch, Oxford, and is reported to have held a public disputation with Carew, the author of the *Survey of Cornwall*; while at college he displayed a remarkable acuteness of intellect and craving for knowledge.

In 1572, Philip Sidney left England, and proceeded on his

---

* Founded by King Edward VI. In our own time, this school has maintained its pre-eminent rank, under the able head-mastership of the Rev. Dr. Butler. The Schoolhouse is situated near the Castle of Shrewsbury, and is built of freestone, in the Italianized Tudor style; it occupies two sides of a quadrangle, with a square pinnacled tower at the angle, which was partly rebuilt in 1831.

travels into France. He was furnished with a license to pass into foreign lands, with three servants and four horses; and was placed under the protection of the Earl of Lincoln, the Lord Admiral.

Sidney was at this time in his eighteenth year, and his boyhood already gave promise of all those graces of mind and of person for which his riper years were so famous. He was tall and well shaped; and even at his early age, skillful in all manly exercises His hair and complexion were very fair, and his countenance soft and pensive as a woman's, and yet full both of intelligence and thoughtfulness Indeed, if the gift of nature descend by inheritance, we cannot wonder that there should be in him a rare union of fine qualities: for his father, Sir Henry, Lord-President of Wales, and afterward Deputy of Ireland, was the very type of a noble English gentleman, excellent as a soldier and a statesman — that is, upright and prudent, brave and loyal. His mother, the Lady Mary, was full worthy to be the wife of such a man She was one of those women who are the richest ornaments of English History; one whose noble nature had been trained by the discipline of sorrow to the highest degree of excellence. She was the daughter of John, Duke of Northumberland; and when her eldest son, Philip, was born, she wore mourning for her father, her brother, and her sister-in-law, the Lady Jane, who had all died on the scaffold. "The clearness of his father's judgment," writes Fulke Greville, "and the ingenious sensibleness of his mother's, brought forth so happy a temper in their eldest son. From the father he had the stout heart, and the strong hand, and keen intelligence, while his mother has set on him the stamp of her own sweet and very gentle nature."—*Life of Sidney, by Steuart A. Pears, M.A.*

Paris was Sidney's first halting-place, and here he was introduced to the dazzling and bewildering splendor of the court of Catharine de Medicis. "Sidney," says Mr. Pears, "had heard much of this queen and her brilliant court: in the quiet days which he had passed at Penshurst, Ludlow, and Oxford, he had often dreamed of such scenes; often too he had talked over the wild doings of the civil wars of France; had his favorite heroes, and in his fancy formed pictures of them — and here he stood in the very midst of these men." But while in the full enjoyment of the pleasure and luxury of Paris, Sidney's mind was horrified by the Massacre of St. Bartholomew — of near 5000 persons — and he fled for shelter to the English embassy: the effect of this tragedy on him was deep, and never effaced. From France he proceeded to Belgium, Germany, Hungary, and Italy. At Frankfort, he first became acquainted with Herbert Languet, and addressed to him a volume of letters in Latin, which Mr. Pears has translated, with a few of Sidney's replies. He observes:

Sidney's letters are not remarkable for the elegance of their style, for he was then only practicing his pen in Latin writing; nor is it the wit and humor of his letters that render them worthy of attention and praise; but there is such a spirit of gentleness through them all, so much manliness of thought, expressed with the greatest modesty and simplicity, that they cannot fail to please those who delight in watching the opening of a fine character. And if they do not possess that profusion of wit which loads the pages of some modern letter-writers, who (to use the words of Sidney himself) "cast sugar and spice upon every dish that is served at table," they have a charm which no mere man of fashion, be he never so brilliant and versed in belles-lettres, can attain or even appreciate. They are full of the quiet play of a heart overflowing with affection. Hence the offensive criticism of Horace Walpole on Sidney's writings.

Sidney next arrived at Vienna, where he perfected himself

in horsemanship and other exercises peculiar to those times. At Venice he became acquainted with Edmund Wotton, brother to Sir Henry Wotton. He is said also to have enjoyed the friendship of Tasso, but this statement cannot be verified. Sidney returned to England in 1573; and, famed aforehand by a noble report of his accomplishments, which, together with the state of his person, framed by a natural propension to arms, he soon attracted the good opinion of all men, and was so highly prized in the good opinion of the queen (Elizabeth), that she "thought the court deficient without him." Connected with this success is Sidney's first literary attempt, a masque entitled *The Lady of May*, which was performed before Queen Elizabeth, at Wanstead House, in Essex.

After Sidney's quarrel at tennis with the Earl of Oxford, he retired from court to Wilton, the seat of his brother-in-law, the Earl of Pembroke: and there, in the companionship of his sister Mary, he wrote, for her amusement, the *Arcadia*, which, probably, received some additions from her pen.

The chivalry of Sir Philip Sidney, his learning, generous patronage of talent, and his untimely fate (he fell at Zutphen, in his thirty-third year), make his character of great interest. "He was a gentleman finished and complete, in whom mildness was associated with courage, erudition mollified by refinement, and courtliness dignified by truth. He is a specimen of what the English character was capable of producing when foreign admixtures had not destroyed its simplicity, or politeness debased its honor. Such was Sidney, of whom every Englishman has reason to be proud. He was the best prose-writer of his time. Sir Walter Raleigh calls him "the English Petrarch," and Cowper speaks of him as "a warbler of poetic prose." He trod, from his cradle to the grave, amidst incense and flowers, and died in a dream of glory.

BOYHOOD OF LORD BACON.

Of the early years of Sir Nicholas Bacon, father of Sir Francis Bacon, the biography is uncertain; but he received his scholastic education at Benet (Corpus Christi) College, Cambridge, and completed his studies abroad. Of his illustrious son, Francis Bacon, born in the Strand, in 1561, we have some interesting early traits. His health was delicate; and by his gravity of carriage, and love of sedentary pursuits, he was distinguished from other boys. While a mere child, he stole away from his play-fellows to a vault in St. James's Fields, to investigate the cause of a singular echo which he had observed there; and when only twelve, he busied himself with speculations on the art of legerdemain.* At thirteen he was entered at Trinity College, Cambridge, which he left after a residence of three years, "carrying with him a profound contempt for the course of study pursued there, a fixed conviction that the system of academic education in England was radically vicious, a just scorn for the trifles on which the followers of Aristotle had wasted their powers, and no great reverence for Aristotle himself." (*Macaulay.*) Such was the foundation of Bacon's philosophy: the influence of his writings has been glanced at in page 116.

THE ADMIRABLE CRICHTON.

The combined genius, learning, and physical advantages which obtained for this celebrated Scotchman the title of Admirable, however oft-told, must be briefly related in this work. James Crichton, son of Robert Crichton, of Eliock, who was Lord Advocate to King James VI., was born in Scotland, in the year, 1561. The precise place of his birth is not mentioned; but, having acquired the rudiments of education at Edinburgh, he was sent to study philosophy and the sciences at St. Andrew's, then the most renowned seminary in Scotland, where the illustrious Buchanan was one of his masters. At the ealy age of fourteen he took his degree of Master of Arts, and was regarded as a prodigy, not only in abilities but actual attainments. He was considered the third reader in the college, and in a short time became complete master of the philosophy and languages of the time, as well as of ten different languages.

It was then the custom for Scotchmen of birth to finish their education abroad, and serve in some foreign army previously to their entering that of their own country. When he was only sixteen or seventeen years old (the date cannot be fixed), Crichton's father sent him to the Continent. He had scarcely arrived in Paris, when he publicly challenged all scholars and philosophers to a disputation at the College of Navarre, to be carried on in any of the twelve specified languages, "in any science, liberal art, discipline, or faculty, whether practical or theoretic; and, as if to show in how little need he stood of preparation, or how lightly he held his adversaries, he spent the six weeks that elapsed between the challenge and the contest in a continued round of tilting, hunting, and dancing." On the

---

* Queen Elizabeth, who was taken with the smartness of Bacon's answers when he was a boy, used to try him with questions on various subjects; and it is said that once when she asked him how old he was, his reply was ingeniously complimentary: "I am just two years younger than your Majesty's happy reign." Elizabeth expressed her approbation by calling the boy her "Young Lord Keeper."

appointed day, however, he encountered "the gravest philosophers and divines," when he acquitted himself to the astonishment of all who heard him, and received the public praises of the president, and four of the most eminent professors. Next day, he was equally victorious at a tilting match at the Louver, where, through the enthusiasm of the ladies of the court, and from the versatility of his talents, his youth, the gracefulness of his manners, and the beauty of his person, he was named *L'Admirable*.

After two years' service in the army of Henry III., Crichton repaired to Italy, and at Rome repeated in the presence of the pope and cardinals the literary challenge and triumph that had gained him so much honor in Paris. From Rome he went to Venice, and in the university of the neighboring city of Padua, reaped fresh honors by Latin poetry, scholastic disputation, an exposition of the errors of Aristotle and his commentators, and (as a playful wind-up of the day's labor) a declamation upon the happiness of ignorance. He next, in consequence of the doubts of some incredulous persons, and the reports that he was a literary impostor, gave a public challenge: the contest, which included the Aristotelian and Platonic philosophies, and the mathematics of the time, was prolonged during three days, before an innumerable concourse of people; when Aldus Manutius, the celebrated Venetian printer, who was present at this "miraculous encounter," states Crichton to have proven completely victorious.

Crichton now pursued his travels to the court of Mantua, but to a combat more tragical than those carried on by the tongue or by the pen. Here he met a certain Italian gentleman "of a mighty able, nimble, and vigorous body, but by nature fierce, cruel, warlike, and audacious, and superlatively expert and dexterous in the use of his weapon." He had already killed three of the best swordsmen of Mantua; but Crichton, who had studied the sword from his youth, and who had probably improved himself in the use of the rapier in Italy, challenged the bravo: they fought; the young Scotchman was victorious, and the Italian left dead on the spot. At the court of Mantua, too, Crichton wrote Italian comedies, and played the principal parts in them himself, with great success. But he was shortly after assassinated by Vincenzo Gonzaga, son of the Duke of Mantua, it is supposed through jealousy. Thus was Crichton cut off in his twenty-second year, without leaving any proof of his genius except a few Latin verses, printed by Aldus Manutius; and the testimonials of undoubted and extreme admiration of several distinguished Itlalian authors who were his cotemporaries and associates.

HOW GEORGE ABBOT, THE CLOTHWEAVER'S SON, BECAME ARCHBISHOP OF CANTERBURY.

In 1562, there was born unto a poor clothworker, at Guildford, in Surrey, a son, under these remarkable circumstances. His mother, shortly before his birth, dreamt that if she could eat a jack or a pike, the child would become a great man. She accordingly sought for the fish; and accidentally, taking up some of the river water (that runs close by the house) in a pail, she also took up the jack, dressed it, and devoured it almost all. This odd affair induced several persons of quality to offer themselves to be sponsors when the child was christened; and this the poverty of the parents induced them joyfully to accept. Such was the tradition of the place, which Aubrey, in 1692, heard on the testimony of the minister, and other trustworthy inhabitants.

In spite of the dream, however, George Abbot would, in all probability, have been a clothworker, like his father, had there not been in those days many admirable institutions for the education of the humbler classes. He was sent to the Free Grammar School, founded by a grocer of London in 1553, for thirty "of the poorest men's sons" of Guildford, to be taught to read and write English, and cast accounts perfectly, so that they should be fitted for apprentices, etc. In 1578 he was removed to Balliol College, Oxford, and in 1597 was elected Master of University College. He was also three times elected Vice-Chancellor of the University, so that his reputation and influence at Oxford must have been considerable. His erudition was great: in 1604 he was one of the persons appointed for the new translation of the Bible; and he was one of eight to whom the whole of the New Testament, except the Epistles, was intrusted. In 1609, he was made Bishop of Lichfield and Coventry; next year, translated to the See of London; and in little more than a month, he was elevated to the Archbishopric of Canterbury. Two other sons of the poor clothworker were almost equally fortunate in advancement. The Archbishop's elder brother and school-fellow, Robert, became Bishop of Salisbury; and his youngest brother, Maurice, was an eminent London merchant, one of the first Directors of the East India Company, Lord Mayor, and representative of the City in Parliament. Archbishop Abbot attended King James in his last illness, and he crowned Charles I. "He founded a fair Hospital, well built, and liberally endowed," at Guildford, for 20 brethren and sisters. He was also a munificent benefactor to the poor of Guilford, Croydon, and Lambeth. The humble cottage tenement in which he was born exists to this day: in 1692 it was a public-house, with the sign of the *Three Mariners.*

SHAKSPEARE AT STRATFORD-ON-AVON.

We have already spoken of King Edward's Free Grammar School, at Birmingham; and, in the same county of Warwick, at Stratford-upon-Avon, is a free grammar-school, founded by a native of the town, in the reign of Henry VI., and celebrated as *the School of Shakspeare.* Immediately over the Guild Hall is the school-room, now divided into two chambers, and having a low flat plaster ceiling in place of the arched roof. Mr. Knight thus argues for the identity of the room:

"The only qualifications necessary for the admission of a boy into the Free Grammar School of Stratford were, that he should be a resident in the town, of seven years of age, and able to read. The Grammar School was essentially connected with the Corporation of Stratford; and it is impossible to imagine that, when the son of John Shakspeare became qualified for admission to a school where the best education of the time was given, literally for nothing, his father in that year being chief alderman, should not have sent him to the school."

Thither, it is held, Shakspeare, born at Stratford in 1564, went about the year 1571. Mr. Knight impressively continues:

"Assuredly the worthy curate of the neighboring village of Luddington, Thomas Hunt, who was also the schoolmaster, would have received his new scholar with some kindness. As his 'shining morning face' first passed out of the main street into that old court through which the upper room of learning was to be reached, a new life would be opening upon him. The humble minister of religion who was his first instructor, has left no memorials of his talents or acquirements; and in a few years another master came after him, Thomas Jenkins, also unknown to fame. All praise and honor be to them; for it is impossible to imagine that the teachers of William Shakspeare were evil instructors, giving the boy husks instead of wholesome aliment."

At Stratford, then, at the free Grammar School of his own town, Mr. Knight assumes Shakspeare to have received in every just sense of the word *the education of a scholar.* This, it is true, is described by Ben Jonson as "small Latin and less Greek;" Fuller states that "his learning was very little;" and Aubrey, that "he understood Latin pretty well." But the question is set at rest by "the indisputable fact that the very earliest writings of Shakspeare are imbued with a spirit of classical antiquity; and that the all-wise nature of the learning that manifests itself in them, whilst it offers the best proof of his familiarity with the ancient writers, is a circumstance which has misled those who never attempted to dispute the existence of the learning which was displayed in the direct pedantry of his cotemporaries." So that, because Shakspeare uses his knowledge skillfully, he is assumed not to have read!

To assume that William Shakspeare did not stay long enough at the grammar-school of Stratford to obtain a very fair proficiency in Latin, with some knowledge of Greek, is to assume an absurdity upon the face of circumstances.
Of Shakspeare's life, immediately after his quitting Stratford, little is positively known. Collier concurs with Malone "in thinking, that after Shakspeare quitted the Free School, he was employed in the office of an attorney. Proofs of something like a legal education are to be found in many of his plays, and it may safely be asserted that they (law phrases) do not occur anything like so frequently in the dramatic productions of any of his cotemporaries."*

"In these days, the education of the universities commenced much earlier than at present. Boys intended for the learned professions, and more especially for the church, commonly went to Oxford and Cambridge at eleven or twelve years of age. If they were not intended for those professions, they probably remained at the Grammar School till they were thirteen or fourteen; and then they were fitted for being apprenticed to tradesmen, or articled to attorneys, a numerous and thriving body in those days of cheap litigation. Many also went early to the Inns of Court, which were the universities of the law, and where there was real study and discipline in direct connexion with the several societies."— *Knight's Life of Shakspeare.*

LORD HERBERT OF CHERBURY, IN SHROPSHIRE.

The celebrated Lord Herbert of Cherbury, born 1581, in his Autobiography, thus describes his early tuition:

"My Schoolmaster in the house of my lady grandmother (at Eyton, in Shropshire). began at the age of seven years to teach me the Alphabet, and afterwards Grammar, and other books commonly read in schools, in which I profited so much, that upon this theme *Audaces fortuna juvat*, I made an oration of a sheet of paper and 50 or 60 verses in the space of one day." . . .

He adds that under Mr. Newton, at Didlebury, in Shropshire, he attained to the knowledge of the Greek Tongue and Logic, in so much that at twelve years old his parents sent him to Oxford to University College, where he disputed at his first coming in Logic, and made in Greek the exercises required in that College, oftener than in Latin. He was a patron of Ben Jonson, who, in a complimentary epigram, addresses him as "all-virtuous Herbert." His *Life of Henry VIII.* is a masterpiece of

* The name "William Shakspere" occurs in a certificate of the names and arms of trained soldiers — trained militia, we should now call them — in the hundred of Barlichway, in the county of Warwick — under the hand of Sir Fulk Greville ("Friend to Sir Philip Sydney"), Sir Edward Greville, and Thomas Spencer. Was our William Shakspere a soldier? Why not? Jonson was a soldier, and had slain his man. Donne had served in the Low Countries. Why not Shakspere in arms? At all events, here is a field for inquiry and speculation. The date is September 23, 1605, the year of the Gunpowder Plot; and the lists were possibly prepared through instructions issued by Cecil in consequence of secret information as to the working of the plot in Warwickshire — the proposed head-quarters of the insurrection.—*State Papers, edited by Mary Anne Everett Green.*

historic biography, worthy to rank with Bacon's *Life of Henry VII.**

ADMIRAL BLAKE AT BRIDGWATER.

Robert Blake, "Admiral and General at Sea," was born in 1598, at Bridgwater, in a house of the Tudor age, which remains to this day; adjoining is the secluded garden, in which "the ruddy-faced and curly-haired boy, Robert Blake, played and pondered, as was his habit, until the age of sixteen." He was sent early to the Bridgwater Grammar School, which had been founded some five-and-forty years before, and endowed by Queen Elizabeth; and was then considered one of the best foundations of its kind in England. "At the Grammar School he made some progress in his Greek and Latin; something of navigation, ship-building, and the routine of sea duties he probably learned from his father, or from his father's factors and servants. His own taste, however, the habit of his mind, and the bent of his ambition, led to literature. He was the first of his race who had shown any vocation to letters and learning, and his father, proud of his talents and his studies, resolved that he should have some chance of rising to eminence. Nor was this early culture thrown away. At sixteen he was already prepared for the university, and at his earnest desire was sent to Oxford, where he matriculated as a member of St. Alban's Hall, in 1615." He removed to Wadham College, and there remained several years, took the usual honors, and completed his education; and in the great dining-hall of Wadham a portrait of the Admiral is shown with pride as that of its most illustrious scholar. Blake, in good time, took his degree of Master of Arts at Oxford; he had read the best authors in Greek and Latin, and wrote the latter language sufficiently well for verse and epigram. Even in the busiest days of his public life, it was his pride not to forget his old studies.†

WALLER'S DULLNESS.

Edmund Waller, the poet, one of the best examples of poetic style and diction, was born at Coleshill, in Berkshire, in 1605, and was sent early to the Grammar School of Market Wickham, where he was said to be "dull and slow in his task." Mr.

---

* Lord Herbert was the elder brother of George Herbert, who studied foreign languages in hopes of rising to be Secretary of State, but being disappointed in his views at court, he took orders, became Prebend of Lincoln, and became Rector of Bemerton, near Salisbury. His poems were printed in 1635, under the title of the *Temple*; of which 20,000 copies were sold in a few years. His best prose work is *The Country Parson*. Lord Bacon dedicated to him his Translation of some Psalms into English verse.

† See Hepworth Dixon's Life of Blake.

Thomas Bigge, of Wickham, who had been Waller's schoolfellow, and of the same form, told Aubrey, that "he little thought that Waller would have made so rare a poet; for he was wont to make his exercise for him." He was removed at an unusually early age to King's College, Cambridge, where his scholastic attainments are said to have led to his being elected member of parliament for the borough of Agmondesham at the age of 16; though this is, with greater probability, attributed to Waller's name and local influence.

This account of Waller's dullness at school is probable; for says Mr. Bell, "it clearly indicates the character of Waller's genius, which demanded time and labor in the accomplishment of the smallest results."

Aubrey describes Waller's writing as "a lamentable hand, as bad as the scratching of a hen;" but this is an exaggeration, and disproved by his autograph, which is, however, very rare.

Waller took his seat in the House of Commons before he was the age of 17. He became (as Bishop Burnet expresses it) "the delight of the House," and, when old, "said the liveliest things of any among them." Being present once, when the Duke of Buckingham was paying his court to the King, by arguing against Revelation, Mr. Waller said; "My Lord, I am a great deal older than your Grace; and have, I believe, heard more arguments for atheism than ever your Grace did; but I have lived long enough to see there is nothing in them; and so, I hope your Grace will." Waller died in 1687, in his 83rd year.

DR. BUSBY, HEAD MASTER OF WESTMINSTER SCHOOL.

This most eminent schoolmaster of his time, who is said in the *Census Alumnorum*, "to have educated the greatest number of learned scholars that ever adorned at one time any age or nation," was born at Luton, in Northamptonshire, in 1606. Having passed through Westminster School, he was elected student of Christ Church, Oxford; but he was so poor that he received the sum of 5*l.* of the parish of St. Margaret, to enable him to proceed bachelor; and 26*l.* 13*s.* 4*d.* to proceed master of arts; as entered in the Churchwarden's accounts. Of this timely aid he made a noble acknowledgment by making a bequest of 50*l.* to poor housekeepers, an estate worth 525*l.*, and in personal property nearly 5000*l.*, to St. Margaret's parish.

Busby achieved a great reputation at Oxford, as an "exact Latinist and Grecian," and likewise for his power of oratory. While still a resident in the university, he acted the part of Cratander, in Cartwright's *Royal Slave*, before the King and Queen at Christchurch, when being more applauded than his fellow-students, his success excited in him so violent a passion for the stage, that he had well nigh engaged himself as an actor.

In 1640 he was appointed master of Westminster School. During the civil War, though he was ejected from his church appointments, but was allowed to retain his studentship of Christchurch, and the chief mastership of the school,—a tribute to his pre-eminent qualities as an instructor. He labored in his mastership during more than half a century; and by his diligence, learning, and assiduity, has become the proverbial representative of his class.

Dr. Busby is said to have been not only witty, learned, and highly accomplished, but also modest and unassuming: his piety was unaffected, and his liberality unbounded. He died in 1695, and was interred in Westminster Abbey. His works were principally for the use of his school, and either consist of expurgated editions of certain classics which he wished his boys to read in a harmless form; or grammatical treatises, mostly metrical. There is a tradition that some of these were the compositions of his scholars, superintended and corrected by himself. Several of his publications, more or less altered, were used in Westminster School until a few years since.

The severity of Busby's discipline is traditional,* but we do not find that it was so; and strange as it may appear, no records are preserved of him in the school over which he so long presided. The charitable intentions of his will are carried into effect by old Westminsters, who meet in the Jerusalem Chamber. The picture, by Riley, of Dr. Busby with one of his scholars, said to be Philip Henry, is in the Hall at Christchurch; there are also other portraits of him, and a bust of him by Rysbrack; all from a cast in plaster taken after death, for during his life he never would sit for his portrait. Bagshaw states that he never spoilt the rod by sparing the child: according to Dr. Johnson, he used to call the rod his "sieve," and to say "whoever did not pass through it was no boy for him." Pope thus commemorates one of the class:

> "Lo! a specter rose, whose index-hand
> Hold forth the virtues of the dreadful wand:
> His beaver'd brow a birchin garland wears,
> Drooping with infants' blood and mothers' tears.
> O'er every vein a shudd'ring horror runs,—
> Eton and Winton shake through all their sons.

---

* Doubtless transmitted by the following passage from Sir Roger de Coverley's visit to Westminster Abbey, in the *Spectator*:
"As we stood before Busby's tomb, the knight uttered himself—'Dr. Busby—a great man! he whipped my grandfather—a very great man! I should have gone to him myself if I had not been a blockhead—a very great man!'"

> All flesh is humbled; Westminster's bold race
> Shriek and confess the genius of the place;
> The pale poy senator yet tingling stands,
> And holds his garments close with quiv'ring hands."

Nevertheless, Busby was much beloved by his scholars, as may be seen by letters from Cowley, Dryden, and others. He is said to have taken especial pains in preparing his scholars for the reception of the Eucharist.

Wood describes him as "eminent and exemplary for piety and justice, an encourager of virtuous and forward youth, of great learning and hospitality, and the chief person that educated more youths that were afterward eminent in the Church and State than any master of his time."

LORD CLARENDON.

Edward Hyde, Earl of Clarendon, one of the illustrious men whose talents were called into action by the Civil Wars, was born in 1608, at Dinton, near Salisbury, where his father enjoyed a competent fortune. He was first instructed at home by the clergyman of the parish, who was also a schoolmaster; but his principal improvement arose from the care and conversation of his father, who had traveled much in his youth. Edward, being a younger son, was destined for the church: and with this view was sent to Magdalen College, Oxford, in his fourteenth year. But on the death of his eldest brother, which soon after took place, his destination was altered; and he was now designed for the profession of the law. He quitted the University with the reputation rather of talents than of industry; and from some dangerous habits in which he had been initiated, he afterward looked on this early removal as not the least fortunate incident of his life.

He commenced his professional studies in the Middle Temple, under the direction of his uncle, Sir Nicholas Hyde, then treasurer of that Society. His early legal studies were impeded by his ill health. Nor was his application considerable after his recovery; he lost another year amidst the pleasures of dissipation; and when his dangerous companions had disappeared, he still felt little inclination to immure himself amidst the records of the law. He was fond of polite literature, and particularly attached to the Latin classics; he therefore bestowed only so much attention on his less agreeable professional studies as was sufficient to save his credit with his uncle.

Nevertheless, Hyde, on his appearance at the bar, greatly surpassed the expectations of his cotemporaries: he had been punctual in the performance of all those public exercises to which he was bound by the rules of his profession. Meanwhile, he had been careful to form high connections; for he had laid it down as a rule to be always found in the best company; and to attain by every honorable means, an intimate friendship with the most considerable persons in the kingdom. While only a student-at-law, he enjoyed the society of Ben Jonson, the most celebrated wit of that age; of Selden, the most skillful of all English lawyers in the ancient constitution and history of his country; and of May, a distinguished scholar, and afterward the historian of the parliament. Among his other friends, he could recount some of the most learned and celebrated divines—Sheldon, Morley, Earles, Hales of Eton, and above all Chillingworth, whose amiable qualities rendered him as beloved by his friends, as his controversial talents caused him to be feared by his antagonists: Edmund Waller, who was not less admired by his cotemporaries as an orator, than by posterity as a poet, was among Clarendon's intimate associates; but the friend whom he regarded with the most tender attachment, and the most unqualified admiration, was Sir Lucius Carey, afterward Lord Falkland, whom he delights to describe as the most accomplished gentleman, scholar, and statesman of his age.* From the conversation of these and other distinguished individuals (the characters of some of whom he has admirably sketched in his works), Clarendon considered himself to have derived a great portion of his knowledge; and he declares that "he never was so proud, or thought himself so good a man, as when he was the worst man in the company."

SIR MATTHEW HALE'S EARLY LIFE.

Sir Matthew Hale, the illustrious lawyer, born in 1609, lost both his parents when he was but an infant: he was educated under a clergyman of Puritanical principles, and at the age of 17 was sent to Magdalen Hall, Oxford, where he soon got rid of his Puritanical notions, and plunged into the extreme dissipation of the college life of that period. He was on the point of

---

* Clarendon says: He (Falkland) was wonderfully beloved by all who knew him, as a man of excellent parts, of a wit so sharp, and a nature so sincere, that nothing could be more lovely.

His house (at Tew), being within little more than ten miles of Oxford, he contracted familiarity and friendship with the most polite and accurate men at that university; who found such an immenseness of wit, and such a solidity of judgment in him, so infinite a fancy, bound in by a most logical ratiocination; such a vast knowledge, that he was not ignorant in anything; yet such an excessive humility, as if he had known nothing, that they frequently resorted and dwelt with him, as in a college situated in a purer air; so that his house was a university in a less volume, whither they came not so much for repose as study, and to examine and refine those grosser propositions, which laziness and consent made current in vulgar conversation.

He was superior to all those passions and affections which attend vulgar minds, and was guilty of no other ambition than of knowledge; and to be reputed a lover of all good men.

A statue of this truly great man is appropriately placed in St. Stephen's Hall, in the New Palace at Westminster.

becoming a soldier in the army of the Prince of Orange, then engaged in the Low Countries, when accident introduced him to Serjeant Glanville, who, perceiving the valuable qualities which the young man possessed, persuaded him to apply himself exclusively to the law. Acting upon this advice, Hale was admitted a student of Lincoln's Inn, and commenced a course of study, extending to sixteen hours every day. One of his companions in a debauch having been taken suddenly and dangerously ill, Hale was so struck with remorse, that he gave up his intemperate habits. He rose to be Chief Justice of the King's Bench, and left a *History* of the Common Law; and a collection of valuable MSS., which he bequeathed to the library of Lincoln's Inn. His "Plan of Instruction" has been detailed at p. 109.

SAMUEL BUTLER AT WORCESTER.

Samuel Butler, the most witty and learned poetical satirist, was born at Strensham, in Worcestershire, in 1612, and received his first rudiments of learning at home: he was afterward sent to the College School at Worcester, then presided over by Mr. Henry Bright, prebendary of that Cathedral, whom Dr. Nash describes as a "celebrated scholar, and many years master of the King's school there; one who made his business his delight; and, though in very easy circumstances, continued to teach for the sake of doing good, by benefiting the families of the neighboring gentlemen, who thought themselves happy in having their sons instructed by him." Butler's father's finances would not allow him to be matriculated at Cambridge, to which university he desired—and his proficiency in learning entitled him —to proceed. Accordingly he engaged as clerk to an eminent justice of the peace, and in his leisure hours studied history, poetry, music, and painting; and obtaining access to the Countess of Kent's well-stocked library, he enjoyed the conversation of the learned Selden. He entered afterward into the service of Sir Samuel Locke, a knight of ancient family in Bedfordshire, who had been one of Cromwell's commanders, and is supposed to have been the prototype of the character of *Hudibras*.[*]

[*] Life of Butler prefixed to *Hudibras*. Bright is buried in Worcester cathedral, where, in the Bishop's Chapel, is a Latin epitaph on him, written by Dr. Joseph Hall, Dean of Worcester. Dr Nash adds:—"I have endeavored to revive the memory of this great and good teacher, wishing to excite a laudable emulation in our provincial schoolmasters; a race of men who, if they execute their trust with ability, industry, and in a proper manner, deserve the highest honor and patronage their country can bestow, as they have an opportunity of communicating learning at a moderate expense to the middle rank of gentry, without the danger of ruining their fortunes, and corrupting their morals or their health."

JEREMY TAYLOR AT CAMBRIDGE.

Jeremy Taylor, the most eloquent and imaginative of English divines, and the Shakspeare and Spenser of our theological literature, was born in 1613, and descended from gentle and even heroic blood. His family had, however, "fallen into the portion of weeds and outworn faces," and Jeremy's father was a barber in Cambridge. He, nevertheless, put his son to college, as a sizar, in his thirteenth year, having himself previously taught him the rudiments of grammar and mathematics, and given him the advantages of the Free Grammar School. In 1631, Jeremy Taylor took his degree of B.A. in Caius College, and entering into sacred orders, removed to London, where his eloquent lectures in St. Paul's Cathedral, aided by "his florid and youthful beauty and pleasant air," procured him the patronage of Archbishop Laud. Such was the commencement of the rise of Jeremy Taylor, whose fortunes suffered "in the great storm which dashed the vessel of the church all in pieces," and from his being in advance of the age in which he lived, and of the ecclesiastical system in which he had been reared.

COWLEY AT WESTMINSTER.

Abraham Cowley, whom Milton declared to be one of the three greatest English poets, was born in Fleet-street, in 1618.* He was sent early to Westminster School: he tells us that he had such a defect in his memory, as never to "bring it to retain the ordinary rules of grammar." Bishop Spratt says:

"However, he supply'd that want by conversing with the books themselves from whence those rules had been drawn. That no doubt was a better way, though much more difficult, and he afterward found this benefit by it, that having got the *Greek* and *Roman* languages as he had done his own, not by precept but use, he practiced them, not as a scholar but a native.

"The first beginning of his studies was a familiarity with the most solid and unaffected Authors of Antiquity, which he fully digested, not only in his memory, but his judgment. By this advantage he learn'd nothing while a boy, that he needed to forget or forsake when he came to be a Man. His Mind was rightly season'd at first, and he had nothing to do, but still to proceed on the same Foundation on which he began."

At Westminster, Cowley "soon obtain'd and increas'd the noble genius peculiar to that place." He wrote his *Piramus and Thisbe* when only ten years old, and his *Constantia and Philetus* when only twelve. They were published, with other pieces, as *Poetical Blossomes*, when he was only fifteen. At Westminster, too, he wrote his comedy of *Love's Riddles;* and his elegy upon the tragical fate of the two sons of Sir Thomas Lyttleton, drowned at Oxford, the elder in attempting to save the younger, in 1635. He had great respect for his master, Dr. Busby, to whom, in

* Cowley's father was a law-writer, or engrosser, and not a grocer, as stated generally.

1662, he presented a copy of his two Books of Plants, with a letter couched in the most affectionate and respectful terms. Dr. Johnson has pithily characterized Cowley as "a man whose learning and poetry were his lowest merits." Cowley, in his Essay "Of Myself," says:

"When I was a very young boy at school, instead of running about on holidays, and playing with my fellows, I was wont to steal from them, and walk into the fields, either alone with a book, or with some one companion. if I could find any of the same temper. I was then, too, so much an enemy to constraint, that my masters could never prevail on me, by any persuasions or encouragements, to learn without book the common rules of grammar, in which they dispensed with me alone, because they found I made a shift to do the usual exercise out of my own reading and observation. That I was then of the same mind as I am now (which, I confess, 1 wonder at myself), may appear at the latter end of an ode which I made when I was but thirteen years old, and which was then printed with many other verses. The beginning of it is boyish, but of part," adds Cowley, "if very little were corrected, 1 should hardly now be much ashamed. You may see by it I was even then acquainted with the poets (for the conclusion is taken out of Horace); and perhaps it was the immature and immoderate love of them which stamped first, or rather engraved, the characters in me." . . . . "I believe I can tell the particular little chance that filled my head first with such chimes of verse, as have never since left ringing there; for I remember when I began to read, and take some pleasure in it, there was wont to lie in my mother's parlor (I know not by what accident, for she never in her life read any book but of devotion); but there was wont to be Spenser's works; this I happened to fall upon, and was infinitely delighted with the stories of the knights, and giants, and monsters, and brave houses, which I found everywhere there (though my understanding had little to do with all this); and by degrees with the tinkling of the rhyme, and dance of the numbers; so that I think I had read him all over before I was twelve years old. With these affections of mind, and my heart wholly set upon letters, I went to the university; but was soon torn from thence by that public violent storm, which would suffer nothing to stand where it did, but rooted up every plant, even from the princely cedar, to me, the hyssop."

At college he was known by the elegance of his exercises, and composed the greater part of his epic, *Davideis*. Before he was 20 years old, he laid the design of this his most masculine work, that he finished long after.

JOHN EVELYN AT ETON AND OXFORD.

John Evelyn, the perfect model of an English gentleman of the seventeenth century, and known as "Sylva Evelyn," from his work with that title, on Forest Trees, was born in 1620, at Wotton House, in the most picturesque district of Surrey. He states in his Diary, that he "was not initiated into any rudiments till he was four years old, and then one Frier taught him at the church porch." When he was eight years old, at which time he resided with his maternal grandmother, he began to learn Latin at Lewes, and was afterward sent to the Free School at South-over, adjoining Lewes. His father, who would willingly have weaned him from the fondness of his grandmother, intended to place him at Eton, but the boy had been so terrified by the report of the severe discipline there, that he was sent back to Lewes. Poor Tusser's* account of Eton, which Evelyn

---

*Thomas Tusser, born about 1523, of ancient family, was the author of the first didactic poem in the language. He had a good education, and commenced life at Court, under the

undoubtedly had in his mind, was quite sufficient to justify him:

> From Pauls I went, to Eton sent,
> To learn straightways the Latin phrase,
> Where fifty-three stripes given to me
> At once I had;
> For fault but small, or none at all,
> It came to pass, thus beat I was;
> See Udall see, the mercy of thee
> To me, poor lad!

No such inhumanity, we may be assured, would be perpetrated at Eton while Sir Henry Wotton was provost; and Evelyn, who says that he afterward a thousand times regretted his perverseness, lost much in not being placed under this admirable man. In 1636, he was admitted into the Middle Temple, though then absent and at school, whence, however, he finally removed in the following year, to Balliol College, Oxford. At school he had been very remiss in his studies till the last year, "so that I went to the university," he says, "rather out of shame of abiding longer at school, than from any fitness, as by sad experience I found, which put me to relearn all I had neglected, or but perfunctorily gained." While at Oxford, Evelyn was "admitted into the dancing and vaulting school," and began also to "look on the rudiments of music," in which, he says, "he afterward arrived to some formal knowledge, though to small perfection of hand, because he was so frequently diverted by inclinations to newer trifles." Having quitted the university, he went to London in 1640, to reside in the Middle Temple, his father having intended that he should adopt the profession of the law, which he denominates an "unpolished study;" but this idea he relinquished, on the death of his father. Storing his mind by travel and study, he entered on a long career of active, useful, and honorable employment. He was the great improver of English gardening; his love of planting, and the want of timber for the Navy, led him to write his "Sylva, a Discourse of Forest Trees,"* the first book printed by order of the Royal Society, of which Evelyn was one of the earliest Fellows; it led to the planting of many millions of forest-trees, and is one of the very few books in the world which completely effected what it was designed to do. Another valuable work by Evelyn, is his Diary, or Kalendarium, a most interesting record of the eventful times in which the writer lived.

patronage of Lord Paget. Afterward he practiced farming successively at Ratwood, in Sussex; Ipswich; Fairsted, in Essex; Norwich, and other places. He died in 1580. He is principally known by his poem entitled *Hundred Go d Points of Husbandrie*, first published in 1557, and consisting of practical directions for farming, expressed in simple verse.

* The best illustration is to be seen to this day in the magnificent woods at Wotton Place.

A short time before the publication of the Memoirs of John Evelyn, in 1817, Mr. Upcott, of the London Institution, was at Wotton, in Surrey, the residence of the Evelyn family; and, sitting after supper with Lady Evelyn and Mrs Molyneux, his attention was attracted to a tippet made of feathers, on which the latter was employed. "Ah, Mrs Molyneux, we have all of us our hobbies," said Mr. Upcott. "Very true, Mr Upcott," rejoined Lady Evelyn, "and may I take the liberty of asking what yours is?" "Why mine, madam, from a very early age, has been the collecting of the handwriting of men of eminence." "What! I suppose." Mrs Molyneux said, "you would care for things like these; unfolding one of her thread-cases, which was formed of a letter written by Sarah, Duchess of Marlborough "Indeed I should, very much " "Oh, if that be your taste," said Lady Evelyn, " we can easily satisfy you This house is full of such matters ; there is a whole clothes-basket full of letters and other papers of old Mr. Evelyn, in the garret, which I was so tired of seeing, that I ordered the housemaid the other day to light the fires with them ; but probably she may not yet have done it " The bell was rung, the basket appeared untouched, and the result was the publication of the *Memoirs and Diary of John Evelyn*.

MARVELL'S SCHOLARSHIP.

Andrew Marvell, prose-writer, poet, and patriot, was born in 1620, at Kingston-upon-Hull, where his father was master of the Grammar School. At the age of 15, he was sent to Trinity College, Cambridge. Milton, writing to Bradshawe, in 1652, thus speaks of Marvell's attainments: "He (Marvell) hath spent four years abroad in Holland, France, Italy, and Spain, to very good purpose as I believe, and the gaining of those four languages; besides, he is a scholar, and well read in the Latin and Greek authors, and no doubt of an approved conversation, for he comes now lately out of the house of the Lord Fairfax, who was general, where he was intrusted to give some instructions in the languages to the lady his daughter."

JOHN AUBREY, IN WILTSHIRE.

Aubrey, born in the parish of Kingston-St.-Michael, in 1625, in his Diary, tells us that in 1633 he " entered into his grammar at the Latin School at Yatton Keynel (Wilts), in the church, where the curate, Mr. Hare, taught the eldest boys Virgil, Ovid, Cicero, etc." Next year Aubrey was removed to the adjoining parish of Leigh-de-la-Mere, under Mr. Robert Latimer, the Rector, who, " at 70, wore a dudgeon, with a knife and bodkin."* He had been the schoolmaster of Thomas Hobbes, the philosopher of Malmesbury. At these schools it was the fashion for the boys to cover their books with parchment—" old manuscript," says Aubrey, " which I was too young to understand; but I was pleased with the elegancy of the writing, and the colored initiall letters." These manuscripts are believed to have been brought

---

* Bodkin was, at this period, a name for a small dagger. In this sense, it occurs in Shakspeare:

   " When he himself might his quietus make
   With a bare bodkin."—*Hamlet*.

Dudgeon was likewise the name for a dagger ;

   " It was a serviceable dudgeon
   Either for fighting or for drudging."—*Hudibras*.

from the Abbey of Malmesbury; and the Rector, "when he brewed a barrell of special ale, his use was to stop the bunghole (under the clay) with a sheet of manuscript. He sayd nothing did it so well, which methought did grieve me then to see." In 1638, Aubrey was "transplanted to Blandford School, in Dorset," "in Mr. Wm. Gardner's time the most eminent school for the education of gentlemen in the West of England." Aubrey has left the following account of his school-days in the manuscript of his *Lives of Eminent Men*, in the Ashmolean Museum, Oxford:

"When a boy bred at Eston (in eremiticall solitude), was very curious, his greatest delight to be with the Artificers that came there, e. g. joyners, carpenters, cowpers, masons, and understood their trades: Noris vacuis, I drew and painted. In 1634, I was entred in Latin gramer by Mr. R. Latimer, a delicate and little person, rector of Leigh-de-la-Mere,— a mile fine walk,—who had an easie way of teaching; and every time we asked leave to go forth, we had a Latin word from him, wch at our returne we were to tell him again: which in a little while amounted to a good number of words. 'Twas my unhappinesse in half a year to lose this good enformer by his death, and afterwards was under severall dull ignorant teachers till 12, 1638, about which time I was sent to Blandford schoole in Dorset, Mr. Sutton, B.D., who was ill natured Here I recovered my health and got my Latin and Grecke. Our usher had (by chance) a Cowper's Dictionary, which I had never seen before. I was then in Terence. Perceiving this method, I read all in the booke where Ter. was. and then Cicero, which was the meanes by which I got my Latin. 'Twas a wonderfull helpe to my phansie in reading of Ovid's Metamorph. In English by Sandys, which made me understand Latin the better. Also I mett accidentally a book of my mother's—*Bacon's Essayes*—which first opened my understanding on the moralls (for Tullies Offices were too crabbed for my young yeares), and the excellent clearnesse of the style, and hints and transitions." He also notes: "at eight I was a kind of Engineer, and then fell to Drawing. Copied pictures in the parlor in a table book. Not very much care for gram."

THE HON. ROBERT BOYLE, A TRUE PATRON AND CULTIVATOR OF SCIENCE.

The early life of the Hon. Robert Boyle presents a remarkable instance of the right employment of wealth and station to obtain an excellent education. He was born in 1627, and was the youngest son of the great Earl of Cork. He tells us that his father, having "a perfect aversion for their fondness who use to breed their children so nice and tenderly that a hot sun or a good shower of rain as much endangers them as if they were made of butter or of sugar," committed him to a nurse away from home, under whose care he formed a vigorous constitution. He adds, that at an early age he acquired a habit of stuttering, from mocking other children. He was taught very young to speak both Latin and French; and his studiousness and love of truth endeared him to his father. At eight years old he was sent to Eton, with his elder brother. Here he became immoderately fond of study from "the accidental perusal of Quintus Curtius, which first made him in love with other than pedantic books;" and the most effectual mode of preventing the ill effects of reading romance, he found to be the extraction of the square and cube roots, and the more laborious operations of algebra. In his eleventh year, he and one of his brothers were sent with a French gentleman to travel on the Continent, and settled at Geneva, where a thunderstorm in the night was the cause of those religious impressions which he retained throughout his life. Here Boyle continued some time, studying rhetoric, logic, and political geography: and he cultivated both Hebrew and Greek, though a professed hater of verbal studies, that he might read the original of the Scriptures. At the same time he was taught fencing and dancing; his recreations were mall and tennis; and the reading of romances, which "assisted by a total discontinuance of the English tongue, in a short time taught him a skill in French somewhat unusual to strangers." The party afterward set off for Italy; at Florence, Boyle made himself master of the Italian language; and became acquainted with the then recent astronomical discoveries of Galileo. He returned to England, and his father being dead, he retired to his family estate in Dorsetshire, and there gave himself up for five years to the study of natural philosophy and chemistry; though he mentions among his occupations, essays in prose and ethics. "How few of the high born and wealthy have employed their advantages so well for the improvement of his mind as did Robert Boyle!" From this time to the end of his life he appears to have been engaged in study. His chemical experiments date from this period. He was one of the first members of "the Invisible College," subsequently the Royal Society; and he was afterward the great improver of the air-pump. It should not be forgotten that he devoted much of his fortune to promoting Christianity in the East.

JOHN BUNYAN, AUTHOR OF "THE PILGRIM'S PROGRESS."

Who has not read *The Pilgrim's Progress?*—"a book," says Southey, "which makes its way through the fancy to the understanding and the heart: the child peruses it with wonder and delight: in youth we discover the genius which it displays; its worth is apprehended as we advance in years; and we perceive its merits feelingly in declining age." Lord Macaulay has said of Bunyan: "though there were many clever men in England during the latter half of the seventeenth century, there were only two great creative minds. One of these minds produced 'The Paradise Lost;' the other, 'The Pilgrim's Progress.'"

John Bunyan was born in the village of Elstow, within a mile of Bedford, in the year 1628, in a cottage which remained in its original state to our time. Bunyan's descent, to use his own words, "was of a low inconsiderable generation; my father's house," he says, "being of that rank that is meanest and most despised of all the families in the land."* He was, as his own statement implies, of a generation of tinkers, and born and bred to that calling, as his father had been before him.† His parents had several other children; but they were able to put their son John to school in an age when very few of the poor were taught to read and write. The boy learnt both, "according to the rate of other poor men's children," but soon lost what little he had been taught, "even," he says, "almost utterly." Southey is of opinion that Bunyan's parents took some pains in impressing him with a sense of his religious duties; otherwise, when, in his boyhood, he having but few equals in cursing, swearing, lying, and blaspheming, he would not have been visited by such dreams and such compunctious feelings as he has described.

"Often," he says, "after I had spent this and the other day in sin, I have in my bed been greatly afflicted, while asleep, with the apprehensions of devils and wicked Spirits, who still, as I then thought, labored to draw me away with them." His waking reflections were not less terrible than these fearful visions of the night : and these, he says, "when I was but a child, but nine or ten years old, did so distress my soul, that then in the midst of my many sports and childish vanities, amidst my vain companions, I was often much cast down, and afflicted in my mind therewith : yet could I not let go my sins."

But these impresssions soon passed away, and were forgotten in the society of Bunyan's village companions: according to his own confession, he ran headlong into the boisterous vices which prove fatal to so many of the ignorant and the brutal. Yet, though he became so far hardened in profligacy, the sense of right and wrong was not extinguished in him, and it shocked him when he saw those who pretended to be religious act in a manner unworthy of their profession. Some providential escapes, during this part of his life, he looked back upon as so many judgments mixed with mercy. Once he fell into a creek of the sea, once out of a boat into the river Ouse, near Bedford, and each time was narrowly saved from drowning. One day an adder crossed his path; he stunned it with a stick, then forced open its mouth with a stick, and plucked out the tongue, which he supposed to be the sting, with his fingers; "by which act," he says, "had not God been merciful unto me, I might, by my desperateness, have brought myself to an end." If this indeed were an adder, and not a harmless snake, his escape from the fangs was more remarkable than he was aware of. A circumstance which was likely to impress him more deeply, occurred in the eighteenth year of his age, when, being a soldier in the Parliament's army, he was drawn out to go to the siege of Leicester; one of the company wished to go in his stead; Bunyan

* "Grace abounding to the Chief of Sinners," by John Bunyan.
† In 1828, there were shown at Elstow the remains of a closet, in which Bunyan had worked as a tinker.

consented to exchange with him; and this volunteer substitute, standing sentinel one day at the siege, was shot through the head with a musket-ball.

Bunyan, probably before he was nineteen, chanced to "light upon a wife," whose father, as she often told him, was a godly man: the young couple began housekeeping without so much as a dish or spoon; but Bunyan had his trade, and she brought for her portion two books which her father had left her at his death: *The Plain Man's Pathway to Heaven* was one; the other was Bayley, Bishop of Bangor's *Practice of Piety*. These books he sometimes read with her; and they begat in him some desire to reform his vicious life, and made him fall in eagerly with the religion of the times, go to church twice a-day with the foremost, and there devoutly say and sing as others did;—yet, according to his own account, retaining his wicked life. How he was first reclaimed through a Puritan sermon against Sabbath-breaking; how he joined a Baptist congregation in Bedford, and became its preacher; was next apprehended for holding "unlawful meetings and conventicles," and was imprisoned in Bedford gaol 12½ years; we have no space to tell. His library, while in prison, consisted but of two books—the Bible, which he read intently, and especially historically; and Fox's *Book of Martyrs*, which copy is now preserved in the Bedfordshire General Library. While in prison, he wrote several works, including *The Holy War*, and *Grace abounding to the Chief of Sinners*, a narrative of his own life and religious experience. But his chief work is *The Pilgrim's Progress from this World to that which is to Come*, which has been translated into most of the European languages.

If it is not a well of English undefiled to which the poet as well as the philologist must repair, if they would drink of the living waters, it is a clear stream of current English, the vernacular speech of his age, sometimes, indeed, in its rusticity and coarseness, but always in its plainness and its strength. To this natural style Bunyan is in some degree beholden for his general popularity; his language is everywhere level to the most ignorant reader, and to the meanest capacity: there is a homely reality about it; a nursery tale is not more intelligible, in its manner of narration to a child.—*Southey*.

ISAAC BARROW AT THE CHARTER-HOUSE.

Dr. Isaac Barrow, the eminent mathematician and divine, was born in 1630, in the city of London, where his father was linen-draper to Charles II. The young Barrow was first sent to the Charter-house, where he was only noted for his idleness and love of fighting; he was on this account removed to a school at Felstead, in Essex, where he abandoned his idle habits, and studied so successfully, that his master made him a sort of tutor to Lord Fairfax, of Ireland, then a boy in the same school. The fortunes of his family had now begun to suffer for their stanch adherence to the royal cause, and the young student must have given up his career of learning had not Dr. Hammond, Canon of Christchurch, given him the means of completing his education. He died 1677, aged 47.

Few persons ever attained such a deserved reputation in such various branches of science and learning, whose life was so short, as the celebrated Isaac Barrow. His sermons will remain specimens of profound erudition, of splendid eloquence, and of the manner in which a subject may be exhausted,—so long as the Church of England and the English language exist. For his mathematical proficiency he received the highest honors from the University of Cambridge; and he was elected to the mastership of Trinity in 1672. He was a great writer of poetry; and at one time studied anatomy, botany, and chemistry, with a view to the practice of physic.

DRYDEN AT WESTMINSTER AND OXFORD.

John Dryden (or Driden), one of the greatest masters of English verse, was born on the 9th of August, 1631, in the parsonage-house of Oldwincle All-Saints, Northamptonshire. The house is still standing, and a small apartment in it is still known as "Dryden's Room." He received the rudiments of his education at Tichmarsh, or at the neighboring grammar-school of Oundle. "We boast," says the inscription at Tichmarsh, on the monument erected by Dryden's relative (Mrs. Creed), "that he was bred and had his first learning here, where he has often made us happie by his kind visits and most delightful conversation." He was afterward admitted a King's scholar at Westminster School, under Dr. Busby, for whom he contracted a warm and lasting regard. He was not, however, indifferent to the Doctor's severity in the use of the rod; for the poet compares his over-correction of some verses to "our Master Busby," who "used to whip a boy so long till he made him a confirmed blockhead." Yet Dryden was so strongly impressed with Busby's high moral character and excellent system of tuition, that he placed two of his sons under him. The Doctor was the first to discover and encourage Dryden's poetical talent; but of his performance in this way when at Westminster, the only record we have is, that he translated the third Satire of Persius as a Thursday night's exercise.* Other pieces of a similar kind were produced, and remained in the hands of Dr. Busby, but were never recovered. Here also, while yet a King's scholar, in

---

* To the end of the third Satire of Persius, Dryden affixed the following note: "I remember I translated this satire when I was a King's scholar at Westminster School, for a Thursday night's exercise; and believe that it and many other of my exercises of this nature, in English verse, are still in the hands of my learned master, the Rev. Dr. Busby."

1649, Dryden wrote an *Elegy on the Death of Lord Hastings*, and some commendatory verses on the *Divine Epigrams* of his friend, John Hoddesdon, both of which were published in the following year.

In the library at Westminster School is a small portion of a form which bears, in upright letters, the name I DRYDEN, believed to have been cut by the boy-poet with a penknife: it is kept cased in glass, and is ornamented with gold and diamonds. There was also within the present century to be seen the poet's name written upon the wall of a room in the Manor House, Chiswick, which was frequently resorted to by Busby and his pupils. Dryden came up as a Westminster scholar to Trinity College, Cambridge, May 11, 1650. Of his career at College, almost the only notice in the archives is dated July 19, 1652: "put out of Commons for a fortnight at least," confined to the walls, and sentenced to read a confession of his crime at the fellows' table during dinner time—this offense being disobedience to the vice-master, and "contumacy in taking the punishment inflicted by him." He took his degree of Bachelor of Arts, and was made Master of Arts, but never became a Fellow of the College; and he always entertained feelings of aversion for Cambridge, which he did not hesitate to avow in the Prologues he wrote many years afterward for delivery at Oxford. Dryden has left these interesting memorials of his early studies:

"For my own part, who must confess it to my shame, that I never read anything but for pleasure, history has always been the most delightful entertainment of my life."—*Life of Plutarch*, 1683.

"I had read Polybius in English, with the pleasure of a boy, before I was ten years of age."—*Character of Polybius*, 1692.

Hence Dryden is concluded to have spent more time over Thucydides, Tacitus, and the rest of the Greek and Roman historians, than he gave up to the poets, ancient or modern. He cultivated slowly the poetical faculty; he was nearly thirty years of age before he published his poem on the death of Cromwell; and his early productions followed each other at long intervals. His *Essay on Dramatic Poesy*, elegantly written, is the earliest regular work of the kind in the language, and contains the manly avowal—the first after the Restoration—of the supremacy of Shakspeare. Dryden's language, like his thoughts, is truly English: his verse flows with natural freedom and magnificence; his satire is keen and trenchant; and the style of his prose is easy, natural, and graceful. He was made Poet-Laureate, but deprived of his office by the Revolution. "The prose of Dryden," says Sir Walter Scott, "may rank with the best in the English language. It is no less of his own formation than his versification; is equally spirited and equally harmonious."

PHILIP HENRY AT WESTMINSTER.

Philip Henry was born on St. Bartholomew's Day, 1631, at Whitehall, where his father was keeper of the orchard, and page of the back-stairs: in these situations he was much respected by Charles I., who remembered him in his sad hour of affliction, and on the way to his trial took an affecting leave of his old servant. Philip had for his sponsors the Earls of Pembroke and Carlisle, and the Countess of Salisbury; he became the playfellow of the young princes, and was kindly noticed by Laud, for whom, when he came to the palace, Philip used to open the water-gate. He was sent, first, to St. Martin's School; then to a school at Battersea; at 12 years old he was removed to Westminster, and placed in the fourth form; and was in due time admitted "Head into college." Busby soon took a great liking to the boy, and employed him, with other favorite scholars, in collecting materials for his Greek Grammar. Philip was early imbued with Puritanical principles by his mother, and with her used to attend all the lectures, which lasted sometimes from eight in the morning till four in the afternoon. Lord Pembroke still continued his patronage to him, and at his election gave him the means of defraying his first expenses at the University. Philip Henry ever retained a great affection for the University, as well as for the school in which he had been first taught; and was wont to allege as an excuse for having been less studious than he should have been, that, "coming from Westminster School, his attainments in school learning were beyond what others generally had that came from other schools, so that he was tempted to think there was no need to keep pace with others."

SIR CHRISTOPHER WREN AT WESTMINSTER AND OXFORD.

Thousands of the indwellers of the capital which Sir Christopher Wren has adorned with no fewer than forty public buildings, are, probably, unacquainted with the extent and variety of the abilities and acquirements of this great architect and excellent man. Seldom has the promise of youth been so well redeemed as in Wren. He was born in 1632, at East Knoyle, in Wiltshire, of which parish his father was then rector. He was a small and weakly child, whose rearing required much care. He was educated at home by his father and a private tutor, until he was placed under the special care of Dr. Busby, at Westminster School, having at the same time Dr. Holder as a mathematical tutor. Aubrey describes young Wren as "a youth of prodigious inventive wit," of whom Holder "was as tender as if he had been his own child, who gave him his first introductions into Geometry and Arithmetic; and when he was a young scholar at the University of Oxford, was a very necessary and kind friend." The first-fruits of young Wren's inventive faculty was put forth in 1645, in his thirteenth year, by the production of a new astronomical instrument, which he dedicated to his father, with a dutiful Latin address, and eighteen hexameter verses. This invention was followed up by an exercise in physics, on the origin of rivers, and by the invention of a pneumatic engine, and a peculiar instrument in gnomonics. His mind ripened early into maturity and strength; he loved the classics; but mathematics and astronomy were from the first his favorite pursuits.

In his fourteenth year, Wren was admitted as a gentleman-commoner at Wadham College, Oxford, where, by his acquirements and inventions, he gained the friendship of Dr. Wilkins, Seth Ward (Bishop of Salisbury), Hooke, whom he assisted in his *Micrographia*, and other eminent scientific men, whose meetings laid the foundation of the Royal Society. In his fifteenth year, he translated Oughtred's Geometrical Dialing into Latin; and about this time he made a reflecting dial for the ceiling of a room, embellished with figures representing astronomy and geometry, with their attributes, tastefully drawn with a pen. He next took out a patent for an instrument to write with two pens at the same time; and he invented a weather-clock, and an instrument wherewith to write in the dark.

In 1654, Evelyn visited Oxford, and went to All-Souls, where he says, "I saw that miracle of a youth, Christopher Wren." He ranked high in his knowledge of anatomical science; he made the drawings for Dr. Wilkins's Treatise on the Brain; and he was the originator of the physiological experiment of injecting various liquors into the veins of living animals. In 1653, he was elected a Fellow of All-Souls; and by the time that he had attained his twenty-fourth year, his name had gone over Europe, and he was considered as one of that band of eminent men whose discoveries were raising the fame of English science. In 1657, he was appointed Professor of Astronomy at Gresham College; three years later, Savilian Professor at Oxford; and received the degree of D.C.L. in 1661. It was after delivering his lecture on Astronomy at Gresham College, on Nov. 28, 1660, that the foundation of the Royal Society was discussed; and its archives bear the amplest testimony to his knowledge and industry, as exhibited in his commentaries on almost every subject connected with science and art. His inventions and discoveries alone are said to amount to fifty-three.

Wren's scientific reputation probably led to his being, in 1661, appointed assistant to Sir John Denham, the Surveyor-General; and in 1663, he was commissioned to survey and report upon St. Paul's Cathedral, with a view to its restoration, or rather, the rebuilding of the body of the fabric. The Great Fire decided the long-debated question whether there should be a new cathedral. He was the worst paid architect of whom we have any record: his salary as architect of St. Paul's was only 200*l.* a year; his pay for rebuilding the churches in the city was only 100*l.* a year; and it is related that on his completion of the beautiful church of St. Stephen, Walbrook, the parishoners presented his wife with 20 guineas!

With all these architectural pursuits, Wren found time to preside at the Royal Society, and take part in experiments: many great men have shed luster upon its chair; few to a greater degree than Sir Christopher Wren.*

DR. SOUTH AT WESTMINSTER.

This celebrated wit and eminent preacher, who has been aptly denominated "the scourge of fanaticism," was born at Hackney in 1633, and was sent early to Westminster School. Here his master, Busby, said of him, with his characteristic penetration, "I see great talents in that sulky boy, and I shall endeavor to bring them out;" a work which he accomplished by severe discipline. When reader of the Latin prayers for the morning, South publicly prayed for King Charles the First by name "but an hour or two at most before his sacred head was cut off."

In his Sermon "prepared for delivery at a solemn meeting of his school-fellows in the Abbey," South, with pride and satisfaction, paid this tribute to his place of early education:

Westminster is a school which neither disposes men to division in Church, nor sedition in State,—a school so untaintedly loyal that I can truly and knowingly aver that, in the worst of times (in which it was my lot to be a member of it) we really were King's Scholars, as well as called so. And this loyal genius always continued amongst us, and grew up with us, which made that noted Coryphæus (D. J. Owen) often say, " that it would never be well with the nation until this school was suppressed."

After South's election to Christchurch, Oxford, he distinguished himself by his classical attainments, and composed an elegant Latin poem addressed to Cromwell, on the conclusion of the Dutch war: for this he was strongly censured, but he, probably, regarded his verses as a college exercise. He was ordained in 1659; and in 1661, was made chaplain to the great

* Weld's History of the Royal Society, vol. I.

Lord Clarendon, whose notice he had attracted by a speech delivered at his investiture as Chancellor of the University.

The sermons of this great man are the most enduring monuments of his wit and learning. Their effect is abundantly evidenced in No. 125 (by Addison) of the *Guardian;* and No. 205 (by Fuller) of the *Tatler;* and in No 6 (by Steele) of the latter, allusion is made to his virtuous life, and constant attendance on public worship.

South died in 1716, aged 82. His remains lay for four days in the Jerusalem Chamber, and were carried thence into the College Hall; they were attended to his grave in the Abbey by the prebendaries, masters, and scholars, and all in any way connected with the royal foundation.

When South's remains lay in the College Hall, Barber, then Captain of the School, spoke a Latin oration over the body before it was interred in Westminster Abbey. This was the oration, for the unlicensed printing of which Curll received his well-known castigation from the Westminster boys, thus related in a letter of the time:—"Being fortunately nabbed within the limits of Dean's Yard by the king's scholars, there he met with a college salutation: for he was first presented with the ceremony of the blanket, in which, when the skeleton had been well shook, he was carried in triumph to the school; and before receiving a grammatical correction for his false concords, he was reconducted to Dean's Yard, and on his knees asking pardon of the aforesaid Mr. Barber for his offense, he was kicked out of the Yard, and left to the huzzas of the rabble."

There is a print, in three compartments, representing the three separate punishments which Curll underwent.

BISHOP KEN AT WINCHESTER.

When the Wykehamists held their 450th anniversary of the opening of Winchester College in 1846, Ken was commemorated in the following lines:

> "In these cloisters holy Ken strengthened with deeper prayer
> His own and his dear scholars' souls to what pure souls should dare;
> Bold to rebuke enthroned sin, with calm undazzled faith,
> Whether amid the pomp of courts, or on the bed of death;
> Firm against kingly terror in his free country's cause,
> Faithful to God's anointed against a world's applause."

Thomas Ken, son of an attorney of Furnival's Inn, Holborn, was born at Little Berkhampstead, in Hertfordshire, in the year 1637. Where he received his first education is not known; nor by whose recommendation he became a scholar on William of Wykeham's college at Winchester. Ken had a musical voice, which had no small recommendation for admission to all ancient ecclesiastical establishments, from their foundation; for, in after life, it is known that no day passed without his singing to his lute his evening and morning hymn, the origin of those beautiful morning and evening hymns sung at this day by the children of every parish. The Rev. W. Lisle Bowles thus sketches his fellow-Wykehamite at Winchester:

At the age of thirteen, the scholastic novitiate at Winchester is probably placed in the form called Junior part of Fifth; and is become, with a band, and black dangling gown, a Junior of Fifth or Sixth Chamber.

As junior, he is up before the other boys of the same chamber. In the glimmering and cold wintry mornings, he would perhaps repeat to himself — watching the slow morning through the grated window — one of the beautiful ancient hymns composed for the scholars on the foundation:

> Jam lucis ordo sydere
> Deum precemur supplices,
> Ut in diurnis actibus,
> Nos servet a nocentibus.

> Now the star of morning light
> Rises on the rear of night;
> Suppliant to our God we pray,
> From ills to guard us through this day.

Rising before the others, he had little to do except to apply a candle to a large fagot, in winter, which had been already laid.

On the fifth or sixth day, our junior is at ease among his companions of the same age: he is found, for the first time, attempting to wield a cricket-bat; and when his hour of play is over, he plies at his *scob*,* the labors of his silent lesson, or sits scanning his "nonsense" verses, which, nonsense as they have been called, have led the way to form the most accurate and elegant scholars, however such rudiments may be derided.

Here cares are soon at an end; the holidays are approaching; and who more blithely than Ken, with his musical voice, can sing the old Wykehamical canticle, *Dulce Domum*, from its style judged to have been written before the Reformation.

Now every boy pants for Whitsuntide, when is sung in choral glee —

> Musa, *libros* mitte, fessa,
> Mitte, *pensa dura*.

Till that day arrives, after the "pensa dura" of four days, the whole train of youthful scholars is seen streaming twice a week, by the side of the station, toward Catharine-hill, a large, round, conical hill, front in the Downs; a scene, since the foundation of the school, dedicated to youthful recreation and short oblivion of school cares.

Ken left Winchester College for Oxford a super-annuate between eighteen and nineteen years of age, 1655–6. As there was no vacancy at New College, he was entered at Hart-hall, afterward Hertford College; but in 1657, he was admitted Probationer Fellow of New College. The Puritans were then in full sway, and Ken did not take his first degree of Bachelor of Arts till 1661; he soon after entered into Orders; and at the proper age commencing Master of Arts, may have employed his time as tutor of the younger members of the college, where, to this day, is pointed out the room in which Ken read and wrote, and accompanied his morning and evening hymn with his lute.

In 1666, Ken being elected Fellow of Winchester, returned

---

* An oaken box, which contains his few books. On each side are places for pens and ink. The outer cover is placed open. The depository of books has another cover, on which the young scholar writes his task, or reads his lesson.

thither; and in 1669, he was promoted to a prebendal stall in Winchester Cathedral, through the influence of his brother-in-law, Izaak Walton, with Morley, Bishop of Winchester. He now composed his devotional Manual for the use of the Winchester scholars; but his most interesting compositions are those affecting and beautiful hymns which were sung by himself, and written to be sung in the chambers of the boys, before chapel in the morning, and before they lay down on their small boarded beds at night. Of Ken's own custom of singing his hymn to the Creator at the earliest dawn, Hawkins, his biographer, relates, "that neither his (Ken's) study might be the aggressor on his hours of instruction, or what he judged duty prevent his improvement, he strictly accustomed himself to but one hour's sleep, which obliged him to rise at one or two o'clock in the morning, or sometimes earlier; and he seemed to go to rest with no other purpose than the refreshing and enabling him with more vigor and cheerfulness to sing his Morning Hymn, as he used to do, to his lute, before he put on his clothes." When he composed those delicious hymns, he was in the fresh morn of life; and who does not feel his heart in unison with that delightful season, when such a strain as this is heard?—

> "Awake, my soul, and with the sun,
> Thy daily stage of duty run;
> Shake off dull sloth, and early rise,
> To pay thy morning sacrifice.
> * * * * * *
> Lord, I my vows to thee renew;
> Disperse my sins as morning dew."

May we not also say that when the Evening Hymn is heard, like the sounds that bid farewell to evening's parting plain, it fills the silent heart with devotion and repose:

> "All praise to thee, my God, this night,
> For all the blessings of the light;
> Keep me, oh! keep me, King of Kings,
> Under thine own Almighty wings.
>
> Forgive me, Lord, for thy dear Son,
> The ills that I this day have done;
> That with the world, myself, and Thee,
> I, ere I sleep, at peace may be."

Ken was, for his faithful discharge of duty, appointed by Charles, Bishop of Bath and Wells. He was earnest and unwearied: he established many schools, and wrote his "Exposition of the Church Catechism" for their use. He was an eloquent and industrious preacher, and James II. said he was the best among the Protestants. He was one of the Seven Bishops committed to the Tower for refusing to read James's declaration in favor of Romanism; and he was suspended and deprived by

William III. for refusing to take the oath of allegiance. But he found an asylum in Lord Weymouth's mansion of Longleat, and here he walked, and read, and hymned, and prayed, and slept to do the same again. The only property he brought from Wells palace was his library, part of which is still preserved at Longleat. In an upper chamber he composed most of his poems of fervid piety. He died in 1711, in his 74th year, and was carried to his grave, in Frome churchyard, by six of the poorest men of the parish, and buried under the eastern window of the church, at *sunrise*, in reference to the words of his Morning Hymn:

"Awake, my soul, and *with the sun.*"

The same words are sung, to the same tune, every Sunday, by the parish children, in the parish church of Frome, and over his grave who composed the words, who sung them himself, to the same air, 187 years ago: yet, Ken sleeps in the churchyard without an inscription or name!

SIR DUDLEY NORTH — HOW HE MADE UP FOR HIS DULLNESS AT SCHOOL.

The history and habits of this remarkable man strongly exemplify the successful pursuit of business and philosophy in one individual.

Sir Dudley North was born in 1641, and having been placed at Bury, to learn Latin, "he made but an indifferent scholar," partly through the severity of his master, who used "to correct him at all turns, with or without a fault," till he was driven almost to despair; and partly to his having "too much spirit, which could not be suppressed by conning his book, but must be rather employed in regular action." It was this "backwardness in school," his brother, Roger North, thinks, "that probably determined his destination." "But the young man himself," he adds, "had a strange bent to traffic, and, while he was at school, drove a subtle trade among the boys by buying and selling. In short, it was considered that he had learning enough for a merchant, but not phlegm enough for any sedentary profession." He was next sent to a writing and arithmetic school for some time, and then bound by his father, Lord North, to a Turkey merchant. Dudley had, however, much time on his hands, and he "took a fancy to the binding of books; and having procured a stitching-board, press, and cutter, fell to work, and bound up books of account for himself, and divers for his friends, in a very decent manner. He had a distinguishing genius toward all sorts of mechanic exercises."

After some time, he was sent out by his master as supercargo, with an adventure to Archangel, where he was to ship another cargo for Smyrna, and then to take up his residence in the latter place as factor. In this trading voyage he had an eye for everything worth observing, and kept a regular journal of all that he saw and befell him, which he transmitted to London, in letters, to his elder brother, Francis, afterward Lord Keeper Guildford. But North greatly complained of the idleness in which he was obliged to pass his time. Having, on his return from Archangel, been detained for some time at Leghorn, he visited Florence, fifty-five miles off, and there and at Leghorn acquired some knowledge of Italian. "The language," he remarks, "is not difficult; and I find the little Latin I have to be an extraordinary help in attaining it."

He began business at Smyrna, and thence removed to Constantinople, where, by industry and perseverance, he became a wealthy man; still showing the same inquisitiveness and love of knowledge, the same activity, and capacity of overcoming difficulties, which had characterized him from his boyhood. He not only made himself master of the political constitution and statistics of the country, but even acquired such skill in the Turkish law, that he tried in the Turkish courts above 500 causes without employing interpreters, but speaking for himself. He spoke the Turkish language fluently, wrote it well, and composed a Turkish dictionary; and "no Frank ever spoke the vulgar idiom so correct and perfect as he did." Upon his return to England, he settled as a merchant in London, and became a member of Parliament, a Commissioner of Customs, and then a Lord of the Treasury. Before this he had learned Algebra, "a new kind of arithmetic, which he had never heard of before."

After the Revolution, he retired from public life, returned to business, and once more withdrew. He then employed himself in illustrating mechanic powers, which he sought among the engines, tackle, etc., used in building St. Paul's Cathedral; Sir Christopher Wren often giving replies to his inquiries. In his leisure, Dudley read such books as pleased him: and (though he was a kind of dunce at school) he now recovered so much Latin as to make him take pleasure in the best classics.

One of North's favorite recreations was swimming in the Thames. "He could," says his brother, "live in the water an afternoon with as much ease as others walk upon land. He shot the bridge (old London bridge) divers times at low water, which showed him not only active, but intrepid; for courage is required to bear the very sight of that tremendous cascade, which few can endure to pass in a boat."

NEWTON AT GRANTHAM AND CAMBRIDGE.

The childhood and education of that master-mind which, by the establishment of the theory of Gravitation, "immortalized his name, and perpetuated the intellectual glory of his country," next demand our attention. Isaac Newton was born in 1642, in the manor-house of Woolsthorpe, close to the village of Colsterworth, about six miles south of Grantham, in Lincolnshire. He was a posthumous child, and was of such a diminutive size when born, that he might have been put into a quart mug. At the usual age he was sent to two small day-schools at Skillington and Stoke, two hamlets near Woolsthorpe, and here he was taught reading, writing, and arithmetic. At the age of twelve he was sent to the grammar-school at Grantham. According to his own confession, Newton was extremely inattentive to his studies, and stood very low in the school. When he was last in the lowermost form but one, the boy above him, as they were going to school, kicked him on the stomach; Newton subsequently challenged the boy to fight, the combat took place in the church-yard, and Newton was the victor; his antagonist still stood above him in the form, until, after many a severe struggle, Newton not only gained the individual victory, but rose to the highest place in the school.

Newton had not long been at school before he exhibited a taste for mechanical inventions. With the aid of little saws, hammers, hatchets, and other tools, during his play-hours, he constructed models of known machines and amusing contrivances; as a windmill, a water-clock, and a carriage, to be moved by the person who sat in it; and by watching the workmen in erecting a windmill near Grantham, Newton acquired such knowledge of its mechanism, that he completed a large working model of it, which was frequently placed upon the top of the house in which Newton lived at Grantham, and was put in motion by the action of the wind upon its sails. Although Newton was at this time a "sober, silent, and thinking lad," who never took part in the games of his school-fellows, but employed all his leisure hours in "knocking and hammering in his lodging-room," yet he occasionally taught the boys to "play philosophically." He introduced the flying of paper kites, and is said to have investigated their best forms and proportions, as well as the number and position of the points to which the string should be attached. He constructed also lanterns of "crimpled paper," in which he placed a candle to light him to school in the dark winter mornings; and in dark nights he tied them to the tails of his kites, which the terrified country-people took for comets. Meanwhile, in the yard of the house where he lived, Newton was frequently observed to watch the motion of the sun; he drove wooden pegs into the walls and roofs of the buildings, as gnomons, to mark by their shadows the hours and half-hours of the day. It does not appear that he knew how to adjust these lines to the latitude of Grantham; but he is said to have succeeded, after some years' observation, in making them so exact, that anybody could tell what o'clock it was by *Isaac's Dial*, as it was called; and, probably, about this time, he carved two dials on the walls of his own house at Woolsthorpe, one of which is now in the museum of the Royal Society. Newton also became expert with his pencil: his room was furnished with pictures, drawn, some from prints, and others from life, in frames made by himself: among the portraits were several of the King's heads; Dr. Donne; Mr. Stokes, his teacher at Grantham; and King Charles I.; also, drawings of "birds, beasts, men, ships, and mathematical diagrams, executed with charcoal on the wall, which remained till the house was pulled down in 1711." Although Newton stated that he "excelled particularly in making verses," no authentic specimen of his poetry has been preserved; and in later years, he often expressed a dislike for poetry. During the seven years which he spent at Grantham, to the society of his school-fellows he preferred that of the young ladies who lived in the same house, and he often made little tables, cupboards, etc., for them to set their dolls and their trinkets upon. One of these ladies, when she had reached the age of 82, confessed that Newton had been in love with her, but that smallness of income prevented their marriage.

When Newton had reached his fifteenth year, he was recalled from the school at Grantham to take charge of his mother's farm: he was thus frequently sent to Grantham market, to dispose of grain and other agricultural produce, which, however, he generally left to an old farm servant who accompanied him, and Newton made his way to the garret of the house where he had lived to amuse himself with a parcel of old books left there; and afterward he would intrench himself on the wayside between Woolsthorpe and Grantham, devouring some favorite author till his companion's return from market. And when his mother sent him into the fields to watch the sheep and cattle, he would perch himself under a tree with a book in his hand, or shaping models with his knife, or watching the movements of an undershot water-wheel. One of the earliest scientific experiments which Newton made was in 1658, on the day of the great storm, when Cromwell died, and when he himself had just entered his 16th year.

Newton's mother was now convinced that her son was not

destined to be a farmer; and this, with his uncle finding him under a hedge, occupied in the solution of a mathematical problem, led to his being again sent to Grantham School, and then to Trinity College, Cambridge, which thence became the real birthplace of Newton's genius. We have not space to detail how he mastered Sanderson's Logic, and Kepler's Optics, before he attended his tutor's lectures upon those works; how he bought a book of Judicial Astrology at Stourbridge Fair, and to understand its trigonometry, purchased an English Euclid, which he soon threw aside for Descartes' Geometry; his long-continued observations upon a comet in 1664; his first discovery of Fluxions in 1665; his first study of Gravity, suggested to him by the fall of an apple from a tree while sitting in his garden at Woolsthorpe; his purchase of a glass prism at Stourbridge Fair; his first application to optical discoveries; his construction of telescopes,* etc. But we cannot leave him without remarking that late in life, ascribing whatever he had accomplished to the effect of patient and continuous thought rather than to any peculiar genius with which nature had endowed him, he looked upon himself and his labors in a very different light from that in which both he and they were regarded by mankind. "I know not," he remarked, a short time before his death, "what I may appear to the world; but to myself I seem to have been only like a boy playing on the sea-shore, and diverting myself in now and then finding a smoother pebble or a prettier shell than ordinary, whilst the great ocean of truth lay all undiscovered before me." How touching is this sense of humility, and contrast of the littleness of human knowledge with the extent of human ignorance!

WILLIAM PENN AT OXFORD.

William Penn, whose name has become "throughout all civilized countries a synonyme for polity and philanthropy," was born October 14, 1644. He grew up into a graceful and promising child at Wanstead, in Essex, and was sent to learn the first rudiments of scholarship at a grammar-school at Chigwell, then recently founded by the Archbishop of York. When he was eleven years old, his father, Admiral Penn, was arrested by order of Cromwell for his alleged share in the failure of an attack on Hispaniola; and young Penn, "a quick-witted and affectionate child, was overwhelmed with melancholy" at his father's arrest. "While in this state of mind, he was one day surprised in his room, where he was alone, with an inward

---

* These particulars of Newton's early years have been abridged from Sir David Brewster's enlarged Life of the great philosopher.

and sudden sense of happiness, akin to a strong religious emotion; the chamber at the same time appearing as if filled with a soft and holy light." This incident has been regarded by some as a miracle,—by others as a delusion; but Mr. Hepworth Dixon, the earnest biographer of Penn, considers the lively and sensitive child being in a morbid condition of mind, and his father being in a few days set at liberty, "it is probable that the glory which filled the room and the feeling which suffused his frame were simply the effects of a sensitive temperament over-excited by the glad tidings of this release." His father then retired with his family into Ireland, where William "rapidly improved, under a private tutor from England, in useful and elegant scholarship. He exhibited already a rare aptitude for business. In person he was tall and slender, but his limbs were well knit, and he had a passionate fondness for field sports, boating, and other manly exercises. In the elementary parts of education he had already made such progress that the Admiral thought him ready to begin his more serious studies at the University; and, after due consideration, it was resolved that he should go to Oxford." After a year's delay, to Oxford he went, where he matriculated as a gentleman commoner at Christchurch, of which Dr. John Owen was Dean: South was Orator to the University; and here were Wilmot, Earl of Rochester, and "the noblest and most notable of all ornaments of Oxford at that day"—John Locke. Penn proved at college a hard student, a skillful boater, and adventurous sportsman; his reading was solid and extensive, and his memory excellent. His great pleasure and recreation while at Christchurch was in reading the doctrinal discussions to which the Puritan idea had given rise; and the preaching of the new doctrines taught by George Fox, and the threatened restoration of popish usages, led Penn and others into forcible opposition to the orders of the Court, for which they were expelled the University. For a boy, he left Oxford with a profound acquaintance with history and theology. Of languages he had more than an ordinary share. Then, and afterward, while at Saumur, (in France), he read the chief writers of Greece and Italy in their native idioms, and acquired a thorough knowledge of French, German, Dutch, and Italian. Later in life he added to his stock two or three dialects of the Red Men. Upon his return to England, Penn's father entered him as a student at Lincoln's Inn, that he might acquire some knowledge of his country's laws. He did not remain long in London, but returned to Ireland; and at Cork, hearing an old Oxford acquaintance preach the doctrines of George Fox, from that night Penn became a Quaker in his heart.

THE GREAT DUKE OF MARLBOROUGH AT ST. PAUL'S.

Among the celebrated Paulines stands prominently the name of John Churchill, Duke of Marlborough, the ablest general and most consummate statesman of his time. He was the second son of Winston Churchill, and was born at Ashe House,* in the parish of Musbury, adjoining Axeminster, Devonshire, in 1650. Part of the "antient and gentile" seat remains; and the bedstead upon which Marlborough was born is preserved in the neighborhood.

"Of the education of a person afterward so illustrious," says Coxe, "we only know that he was brought up under the care of his father, who was himself a man of letters, and author of a political history of England, entitled *Divi Britannici*. He was also instructed in the rudiments of knowledge by a neighboring clergyman of great learning and piety; and from him, doubtless, imbibed that due sense of religion, and zealous attachment to the Church of England, which were never obliterated amidst the dissipation of a court, the cares of political business, or the din of arms."

He was next removed to the metropolis, and placed in the school of St. Paul's, but for a short period. This fact is thrice mentioned in the Life of Dean Colet, the founder of the school, by Dr. Knight, who had been himself a scholar, and published his work soon after the death of Marlborough. He is said to have imbibed his passion for a military life from the reading of *Vegetius de re Militari*, which was then in the school library. The anecdote is thus recorded by the Rev. George North, rector of Colyton, in his copy of Vegetius, presented to the Bodleian Library by the late Mr. Gough:

"From this very book, John Churchill, scholar of this school, afterward the celebrated Duke of Marlborough, first learnt the elements of the art of war, as was told to me, George North, on St Paul's Day, 1724-25, by an old clergyman, who said he was a cotemporary scholar, was then well acquainted with him, and frequently saw him read it. This I testify to be true. G. NORTH."

This tradition is, however, not thought very probable, Vegetius being a difficult book for a boy to read at so early an age, particularly as we can trace no indication that Marlborough possessed such an intimate acquaintance with the Latin tongue as the study of this author must have required. The restless curiosity of youth might, however, have prompted him to look into this book, which contains some amusing prints, not unlikely to attract his attention.†

* A view of Ashe House forms one of the illustrations to Pulman's *Book of the Axe*, a very intelligent and agreeable companion to that far-famed stream.

† Note to Coxe's Life, by John Wade. Bohn's Edit. 1847.

Notwithstanding he remained but a short time at St. Paul's, he gave early indications of spirit and intelligence. He was appointed page of honor to the Duke of York, who asking Churchill what profession he preferred, and in what manner he should provide for him, the youth threw himself upon his knees, and warmly petitioned that he might be appointed to a pair of colors in one of those fine regiments whose discipline he had admired. The request was graciously received: the youth was gratified with the colors, and thus was opened to "the handsome young Englishman" a career of military renown, which may almost be said to have commenced with his first campaign.

MATTHEW PRIOR AT WESTMINSTER.

This celebrated poet was born about 1666, at Wimborne Minster, Dorset: his parents died when he was very young, and he was intrusted to the care of his uncle, Samuel Prior, who kept "the Rummer" tavern, between Whitehall and Charing Cross. At his uncle's charge, Matthew was sent to Westminster School; but from his lines to Fleetwood Shepheard, the future poet assisted his uncle in his business:

> My uncle, rest his soul, when living,
> Might have contriv'd me ways of thriving:
> Taught me with cider to replenish
> My vats, or ebbing tide of Rhenish.
> So when for hock I drew prickt white-wine,
> Swear't had the flavor, and was white-wine.

Tradition relates that the boy was found in his uncle's tavern by the Earl of Dorset, in the act of reading Horace. The Earl sent the lad to St. John's College, Cambridge, where he was admitted in 1683, and was next day appointed a scholar of that house, on the Duchess of Somerset's foundation, by her own nomination. In that year he contributed some verses to the academical congratulations on the marriage of the Princess Anne with Prince George of Denmark. In 1686, he took his degree of B.A., and was chosen fellow of his college; and in 1688, he wrote the Ode to the Deity for a college exercise. In the same year, he and Charles Montague produced "The City Mouse and the Country Mouse;" and with his associate in that composition, Prior left Cambridge, and came up to London to seek his fortune. Late in life he collected his poems, which he published with a dedication to the Duke of Dorset, in gratitude to the memory of that nobleman's father — to whose timely munificence he was indebted for the completion of his education.

ADDISON AT LICHFIELD, CHARTER-HOUSE, AND OXFORD.

Joseph Addison, one of our greatest writers in prose, was educated with great care. He was born at Milston, Wilts, May 1, 1672, of which place his father was rector, and a man of considerable learning. He sent young Joseph to the school of the Rev. Mr. Naish, at Ambresbury; but he was soon removed to Salisbury, under the care of Mr. Taylor; and thence to the grammar-school at Lichfield, in his 12th year. Dr. Johnson relates a story of Addison being here a ringleader in a *barring out;* which was told to Johnson, when he was a boy, by Andrew Corbett, of Shropshire, who had it from Mr. Pigot, his uncle, Addison's school-fellow. There is also a tradition that Addison ran away from school, and hid himself in a wood, where he fed on berries, and slept in a hollow tree, till after a long search he was discovered and brought home. From Lichfield, Addison was removed to the Charter-house, under Dr. Ellis, where he first became acquainted with his afterward celebrated friend Steele. At 15, he was not only fit for the university, but carried thither a classical taste and a stock of learning which would have done honor to a Master of Arts. He was entered at Queen's College, Oxford; but, in a few months, some of his Latin verses falling by accident into the hands of Dr. Lancaster, Dean of Magdalen College, he was so pleased with their diction and versification, that he procured for young Addison admittance to Magdalen, where he resided during ten years. A warm admirer says: "There is no passing through the cloisters of Magdalen College, Oxford, without casting an eye up to the study-window of Mr. Addison, from whence his genius first displayed itself."

"Addison was, at first, one of those scholars who are called Demies, but was subsequently elected a fellow. His college is still proud of his name; his portrait hangs in the hall; and strangers are still told that his favorite walk was under the elms which fringe the meadow on the banks of the Cherwell. It is said, and is highly probable, that he was distinguished among his fellow-students by the delicacy of his feelings, by the dryness of his manners, and by the assiduity with which he often prolonged his studies far into the night. It is certain that his reputation for ability and learning stood high. Many years later, the ancient Doctors of Magdalen continued to talk in the common room of his boyish compositions, and expressed their sorrow that no copy of exercises so remarkable had been preserved."

Lord Macaulay, from whose review of Addison's Life and Writings we quote the above passage, considers his knowledge of the Latin poets, from Lucretius and Catullus down to Claudius and Prudentius, to have been singularly exact and profound, but his knowledge of other provinces of ancient literature slight. "He does not appear to have attained more than an ordinary acquaintance with the political and moral writers of Rome, nor was his own Latin prose by any means equal to his Latin verse.

His knowledge of Greek, though doubtless such as was, in his time, thought respectable at Oxford, was evidently less than that which many lads now carry away every year from Eton and Rugby." Yet he was an accomplished scholar, and a master of pure English eloquence; and a consummate painter of life and manners; and in his *Tatlers, Spectators,* and *Guardians,* he laid the foundation of a new school of popular writing.

DR. ISAAC WATTS—HIS SCHOOLS, AND EDUCATIONAL WORKS.

Watts has been with propriety styled a classic of the people. His hymns for children have exercised an influence on the minds of the young far beyond the Dissenting body, for whom they were written. His verse is generally smooth, sometimes nervous; and the matter is always judicious, sometimes touching, sometimes approaching to eloquence. His "Logic" was once a text-book at Oxford. He was an efficient promoter of charity-schools; and he wrote many books of education, from the simple hymns for children to works upon abstract subjects.

He was born at Southampton in 1674, where his father, who was a man of strong devotional feeling, and a rigid nonconformist, kept a boarding-school. He was imprisoned on account of his religion, and during his confinement his wife sat on a stone at the prison-door, with little Isaac, then an infant, at her breast. The child showed a taste for books at a very early age: he was taught the learned languages in the free grammar-school of Southampton in his fourth year. The little money he received in presents he spent upon books; and his leisure hours he passed in reading, instead of joining the other boys at play. When only seven or eight years old, he composed some devotional pieces to please his mother. His gentle yet vivacious disposition obtained him friends, who offered to support him at one of the universities; but having been bred a nonconformist, he determined to remain one. He was, therefore, sent in his sixteenth year to an academy in London, at that time kept by Mr. Thomas Rowe, minister of an Independent meeting-house at Haberdashers' Hall. He remained here three years, pursuing his studies with intemperate ardor, allowing himself no time for exercise, and curtailing the period usually allotted to sleep. He thus irremediably injured his constitution. He used to mark all the books he read, to abridge some of them, and annotate others, which were interleaved for the purpose. Dr. Johnson says of his classical acquirements:—"Some Latin essays, supposed to have been written as exercises at his academy, show a degree of knowledge, both philosophical and theological, such as very few attain by a much longer course of study;" and, "in his youth he appears to have paid attention to Latin poetry: his verses to his brother in the glyconic measure, written when he was seventeen, are remarkably easy and elegant." He also made some proficiency in the study of Hebrew, of logic, and scholastic divinity. His acquirements in mathematical and physical science appear to have been inconsiderable. Mr. Rowe was accustomed to say that he never had occasion to reprove Watts, and he often held him up as a pattern to his other pupils.

Watts returned to his father's house in 1694, and spent the next two years of his life in private study. Probably most of his juvenile works were composed during this time. No compositions of the kind have obtained such extensive use as his *Hymns and Songs for Children*. Doddridge relates, in a letter to Watts, an affecting incident regarding one of his Hymns:

> I was preaching to a large assembly of plain country-people at a village, when, after a sermon from Hebrews vi. 12, we sung one of your hymns (which, if I remember right, was the 140th of the second book), and at that part of the worship I had the satisfaction to observe tears in the eyes of several people; after the service was over, some of them told me they were not able to sing, so deeply were their minds affected; and the clerk, in particular, said he could hardly utter the words as he gave them out.

The Hon. Mrs. Norton thus touchingly apostrophizes the memory of this excellent man;

> Oh, Watts! gentle-hearted old man! Did you ever foresee the universal interest which would link itself to your name among the innocent hearts of earth? Did angels reveal to you in your death-hour, how many a dying child would murmur your pleasant hymns as its farewell to earth? how many living creatures repeat them as their most familiar notions of prayer? Did you foresee that in your native land, and wherever its language is spoken, the purer and least sinful portion of the ever-drifting generations would be trained with your words? And now, in that better world of glory, do the souls of young children crowd round you? Do you hold sweet converse with those who, perhaps, were first let into the track of glory by the faint light which the spark of your soul left on earth? Do they recognize you, the souls of our departed little ones—souls of the children of the long ago dead—souls of the children of the living—lost and lamented, and then fading from memory like sweet dreams? It may be so; and that when the great responsible gift of authorship is accounted for, your crown will be brighter than that bestowed upon philosophers and sages!

POPE'S SCHOOLS AND SELF-TUITION.

Alexander Pope has been ably characterized by his latest biographer* to have followed closely and reverently in the footsteps of Dryden, "copying his subjects, his manner and versification, and adding to them original powers of wit, fancy, and tenderness, and a brilliancy, condensation, and correctness which even his master did not reach, and which still remain unsurpassed."

Pope was born in London, in the memorable year of the Revolution, 1688. His father carried on the business of a linen-merchant in Lombard-street: he was "an honest merchant, and dealt in Hollands wholesale," as his widow informed Mr.

* Mr. Robert Carruthers, in his Life of Pope. 2nd edit. 1857.

Spence. The elder Pope was a Roman Catholic, and having been successful in business, when the Revolution endangered the lives and property of the sect to which he belonged, he withdrew from trade and the city, first to Kensington, and afterward to Binfield, a skirt of Windsor Forest. The Pope dwelling, a little low house, has been transformed into a villa; but the poet's study has been preserved, with a cypress-tree on the lawn, said to have been planted by him.

"From his infancy, Pope was considered a prodigy," says Mr. Carruthers. "He had inherited from his father a crooked body, and from his mother a sickly constitution, perpetually subject to severe headaches; hence great care and tenderness were required in his nurture. His faithful nurse, Mary Beach, lived to see him a great man; and when she died, in 1725, the poet erected a stone over her grave at Twickenham, to tell that Alexander Pope, whom she nursed in infancy, and affectionately attended for twenty-eight years, was grateful for her services. He had nearly lost his life when a child, from a wild cow, that threw him down, and with her horns wounded him in the throat. He charmed all the household by his gentleness and sensibility, and in consequence of the sweetness of his voice was called 'the Little Nightingale.' He was taught his letters by an old aunt, and he taught himself to write by copying from printed books. This art he retained through life, and often practiced with singular neatness and proficiency. . . . . His letters to Henry Cromwell (the originals of which still exist), his letters to ladies, and his inscriptions in books presented to his friends, are specimens of fine, clear, and scholar-like penmanship."

In his eighth year Pope was put under the tuition of the family priest, who taught him the accidence and first parts of grammar, by adopting the measure followed in the Jesuits' schools of teaching the rudiments of Latin and Greek together. He then attended two little schools, at which he learned nothing. The first of these, Mr. Carruthers considers to have been the Roman Catholic seminary, at Twyford, on the river Loddon, near Binfield: here "he wrote a lampoon upon his master for some faults he had discovered in him, so early had he assumed the characters of critic and satirist!" He was flogged for the offense, and his indulgent father removed him to a school kept by a Roman Catholic convert named Deane, who had a school, first, in Marylebone, and afterward at Hyde Park Corner, at both which places Pope was under his charge.

"I began writing verses of my own invention," he says, "farther back than I can well remember." Ogilby's translation of H mer was one of the first large poems he read, and, in after-life, he spoke of the rapture it afforded him. "I was then about eight years old. This led me to Sandy's Ovid, which I liked extremely, and so I did a translation of a part of Statius by some very bad hand. When I was about twelve I wrote a kind of play, which I got to be acted by my school-fellows. It was a number of speeches from the Iliad, tacked together with verses of my own." Ruffhead says, the part of Ajax was performed by the master's gardener.

Deane had been a Fellow of University College, Oxford, deprived, declared "non socius," after the Revolution. Wood says: "Deane was a good tutor in the College;" Pope, that he was a bad tutor out of it, for he nearly forgot under him what he had learnt before; since, on leaving school, he was only able, he says, to construe a little of Tully's Offices.

Pope was better acquainted with Dryden than with Cicero,

and his boyish admiration and curiosity led him to obtain a sight of the living poet. "I saw Mr. Dryden when I was twelve years of age. (This must have been in the last year of Dryden's life.) I remember his face well, for I looked upon him even then with veneration, and observed him very particularly." Dr. Johnson finely remarks: "Who does not wish that Dryden could have known the value of the homage that was paid him, and foreseen the greatness of his young admirer?"

"My next period," says Pope, " was in Windsor Forest, where I sat down with an earnest desire of reading, and applied as constantly as I could to it for some years. I was between twelve and thirteen when I went thither, and I continued in close pursuit of pleasure and languages till nineteen or twenty. Considering how very little I had when I came from school, I think I may be said to have taught myself Latin as well as French or Greek, and in all these my chief way of getting them was by translation." He afterward said of himself,

> Bred up at home, full early I begun
> To read in Greek the wrath of Peleus's son.

This scheme of self-instruction in the language of Homer did not, however, perfectly succeed; and we agree with Mr. Carruthers, that Pope's "case may be held to support the argument in favor of public schools; but at the same time it affords an animating example to the young student who has been denied the inestimable advantage of early academical training and discipline."

To vary the studies, Pope's father used to set him to make verses, and he often sent him back to "new turn" them, as they were not "good rhymes." The pupil, however, soon shot ahead of his master. His Ode on Solitude was written before the age of twelve, his satirical piece on Elkanah Settle at the age of fourteen; and some of his translations, of nearly the same period, are skillfully polished in versification. "Pope as a versifier was never a boy," says Mr. Carruthers: "he was born to refine our numbers, and to add the charm of finished elegance to our poetical literature, and he was ready for his mission at an age when most embryo poets are laboring at syntax, or struggling for expression."

Waller, Spenser, and Dryden were Pope's favorite poets, and when a boy, he said he could distinguish the difference between softness and sweetness in their versification. The Eclogues of Virgil he thought the sweetest poems in the world. Pope tells us that a little after he was twelve he began an epic poem, Alexander, Prince of Rhodes, which occupied him two years: the aim was to collect all the beauties of the great epic poets in one piece; he wrote four books toward it, of about a thousand verses each, and had the copy by him till he burnt it. His next work was his Pastorals; and about this time he translated above a quarter of the Metamorphoses, part of Statius, and Tully's piece *De Senectute.* Such were the early tastes and indefatigable application of Pope. None of his juvenile poems, however, were published before he was in his twentieth year; and they are thought to have been first carefully corrected. Pope has himself told us that he "lisp'd in numbers." The Ode to Solitude, he said, in a letter to Cromwell, was written when he was not twelve years old. Dodsley, however, who was intimate with and indebted to Pope, mentioned that he had seen several pieces of an earlier date,—and it is possible that the following may have been one of them, although, according to the literal interpretation of the words of the poet prefixed, it must rank the second of his known works. The copy before us is in that beautiful print hand, with copying which Pope all his life occasionally amused himself.*

A
PARAPHRASE on
Thomas à Kempis; L. 3, C. 2.
Done by the Author at 12 years old.

SPEAK, Gracious Lord, oh speak: thy Servant hears;
   For I'm thy Servant, and I'll still be so:
Speak words of Comfort in my willing Ears;
   And since my Tongue is in thy praises slow,
And since that thine all Rhetorick exceeds;
   Speak thou in words, but let me speak in deeds!

Nor speak alone, but give me grace to hear
   What thy coelestial sweetness does impart;
Let it not stop when entred at the Ear
   But sink, and take deep rooting in my heart.
As the parch'd Earth drinks Rain (but grace afford)
With such a Gust will I receive thy word.

Nor with the Israelites shall I desire
   Thy heav'nly word by Moses to receive,
Lest I should die; but Thou who didst inspire
   Moses himself, speak thou, that I may live.
Rather with Samuel I beseech with tears
Speak, gracious Lord, oh speak; thy Servant hears.

Moses indeed may say the words, but Thou
   Must give the Spirit, and the Life inspire
Our Love to thee his fervent Breath may blow,
   But 'tis thyself alone can give the fire;
Thou without them may'st speak and profit too;
But without thee, what could the Prophets do?

They preach the Doctrine, but thou mak'st us do 't;
   They teach the misteries thou dost open lay;
The trees they water, but thou giv'st the fruit;
   They to Salvation show the arduous way,
But none but you can give us Strength to walk;
You give the Practise, they but give the Talk.

Let them be Silent then; and thou alone
   (My God) speak comfort to my ravish'd ears;
Light of my eyes, my Consolation,
   Speak when thou wilt, for still thy Servant hears.
What-ere thou speak'st, let this be understood:
Thy greater Glory, and my greater Good!

---

* From the Athenæum, No. 1394.

JOHN GAY AT BARNSTAPLE.

This lively poet, whose charming Fables are the best we possess, was descended from an old Devonshire family, and was born at Barnstaple, in 1688, as proved by some MS. found in the secret drawer of an arm-chair which once belonged to the poet. He was educated at the grammar-school of his native town, and had for his master one Mr. Luck, who probably fostered though he could not create in his pupil a taste for poetry, by a volume of Latin and English poems, which he published before he retired from the mastership of the school. When Gay quitted it, his father being in reduced circumstances, the young poet was bound apprentice to a silk-mercer in the Strand, London; but he disliked this employment, and obtained his discharge from his master. His joy at this change may be traced in the following passage from his *Rural Sports,* which he, in 1711, dedicated to Mr. Pope, and thus established an acquaintance which ripened into a lasting friendship:

> But I, who ne'er was blessed by Fortune's hand,
> Nor brightened ploughshares in paternal land;
> Long in the noisy town have been immured,
> Respired its smoke, and all its cares endured.
> Fatigued at last, a calm retreat I chose,
> And soothed my harassed mind with sweet repose,
> Where fields, and shades, and the refreshing clime,
> Inspire the sylvan song, and prompt my rhyme.

Gay's Fables,* written in 1726, were designed for the special improvement of the young Duke of Cumberland; but the poet was meanly rewarded, and his fable of *The Hare with many Friends* is, doubtless, drawn from Gay's own experience. He was equally beloved by Swift and Pope: the former called Gay his "dear friend;" and the latter characterized him as—

> Of manners gentle, of affections mild,
> In wit a man, simplicity a child.

HOW EDMUND STONE TAUGHT HIMSELF MATHEMATICS.

Stone was born about the year 1700; his father was gardener to the Duke of Argyle, who, walking one day in his garden, observed a Latin copy of Newton's *Principia* lying on the grass, and thinking it had been brought from his own library, called some one to carry it back to its place. Upon this, Stone, who was then in his eighteenth year, claimed the book as his own. "Yours!" replied the Duke; "do you understand geometry, Latin, and Newton?" "I know a little of them," replied the

---
* The Fables of Gay were beautifully illustrated by William Harvey, in 1854, and published with a Memoir and Notes by Octavius Freire Owen, M.A., F.S.A.

young man. The Duke was surprised; and, having a taste for the sciences, conversed with the young mathematician, and was astonished at the force, the accuracy, and the candor of his answers. "But how," said the Duke, "came you by the knowledge of all these things?" Stone replied: "A servant taught me ten years since to read. Does one need to know anything more than the twenty-four letters in order to learn everything else that one wishes?" The Duke's curiosity redoubled: he sat down on a bank, and requested a detail of the whole process by which he had become so learned.

"I first learned to read," said Stone; "the masons were then at work upon your house. I approached them one day, and observed that the architect used a rule and compasses, and that he made calculations. I inquired what might be the meaning and the use of these things, and I was informed that there was a science called arithmetic. I purchased a book of arithmetic, and I learned it. I was told there was another science called geometry; I bought the necessary books and I learned geometry. By reading, I found that there were good books of these two sciences in Latin; I bought a dictionary, and I learned Latin. I understood also that there were good books of the same kind in French; I bought a dictionary, and I learned French. And this, my Lord, is what I have done: it seems to me that we may learn everything when we know the twenty-four letters of the alphabet."

Under the patronage of the Duke of Argyle, Stone, some years afterward, published in London a Treatise on Mathematical Instruments, and a Mathematical Dictionary, was chosen a Fellow of the Royal Society, and became a distinguished man of science.

JOHN WESLEY AT THE CHARTER-HOUSE AND OXFORD.

The founder of the Methodists, John Wesley, was the second, or the second who grew up to manhood, of the sons of the Rev. Samuel Wesley, of Epworth, Lincolnshire, and was born there in (O. S.) 1703.* When in his sixth year, he nearly lost his life in a fire which consumed his father's parsonage; and John remembered this providential deliverance through life with the

* Samuel, the eldest son, was first under-master of Westminster School afterward head of a free-school at Tiverton. The third son, Charles, was at Westminster School, when an Irish gentleman, Garrett Wellesly (or Wesley), Esq., of Dunganon, M.P., considering the boy of his own family, offered to make him his heir if he would consent to go with him to Ireland. The young man, who was just chosen student of Christchurch from Westminster School, preferred his projects there to a life of dependence on a stranger; and the favor of his namesake was in consequence transferred, and his fortune bequeathed, to Richard, second son of Sir Henry Colley, who assumed the name of Wellesley, was afterward Earl of Mornington, and was grandfather of the Marquis Wellesley and the Duke of Wellington.

deepest gratitude. In reference to it, he had a house in flames engraved as an emblem under one of his portraits, with these words for the motto, "Is not this a brand plucked out of the burning?" Peculiar care was taken of his religious education by his mother, which, with the habitual and fervent piety of both his parents, and his own surprising preservation, at an age when he was perfectly capable of remembering all the circumstances, combined to foster in the child that disposition which afterward developed itself with such force, and produced such important effects.

At an early age John was sent to the Charter-house, where he suffered under the tyranny which the elder boys were permitted to exercise. The boys of the higher forms were then in the practice of taking their portion of meat from the younger ones, by the law of the strongest; and during great part of the time that Wesley remained there, a small daily portion of bread was his only food. He strictly performed an injunction of his father's, that he should run round the Charter-house green three times every morning. Here, for his quietness, regularity, and application he became a favorite with the master, Dr. Walker; and through life he retained so great a predilection for the place, that on his annual visit to London, he made it a custom to walk through the scene of his boyhood.

At the age of seventeen, Wesley proceeded to Christchurch, Oxford. He had previously acquired some knowledge of Hebrew under his brother Samuel's tuition. At college he continued his studies with all diligence, and was noticed there for his attainments, and especially for his skill in logic; no man, indeed, was ever more dextrous in the art of reasoning. He was no inexpert versifier, and at one time seemed likely to have found his vent in poetry. When he was an under-graduate, his manners were free and cheerful; and his active disposition displayed itself in wit and vivacity. As, however, he was destined by the wishes of his family, and the situation which he held in the university, to become a candidate for orders, his parents directed his attention to the studies which concerned his profession, and more particularly to books of a devotional spirit. Among the works which he read in this preparation were the famous treatise *De Imitatione Christi*, ascribed to Thomas à Kempis; but the impression which this writer failed to make, was produced by the work of a far more powerful intellect, and an imagination infinitely more fervent—Jeremy Taylor's *Rules of Holy Living and Dying*. Wesley now got rid of all his acquaintances whose conversation he did not think likely to promote his spiritual improvement. In 1725, he was ordained; and in the following spring was elected to a fellowship at Lincoln College.

From this time Wesley began to keep a diary, in which he conveys a lively picture of himself; registering not only his proceedings, but his thoughts, his studies, and his remarks upon men and books, and miscellaneous subjects, with a vivacity which characterized him to the last. He was next apppointed Moderator of the Logical Disputations and Greek Lecturer. He now formed for himself a scheme of studies: Mondays and Tuesdays were allotted for the classics; Wednesdays to logic and ethics; Thursdays to Hebrew and Arabic; Fridays to metaphysics and natural philosophy; Saturdays to oratory and poetry, but chiefly to composition in those arts; and the Sabbath to divinity. It appears by his diary, also, that he gave great attention to mathematics. Full of business as he now was, he found time for writing by rising an hour earlier in the morning, and going into company an hour later in the evening. At the desire of his father, he next resided at Wroote, one of his livings; he officiated there for two years as his curate, and obtained priests' orders.

He now returned to take up his abode at Lincoln College, became a tutor there, and presided as Moderator at the Disputations. At this time a decided color was given to Wesley's destiny, and the foundation laid of Methodism. During his absence at Wroote, his younger brother, Charles, had drawn together in Oxford a small society of young men, of similar views, who received the sacrament weekly at St. Mary's, and assembled daily in each other's rooms, for the purpose of prayer and study. John was invited to join their party, and his superior age, though he too was very young, together with his station in the University, his character for learning, and above all, his being in priests' orders, combined to give him the direction of the little brotherhood. Nothing was further from his thoughts, or theirs, than the idea of separation from the church: they were, indeed, completely high church in their principles and practice. John Wesley added a remarkable plainness of dress, and an unusual manner of wearing his long flaxen hair; and the name of Methodists (a term not taken, as is generally supposed, from the ancient school of physicians so called, but from a religious sect among the puritans of the seventeenth century) was the least offensive term applied to them. They were in no way molested by the public authorities, either of the University or the Church of England; but their character for unusual piety conciliated the good-will of their ecclesiastical superiors till some of them excited opposition by doctrines decidedly at variance with the prevailing opinions of the church.

We have now sketched the school and college life of John

Wesley, unquestionably a man of very eminent talents and acquirements.

His genius, naturally clear and vivid, had been developed and matured during his residence at Oxford, by an unremitting attention to the studies of the place. His industry and management of time few have equaled. He always rose, for above fifty years together, at four in the morning He read even while on horseback; and during the latter part of his life, when his long journeys were made in a carriage, he boasted that he had generally from ten to twelve hours in the day which he could devote to study and composition Accordingly, besides the ancient languages, he was competently skilled in many of the tongues of modern Europe, and his journals display throughout a remarkable and increasing familiarity with the general reading, the poetry, and the ephemeral productions of his day.—*Abridged from the Quarterly Review, No. 47.*

LORD MANSFIELD AT WESTMINSTER.

"Of all the illustrious characters" (says the *Queen's Scholars' List*) "who have received their education at Westminster, there is perhaps none that holds out a brighter example for the imitation of youth than the accomplished lawyer and statesman, William Murray." He was born at Perth in 1704; at the age of three, was removed to London; and in 1719, was admitted a King's Scholar at Westminster. Here he distinguished himself, not so much in his poetry as in his other exercises, especially in his declamation, prognosticating that eloquence which was matured at the bar, and in both Houses of Parliament. He was elected to Oxford in 1723, and had taken his degree of B.A. in 1727, when he wrote a poem on the Death of George I. and Accession of George II., which won his first prize given on the occasion. He took his degree of M.A. in 1730, and in the following year was called to the bar by the Society of Lincoln's Inn, of which he had been a student since 1724. In early life he associated much with "the men of wit about town." Dr. Johnson said of him that "when he first came to town, he drank champagne with the wits." He was intimate with Pope:

"How sweet an Ovid, Murray was our boast."
Dunciad, iv. 169.

As a lawyer, he was self-taught, and had never gone through the process of a special pleader's or conveyancer's office. He studied oratory, as well at Oxford as in debating-clubs in London. Pope, in the Epistle dedicated to him, says:

"Grac'd as thou art with all the power of words,
So known, so honor'd, in the house of Lords."

Lord Mansfield's attachment to Westminster continued through life; and as long as his strength would permit him, he attended regularly the plays and annual meetings, which have for so many years been venerated customs of the school. At the Election dinner of 1793, his death was feelingly lamented, in some elegant verses written by Dean Vincent, and spoken by the Captain, Dr. Kidd.

LORD CHATHAM AT ETON AND OXFORD.

This illustrious statesman was born in Westminster, in 1708. He was sent early to Eton, where his high qualities were soon discerned by the head-master, Dr. Bland; and he there became eminent among a group, every member of which in manhood acquired celebrity. George (afterward Lord) Lyttleton, Henry Fox (afterward Lord Holland), Sir Charles Hanbury Williams, Henry Fielding, Charles Pratt (afterward Lord Camden), were among Pitt's young friends and competitors at Eton. His biographer, Thackeray, justly remarks, that "among the many recommendations which will always attach to a public system of education, the value of early emulation, the force of example, the abandonment of sulky and selfish habits, and the acquirement of generous, manly dispositions, are not to be overlooked. All these I believe to have had weight in forming the character of Lord Chatham."*

Pitt's studies were not neglected during his school vacations; for his father provided for him an able tutor at home during these periods, and himself assisted in this continuous tuition. The late Lord Stanhope stated that "Pitt being asked to what he principally ascribed the two qualities for which his eloquence was most conspicuous, namely, the lucid order of his reasonings, and the ready choice of his words, answered, that he believed he owed the former to an early study of the Aristotelian logic, and the latter to his father's practice in making him every day, after reading over to himself some passage in the classics, translate it aloud and continuously into English prose." That he cultivated Latin versification early is attested by the Latin hexameters on the Death of George the First, which he wrote in the first year after he was admitted a gentleman commoner at Trinity College, Oxford, in 1726. He was a most assiduous student of the classics: Demosthenes was his favorite; and he appears to have strongly recommended for the studies of his second son, afterward the celebrated minister, the first book of Thucydides and Polybius.

Lord Chatham's studies in youth were not exclusively the classics of antiquity. He read diligently the best English authors for style; his memory was excellent, and he is said to have known some of Dr. Barrow's sermons by heart.

DR. JOHNSON AT LICHFIELD, STOURBRIDGE, AND OXFORD.

Lichfield, in Staffordshire, is scarcely less proud of Samuel Johnson, than is Stratford-upon-Avon, in Warwickshire, of

* Creasy's Eminent Etonians, p. 212.

Shakspeare. In each town is shown the natal home and school of its genius; and though Johnson rests not, like Shakspeare, in the church of his birthplace, the people of Lichfield have testified their veneration of their illustrious townsman by his statue, while Stratford boasts of no such memorial of its master-mind.

Samuel Johnson was born in 1709. His father was a bookseller and stationer, and lived in a house in the market-place at Lichfield, which remains to this day. Johnson's mother was a woman of superior understanding and much piety, to which are ascribed the early impressions of religion which were made upon the mind of her son. When he was a child in petticoats, and had learned to read, Mrs. Johnson one morning put the Common Prayer-book into his hands, pointed to the collect for the day, and said, "Sam, you must get this by heart." She went up-stairs, but by the time she had reached the second floor, she heard him following her. "What's the matter?" said she. "I can say it," he replied, and repeated it distinctly, though he could not have read it more than twice.

Samuel was afflicted with the scrofula, or king's evil; and his mother, by advice of a physician in Lichfield, took the child to London in the Lent of 1712, to be *touched* by Queen Anne, but the ceremony was ineffectual. Johnson was then only thirty months old; but he used to relate in after years, that they went in a stage-coach, and returned in a wagon; and that the queen wore diamonds and a long black hood.

He first learned to read of his mother, and her old maid Catharine, in whose lap he well remembered sitting, to hear the story of St. George and the Dragon. Dame Oliver, a widow, who kept a school for little children in Lichfield, was his next teacher, and said he was the best scholar she ever had. His next instructor in English was one "Tom Brown," who published a spelling-book, and dedicated it to "the Universe." At the age of ten, he began to learn Latin with Mr. Hawkins, under-master of Lichfield grammar-school; in two years Johnson rose to be under the care of Mr. Hunter, the head-master, who, he relates, was "wrongheaded and severe," and used to beat the boys unmercifully, to save them, as he said, from the gallows; but Johnson was sensible that he owed much to this gentleman, and invariably expressed his approbation of enforcing instruction by the rod. Under Mr. Hunter, Johnson made good progress; he seemed to learn (says one of his school-fellows) by intuition; for though indolence and procrastination were inherent in his constitution, whenever he made an exertion he did more than any one else; and he was never corrected at school, but for talking and diverting other boys from their business.

His favorites received very liberal assistance from him; and three of his juvenile associates used to come in the morning, and carry him to school. One in the middle stooped, while Johnson sat upon his back, and one on each side supported him; and thus he was borne triumphant. At school he was uncommonly inquisitive; and he never forgot anything that he had either heard or read. In consequence of his defective sight, he did not join the other boys in their amusements. His only diversion was in winter, when he was fond of being drawn upon the ice by one of his companions barefooted, who *pulled* him along by a garter tied round his middle; no very easy operation, as he was remarkably large.

Dr. Percy, editor of the *Reliques of Ancient Poetry*, relates that Johnson, at this period, was immoderately fond of reading romances of chivalry; and he attributed to such extravagant fictions that unsettled turn of mind which prevented his ever fixing in any profession. From his earliest years he loved poetry, but hardly ever read any poem to the end; he perused Shakspeare at a period so early, that the speech of the ghost in *Hamlet* terrified him when alone. One day, imagining that his brother had hid some apples behind a large folio in his father's shop, Samuel climbed up to search for them: there were no apples; but the large folio proved to be Petrarch, whom he had seen mentioned in some preface as one of the restorers of learning: his curiosity was excited—he sat down, and read a great part of the book.

Johnson was next removed to the school of Stourbridge, Worcestershire, where he did not derive much benefit, but acted as an assistant to the master, in teaching the younger boys. He subsequently discriminated his progress at the two grammar-schools thus: "at one I learned much in the school, but little from the master; in the other I learned much from the master, but little in the school." At Stourbridge he was admitted into the best company of the place; he remained little more than a year, and then returned home, to learn his father's business; but he lacked application. He, however, read much in a desultory way, as he afterward told Boswell, his biographer: "all literature, sir; all ancient writers, all manly; though but little Greek, only some Anacreon and Hesiod; but in this irregular manner I had looked into a great many books which were not commonly known at the universities, where they seldom read any books but what are put into their hands by their tutors; so that when I came to Oxford, Dr. Adams, now Master of Pembroke College, told me I was the best qualified for the University he had ever known come there."

Johnson had already given several proofs of his poetical genius, both in his school exercises and other occasional compositions, of which Boswell quotes specimens.

In 1728, Johnson, being then in his nineteenth year, was entered as a commoner at Pembroke College: his father accompanied him, and introduced him to his tutor as a good scholar, and a poet who wrote Latin verses; Johnson behaved modestly, and sat silent; till, upon something which occurred in the course of conversation, he suddenly struck in, and quoted Macrobius; and thus he gave the first impression of that more extensive reading in which he had indulged himself. Johnson describes his tutor as "a very worthy man, but a very heavy man." Upon occasion of being fined for non-attendance, he said to the tutor, "Sir, you have scored me twopence for non-attendance at a lecture not worth a penny." Nevertheless, Johnson attended his tutor's lectures, and also the lectures in the college, very regularly. At his request he translated Pope's *Messiah* into Latin verse, as a Christmas exercise, with uncommon rapidity and ability; and it obtained for him not only the applause of his college and university, but of Pope himself, who is said to have remarked: "The writer of this poem will leave it a question with posterity, whether his or mine be the original."

Johnson's line of reading at Oxford, and during the vacations, cannot be traced. He told Boswell that what he read *solidly* at the university was Greek; not the Grecian historians, but Homer and Euripides, and now and then a little epigram; that the study of which he was most fond was metaphysics, but that he had not read much even in that way. It is, however, certain, both from his writings and conversation, his reading was very extensive. He appears, at various times, to have planned a methodical course of study. Like Southey, he had a peculiar faculty in seizing at once what was valuable in any book, without reading it through. He wrote at all times impatiently and in a hurry: he wrote his first exercise at college twice over, but never took that trouble with any other composition, and his best works were "struck off in a heat with rapid exertion." From his being short-sighted, writing was inconvenient to him; therefore, he never committed a foul draft to paper, but revolved the subject in his mind, and turned and formed every period, till he had brought the whole to the highest correctness and the most perfect arrangement—when he wrote it; and his uncommonly retentive memory enabled him to deliver a whole essay, properly finished, whenever it was called for.

Johnson was a great favorite with his college companions; and he might often be seen lounging at the gate of Pembroke

College amidst a circle of students, whom he was entertaining with his wit, and keeping from their studies, if not spiriting them to rebellion against the college discipline. The secret of this seeming levity and insubordination will be stated best in Johnson's own words: "I was mad and violent. It was bitterness which they mistook for frolic. I was miserably poor, and I thought to fight my way by my literature and my wit; so I disregarded all power and all authority." Johnson did not form any close intimacies with his fellow-collegians, though he loved Pembroke to the last. He boasted of the many eminent men who had been educated there, and how many poets had been Pembroke men, adding, "Sir, we were a nest of singing birds." But, Johnson's university education, through his scanty supply of funds from home, and the shortcomings of a friend, was left uncompleted; and he *personally* left college without a degree, December 12, 1729, though his *name* remained on the books till October 8, 1731.

Whatever instruction Johnson received from his mother in the doctrines and duties of Christianity, does not appear to have been followed up; and it was not until his going to Oxford that he became a sincerely pious man. When at the University, he took up the Nonjuror Law's *Serious Call to a Holy Life*, and was so affected and convinced by its contents, that from this time religion was the predominant object of his thoughts and affections.

But he returned to Lichfield from the University with gloomy prospects. In 1731, he made an unsuccessful effort to procure the appointment of usher in the grammar-school of Stourbridge, where he had been partly educated. In the summer following he obtained a situation in the school of Market Bosworth, Leicestershire, to which he went on foot: the employment was, however, irksome to him, and he soon quitted it. Soon after this he went to Birmingham, and undertook, for the first bookseller established there, a translation and abridgment of a *Voyage to Abyssinia*, by Lobo, a Portuguese Jesuit, for which he received five guineas!

Johnson now returned to Lichfield, and in 1736 married Mrs. Porter, a widow, with whom he opened a private academy at Edial Hall, near Lichfield; but the establishment did not succeed; he had only three pupils, two of whom were David Garrick and his brother. Meanwhile he was storing his mind, and employed on his tragedy of *Irene*. Next year, accompanied by Garrick, he repaired to London, to try his fortune in "that great field of genius and exertion."

At Lichfield, the house in which Johnson was born is incessantly visited by pilgrims from all parts of the world. Opposite is the statue of the Doctor, its pedestal sculptured with bass-reliefs of incidents in his life; and near a footpath in the town is a willow, from a shoot of the tree planted by Johnson's hands. These are trifling memorials compared with the works which his genius, learning, and understanding produced in the service of religion and virtue, and which have led even his most grudging critic to pronounce Johnson to have been "both a great and a good man."

HOW JAMES FERGUSON TAUGHT HIMSELF THE CLASSICS AND ASTRONOMY.

Ferguson has been characterized as literally his own instructor in the very elements of knowledge; without the assistance either of books or a living teacher. He was born in 1710, in Banffshire, where his father was a day-laborer, but religious and honest. He taught his children to read and write, as they reached the proper age; but James was too impatient to wait till his regular turn came, and after listening to his father teaching his elder brother, he would get hold of the book, and try hard to master the lesson which he had thus heard gone over; and, ashamed to let his father know what he was about, he used to apply to an old woman to solve his difficulties. In this way he learned to read tolerably well before his father suspected that he knew his letters.

When about seven or eight years of age, Ferguson, seeing that to raise the fallen roof of his cottage, his father applied to it a beam, resting on a prop, in the manner of a lever, the young philosopher, by experiment with models which he made by a simple turning-lathe and a little knife, actually discovered two of the most important elementary truths in mechanics—the lever, and the wheel and axle; and he afterward hit upon other discoveries, without either book or teacher to assist him. While tending sheep in the fields, he used to make models of mills, spinning-wheels, etc.; and at night, he used to lie down on his back in the fields, observing the heavenly bodies. "I used to stretch," says he, "a thread with small beads on it, at arms-length, between my eye and the stars; sliding the beads upon it till they hid such and such stars from my eye, in order to take their apparent distances from one another; and then laying the thread down on a paper, I marked the stars thereon by the beads." His master encouraged him in these and similar pursuits; and, says Ferguson, "often took the threshing flail out of my hands and worked himself, while I sat by him in the barn, busy with my compasses, ruler, and pen." He also tells us how he made an artificial globe from a description in Gordon's *Geographical Grammar;* a wooden clock, with the neck of a broken bottle for the bell; and a timepiece or watch, moved by a spring of whalebone. After many years he came to London, became a popular lecturer on astronomy, and had George III., then a boy, among his auditors: Ferguson was elected a Fellow of the Royal Society, and wrote several works valuable for the simplicity and ingenuity of their elucidations.

LORD CAMDEN AT ETON AND CAMBRIDGE.

Charles Pratt, Lord Camden, the profound jurist and enlightened statesman, was born of good family, in 1714, at Colhampton, in Devonshire. His father, Sir John Pratt, Chief Justice of the King's Bench, in George the First's reign, died when his son Charles was ten years old; soon after, he was sent to Eton, and elected on the foundation. He pursued his classical studies with great diligence. Here he was a bosom friend of William Pitt, afterward Earl of Chatham: this friendship did not cease with their college days, for Pratt owed to Pitt his first legal promotion, his introduction to political life, and his Chancellorship; and in return, Lord Camden proved "a tower of strength" to Chatham in his constitutional campaigns.

Pratt left Eton for King's College, Cambridge, in 1731: here "he read with genius;" his favorite authors being Livy and Claudian. He had been, when a little child, destined by his father for the bar; he had entered at the Inner Temple before he went to Cambridge; and at the university, as the best basis for legal excellence, he studied the English history and constitution, the science of jurisprudence, and the masterpieces of Greece and Rome. Having taken his degree, in 1735, he left Cambridge for London, and was called to the bar in 1738.

SHENSTONE'S "SCHOOLMISTRESS."

William Shenstone, "the poet of the Leasowes," was born upon that estate, at Hales-Owen, Shropshire, in 1714. He learned to read at what is termed a dame-school, and his venerable teacher has been immortalized in his poem of "The Schoolmistress." He soon received such delight from books, that he was always calling for fresh entertainment, and expected that when any of the family went to market, a new book should be brought to him, which, when it came, was in fondness carried to bed, and laid by him. It is related that when his request had been neglected, his mother wrapped up a piece of wood of the same form, and pacified him for the night. As he grew older, he went for a time to the grammar-school at Hales-Owen, and was afterward placed with an eminent schoolmaster at Solihull, where he distinguished himself by the quickness of his progress. He was next sent to Pembroke College, Oxford, where he continued his name in the book ten years, but took no degree. At Oxford, in 1737, he published his first work, a small poetical miscellany, without his name. In 1740, appeared his Judgment of Hercules; and in two years afterward his pleasing poem, in the stanza of Spenser, entitled the Schoolmistress, "so delightfully quaint and ludicrous, yet true to nature, that it has all the force and vividness of a painting by Teniers or Wilkie." The cottage of the dame was long preserved as a picturesque memorial of the poet. How vividly has he portrayed the teacher of a bygone age in these stanzas!

> In every village marked with little spire,
> Embowered in trees, and hardly known to fame,
> There dwells in lowly shed and mean attire,
> A matron old, whom we schoolmistress name;
> Who boasts unruly brats with birch to tame:
> They grievous sore, in piteous durance pent,
> Awed by the power of this relentless dame;
> And ofttimes on vagaries idly bent,
> For unkempt hair, or task unconned, are sorely shent.
>
> And all in sight doth rise a birchen tree,
> Which learning near her little dome did stowe;
> Whilom a twig of small regard to see,
> Though now so wide its waving branches flow,
> And work the simple vassals mickle wo;
> For not a wind might curl the leaves that blew,
> But their limbs shuddered, and their pulse beat low;
> And as they looked, they found their horror grew,
> And shaped it into rods, and tingled at the view.
>
> Near to this dome is found a patch so green,
> On which the tribe their gambols do display;
> And at the door imprisoning board is seen,
> Lest weakly wights of smaller size should stray;
> Eager, perdie, to bask in sunny day!
> The noises intermixed, which thence resound,
> Do learning's little tenement betray;
> Where sits the dame disguised in look profound,
> And eyes her fairy throng, and turns her wheel around.
>
> Her cap far whiter than the driven snow,
> Emblem right meet of decency does yield:
> Her apron, dyed in grain, as blue, I trow,
> As is the harebell that adorns the field;
> And, in her hand, for sceptre, she does wield
> Tway birchen sprays; with anxious fear entwined,
> With dark distrust, and sad repentance filled;
> And steadfast hate, and sharp affliction joined,
> And fury uncontrolled, and chastisement unkind.
> * * * *
> Yet, nursed with skill, what dazzling fruits appear!
> Even now sagacious foresight points to show
> A little bench of heedless bishops here,
> And there a chancellor in embryo,
> Or bard sublime, if bard may e'er be so,
> As Milton, Shakspeare,—names that ne'er shall die!
> Though now he crawl along the ground so low,
> Nor weeting how the Muse should soar so high,
> Wisheth, poor starveling elf, his paper kite may fly.*

---

* This stanza is thought to have suggested to Gray the fine reflection in his Elegy—
"Some mute inglorious Milton here may rest," etc.

Shenstone wrote also some graceful letters and essays; and showed much taste in embellishing the Leasowes. He died, here, in the prime of life, in 1763.

GRAY AT ETON AND CAMBRIDGE.

Thomas Gray, of all English poets, the most finished artist, was born in Cornhill, in 1716, and was the only one of twelve children who survived the period of infancy. His father was a money-scrivener, and of harsh and violent disposition, whose wife was forced to separate from him; and to the exertions of this excellent woman, as partner with her sister in a millinery business, the poet owed the advantages of a learned education, toward which his father had refused all assistance. He was sent to be educated at Eton, where a maternal uncle, named Antrobus, was one of the assistant-masters. He remained here six years, and made himself a good classic; he was an intimate associate of the accomplished Richard West, this being one of the most interesting school-friendships on record. West went to Oxford, whence he thus wrote to Gray:

> "You use me very cruelly: you have sent me but one letter since I have been at Oxford, and that too agreeable not to make me sensible how great my loss is in not having more. Next to seeing you is the pleasure of seeing your handwriting; next to hearing you is the pleasure of hearing from you. Really and sincerely, I wonder at you, that you thought it not worth while to answer my last letter. I hope this will have better success in behalf of your quondam school-fellow; in behalf of one who has walked hand in hand with you, like the two children in the wood,
>
> > Thro' many a flow'ry path and shelly grot,
> > Where learning lull'd her in her private* maze.
>
> The very thought, you see, tips my pen with poetry, and brings Eton to my view."

Another of Gray's associates at Eton was Horace Walpole; they removed together to Cambridge; Gray resided at Peterhouse from 1735 to 1738, when he left without a degree. The spirit of Jacobitism and its concomitant hard drinking, which then prevailed at Cambridge, ill suited the taste of Gray; nor did the uncommon proficiency he had made at Eton hold first rank, for he complains of college impertinences, and the endurance of lectures, daily and hourly. "Must I pore into metaphysics?" asks Gray. "Alas, I cannot see in the dark; nature has not furnished me with the optics of a cat. Must I pore upon mathematics? Alas, I cannot see in too much light: I am no eagle. It is very possible that two and two make four, but I would not give four farthings to demonstrate this ever so clearly; and if these be the profits of life, give me the amusements of it." Yet Gray subsequently much regretted that he had never applied his mind to the study of mathematics; and once, rather late in

---

* This expression prettily distinguishes their studies when out of the public school, which would, naturally, at their age, be vague and desultory.—*Mason*.

life, had an intention to undertake it. His time at Cambridge was devoted to classics, modern languages, and poetry; and a few Latin poems and English translations were made by him at this period. In "the agonies of leaving college," he complains of "the dust, the old boxes, the bedsteads, and tutors," that were about his ears. "I am coming away," he says, "all so fast, and leaving behind me without the least remorse, all the beauties of Stourbridge Fair. Its white bears may roar, its apes may wring their hands, and crocodiles cry their eyes out, all's one for that; I shall not once visit them, nor so much as take my leave."

> In a letter to Mr. West, he says: "I learn Italian like any dragon, and in two months am got through the 16th Book of Tasso, whom I hold in great admiration; I want you to learn too, that I may know your opinion of him; nothing can be easier than that language to any one who knows Latin and French already, and there are few so copious and expressive." In the same letter he tells him, "that his college has set him a versifying on a public occasion (viz., those verses which are called Tripos), on the theme of *Luna est habitabilis*." The poem is to be found in the *Musæ Etonenses*. (vol. ii, p 107.) . . . . "His hexameters are, as far as modern ones can be, after the manner of Virgil. They move in the succession of his pauses, and close with his elisions."—*Mason*.

In 1739, Gray accompanied Horace Walpole on a tour through France and Italy; but, as they could not agree, Gray being, as Walpole has it, "too serious a companion," the former returned to England in 1741. He next went to Cambridge, to take his degree in Civil Law. He now devoted himself to the classics, and at the same time cultivated his muse. At Cambridge he was considered an unduly fastidious man, and the practical jokes and "incivilities" played off upon him by his fellow-inmates at Peterhouse—one of which was a false alarm of fire, through which he descended from his window to the ground by a rope—was the cause of his migrating to Pembroke Hall. He subsequently obtained the professorship of Modern History in the University. He usually passed the summer with his mother at Stoke, near Eton, in which picturesque locality he composed his two most celebrated poems—the Ode on a Distant Prospect of Eton College, and his Elegy written in a Country Churchyard. In the Ode, he exclaims with filial fervor to the College where he had spent six years of his life as a boy:

> Ye distant spires, ye antique towers,
>   That crown the wa'ery glade,
> Where grateful Science still adores
>   Her Henry's holy shade;
> And ye, that from the stately brow
> Of Windsor's heights, th' expanse below
>   Of grove, of lawn, of mead survey,
> Whose turf, whose shade, whose flowers among
> Wanders the hoary Thames along
>   His silver-winding way:
>
> Ah, happy hills! ah, pleasing shade!
>   Ah, fields beloved in vain!

> Where once my careless childhood stray'd,
> A stranger yet to pain!
> I feel the gales that from ye blow
> A momentary bliss bestow,
> As waving fresh their gladsome wing,
> My weary soul they seem to soothe,
> And, redolent of joy and youth,
> To breathe a second spring.
>
> Say, Father Thames, for thou hast seen
> Full many a sprightly race
> Disporting on thy margent green,
> The paths of pleasure trace;
> Who foremost now delight to cleave,
> With pliant arm thy glassy wave?
> The captive linnet which enthrall!
> What idle progeny succeed
> To chase the rolling circle's speed,*
> Or urge the flying ball?

Gray continued to reside at Cambridge (it is considered) principally on account of the valuable libraries of the University—for he was one of the greatest readers, though the most sparing of writers. While at dinner one day in the College-hall, he was taken ill, and after six days' suffering, he expired July 30, 1771: he was buried according to his desire, by the side of his mother, at Stoke. Gray was a profound as well as elegant scholar; "he attained the highest degree of splendor of which poetical style seems to be capable; he is the only modern English writer whose Latin verses deserve general notice; in his letters he has shown the descriptive powers of a poet; in new combinations of generally familiar words he was eminently happy; and he was the most learned poet since Milton." (*Sir James Mackintosh.*) Gray was also an excellent botanist, zoologist, and antiquary.

The accomplished Earl of Carlisle, who has elegantly commemorated the genius of this poet, feeling the identification which his celebrated Ode gives to his muse with the memory of Eton, has presented to the College a bust of Gray, which has been added to the collection of the busts of other worthies placed in the Upper School-room.

HOW BRINDLEY TAUGHT HIMSELF THE RUDIMENTS OF MECHANICS.

James Brindley, the sagacious engineer, was born in Derbyshire, in 1716, and was employed when a boy in field labor. His father, who had reduced himself to extreme poverty by his dissipated habits, allowed his son to grow up without any education; and to the end of his life this great genius was barely able to read, and could write little more than his own name. At the age of 17, he apprenticed himself to a millwright at Macclesfield,

---

* "To chase the hoop's elusive speed."—MS.

a few miles from his native place. He was sadly neglected by his master, who frequently left him for whole weeks together, to execute works concerning which he had not given him any instruction. These works Brindley finished in his own way, greatly to the surprise of his master, who was often astonished at the improvements his apprentice from time to time introduced into the millwright business. He rose to be the greatest engineer of his day, not only in mill machinery, but in drainage works, and the improvement of our inland navigation by canals. It was when being examined before a Committee of the House of Commons, and being asked for what objects rivers were created, he gave the ready answer, "To feed navigable canals."

Brindley's designs were the resources of his own mind alone. When he was beset with any difficulty, he secluded himself, and worked out unaided the means of accomplishing his schemes. Sometimes he lay in bed for two or three days; but when he arose, he proceeded at once to carry his plans into effect, without the help of drawings or models.

WILLIAM COLLINS AT WINCHESTER AND OXFORD.

William Collins, whose odes exhibit vast powers of poetry, and who is inferior to no English poet of the 18th century, except Gray, was born at Chichester, in 1721.* His father was a hatter, and at the time of the poet's birth, mayor of Chichester. He was sent, when very young, to the prebendal school there, an ancient institution founded by Bishop Storey, in the reign of Edward IV.; here also were educated Selden, Bishop Juxon, and Hurdis. Collins was early designed by his parents for the church. He was removed from Chichester, and admitted a scholar on the foundation of Winchester College in 1733.

In this venerable institution—where the scholars on the foundation wear the dress prescribed by the rules of the founder, in which rejoicings over a holiday are sung in ancient Latin verse, and terms and phrases long fallen into disuse without its walls, are still the current talk of healthy boys—Collins remained seven years. The master was then Dr. Burton, a name that will long be associated with the college. Among Collins's schoolfellows were William Whitehead and Joseph Warton, the poets, and Hampton, afterward

---

* Collins, in his "Ode to Pity," alludes to his "native plains," which are bounded by the South Downs, and to the small river Arun, one of the streams of Sussex, near which Otway also was born :

> But wherefore need I wander wide
> To old Ilissus's distant side?
> Deserted stream and mute!
> Wild Arun, too, has heard thy strains,
> And Echo 'midst my native plains
> Been soothed by Pity's lute.

translator of Polybius —*Life, by Mr. Moy Thomas, prefixed to new edition of Collins's Poetical Works.* 1858.*

About September, 1733, Lord Peterborough paid a visit to Winchester College, with Pope, who proposed a subject for a poem. Collins was then too young to contest the prizes, which were carried off by Whitehead and Hampton; but he must have seen Pope on that occasion. Johnson speaks of verses published five years later as those by which Collins "first courted the notice of the public;" but he appears to have made verses as early as Pope. He is said at twelve years old to have written a poem "On the Battle of the School-books," at Winchester, probably suggested by Swift's satire, of which the line —

"And every Gradus flapped his leathern wing"—

was afterward remembered.

At Winchester, when about seventeen years old, Collins wrote his Persian Eclogues, after reading that volume of Salmon's *Modern History* which describes Persia. In January, 1733, some lines, by Collins, appeared in the *Gentleman's Magazine;* and in October of that year, the Editor inserted a Sonnet from Collins, together with some verses of Joseph Warton, and another school-fellow at Winchester, which came, he tells us, "in one letter;" and in the next number of the Magazine appeared a criticism on the above three poems, written by Dr. Johnson, then toiling in poverty and obscurity, for Cave: he gives the palm to Collins's Sonnet.

On March 21, 1740, Collins was formally admitted a commoner of Queen's College; but he did not go to Oxford until some time afterward. In the summer of the same year, Collins was elected at Winchester, and placed first on the roll for admission in the succeeding year to New College, Oxford; but no vacancy occurred — a rare misfortune, — which, however, had befallen the poet Young some years before.

Next year, Collins was admitted a Demy of Magdalen College, where he continued to devote himself to poetry. Langhorne states that he was at this time distinguished for genius and indolence, and that the few exercises which he could be induced to write bore evident marks of both qualities. Among his college acquaintances were Hampton and Gilbert White, and his constant friends the two Wartons. On November 18, 1743, Collins took the degree of Bachelor of Arts: he quitted the college at some time before the July election in 1744. He obtained a curacy, but soon gave up all views in the church,

* Aldine Poets. Published by Bell and Daldy. This edition has a portrait of Collins at the age of fourteen, from a drawing : no other portrait of Collins is known to exist.

and preferred the precarious profession of a man of letters. His irresolution soon led him into difficulties. But his studies were extensive, and his scholarship great. His Odes have always been the favorite of poets; and they won for him the praises he prized most. He enjoyed the friendship and affection of Johnson; and the intimacy of Thomson. But the latter part of his short life must be remembered with pity and sadness: he languished for some years under depression of mind, and was for a time bereft of reason. He died in 1756, at Chichester, and is buried in the Cathedral, where a monument, by Flaxman, has been erected to his memory. The poet is represented reading an English Testament, such as at one period he invariably traveled with; it is referred in the inscription on the tablet by the poet Hayley and Mr. John Sargent:

Who joined pure faith to strong poetic powers;
Who, in reviving reason's lucid hours,
Sought on one book his troubled mind to rest,
And rightly deemed the book of God the best.

LORD CLIVE—HIS DARING BOYHOOD.

Robert Clive, the founder of the British empire in India, was born in 1726, at Styche, near Market Drayton, in Shropshire, where his family had been settled since the twelfth century.

Some lineaments of the character of the man (says Lord Macaulay) were early discerned in the child. There remain letters written by his relations when he was in his seventh year; and from these letters it appears that, even at that early age, his strong will and his fiery passions, sustained by a constitutional intrepidity which sometimes seemed hardly compatible with soundness of mind, had begun to cause great uneasiness to his family. "Fighting," says one of his uncles, "to which he is out of measure addicted, gives his temper such a fierceness and imperiousness, that he flies out on every trifling occasion." The old people in the neighborhood still remember to have heard from their parents how Bob Clive climbed to the top of the lofty steeple of Market Drayton, and with what terror the inhabitants saw him seated on a stone spout near the summit. They also relate how he formed all the idle lads of the town into a kind of predatory army, and compelled the shopkeepers to submit to a tribute of apples and halfpence, in consideration of which he guaranteed the security of their windows. He was sent from school to school, making very little progress in his learning, and gaining for himself everywhere the character of an exceedingly naughty boy. One of his masters, it is said, was sagacious enough to prophesy that the idle lad would make a great figure in the world. But the general opinion seems to have been that poor Robert was a dunce, if not a reprobate. His family expected nothing good from such slender parts and such a headstrong temper. It is not strange, therefore, that they gladly accepted for him, when he was in his eighteenth year, a writership in the service of the East India Company, and shipped him off to make a fortune, or die of fever at Madras.

Clive arrived at Madras in 1744, where his situation was most painful: his pay was small, he was wretchedly lodged, and his shy and haughty disposition withheld him from introducing himself to strangers. The climate affected his health and spirits, and his duties were ill-suited to his ardent and daring character. "He pined for his home, and in his letters to his relations expressed his feelings in language softer and more pensive than we should have expected from the waywardness of his boyhood, or from the inflexible sternness of his later years. 'I have not enjoyed,' says he, 'one happy day since I left my native country;' and again, 'I must confess at intervals, when I think of my dear native England, it affects me in a very particular manner.'" Clive, however, found one solace. The Governor of Madras possessed a good library, and permitted Clive to have access to it: he devoted much of his leisure to reading, and acquired at this time almost all the knowledge of books that he ever possessed. As a boy he had been too idle, as a man he had become too busy, for literary pursuits.

His career of prosperity and glory, of wounded honor and bodily affliction, has been vividly drawn by Lord Macaulay, who considers him entitled to an honorable place in the estimation of posterity. From his first visit to India, dates the renown of the English arms in the East; from his second visit, the political ascendancy of the English in that country; and from his third visit, the purity of the administration of our Eastern empire, which, since this was written, the wicked ingratitude of revolt has done so much to endanger.

CAPTAIN COOK'S EDUCATION ON BOARD SHIP.

It was at sea that Cook acquired those high scientific accomplishments by which he became the first circumnavigator of his day. He was born in 1728, and was the son of an agricultural laborer and farm-bailiff, at Marton, near Stockton-upon-Tees. All the school education he ever had was a little reading, writing, and arithmetic, for which he was indebted to the liberality of a gentleman in the neighborhood. He was apprenticed, at the age of 13, to a haberdasher at the fishing-town of Staiths, near Whitby; while in this situation he was first seized with a passion for the sea; and having procured a discharge from his master, he apprenticed himself to a firm in the coal trade at Whitby, on board a coasting-vessel. In this service he rose to be mate, when, in 1755, being in the Thames, he entered as a volunteer in the royal navy. He soon distinguished himself so greatly that in three or four years afterward he was appointed master of the *Mercury*, which belonged to a squadron then proceeding to attack Quebec. Here he first showed the proficiency he had already made in the scientific part of his profession by constructing an admirable chart of the river St. Lawrence. He felt, however, the disadvantages of his ignorance of mathematics; and while still assisting in the hostile operations carrying on against the French on the coast of North America, he applied himself to the study of Euclid's Elements, which he soon mastered, and then began to study astronomy. A year or two after, while stationed in the same quarter, he communicated to the Royal Society an account of a solar eclipse, which took place August 5, 1766; deducing from it, with great exactness and skill, the longitude of the place of observation. He had now completely established his reputation as an able and scientific seaman; and was next appointed to the command of the *Endeavour*, fitted out by Government for the South Sea, to observe the approaching transit of the planet Venus over the sun's disc, which he most satisfactorily recorded, besides a large accession of important geographical discoveries. He was next appointed to an expedition to the same regions, to determine the question of the existence of a south polar continent. Of this voyage, Cook drew up the account, which is esteemed a model in that species of writing.

JOHN HUNTER'S WANT OF EDUCATION.

The well-known John Hunter, one of the greatest anatomists that ever lived, scarcely received any education whatever until he was twenty years old. He was born in 1728, in Lanarkshire, and was the youngest of a family of ten. When he was only ten years old, his father died, and the boy was left to act as he chose. Such was his aversion at this time to anything like regular application, that he could scarcely be taught even the elements of reading and writing; while an attempt that was made to give him some knowledge of Latin (according to the plan of education then almost universally followed in regard to the sons of even the smallest landed proprietors in Scotland), was, after a short time, abandoned altogether. Thus Hunter grew up, spending his time merely in country amusements, until there was no provision for maintaining him longer in idleness. So destitute was he of all literary acquirements, that he could only look for employment of his hands, rather than his head. He was accordingly apprenticed to his brother-in-law, a carpenter, in Glasgow, with whom he learned to make chairs and tables; and this, probably, might have been for life Hunter's employment, but for the failure of his master, when John was thrown out of work. He then applied to his elder brother, Dr. William Hunter, already settled in London, and distinguished as a lecturer and anatomical demonstrator. John offered his services as an assistant in the dissecting-room, adding, that if his proposal should not be accepted, he meant to enlist in the army. Fortunately for science, his letter was answered in the way he wished: he came to London, began by dissecting an arm, and so succeeded, that Dr. Hunter foretold he would become an excellent anatomist. This was verified; but he never entirely overcame the disadvantages entailed upon him by neglect in his early years. He attained little acquaintance with the literature of his own profession, and he continued to the end of his life an awkward writer. "If these," says Mr. Craik,* "were heavy penalties, however, which he had to pay for what was not so much his fault as that of others, the eminence to which he attained in spite of them is only the more demonstrative of his extraordinary natural powers, and his determined perseverance."

EDMUND BURKE AT BALLITORE AND DUBLIN.

This renowned orator and statesman was born in Dublin, on the 1st of January, 1730, or, as the register of Trinity College, Dublin, states, 1728. His father, Richard Burke, or Bourke, a Protestant, and of good family, was an attorney in large practice. His mother was a Miss Nagle, a Roman Catholic lady, and great-niece of Miss Ellen Nagle, who married Sylvanus Spenser, the eldest son of the poet; the name of Edmund may possibly, therefore, have been adopted from the author of the *Faerie Queene* by the subject of the present memoir.

During his boyhood, Burke's health was very delicate, even to the risk of consumption. His first instructor was his mother, a woman of strong mind, cultivated understanding, and fervent piety. Many years of his childhood were passed among his maternal relatives in the south of Ireland, especially with his grandfather at Castletown Roche, in a locality teeming with the romance of history; for here, at Kilcolman Castle, Spenser wrote his *Faerie Queene;* and here lived Essex and Raleigh. It is but natural to suppose that here, upon the beautiful banks of the Blackwater, England's future orator imbibed in the poetry of the *Faerie Queene* that taste for ornate and eastern imagery which gave such splendor to his eloquence; and here, amid the memories hanging around the ruins of Kilcolman, he thirsted for the historic knowledge which he afterward threw with such power and prophetic force into his reasoning and his language."† He was an ardent admirer of the epic poet: "Whoever relishes and reads Spenser as he ought to be read," said Burke in after-life, "will have strong hold of the English language;" and there are many coincidences of expression between Burke and Spenser.

Young Burke learned the rudiments of Latin from a schoolmaster in the village of Glanworth, near Castletown Roche. This teacher, O'Halloran, afterward boasted that "No matter how great Master Edmund was, *he* was the first who had ever

---

* Pursuit of Knowledge, vol. 1.   † Life of Burke. By Peter Burke. 1853.

put a Latin grammar into his hands." In his twelfth year he was sent with his brothers, Garrett and Richard, to the classical school of Ballitore, in the county of Kildare, then kept by Abraham Shackleton, a member of the Society of Friends, and a man of high classical attainments. The master liked his pupil, and the pupil became fond of his master; and during the two years that Burke remained at Ballitore, he studied diligently, and laid the foundation of a sound classical education.. Burke was ever grateful to his excellent tutor.

In the House of Commons he paid a noble tribute to the memory of Abraham Shackleton, declaring that he was an honor to his sect, though that sect was one of the purest. He ever considered it as one of the greatest blessings of his life that he had been placed at the good Quaker's academy, and readily acknowledged it was to Abraham Shackleton that he owed the education that made him worth anything.* A member of the Society of Friends had always peculiar claims on his sympathy and regard.† Burke's bosom friend at Ballitore was Richard Shackleton, the schoolmaster's son : they read together, walked together, and composed their first verses together ; unlike most school-boy ties, which seldom endure the first rough contact with the world, the friendship of Burke and Shackleton remained fresh, pure, and ardent, until the close of their existence.‡

Burke entered Trinity College, Dublin, in the spring of 1743. He became, in 1746, a scholar of the house, which is similar to being a scholar of Christchurch, Oxford. Oliver Goldsmith, who was at Trinity with Burke, states that he did not distinguish himself in his academical exercises; and Dr. Leland, another of his cotemporaries, supports Goldsmith's statement. But Burke undoubtedly acquired at Ballitore a good knowledge of the ordinary classics; and, says Mr. Macknight, his miscellaneous reading gave him more extensive views than could be acquired from the usual text-books of the college. Burke, says the same biographer, seems never to have thought of applying himself systematically to one branch of study, or seriously labored to acquire gold medals, prize-books, and worldly distinctions. But the longer he remained at college, the more desultory his course of study became : he took up violently with natural philosophy—his *furor mathematicus;* then he worked at

* In one of his speeches, when he was 50 years old, he said: " I was educated a Protestant of the Church of England by a Dissenter who was an honor to his sect. Under his eye, I read the Bible morning, noon, and night; and I have ever since been a happier and a better man for such reading."—Works and Correspondence, vol. i. p. 17, quoted in *The Life and Times of Edmund Burke*, by Thomas Macknight. 1858.

† When Mr. Burke was informed that Mr. West was a Quaker, he said that he always regarded it among the most fortunate circumstances of his life that his first preceptor was a member of the Society of Friends.—*Early Life and Studies of Benjamin West*, vol. ii. p. 8.

‡ There is a pleasing anecdote connected with Edmund Burke's subsequent intercourse with the Shackletons. In the early part of his political career, he was officially installed in apartments in Dublin Castle. No sooner was he there, than his good friends the Shackletons hastened to pay him a visit; and, of course, expected to find the incipient statesman, whose industry was already a public theme, immersed in Government affairs. What was their surprise when, on entering his room, they caught him at play with his children : he was on all-fours, carrying one of them on his back round the room, whilst the other, a chubby infant, lay crowing with delight upon the carpet. The incident recalls a similar story told of the famous Bourbon prince, Henry the Fourth.

logic—his *furor logicus;* to this succeeded his *furor historicus,* which subsided into his old complaint, *furor poeticus,* the most dangerous and difficult to cure of all these forms of madness.

Of Burke's favorite authors, many accounts have been given. His letters show that of the Roman historians Sallust was his delight. He preferred Cicero's Orations to his Epistles; and his frequent quotation of Virgil, Horace, and Ovid, shows how deeply his mind was imbued with their classic imagery. There are few indications of his application to Greek literature. Of modern authors he took most pleasure in Milton, whom he delighted to illustrate at his Debating Society; yet, he greeted Ossian's song of the Son of Fingal with more applause than he bestowed on Shakspeare.* He loved Horace and Lucretius; and defended against Johnson the paradox that though Homer was a greater poet than Virgil, yet the Æneid was a greater poem than the Iliad.

While at college, Burke was a member of that excellent institution of juvenile debate for the use of the students of Trinity, called the Historical Society, which was the arena not only of his incipient oratory, but of that of many others among the greatest men Ireland has produced.

In 1748, Burke took his degree of B.A.; that of M.A. he obtained in 1751; and he was presented with the further degree of LL.D. in 1791. Meantime, having been intended for the English bar, he had entered at the Middle Temple in 1747; and early in 1750, he left Dublin for London.

Burke's college career was free from vice or dissipation.

<small>A high moral tone and dignified bearing, tempered as they were by an extreme urbanity of manner, and a wonderful power of charming in conversation, had already become his characteristics; already, too, his company was sought among the fashionable, as much as among the learned. He had that great art of good breeding which rendered men pleased with him and with themselves. He had an inexhaustible fund of discourse, either serious or jocose, seasoned with wit and humor, poignant, strong, delicate, sportive, as answered the purpose or occasion. He had a vast variety of anecdotes and stories, which were always well adapted and well told; he had also a constant cheerfulness and high spirits. His looks and voice were in unison with the agreeable insinuation and impressiveness of his conversation and manners. Possessing these attractions—his lasting possessions—it was no wonder that at all times Burke found it easy to have whatever associates he liked; and he always chose the best.—*Peter Burke.*</small>

<small>* Yet, Burke perfected his oratory by studying Shakspeare. He is thought to have overrated Ossian to please Macpherson, who, being the agent of the Nabob of Arcot, had probably laid Burke under obligation by affording him information on Indian affairs.

Burke was more of a versifier in his youth than was ever supposed until some time after his death. When Sir James Mackintosh said that had Burke ever acquired the habit of versification, he would have poured forth volumes of sublime poetry (*Mackintosh's Memoirs,* by his Son), he little suspected that while he was at Trinity College, the great statesman and philosopher was the most inveterate of versifiers. He seldom wrote a letter to a friend without inclosing him some specimens of his verse which, though rarely above commonplace, breathe a sincere love of all that is virtuous, beautiful, and pious; he continued his poetical efforts longer, and met with less success, than any man who ever engaged in political life with a tenth part of his qualifications.—*Macknight,* vol. i. p. 26.</small>

COWPER AT WESTMINSTER.

William Cowper, "the most popular poet of his generation, and the best of English letter-writers," was the son of Dr. John Cowper, rector of Great Berkhampstead, Herts, and was born at the parsonage-house, in 1731. In his sixth year he lost his mother, of whom he always retained the most affectionate recollection: the deprivation of her tenderness laid the seeds of those infirmities which afterward afflicted his manhood. In the year of his mother's death, he was, as he himself describes it, "taken from the nursery, and from the immediate care of a most indulgent mother," and sent out of his father's house to a considerable school kept by a Dr. Pitman, at Market-street. Here for two years he suffered much from ill-treatment by his rough companions: his sensibility and delicate health were the objects of their cruelty and ridicule; and one boy so relentlessly persecuted him that he was expelled, and Cowper was removed from the school. Cowper retained in late years a painful recollection of the terror with which this boy inspired him. "His savage treatment of me," he says, "impressed such a dread of his figure on my mind, that I well remember being afraid to lift my eyes upon him higher than his knees; and that I knew him better by his shoe-buckle than by any other part of his dress." To the brutality of this boy's character, and the general impression left upon Cowper's mind by the tyranny he had undergone at Dr. Pitman's, may be traced Cowper's prejudice against the whole system of public education, so forcibly expressed in his poem called *Tirocinium; or, a Review of Schools.*

About this time Cowper was attacked with an inflammation in the eyes, and was placed in the house of an oculist, where he remained two years, and was but imperfectly cured.

At the end of this time, at the age of ten, he was removed to Westminster School. The sudden change from the isolation of the oculist's house to the activity of a large public school, and the collision with its variety of characters and tempers, helped to feed and foster the moods of dejection to which Cowper was subject. His constitutional despondency was deepened by his sense of solitude in being surrounded by strangers; and thus, thrown in upon himself, he took refuge in brooding over his spiritual condition. This tendency had first manifested itself at Dr. Pitman's school, and next at Westminster. Passing one evening through St. Margaret's churchyard, he saw a light glimmering at a distance from the lantern of a grave-digger, who, as Cowper approached, threw up a skull that struck him on the leg. "This little incident," he observes, "was an alarm to my conscience; for the event may be remembered among the best religious documents I received at Westminster." He sought hope in religious consolations, and then hopelessly abandoned them; and he was struck with lowness of spirits, and intimations of a consumptive habit, which the watchful sympathies of home might possibly have averted or subdued.

Nevertheless, Cowper appears to have been sufficiently strong and healthy to excel at cricket and football; and he persevered so successfully in his studies, that he stood in high favor with the master for his scholarship. Looking back many years afterward on this part of his life, he only regretted the lack of his religious instruction. Latin and Greek, he complains, were all that he acquired. The duty of the school-boy absorbed every other, with the single exception of the periodical preparations for confirmation, to which we find this interesting testimony in his letters:

"That I may do justice to the place of my education, I must relate one mark of religious discipline, which, in my time, was observed at Westminster; I mean the pains which Dr. Nichols took to prepare us for confirmation. The old man acquitted himself of this duty like one who had a deep sense of its importance; and I believe most of us were struck by his manner, and affected by his exhortations."

Cowper translated twenty of Vinny Bourne's poems into English, and his allusions to his old favorite usher of the fifth form at Westminster are frequent.*

"I remember (says Cowper) seeing the Duke of Richmond set fire to Vinny's greasy locks, and box his ears to put it out again." And again, writing to Mr. Rose, Cowper says: "I shall have great pleasure in taking now and then a peep at my old friend, Vincent Bourne; the neatest of all men in his versification, though, when I was under his ushership at Westminster, the most slovenly in his person. He was so inattentive to his boys, and so indifferent whether they brought good or bad exercises, or none at all, that he seemed determined, as he was the best, so he should be the last, Latin poet of the Westminster line; a plot, which I believe he exercised very successfully: for I have not heard of any one who has at all deserved to be compared with him." Even in the time of his last illness, we find that Cowper's dreary thoughts were, for the moment, charmed away by the poems of his old favorite, Vincent Bourne.

Among Cowper's cotemporaries at Westminster were William (afterward Sir William) Russell, whose premature death he had early occasion to deplore; Cumberland, the essayist, with whom

---

* Vincent or Vinny Bourne, the elegant Latin poet, and usher of Westminster School, where he was educated, died in 1747. Cowper has left also this feeling tribute to his old tutor:

"I love the memory of Vinny Bourne. I think him a better Latin poet than Tibullus, Propertius, Ausonius, or any of the writers in *his* way, except Ovid, and not at all inferior to *him*. . . . . It is not common t , meet with an author who can make you smile, and yet at nobody's expense; who is always entertaining, and yet always harmless; and who, though always elegant, and classical in a degree not always found even in the classics themselves, charms more by the simplicity and playfulness of his ideas than by the neatness and purity of his verse; yet such was poor Vinny."

Vinny's Latin translations of the ballads of "Tweedside," "William and Margaret," and Rowe's "Despairing beside a Clear Stream," in sweetness of numbers and elegant expressions equal the originals, and are considered scarcely inferior to anything in Ovid or Tibullus.

he lodged; Impey, and Hastings, afterward distinguished in India; and G. Colman, Lloyd, and Churchill; these, with a few other Westminster men, limited to seven, formed the Nonsense Club. Cowper likewise speaks of the five brothers Bagot, his school-fellows, as "very amiable and valuable boys." With one of them, Walter Bagot, he renewed his intimacy twenty years after they left school: "I felt much affection for him," says Cowper; and the more so, because it was plain that after so long a time he still retained his for me." Such a renewal of school-friendship is very rare.

Cowper was taken from Westminster at eighteen. He has left, amidst many recollections of a less cheerful cast, the following pleasing picture:

> Be it a weakness, it deserves some praise,
> We love the play-place of our early days;
> The scene is touching, and the heart is stone
> That feels not at the sight, and feels at none.
> The walls on which we tried our graving skill,
> The very name we carved, subsisting still;
> The bench on which we sat while deep employed,
> Though mangled, hacked, and hewed, not yet destroyed;
> The little ones, unbuttoned, glowing hot,
> Playing our games, and on the very spot;
> As happy as we once, to kneel and draw
> The chalky ring, and knuckle down at taw;
> To pitch the ball into the grounded hat,
> Or drive it devious with a dextrous pat;
> The pleasing spectacle at once excites
> Such recollection of our own delights,
> That, viewing it, we seem almost to attain
> Our innocent, sweet simple years again.
> This fond attachment to the well-known place,
> Whence first we started into life's long race,
> Maintains its hold with such unfailing sway,
> We feel it even in age, and at our latest day.

WARREN HASTINGS AT WESTMINSTER.

Few men stand so prominently from the historic canvas of the eighteenth century as Warren Hastings, the first Governor-General of Bengal. He was born in 1732, and left a little orphan, destined to strange and memorable vicissitudes of fortune. Of his childhood, Lord Macaulay has painted this impressive picture:

"The child was sent early to the village school (of Daylsford, in Worcestershire), where he learned his letters on the same bench with the sons of the peasantry; nor did anything in his garb or fare indicate that his life was to take a widely different course from that of the young rustics with whom he studied and played. But no cloud could overcast the dawn of so much genius and so much ambition. The very plowmen observed, and long remembered, how kindly little Warren took to his book. When he was eight years old he went up to London, and was sent to a school at Newington, where he was well taught but ill fed. He always attributed the smallness of his stature to the hard and scanty fare of this seminary. At ten, he was removed to Westminster school. Vinny Bourne was one of the masters. Churchill, Colman, Lloyd, Cumberland, Cowper, were among the students. Warren was distinguished among his comrades as an excellent swimmer, boatman, and scholar. At fourteen, he was first in the examination for the foundation. His name in gilded letters on the walls of the dormitory still attests his victory over many elder compeers. He stayed two years longer at the school, and was looking forward to a studentship at Christchurch, when he was removed from Westminster to fill a writership obtained for him in the service of the East India Company. He was placed for a few months at a commercial academy, to study arithmetic and book-keeping; and in January, 1750, a few days after he had completed his seventeenth year, he sailed for Bengal, and arrived at his destination in the October following."

It is worthy of remark, that Warren Hastings was removed from Westminster through the death of his uncle, who bequeathed him to the care of a friend, who was desirous to get rid of his charge as soon as possible. Dr. Nichols, the head-master at Westminster, made strong remonstrances against the removal of a youth who seemed likely to be one of the first scholars of the age. He even offered to bear the expense of sending his favorite pupil to Oxford. But the guardian was inflexible, obtained for the youth the writership, and he was sent to India. Here he rose through indomitable force of will, which was the most striking peculiarity of his character, to be Governor-General of Bengal. Lord Macaulay touchingly says:

"When, under a tropical sun, he ruled fifty millions of Asiatics, his hopes, amidst all the cares of war, finance, and legislation, still pointed to Daylsford. And when his long public life, so singularly chequered with good and evil, with glory and obloquy, had at length closed for ever, it was to Daylsford he retired to die."

GIBBON, THE HISTORIAN — HIS SCHOOLS AND PLAN OF STUDY.

Edward Gibbon, the celebrated historian, was born at Putney, in Surrey, 1737, in a house situated between the roads which lead to Wandsworth and Wimbledon.

From his own account we learn that in childhood Gibbon's health was delicate, and that his early education was principally conducted by his aunt, Mrs. Porter. At the age of nine, he was sent to a boarding-school at Kingston-upon-Thames, where he remained two years, but made little progress, on account of his ill-health. The same cause prevented his attention to study at Westminster School, whither he was sent in 1749; and "his riper age was left to acquire the beauties of the Latin and the rudiments of the Greek tongue." After residing for a short time with the Rev. Philip Francis, the translator of Horace, he was removed, in 1752, to Oxford, where he matriculated as a gentleman commoner of Magdalen College, in his fifteenth year. Though his frequent absence from school had prevented him from obtaining much knowledge of Latin and Greek, his love of reading had led him to peruse many historical and geographical works; and he arrived at Oxford, according to his own account, "with a stock of erudition that might have puzzled a doctor, and a degree of ignorance of which a school-boy would have been ashamed." His imperfect education was not improved during his residence at Oxford: his tutors he describes as easy men, who preferred receiving their fees to attending to the instruction of their pupils; and after leading a somewhat dissipated life for fourteen months, he embraced the Roman Catholic faith.

With the object of reclaiming Gibbon to Protestantism, his father sent him to Lausanne, in Switzerland, to reside with M. Pavillard, a Calvinist minister, whose arguments and Gibbon's own studies led him in the following year to profess his belief in the doctrines of the Protestant church. He remained in Switzerland for five years, during which time he studied hard, to remedy the defects of his early education. He had now become perfectly acquainted with the French language, in which he composed his first work. His biographer, Lord Sheffield, observes that "Gibbon's residence at Lausanne was highly favorable to his progress in knowledge, and the formation of regular habits of study;" to this fortunate period of retirement and application, he was chiefly indebted for his future reputation as a writer and a thinker; and for his production of the *History of the Decline and Fall of the Roman Empire*, the most brilliant work in modern historical literature.

ARCHDEACON PALEY AT CAMBRIDGE.

Paley was fortunate in his education. He was born at Peterborough, in 1743: during his infancy, his father removed to Giggleswick, in Yorkshire, having been appointed head-master of King Edward's School, in that place. He was educated under his paternal roof, and soon distinguished himself by great abilities, a studious disposition, and a rare ripeness of intellect. In his seventeenth year he was entered a sizar of Christ's College, Cambridge; when his father declared that he would turn out a very great man, for he had by far the clearest head he had ever met with in his life. The event fully verified his parent's declaration. He graduated in 1763, and was senior wrangler. After completing his academical course, he became tutor in an academy at Greenwich; next curate of Greenwich; and fellow of his College, and lectured in the University on Moral Philosophy and the Greek Testament. Among his preferments he received the archdeaconry of Carlisle. As a writer he is distinguished for power of intellect, skill in argument, and strong, exact, and clear style. His great works are on Moral and Political Philosophy, the Evidences of Christianity, and Natural Theology. Both in his metaphysical and ethical views, Paley was a follower of Locke. His merits are thus summed up by Bishop Turton:

"It has long been deemed the glory of Socrates, that he brought Philosophy from the schools of the learned to the habitations of men—by stripping it of its technicalities, and exhibiting it in the ordinary language of life. There is no one in modern times who has possessed the talent and disposition for achievements of this kind to an equal extent with Paley; and we can scarcely conceive any one to have employed such qualities with greater success. The transmutation of metals into gold was the supreme object of the alchymist's aspirations. But Paley had acquired a more enviable power. Knowledge, however abstruse, by passing through his mind, became plain common sense—stamped with the characters which insured it currency in the world."

Paley thus strikingly remarks on Teaching:

Education, in the most extensive sense of the word, may comprehend every preparation that is made in our youth for the sequel of our lives; and in this sense I use it. Some such preparation is necessary for all conditions, because without it they must be miserable, and probably will be vicious when they grow up. either from the want of the means of subsistence, or from want of rational and inoffensive occupation. In civilized life, everything is effected by art and skill. Whence, a person who is provided with neither (and neither can be acquired without exercise and instruction) will be useless; and he that is useless will generally be at the same time mischievous to the community So that to send an uneducated child into the world, is injurious to the rest of mankind; it is little better than to turn out a mad dog or a wild beast into the streets.

SIR JOSEPH BANKS AT ETON.

This distinguished naturalist, and great friend to the advancement of science, was born in Argyle-street, London, in 1743. He received his earliest education under a private tutor; at nine years of age, he was sent to Harrow School, and was removed, when thirteen, to Eton. He is described in a letter from his tutor as being well-disposed and good-tempered, but so immoderately fond of play, that his attention could not be fixed to study. When fourteen, he was found, for the first time, reading during his hours of leisure. This sudden turn, Banks, at a later period, explained to his friend, Sir Everard Home. One fine summer evening, he bathed in the Thames, as usual, with other boys, but having stayed a long time in the water, he found, when he came to dress himself, that all his companions were gone: he was walking leisurely along a lane, the sides of which were richly enameled with flowers; he stopped, and looking round, involuntarily exclaimed, "How beautiful!" After some reflection, he said to himself, "it is surely more natural that I should be taught to know all these productions of nature, in preference to Greek and Latin; but the latter is my father's command, and it is my duty to obey him: "I will, however, make myself acquainted with all these different plants for my own pleasure and gratification." He began immediately to teach himself botany; and for want of more able tutors, submitted to be instructed by the women employed in "culling simples," to sup'y the druggists' and apothecaries' shops; he paid sixpence for every material piece of information. While at home for the ensuing holidays, he found in his mother's dressing-room, to his great delight, a book in which all the plants he had met with were not only described, but represented by engravings. This proved to be Gerard's *Herbal*, which, although one of the boards was lost and several leaves were torn out, young Banks carried with him to Eton, where he continued his collection of plants, and also made one of butterflies and other insects. Lord Brougham states that his father, who was Banks's intimate friend, describes him as "a remarkably fine-looking, strong, and active boy, whom no fatigue could subdue, and no peril daunt; and his whole time, out of school, was given up to hunting after plants and insects, making a *hortus siccus* of the one, and forming a cabinet of the other. As often as Banks could induce him to quit his task in reading or in verse-making (says Lord Brougham), he would take him on his long rambles; and I suppose it was from this early taste that we had at Brougham so many butterflies, beetles, and other insects, as well as a cabinet of shells and fossils; but my father always said that his friend Joe cared mighty little for his book, and could not understand any one taking to Greek and Latin."

Banks left Eton at eighteen, and was entered a gentleman-commoner at Christchurch, Oxford, in December, 1760. His love of botany, which commenced at school, increased at the University, and there his mind warmly embraced all other branches of natural history. Finding there were no lectures given on botany, by permission, he engaged a botanical professor from Cambridge, to lecture at Oxford, his remuneration to be derived from the students who formed his class. Mr. Banks soon made himself known in the University by his superior knowledge of natural history.

"He once told me," says Everard Home, "that when he first went to Oxford, if he happened to come into any party of students in which they were discussing questions respecting Greek authors, some of them would call out 'Here is Banks, but he knows nothing of Greek!' To this rebuke he would make no reply, but said to himself, I will very soon excel you all in another kind of knowledge, in my mind of infinitely greater importance ; and not long after, when any of them wanted to clear up a point of natural history, they said, 'We must go to Banks!'"

He left Oxford at the end of 1763, after having taken an honorary degree. His election into the Royal Society, and his presidency, and the extension of science, were the leading objects of his after-life, during the last thirty years of which all the voyages of discovery made under the auspices of Government had either been suggested by him (Sir Joseph), or had received his approbation and support. He died in his 78th year.

SIR WILLIAM JONES AT HARROW.

This great Oriental scholar was born in London, in 1746: his father, an eminent mathematician, dying when his son was only three years old, the education of young Jones devolved upon his mother, a woman of extensive learning. When in his fifth year, the imagination of the young scholar was caught by the sublime description of the angel in the 10th chapter of the Apocalypse, and the impression was never effaced. In 1753, he was placed at Harrow School, under Dr. Thackeray, and continued under Dr. Sumner.

<small>Lord Teignmouth relates that, when a boy at Harrow, Sir W. Jones invented a political play, in which Dr. William Bennett, Bishop of Cloyne, and Dr. Parr, also boys, were his principal associates. They divided the fields in the neighborhood of Harrow according to a map of Greece, into states and kingdoms: each fixed upon one as his dominions, and assumed an ancient name. Some of the school-fellows, as barbarians, invaded their territories, and attacked their hillocks or fortresses. The chiefs defended their respective domains against the incursions of the enemy; and in these imitative wars the young statesmen held councils; all doubtless very boyish, but admirably calculated to fill their minds with ideas of legislation and civil government. In these amusements, Jones was ever the leader.</small>

In 1764, he was entered of University College, Oxford: here his taste for Oriental literature continued, and he engaged a native of Aleppo, whom he had discovered in London, to act as his preceptor; he also assiduously read the Greek poets and historians. After the completion of his academical career, through his intimacy with Dr. Sumner and Dr. Parr, Jones returned to Harrow as private tutor to Lord Althorpe, afterward Earl Spencer. A fellowship of Oxford was also conferred upon him.

Sir W. Jones, in addition to great acquirements in other departments of knowledge, made himself acquainted with no fewer than twenty-eight different languages. He was from his boyhood a miracle of industry. He used to relate that when he was only three or four years of age, if he applied to his mother, a woman of uncommon intelligence and acquirements, for information upon any subject, her constant answer to him was, "Read, and you will know." He thus acquired a passion for books, which only grew in strength with increasing years. Even at school his voluntary exertions exceeded in amount his prescribed tasks; and Dr. Thackeray, one of his masters, was wont to say of him, that he was a boy of so active a mind, that if he were left naked and friendless upon Salisbury Plain, he would nevertheless find the road to fame and riches. At this time he often devoted whole nights to study, when he generally took coffee or tea to keep off sleep. To divert his leisure, he commenced the study of the law; and he is said to have often surprised his mother's legal acquaintances by putting cases to them from an abridgment of Coke's Institutes, which he had read and mastered. In after-life his maxim was never to neglect any opportunity of improvement which presented itself. In conformity with this rule, while making the most wonderful exertions in the study of Greek, Latin, and the Oriental languages, at Oxford, he took advantage of the vacations to learn riding and fencing, and to read all the best authors in Italian, Spanish, Portuguese, and French; thus—to transcribe an observation of his own — "with the fortune of a peasant, giving himself the education of a prince."

When in his thirty-third year, Sir William Jones resolved, as appears from a scheme of study found among his papers, "to learn no more rudiments of any kind; but to *perfect* himself in, first, twelve languages, as the *means* of acquiring accurate knowledge of history, arts, and sciences." These were the Greek, Latin, Italian, French, Spanish, Portuguese, Hebrew, Arabic, Persian, Turkish, German, and English: but he eventually extended his researches beyond even these ample limits. He made himself not only completely master of Sanscrit, as well as less completely af Hindostanee and Bengalee, but to a considerable extent also of the other Indian dialects. The languages which he describes himself to have studied least perfectly were the Chinese, Russian, Runic, Syrian, Ethiopic, Coptic, Dutch, Swedish, and Welsh. Yet, Sir William Jones died at the early age of forty-seven.

HOW DR. PARR BECAME A PARSON INSTEAD OF A SURGEON.

Samuel Parr was born at Harrow-on-the-Hill, in 1747, where his father was a surgeon and apothecary. It was the accident of his birthplace that laid the foundation of his fame; for he was sent to the grammar-school at Harrow in his sixth year. In his boyhood he wrs studious after a fashion, delighting in Mother Goose and the Seven Champions, and little caring for boyish sports. One day he was seen sitting on the churchyard gate at Harrow, with great gravity, whilst his school-fellows were all at play. "Sam, why don't you play with the others?" cried a friend. " Do not you know, sir," said Parr, with vast solemnity, "that I am to be a parson?" When nine or ten years old, he would put on one of his father's shirts for a surplice, and read the church service to his sisters and cousins, after they had been duly summoned by a bell tied to the banisters; preach them a sermon; and even in spite of his father's remonstrance, would bury a bird or a kitten (Parr had always a great fondness for animals), with the rites of Christian burial. At school, his masters predicted his future eminence; but, at the age of 14, when he was at the head of the school, he was removed from it, and placed in his father's shop. Here he criticised the Latin of the apothecary's prescriptions, and showed great dislike of the business; while he continued his classical studies, by getting one of his former companions to report to him the master's remarks on the lesson of every day, as it was read; and Parr, having in vain tried to reconcile himself to the business for three years, was, at length, sent to Emmanuel College, Cambridge, where he studied hard in the classics and philology. Soon after, his father died, and he was compelled, before he had taken a degree, to relinquish his academic career, when he became an under-master of Harrow School. He now took deacon's orders: he continued assistant-master at Harrow five years, when he became a candidate for the head-mastership, but was defeated: a rebellion ensued among the boys, many of whom took Parr's part, and he withdrew to Stanmore, a village in the neighborhood, where he set up a school, followed by 40 of the young rebels. Here ensued many disappointments and struggles with misfortune, which did not, however, prevent Parr from becoming one of the greatest scholars of his time.

Parr himself used to tell of Sir William Jones, another of his school-fellows, that as they were one day walking together near Harrow, Jones suddenly stopped short, and looking hard at him, cried out, "Parr, if you should have the good luck to live forty years, you may stand a chance of overtaking your face."

Dr. Parr quitted Cambridge with deep regret.

"I left Emmanuel College (he says), as must not be dissembled, before the usual time, and in truth had been almost compelled to leave it, not by the want of a proper education, for I had arrived in the first place of the first form of Harrow School when I was not quite fourteen; not for the want of useful tutors, for mine were eminently able, and to me had been uniformly kind; not for the want of ambition, for I had begun to look up ardently and anxiously to academical distinctions; not for the want of attachment to the place, for I regarded it then, as I continue to regard it now, with the fondest and most unfeigned affection; but by another want which it was unnecessary to name, and for the supply of which, after some hesitation, I determined to provide by patient toil and resolute self-denial, when I had not completed my twentieth year. I ceased, therefore, to reside, with an aching heart; I looked back with mingled feelings of regret and humiliation to advantages of which I could no longer partake, and honors to which I could no longer aspire. The unreserved conversation of scholars, the disinterested offices of friendship, the use of valuable books, and the example of good men, are endearments by which Cambridge will keep a strong hold upon my esteem, my respect, and my gratitude to the last moment of my life."

Dr. Parr has left this striking illustration, enjoining upon children Tenderness to Animals:

"He that can look with rapture upon the agonies of an unoffending and unresisting animal, will soon learn to view the sufferings of a fellow-creature with indifference; and in time he will acquire the power of viewing them with triumph, if that fellow-creature should become the victim of his resentment, be it just or unjust. But the minds of children are open to impressions of every sort, and, indeed, wonderful is the facility with which a judicious instructor may habituate them to tender emotions. I have, therefore, always considered mercy to beings of an inferior species as a virtue which children are very capable of learning, but which is most difficult to be taught if the heart has been once familiarized to spectacles of distress, and has been permitted either to behold the pangs of any living creature with cold insensibility, or to inflict them with wanton barbarity."

LORDS ELDON AND STOWELL AT NEWCASTLE AND OXFORD.

John Scott, Earl of Eldon, the greatest lawyer of his time, and Lord High Chancellor of England for seven-and-twenty years, was the son of Mr. John Scott, coalfitter, in Newcastle-upon-Tyne, and was born in that town in 1751. His elder brother, Lord Stowell, was born in 1645, under circumstances of some peculiarity, which had a remarkable effect on the fortunes of the two brothers in after-life. The story is thus told:

> In 1745, the city of Edinburgh having surrendered to the Pretender's army, his road to London lay through Newcastle, the town-walls of which bristled with cannon, and the place was otherwise prepared for a siege. Mrs Scott was, at that time, in such a condition as made her anxious to be removed to a more quiet place. This, however, was a matter of some difficulty; for Mr. Scott's house was situated in one of the narrow lanes of Newcastle, between which and the river Tyne ran the town-wall, the gates of which were closed and fortified. In this dilemma, Mrs Scott was placed in a basket, and, by aid of a rope, hoisted over the wall to the water-side, whence a boat conveyed her to Haworth, a village about four miles from Newcastle, but on the southern bank of the Tyne: and here, within about two days after the above removal, Mrs. Scott gave birth to the twins, William and Barbara.

Lord Stowell having been thus born in the county of Durham, was eligible for a scholarship, which fell vacant for that diocese, in Corpus Christi College, Oxford, which he succeeded in obtaining; and thus laid the foundation, not only of his own, but of his still more successful brother's prosperity.

Lord Eldon was carefully educated at home, after the fashion of the old school, the birch being freely applied, especially for his habit of telling direct untruths, but without effecting contrition for the offense. This is stated upon the authority of his anecdote-book, where he recounts sundry instances of sturdy lying, apparently with some pride; yet, there was constant serious observance at home. "I believe," said Lord Eldon, "I have preached more sermons than any one that is not a clergyman. My father always had the Church Service read on the Sunday evenings, and a sermon after it. Harry and I used to take it in turns to read the prayers or to preach: we always had a shirt put over our clothes to answer for a surplice."

John and William were sent to the free grammar-school at Newcastle,* where John seems to have been noted as a lad of great abilities, and to have indicated early that constant activity of mind which was his characteristic throughout life. On their teacher in the school, the Rev. Hugh Moises, the Scotts appear to have produced a feeling of very deep and lasting affection. With great pride did the provincial schoolmaster watch the rising footsteps of his two favorite pupils; and, to do them justice,

---

* At this school, founded and endowed by the Mayor of Newcastle, in 1525, Bishop Ridley, the poet Akenside, Lord Collingwood, and other eminent persons, received the earlier part of their education.

they seem to have reciprocated the attachment. Lord Eldon kept up his correspondence with his old preceptor, amid all the honors and distinctions which future years showered on him. One of the first acts of his Chancellorship was to make Mr. Moises one of his chaplains. He twice afterward offered him still more substantial preferment; this the old man declined, but the patronage was bestowed upon his family.

Lord Stowell having gone to Oxford, and commenced his career with great success, it was intended that John should follow his father's occupation. His brother, however, who knew his great abilities, would not allow them to be so buried. "Send Jack here," he wrote from Oxford; "I can do better for him." And to Oxford Jack was sent accordingly, and entered as a commoner of University College, in the year 1766, under the tutorship of his brother.

The only distinction which Lord Eldon acquired at Oxford, was gaining the Lichfield prize by an "Essay on the Advantages and Disadvantages of Foreign Travel." He took his Bachelor's degree, and intended to prosecute his studies for the Church. But an event, fortunately as it turned out, averted the whole current of his life. He fell in love with the daughter of a townsman of his father's, and we trace half-stifled lamentations in his letters to his companions from Oxford. At last, he eloped with the lady to Scotland: the relations were highly displeased with the match, and the fortunes of the bridegroom were supposed to be so completely marred by this exploit, that a wealthy grocer in Newcastle offered to his father to take him into partnership, as the only means of establishing him respectably. The proposal was so far entertained as to be referred to William Scott for his opinion; but his answer in the negative preserved his brother for greater things. Lord Eldon's marriage, however, rendered it impossible for him to prosecute his views toward the church with any chance of success, unless a living should fall vacant to his College during the first year: he accordingly resolved to turn himself to the law, and entered in the Middle Temple, in January, 1773. The year of grace passed without any College living becoming vacant, and thus was his destiny conclusively fixed. While keeping his terms in the Temple, he continued his residence at Oxford, assiduously prosecuting his legal studies, and employed partly as tutor of University College, during 1774–75, and partly as Deputy Professor of Law, for which service he received 60*l.* a year. He relates that immediately after he was married, the Law Professor sent him the first lecture to read *immediately* to the students, and this he began without knowing a single word that was in it. It was upon the statute of young men running away with young maidens. "Fancy me," he says, "reading, with about one hundred and forty boys and young men all giggling at the Professor. Such a tittering audience no one ever had!"

Lord Eldon well remembered Johnson in college at Oxford. He relates of the Doctor:

"If put out of temper, he was not very moderate in the terms in which he expressed his displeasure. I remember that in the common-room of University College, he was dilating upon some subject, and the then head of Lincoln College, Dr. Mortimer, was present. Whilst Johnson was stating what he proposed to communicate, the Doctor occasionally interrupted him, saying, 'I deny that!' This was often repeated, and observed upon by Johnson, as it was repeated, in terms expressive of exceeding displeasure and anger. At length, upon the Doctor's repeating the words 'I deny that,' 'Sir, sir,' said Johnson, 'you must have forgot that an author has said, *Plus negabit unus asinus in una hora, quam centum philosophi probaverint in centum annis.*'"

Lord Eldon finally removed to London in 1775, but with gloomy prospects, being almost without a sixpence he could call his own, and receiving little attention from his father and other relations. Indeed, the generosity and kindness of his brother William, for which in after-life he was always deeply grateful, were chiefly instrumental in enabling him to prosecute his views for the bar. He first lived in Cursitor-street, of which he used to say: "Many a time have I run down from Cursitor-street to Fleet-market, to get sixpennyworth of sprats for supper." Lord Eldon was called to the bar in 1776. He waited long in vain for clients, and had resolved to quit Westminster Hall, to seek his native city; when the accident of a leading counsel's sudden indisposition introduced him to the notice of the profession, and his success at the bar became thenceforth certain.*

THE TWO BROTHERS MILNER.

These eminent churchmen were originally Yorkshire weavers, but were, by fortuitous circumstances, well educated. Joseph Milner, born in 1744, was sent to the grammar-school at Leeds, where, by his industry and talents, among which a memory of most extraordinary power was conspicuous, he gained the warm regard of his instructor, who resolved to have him sent to college. This plan was nearly frustrated by the death of Milner's father, in very narrow circumstances; but by the assistance of some gentlemen in Leeds, whose children Milner had lately engaged in teaching, he was sent to Catherine Hall, Cambridge, at the age of 18. He afterward became head-master of Hull

* At Vauxhall, a Public School for 140 boys was founded in 1820, by Mr. Charles Francis, of Belgrave House, "to perpetuate the memory of the Earl of Eldon, and to commemorate his able, zealous, and constant defense of the Protestant Reformed Religion against every innovation." The School-house, a Tudor building, is adorned with a statue of Lord Eldon, upon the anniversary of whose birthday, June 4, the public examination of the boys takes place.

grammar-school, and vicar of that parish, and wrote many learned works, of which his *History of the Church of Christ* is the principal.

His brother, Isaac Milner, Dean of Carlisle, born in 1751, at the age of six accompanied him to the Leeds grammar-school; but at his father's death, he was taken away to learn the woolen manufacture. When Joseph Milner was appointed to the headmastership of the Hull grammar-school, he released his brother from his engagements at Leeds, and took him under his own tuition, employing him as his assistant in teaching the younger boys. In the Life of his brother, the Dean expresses his sense of this kindness with affectionate warmth. In 1770, Isaac Milner entered Queen's College, Cambridge: here he rose to be Lucasian Professor of Mathematics, and he was twice Vice-Chancellor. He became the intimate friend of Mr. Wilberforce and Mr. Pitt. He was a man of extensive and accurate learning; wrote several works; and greatly assisted his brother Joseph in his History of the Church.

HOW WILLIAM GIFFORD BECAME A SCHOLAR AND CRITIC.

William Gifford, the eminent critic, was born in 1755, at Ashburton, in Devonshire; and by the early death of both parents, was left, at the age of 13, penniless, homeless, and friendless. He had learned reading, writing, and a little arithmetic, when his godfather took charge of him, sent him again to school; but just as Gifford was making considerable progress in artithmetic, his patron grew tired of the expense, and took him home to employ him as a plow-boy, for which, however, he was unfit. It was next resolved that he should be sent to Newfoundland to assist in a storehouse; but for this he was declared "too small." He was then sent as a cabin-boy, on board a coasting vessel, where he remained about a twelvemonth, during which time the only book he saw was the "Coasting Pilot." His godfather then took him home, and sent him again to school, where, in a few months, he became head boy. His godfather now thought he "had learned enough, and more than enough, at school," and apprenticed him to a shoemaker at Ashburton. But Gifford's strong thirst for knowledge had not abated: mathematics at first were his favorite study; and he relates that, for want of paper, he used to hammer scraps of leather smooth, and work his problems on them with a blunt awl: for the rest, his memory was tenacious, and he could multiply and divide by it to a great extent. His master finding his services worth nothing, used harsh means to wean him from his literary tastes; and Gifford, hating his business, sank into a sort of savage melancholy. From this state he was withdrawn by the active kindness of Mr. Cookesly, a surgeon, of Ashburton, who had seen some rhymes by Gifford, and with his sad story, conceived a strong regard for him, and raised "a subscription for purchasing the remainder of the time of William Gifford, and for enabling him to improve himself in writing and English grammar." Enough was collected to free him from his apprenticeship; he was placed at school, and in two years sent to Exeter College, Oxford. Not long after, Mr. Cookesley died; but a more efficient patron was raised up in Earl Grosvenor, who gave Gifford a home in his own mansion. A long and prosperous life followed: he executed translations of Latin poets; edited the works of Massinger, Ben Jonson, Ford, and Shirley; and was appointed editor of the *Quarterly Review* upon its first establishment. He died in 1826, leaving the bulk of his fortune to the son of his first patron, Mr. Cookesley.

LORD NELSON'S SCHOOLS IN NORFOLK.

Horatio Nelson was born with a quick good sense, an affectionate heart, and a high spirit, by which qualities his boyhood was strongly marked. He was the fifth son and the sixth child of Edmund and Catherine Nelson; his birth took place in 1758, in the parsonage-house of Burnham Thorpe, a village in the county of Norfolk, of which his father was rector. The maiden name of his mother was Suckling;* her grandmother was an elder sister of Sir Robert Walpole, and this child was named after his godfather, the first Lord Walpole. Horatio "was never of a strong body," says Southey; "and the ague, which was at that time one of the most common diseases in England, had greatly reduced his strength;" yet he very early gave proofs of that resolute heart and nobleness of mind which, during his whole career of labor and of glory, so eminently distinguished him. When a mere child, he strayed a bird's-nesting from his grandmother's house, in company with a cow-boy; the dinner-hour elapsed, he was absent, and could not be found; when the alarm of the family became very great, for they apprehended that he might have been carried off by gipsies. At length, after search had been made for him in various directions, he was discovered alone, sitting composedly by the side of a brook which he could not get over. "I wonder, child," said the old lady when she saw him, "that hunger and fear did not drive you home." "Fear! grandmamma," replied the future hero; "I never saw fear—what is it?"

* A descendant of Sir John Suckling, the poet. One of the family married a descendant of Inigo Jones.

Nelson was first sent to a small school at Downham; and in the market-place, as often as he could get there, he might be seen, working away, in his little green coat, at the pump, till, by the help of his school-fellows, a sufficient pond was made for floating the little ship which he had cut with a knife, and rigged with a paper sail. An incident, showing Nelson's compassionate disposition, is related of him at this age. A shoemaker of Downham had a pet-lamb, which he kept in his shop; and one day Nelson accidentally jammed the animal between the door and the door-post, when the little fellow's sorrow for the pain he had unwittingly inflicted was excessive, and for some time uncontrollable.

Horatio was next sent, with his brother William, to a larger school at North Walsham, where another characteristic incident occurred. There were some fine pears growing in the schoolmaster's garden, which the boys regarded as lawful booty, and in the highest degree tempting; but the boldest among them was afraid to venture for the fruit. Horatio volunteered upon the service: he was lowered down at night from the bed-room window by some sheets, he plundered the tree, and was drawn up with the pears, which he distributed among his school-fellows, without reserving any for himself—"I only took them," he said, "because every other boy was afraid."

Nelson's mother died in 1767, leaving eight out of eleven children. Her brother, Captain Maurice Suckling, of the Navy, visited the widow upon this event, and promised to take care of one of the boys. Three years afterward, when Horatio was only twelve years of age, being at home for the Christmas holidays, he read in the county newspaper that his uncle was appointed to the *Raisonnable*, of 64 guns. "Do, William," said he to a brother who was a year and a half older than himself, "write to my father, and tell him that I should like to go to sea with uncle Maurice." Mr. Nelson was then at Bath: his circumstances were straitened, and he knew that it was the wish of providing for himself by which Horatio was chiefly actuated; he did not oppose his resolution; he understood the boy's character, and had always said that in whatever station he might be placed, he would climb, if possible, to the very top of the tree. Accordingly, Captain Suckling was written to: "What," said he, in his answer, "has poor Horatio done, who is so weak, that he, above all the rest, should be sent to rough it out at sea?— But let him come, and the first time we go into action, a cannonball may knock off his head, and provide for him at once."

The brothers returned to their school at North Walsham. Not

long after, early on a cold and dark spring morning, Mr. Nelson's servant arrived with the expected summons for Horatio to join his ship. The parting from his brother William, who had been so long his playmate, was a painful effort. He accompanied his father to London. The *Raisonnable* was lying in the Medway. He was put into the Chatham stage, and on its arrival was set down with the rest of the passengers, and left to find his way on board as he could. After wandering about in the cold without being able to reach the ship, an officer, observing the forlorn appearance of the boy, questioned him; and happening to be acquainted with his uncle, took him home and gave him some refreshment. When he got on board, Captain Suckling was not in the ship, nor had any person been apprised of the boy's coming. He paced the deck the whole remainder of the day, without being noticed by any one; and it was not till the second day that somebody, as he expressed it, "took compassion on him." Mr. Southey feelingly adds:

"The pain which is felt when we are first transplanted from our native soil, when the living branch is cut from the parent tree, is one of the most poignant griefs which we have to endure through life. There are after-griefs which wound more deeply, which leave behind them scars never to be effaced, which bruise the spirit, and sometimes break the heart : but never do we feel so keenly the want of love, the necessity of being loved, and the sense of utter desertion, as when we first leave the haven of home, and are, as it were, pushed off upon the stream of life. Added to these feelings, the sea-boy has to endure physical hardships, and the privation of every comfort, even of sleep. Nelson had a feeble body and an affectionate heart, and he remembered through life his first days of wretchedness in the service.

In Arthur's Life of the hero, we have Nelson's own account of his birth and early life: "I was born Sept. 29th, 1758, in the parsonage-house; was sent to the High-school at Norwich, and afterward removed to Northway, from whence, on the disturbance with Spain relative to the Falkland Islands, I went to sea with my uncle, Captain Maurice Suckling, in the *Raisonnable*, of 64 guns; but the business with Spain being accommodated, I was sent in a West India ship belonging to the house of Hibbert Purrier Horton, with Mr. John Rathbone, who had formerly been in the navy, in the *Dreadnought*, with Captain Suckling. From this voyage I returned to the *Triumph*, at Chatham, in July, 1772; and if I did not improve in my education, I returned a practical seaman, with a horror of the Royal Navy, and with a saying, then constant with the seamen—'*Aft the most honor, forward the better man.*'"

Such was the start in life of one of the greatest heroes in the annals of British history, or perhaps in the annals of the world, whose great deeds are so numerous, splendid, and important as to "confound the biographer *with excess of light*," and whose death was felt in England as a public calamity; "yet," says

Southey, "he cannot be said to have fallen prematurely whose work was done, or ought he to be lamented who died so full of honors, and at the height of human fame."

ROBERT BURNS, "THE AYRSHIRE PLOWMAN."

Robert Burns, whom his countrymen delight to honor as the Shakspeare of Scotland, was born in 1759, in the parish of Alloway, near Ayr. His father was a poor farmer, who gave his son what education he could afford. Burns tells us that "though it cost the schoolmaster some thrashings," he made an excellent English scholar; and by the time he was ten or eleven years of age, he was a critic in substantives, verbs, and particles. In his infant and boyish days, too, he was much with an old woman who resided in the family, and was remarkable for her ignorance, credulity, and superstition. She had the largest collection in the country of tales and songs concerning demons, ghosts, fairies, brownies, witches, kelpies, elf-candles, dead-lights, wraiths, apparitions, cantraips, giants, enchanted towers, dragons, and other trumpery. This cultivated the latent seeds of poetry, but had so strong an effect on Burns's imagination, that after he had grown to manhood, in his nocturnal rambles he sometimes kept a sharp look-out in suspicious places, and it often took an effort of philosophy to shake off these idle terrors.* He says: "The earliest composition that I recollect taking pleasure in, was *The Vision of Mirza*, and a hymn of Addison's, beginning, 'How are thy servants blest, O Lord!' I particularly remember one stanza, which was music to my boyish ear:

'For though on dreadful whirls we hung
High on the broken wave.'

I met with these pieces in Mason's *English Collection*, one of my school-books. The two first books I ever read in private, and which gave me more pleasure than any two books I ever read since, were *The Life of Hannibal*, and *The History of Sir William Wallace*. Hannibal gave my young ideas such a turn, that I used to strut in rapture up and down after the recruiting drum and bagpipe, and wish myself tall enough to be a soldier; while the story of Wallace poured a Scottish prejudice into my veins, which will boil along there till the flood-gates of life shut in eternal rest."

While Burns lived on his father's little farm, he tells us that he was, perhaps, the most ungainly, awkward boy in the parish. He continues:

* See the Life and Works of Robert Burns. Library Edition. Edited by Robert Chambers.

"What I knew of ancient story was gathered from Salmon's and Guthrie's *Geographical Grammars;* and the ideas I formed of modern manners, literature, and criticism, I got from the *Spectator.* These, with Pope's *Works*, some *Plays* of Shakspeare, Tull and Dickson on *Agriculture*, the *Pantheon*, Locke *On the Human Understanding*, Stackhouse's *History of the Bib'e*, Justice's *British Gardener's Directory*, Bayle's *Lectures*, Allan Ramsay's *Works*, Taylor's *Scripture Doctrine of Original Sin*, *A Select Collection of English Songs*, and Hervey's *Meditations*, had formed the whole of my reading. The Collection of Songs was my vade-mecum. I pored over them driving my cart, or walking to labor, song by song, verse by verse—carefully noting the true, tender, and sublime, from affectation and fustian. I am convinced I owe to this practice much of my critic craft, such as it is."

Burns's father was a man of uncommon intelligence for his station in life, and was anxious that his children should have the best education which their circumstances admitted of. Robert was, therefore, sent in his sixth year to a little school at Alloway Mill, about a mile from their cottage: not long after, his father took a lead in establishing a young teacher, named John Murdoch, in a humble temple of learning, nearer hand, and there Robert and his younger brother, Gilbert, attended for some time. "With him," says Gilbert, "we learned to read English tolerably well, and to write a little. He taught us, too, the English Grammar. I was too young to profit much from his lessons in grammar, but Robert made some proficiency in it; a circumstance of considerable weight in the unfolding of his genius and character, as he soon became remarkable for the fluency and correctness of his expression, and read the few books that came in his way with much pleasure and improvement; for even then he was a reader when he could get a book." Gilbert next mentions that *The Life of Wallace*, which Robert Burns refers to, "he borrowed from the blacksmith who shod our horses."

The poet was about seven years of age when (1766) his father left the *clay bigging* at Alloway, and settled in the small upland farm at Mount Oliphant, about two miles distant. He and his younger brother continued to attend Mr. Murdoch's school for two years longer, when it was broken up. Murdoch took his leave of the boys, and brought, as a present and memorial, a small compendium of English Grammar, and the tragedy of Titus Andronicus; he began to read the play aloud, but so shocked was the party at some of its incidents, that Robert declared if the play were left, he would burn it; and Murdoch left the comedy of the *School for Love* in its place.

The father now instructed his two sons, and other children: there were no boys of their own age in the neighborhood, and their father was almost their only companion: he conversed with them as though they were men; he taught them from Salmon's *Geographical Grammar* the situation and history of the different countries of the world; and from a book-society in Ayr he procured Durham's *Physico and Astro Theology*, and Ray's *Wisdom of God in the Creation,* to give his sons some idea of astronomy and natural history. Robert read all these books with an avidity and industry scarcely to be equaled. From Stackhouse's *History of the Bible,* then lately published in Kilmarnock, Robert collected a competent knowledge of ancient history; "for," says his brother, "no book was so voluminous as to slacken his industry, or so antiquated as to damp his researches." About this time a relative inquired at a bookseller's shop in Ayr for a book to teach Robert to write letters, when, instead of the *Complete Letter Writer,* he got by mistake a small collection of letters by the most eminent writers, with a few sensible directions for attaining an easy epistolary style, which book proved to Burns of the greatest consequence.

Burns was about thirteen or fourteen, when, his father regretting that he and his brother wrote so ill, to remedy this defect sent them to the parish school of Dalrymple, between two and three miles distant, the nearest to them. Murdoch, the boys' former master, now settled in Ayr, as a teacher of the English language: he sent them Pope's Works, and some other poetry, the first they had an opportunity of reading, except that in the English Collection, and in the *Edinburgh Magazine* for 1772. Robert was now sent to Ayr, "to revise his English grammar with his former teacher," but he was shortly obliged to return to assist in the harvest. He then learned surveying at the parish school of Kirkoswald. He had learned French of Murdoch, and could soon read and understand any French author in prose. He then attempted to learn Latin, but soon gave it up. Mrs. Paterson, of Ayr, now lent the boys the *Spectator,* Pope's Translation of Homer, and several other books that were of use to them.

Thus, although Robert Burns was the child of poverty and toil, there were fortunate circumstances in his position: his parents were excellent persons; his father exerted himself as his instructor, and, cottager as he was, contrived to have something like the benefits of private tuition for his two eldest sons; and the young poet became, comparatively speaking, a well-educated man. His father had remarked, from a very early period, the bright intellect of his elder-born in particular, saying to his wife, "Whoever may live to see it, something extraordinary will come from that boy!"

It was not until his twenty-third year that Burns's reading was enlarged by the addition of Thomson, Shenstone, Sterne, and Mackenzie. Other standard works soon followed. The great advantage of his learning was, that what books he had, he read and studied thoroughly—his attention was not distracted by a multitude of volumes, and his mind grew up with original and robust vigor; and in the veriest shades of obscurity, he toiled, when a mere youth, to support his virtuous parents and their household; yet all this time he grasped at every opportunity of acquiring knowledge from men and books.

Burns, says Mr. Carruthers, came as a potent auxiliary or fellow-worker with Cowper, in bringing poetry into the channels of truth and nature. There were only two years between the *Task*, and the *Cotter's Saturday Night*. No poetry was ever more instantaneously or universally popular among a people than that of Burns in Scotland. There was the humor of Smollett, the pathos and tenderness of Sterne or Richardson, the real life of Fielding, and the description of Thomson—all united in the delineations of Scottish manners and scenery by the Ayrshire plowman. His master-piece is Tam o'Shanter: it was so considered by himself, and the judgment has been confirmed by Campbell, Wilson, Montgomery, and by almost every critic.

RICHARD PORSON, "THE NORFOLK BOY," AT HAPPESBURGH, ETON, AND CAMBRIDGE.

Richard Porson was born in 1759, at East Ruston, near North Walsham, Norfolk: he was the eldest son of the parish-clerk of the place, who was a worsted-weaver, and is described as clever in his way. Porson's mother was the daughter of a shoemaker: she was shrewd and lively, and had considerable literary taste, being familiar with Shakspeare and other standard English authors, from her access to a library in a gentleman's house where she lived servant.

Porson, when a boy, was put to the loom at once, and probably helped his mother in the corn-fields in harvest-time. He was next sent to the neighboring school of Happesburgh, the master of which was a good Latin scholar. When the father took his son to school, he said to the master: "I have brought my boy Richard to you, and just want him to make (*sic*) his own name, and then I shall take him into the loom." The master, however, took great pains with the boy, making him at night repeat the lessons he had learnt during the day, and thus, probably, laid the foundation of Porson's unrivaled memory. He had previously been for a short time at a school at Bacton, but was unable to bear the rough treatment of the boys. At Happesburgh, he learnt rapidly—especially arithmetic, of which he continued all his life very fond; and his penmanship was very skillful. His memory was wonderful: he would repeat a lesson which he had learnt one or two years before, and had never seen in the interim. He had only such books as his father's cottage supplied—a volume or two of Arithmetic, Greenwood's *England,* Jewell's *Apology;* an odd volume of Chambers's *Cyclopædia,* picked up from a wrecked coaster; and eight or ten volumes of the *Universal Magazine.*

The remarkable aptitude of Porson soon became noticed: at the age of eleven, Mr. Hewitt, the curate of East Ruston, took charge of his education, and continued to instruct him till the age of thirteen, when his fame as a youthful prodigy, through Mr. Hewitt, became known to Mr. Norris, the founder of the Norrisian Professorship at Cambridge, who said, however: "Well, I see nothing particular in this heavy-looking boy, but I confide in your account of his talents." Porson was then sent to Cambridge, where the Greek Professor, and three tutors of Trinity College, having examined him, reported of him so favorably that Mr. Norris had him entered on the foundation at Eton, in 1774.

Hr. Hewitt, writing to the Cambridge Professor, speaks of having had "the orderly and good boy under his care for almost two years, chiefly on Corderius's Colloquies, Cæsar, Ovid, Horace, and Virgil, and Mathematics. In Greek he was only learning the verbs." *

Of his Eton days, Porson only recollected with pleasure the rat-hunts in the Long Chamber. His promise of excellence appears at this time to have rather diminished: his composition was weak, and his ignorance of quantity kept him behind his inferiors in other respects. He was also prone to conceit in his verses, and fond of mixing Greek with his Latin. He went too late to Eton to have any chance of succeeding to a scholarship at King's. He was popular among his school-fellows, and two dramas which he wrote for performance in the Long Chamber are still remembered. He seems, however, at first to have somewhat disappointed his friends, as Lord Nelson's brother, who was at Eton with Porson, brought back word that they thought nothing of the Norfolk boy. At the same time, his unrivaled memory was noticed at school, and exemplified in the oft-repeated story of his construing Horace from memory, when his book had been abstracted, and Ovid put in its place. And his promise must have been remarkable, as when he left Eton, contributions from Etonians to aid the funds for his maintenance at the University were readily subscribed.

At Eton he remained some four years, and in October, 1778,

---

* These leading details of Porson's life and career of learning have been selected and condensed from a very able paper by H. R. Luard, M.A., in the *Cambridge Essays, contributed by Members of the University.* 1857.

through the aid of Sir George Baker, the celebrated physician (Mr. Norris had died in the previous year), Porson became a member of Trinity College, Cambridge; was elected Scholar in 1780, and Craven University Scholar in 1781. Next year he graduated as third senior optime, and obtained soon after the first Chancellor's medal; and in the same year he was elected Fellow of Trinity, a very unusual thing at that time for a Junior Bachelor of Arts. He seems to have begun his critical career while an undergraduate, and it was, doubtless, during his residence at Cambridge that he laid up his marvelous stores of learning for future use. He now turned his thoughts to publication; and is said to have first appeared in print in a short critique on Schutz's *Æschylus*, in a review started by his friend Maty, a Fellow of Trinity, in 1783; and he contributed to this journal some four years, until it was discontinued. "His review of Brunck's *Aristophanes* is a striking specimen of that strong nervous English for which all Porson's writings are remarkable, and nowhere else are the chief excellencies and defects of the great comic poet so well summed up." But at this period, his chief attention was devoted to *Æschylus*: his restoration of two passages in Plutarch and Æschylus, by each other's help, is one of the earliest as well as one of the most brilliant of all Porson's emendations. "If it be remembered that this was done by a young man at the age of twenty-three, it shows an amount of learning, mingled with the power of applying it, at that age, that it would be vain to seek elsewhere." (*H. R. Luard.*)

In 1786, Porson communicated to a new edition of Hutchinson's *Anabasis of Xenophon* a few annotations which give the first specimen of that neat and terse style of Latin notes in which Porson was afterward to appear without a rival. They also show already his intimate acquaintance with his two favorite authors, Plato and Athenæus, and a familiarity with Eustathius's Commentary on Homer. Next year were written his *Notæ breves* prefixed to the Oxford reprint of Toup, which first made his name known, generally, as a critic of the highest rank. In the same year appeared the most perfect specimen of Porson's wonderful power of humor—the three panegyrical letters in the *Gentleman's Magazine*, on Hawkins's *Life of Johnson*, in which wonderful compositions Porson's force of pleasantry and delicate touches of satire show his extensive acquaintance with the English dramatists, especially with Shakspeare. The whole is an admirable specimen of Porson's peculiar ironical humor.

Porson became better known by his series of Letters to Archdeacon Travis, on the contested verse, 1 John v. 7—in the words of Gibbon, "the most acute and accurate piece of criticism which had appeared since the days of Bentley." Porson also gained great celebrity in the learned world by his discovery of the new canons respecting the Iambic metre of the Greek tragedians, which he announced in the preface to his second edition of the *Hecuba* of Euripides.

We have not space to glance further at Porson's masterly criticisms, or his classical contributions to periodical literature. He resigned his Fellowship through his religious opinions, and was subsequently supported by subscription. He was afterward elected to the Regius Professorship of Greek at Cambridge.

Meanwhile, he lived in Chambers in Essex-court, Temple; and occasionally visited Dr. Goodall, at Eton; and Dr. Parr. While at Hatton, he generally spent his mornings in the library, and in the evening would pour fourth from the rich stores of his memory pages of Barrow, whole letters of Richardson, whole scenes of Foote, recitations from Shakspeare, and etymologies and dissertations on the roots of the English language. His wonderful power of retaining accurately what he had read, and being able to produce it always when called for, never forsook him. Nothing came amiss to his memory: he would set a child right in his twopenny fable-book, repeat the whole of the moral tale of the Dean of Badajos, or a page of Athenæus on cups, or Eustathius on Homer. Sometimes he would recite forgotten Vauxhall songs, and spend hours in making charades or conundrums for ladies, with whom he was a great favorite.

It has been observed of Porson by one who saw much of him, that to the manners of a gentleman, and the most gigantic powers of learning and criticism, he joined the inoffensiveness of a child; and, among his many good qualities, one was, *never to speak ill of the moral character of any man.*

It is not difficult to trace in Porson's habits of thought the influence which the study of mathematics had upon him. He was to his dying day very fond of these studies. There are still preserved many papers of his scribbled over with mathematical calculations; and when the fit seized him in the street which caused his death, an equation was found in his pocket.

Dr. Young has said of him, that "as far as regards the possession of a combination of the faculties which Porson did cultivate, he appears to have been decidedly the most successful of any man on record in the same department."

"To him chiefly," says Mr. Luard, in his excellent paper in the *Cambridge Essays*, "English scholarship (especially Cambridge scholarship) owes its accuracy and its certainty: and this as a branch of education — as a substratum on which to rest other branches of knowledge often infinitely more useful in themselves—really takes as high a rank as any of those studies which can contribute to form the character of a well-educated English gentleman."

How painful is it to add, that a man of such amiable nature and surpassing intellect should have been addicted for many years of his life to the degrading habit of hard-drinking.

THE MARQUIS WELLESLEY AL ETON AND OXFORD.

In the foremost rank of high scholarship at Eton is Richard Marquis Wellesley, the eldest son of the Earl of Mornington, "a person of talents and virtue, and his taste in music being cultivated in an extraordinary degree, he was the author of some beautiful compositions, which still retain their place in the favor of the musical world." Richard was born at Dangan Castle, in the county of Meath, in 1760: his mother, a daughter of Lord Dungannon, lived to an extreme old age: "she saw all the glories of Hindostan, of Spain, and of Waterloo; and left four sons sitting in the House of Lords, not by inheritance, but by merit raised to that proud eminence." *

Richard, who, at his father's death, had nearly attained majority, was sent first to Harrow, and there took part in a great rebellion that had well nigh broken up the school. This occasioned his expulsion, and he then, in his 11th year, went to Eton, where, says his biographer, Lord Brougham, " he was distinguished above all the youths of his time."

When Dr Goodall, his cotemporary, and afterward Head-Master, was examined in 1818, before the Education Committee of the House of Commons respecting the alleged passing over of Porson in giving promotion to King's College, he at once declared that the celebrated Grecian was not by any means at the head of the Etonians of his day; and being asked by me (as chairman) to name his superior, he at once said, Lord Wellesley.—*Lives of Statesmen*, by *Lord Brougham*, who adds in a note, "Some of the Committee would have had this struck out of the evidence, as not bearing upon the subject of the inquiry, the Abuse of Charities; but the general voice was immediately pronounced in favor of retaining it, as a small tribute of our great respect for Lord Wellesley; and I know that he highly valued this tribute."

Dr. Davis was Lord Wellesley's tutor when he entered Eton School; and, in after-life, the Marquis described the Doctor to have always bestowed on his education the solicitude and affection of a kind parent. The pupil greatly excelled in classical studies: some of his verses in the *Musæ Etonenses* have great merit, as examples both of pure Latinity and poetical talent: the Lines on Bedlam, especially, are of distinguished excellence. Some of his Latin poems were published about this early period.

* The Marquis Wellesley, Lord Maryborough, the Duke of Wellington, and Lord Cowley.

On leaving Eton, Lord Wellesley went to Christchurch, Oxford, and here, under Dr. W. Jackson, afterward Bishop of Oxford, he continued his classical studies. His poem on the Death of Captain Cook showed how entirely he had kept up his school reputation: it justly gained the University prize. At college he formed with Lord Grenville a friendship which continued during their lives, and led to his intimacy with Lord Grenville's great kinsman, Mr. Pitt, upon their entering into public life.* Yet the young minister never deemed it worth while to promote Lord Wellesley, whose powers as a speaker were of a high order, and with whom Mr. Pitt lived on the most intimate footing. The trifling place of a junior Lord of the Treasury, and a member of the India Board, formed all the preferment which he received before his appointment as Governor-General of India, although that important nomination sufficiently shows the high estimate which Mr. Pitt had formed of his capacity. In 1781, before taking his degree, Lord Wellesley was called away to Ireland in consequence of the death of his father: subsequently he attended to the education of his younger brothers. Lord Wellesley (says Pearce, his biographer) "was deeply attached throughout his long life to Eton. Some of the latest productions of his lordship's pen were dedicated to his beloved Eton; and in testimony of the strong affection which he entertained toward the place where he received his first impressions of literary taste, and in accordance with his desire expressed before his death, his body was deposited in a vault of Eton Chapel."

In his riper years, Lord Wellesley retained the same classical taste which had been created at school and nurtured at college. As late as a few weeks before his death, he amused himself with Latin verses, was constant in reading the Greek orators and poets, and corresponded with the Bishop of Durham upon a favorite project which he had formed of learn-

* When Mr. Pitt was a youth, some law-lord (could it be Lord Mansfield?) one morning paid a visit to Lord Chatham at his country residence. Whilst they were conversing, his son William came through the library. Lord ——— asked who is that youth? Lord Chatham said, "That is my second son—call him back and talk to him. They did so, and Lord ——— was struck by a forwardness of knowledge, a readiness of expression, and unyieldingness of opinion, which even then was remarkable in the future minister. When he had left them, Lord Chatham said: "That is the most extraordinary youth I ever knew. All my life I have been aiming at the possession of political power, and have found the greatest difficulty in getting or keeping it. It is not on the cards of fortune to prevent that young man's gaining it, and if ever he does so, he will be the ruin of his country."—*Blackwood's Edinburgh Magazine*, 1825.

Pitt was born in 1759. Lord Brougham gracefully says of Pitt: "At an age when others are but entering on the study of state affairs and the practice of debating, he came forth a mature politician, a finished orator, even, as if by inspiration, an accomplished debater. His knowledge, too, was not confined to the study of the classics, though with these he was familiarly conversant; the more severe pursuits of Cambridge had imparted to him some acquaintance with the stricter sciences which have had their home upon the banks of the Granta since Newton made them his abode; and with political philosophy he was more familiar than most Englishmen of his own age." In honor of this great Statesman there was founded, in 1813, in the University of Cambridge, a Classical "Pitt Scholarship."

ing Hebrew, so that he might be able to relish the beauties of the Sacred Writings, particularly the Psalmody, an object of much admiration with him. His exquisite lines on the "Babylonian Willow,* transplanted from the Euphrates a hundred years ago," were suggested by the delight he took in the 137th Psalm, the most affecting and beautiful of the inspired King's whole poetry. This fine piece was the production of his eighteenth year.—*Lord Brougham.*

LORD-CHIEF-JUSTICE TENTERDEN AT CANTERBURY AND OXFORD.

The vicissitudes of life, and the contrast presented by great elevation from a very humble origin, are strikingly exemplified in the history of this able and impartial judge.

Charles Abbott, Baron Tenterden, was born in 1762, at Canterbury, where his father was a hair-dresser, "a very decent, well-behaved man, much respected in his neighborhood," who did his best, with decent humility, to obtain for his son a good education. Young Abbott was sent to the King's School in Canterbury Cathedral, of which he became the captain, and where he so distinguished himself that the trustees of the school came to a special vote to send him as an exhibitioner to the University of Oxford. This assistance he afterward repaid from his private purse, by opening it to the same trustees in a similar exigency. While he was at Canterbury school, his master, Dr. Osmond Beauvoir, it is said, proud of his proficiency, showed his verses to the clergy of the neighborhood, boasting that "the son of the Canterbury barber was qualified to carry off a classical prize from any aristocratic versifier at Westminster, Winchester, or Eton."

He obtained remarkable honors at Oxford. The Class List was not established till the commencement of this century, and young Abbott took his bachelor's degree in 1785: consequently, there being yet no *tripos*, he was obliged to content himself with all the honors which were open to him. He had gained a scholarship at Corpus after he had been a week in Oxford, and he gained in 1784 the Latin prize poem, subject, "*Globus aërostaticus;*" and in 1786, the English prize essay, subject, *The Use and Abuse of Satire*—so that, as the Latin essay and English poem were yet unknown, he gained all he could gain.

Abbott lost his father while at the University; his mother then became in a measure dependent on his assistance, and he was obliged, in consequence, to decline an advantageous offer to go as tutor to a rich gentleman of Virginia; his small means were straitened by the performance of his filial duties; he was obliged to dress plainly, to forego the enjoyment of society,

* Salix Babylonica.

and to sustain himself hardly, yet becomingly, on his limited resources.

The first practical result of young Abbott's efforts was his election as Fellow, and his appointment as junior tutor of his college. He was already destined for the church, when he was invited to become tutor to the son of Mr. Justice Buller. This connection introduced him to the judge, who soon discovered his intellectual powers and peculiar fitness for law, and recommended him to attempt it. The advice was taken; and we have the authority of Lord Campbell for adding that Abbot became the very best lawyer of his generation in England, as he had already become the finest classical scholar. Lord Campbell adds:

"The scrubby little boy who ran after his father, carrying for him a pewter basin, a case of razors, and a hair-powder bag, through the streets of Canterbury, became Chief Justice of England, was installed among the peers of the United Kingdom, attended by the whole profession of the law, proud of him as their leader: and when the names of orators and statesmen illustrious in their day have perished with their frothy declamations, Lord Tenterden will be respected as a great magistrate, and his judgments will be studied and admired." *

Lord Tenterden died in 1832, and was buried in the chapel of the Foundling Hospital, of which he was Vice-President.† At the extreme entrance to the chapel is a marble bust of his Lordship, and beneath it a Latin inscription, which, after describing his humble origin, and judicial eminence, concludes with these emphatic words: "Learn, Reader, how much in this country may, under the blessing of God, be attained by honest industry."

HOW ROBERT BLOOMFIELD WROTE HIS "FARMER'S BOY" IN THE HEART OF LONDON.

This true poet of nature was born in 1766, at a small village in Suffolk: his father died in the same year, leaving his widow five other children besides Robert. To obtain a maintenance, she opened a school, and taught her own children the elements of reading along with those of her neighbors. Besides this education, Bloomfield was taught to write for two or three months at a school in the town of Ixworth. At the age of eleven he went to work upon his uncle's farm, receiving only his board for his labor. In his fifteenth year he removed to London, to

---
* Lives of the Lord Chief-Justices.
† Some verses written by his lordship to be set to music, are annually sung at the commemorative festivals of the Governors of the Hospital.

join his two brothers in making shoes, in a garret in Bell-alley, Coleman-street. At this time he read about as many hours every week as boys generally spend in play. He next wrote a few verses, which were printed in the *London Magazine;* and he was observed to read with much avidity a copy of Thomson's *Seasons,* which first inspired Bloomfield with the thought of composing a long poem, such as the *Farmer's Boy,* the idea being favored by a visit of two months to his native district, where he had often held the plow, driven a team, and tended sheep. He returned to London and shoemaking; but some years elapsed before he produced his *Farmer's Boy,* which he composed while he sat at work in his garret in Bell-alley, with six or seven other workmen; and nearly 600 lines were completed before Bloomfield committed a line to paper. The poem was published in 1800, was translated into French and Italian, and partly into Latin; 26,000 copies were sold in three years; and it was the dearest of the lowly-born poets gratifications, when his book was printed, to present a copy of it to his mother, to whom he then had it in his power, for the first time, to pay a visit, after twelve years' absence from his native village.

Bloomfield was a little boy for his age. " When I met him and his mother at the inn,'' (in town), says his brother, "he strutted before us just as he came from keeping sheep, hogs, etc., his shoes filled full of stumps in the heels. He, looking about him, slipped up; his nails were unused to a flat pavement. I remember viewing him as he scampered up—how small he was. I hardly thought that little fatherless boy would be one day known and esteemed by the most learned, the most respected, the wisest, and the best men of the kingdom."

PRECOCITY OF SIR THOMAS LAWRENCE.

We have few instances of the precocious development of talent so striking as are presented by the boyhood of this great artist. He was born in 1769, at Bristol, where his father kept the White Lion inn, and was more noted for his love of poetry, and writing rhyme, than for his success in business. His son Thomas was a very beautiful boy, and had been remarkable from infancy for his sprightly and winning manners. His father taught him to recite poetry; and when the child was only four or five years old, it was common for him to be presented by his parent to strangers who visited the inn at Bristol, and subsequently at the Black Bear at Devizes, whither he had removed. At four years old, young Lawrence could recite the poem of Joseph and his Brethren; at five, Addison's Nymphs of Solyma; and at seven, Milton's Lycidas. He was already able to use his pencil, and to take likenesses, which art he had acquired entirely of himself. The portraits which he thus sketched are affirmed to have been generally successful: among them was a portrait of Lady Kenyon, which was recognized by a friend twenty-five years after.

At the age of six, Lawrence was sent to school near Bristol, where he remained scarcely two years; and this, with a few lessons in Latin and French, was all the education he ever received. At the age of eight years, he contributed verses to the magazines; and many of his pieces may be found in the European and Lady's Magazines from 1780 to 1787. Daines Barrington relates that at the age of nine, without instruction from any one, Lawrence copied historical pictures in a masterly style, and succeeded amazingly in compositions of his own, particularly that of Peter denying Christ. In about seven minutes he scarcely ever failed to draw a strong likeness of any one present, which had generally much freedom and grace. He was also then an excellent reader of blank verse, and would immediately convince any one that he both understood and felt the striking passages of Milton or Shakspeare.

Young Lawrence's early talent soon made him generally known. His father would neither permit him to go to Rome to study, nor to take lessons at home, lest it should cramp his genius. He allowed him, however, to visit the houses of some of the neighboring gentry, where he saw some good pictures, which first gave him an idea of historical painting; he copied several, and at last produced original compositions of his own. When he was ten years old, his father took him from Devizes to Oxford, where the boy's qualifications were announced, and numbers thronged to him to have their likenesses taken. From Oxford they removed to Salisbury, and thence to Weymouth, at both which places the talents of the young artist were very profitable. At last his father settled at Bath, Thomas being then in his thirteenth year. Here sitters came to him in such numbers that he raised the price of his crayon portraits from a guinea to a guinea and a half. He also made copies of pictures; and one of the Transfiguration of Raphael, which Lawrence sent to the Society of Arts, was rewarded with a silver-gilt palette and five guineas. He remained at Bath about six years, and was the sole support of his father and family. They removed to London when Thomas was in his eighteenth year: he became a student of the Royal Academy; was kindly received by Sir Joshua Reynolds; and on his death, in 1792, was appointed his successor as painter to his Majesty and to the Dilettanti Society. Thence his reputation grew steadily till he became the first portrait-painter of the age: he succeeded Mr. West as President of the Royal Academy in 1820. Of his earlier career it has been truly said that Art presents no parallel case of an equal degree of excellence, attained so rapidly, and so exclusively without instruction, or opportunity of study.

THE DUKE OF WELLINGTON'S SCHOOLS.

Arthur Wellesley, the illustrious soldier-statesman, was born at Dangan Castle,* at Trim, about twenty miles from Dublin, in 1769, the year which ushered also Napoleon Bonaparte and Cuvier into the world. The castle has been nearly destroyed by a conflagration; but the chamber in which the Duke was born is pointed out to this day. Adjoining the castle is the humble church of Laracor, of which village Swift was vicar; a tall, thick wreck of a wall is all that remains of the Dean's vicarage-house. At a little distance, on the fair-green of the town, is a Corinthian column in memory of Wellington's fame, and surmounted by a statue of the hero. The present parsonage at Trim was a favorite residence of Maria Edgeworth. The town is sad and dreary to look at in its state of crumbling decay; yet, while it can bring remembrance of Swift and Miss Edgeworth, and while men can say of it, "here Wellington was born," it will continue as noted as one of the greatest landmarks in the world.

The Earl and Countess of Mornington, young Arthur's parents, placed him early at a school at Trim: he must then have been a very little boy, for one of his school-fellows relates that when Crosbie, afterward Sir Edward, of balloon notoriety, had climbed to the top of "the Yellow Steeple," and had thrown down his will, disposing of his game-cocks and other boyish valuables, in case he should be killed in coming down—little Arthur Wellesley began to shed tears when he found that nothing had been left him.

When about ten years old, Arthur was placed under the tuition of the Rev. William Gower, at Chelsea. His health was indifferent, but improved as he grew up. Occasional illness produced an indolent and careless manner, and often a degree of heaviness. Unlike boys of his age, Arthur was rarely seen to play, but generally came lagging out of the school-room into the play-ground: in the centre of it was a large walnut-tree, against which he used to lounge and lean, observing his school-fellows playing around him. If any boy played unfairly, Arthur quickly gave intelligence to those engaged in the game: on the delinquent being turned out, it was generally wished that he,

---

* It is also stated that the Duke first saw the light in the town residence of his parents, Mornington House, in the centre of the eastern side of Upper Merrion Street, Dublin. The proof of Dangan Castle being the Duke's birthplace is, however, more circumstantial. The most notable point in the question is the indifference with which it was treated by the person most immediately concerned. The Duke kept his birthday on the 18th of June.

Arthur, should supply his place, but nothing could induce him to do so; when beset by a party of five or six, he would fight with the utmost courage and determination, until he freed himself from their grasp; he would then retire again to his tree, and look about him as quiet, dejected, and observant as he had been before. This anecdote was communicated to the *British and Foreign Review*, in 1840, by one of Arthur's school-fellows at Chelsea.

The Duke and his brother, the Marquis Wellesley, passed much of their boyhood at Brynkinalt, in North Wales. On one occasion they met a playfellow, David Evans, and his sister, returning from school, when Arthur commenced a game at marbles with the boy, while his sister walked on. Presently, her brother called her to his assistance, as Arthur, he said, had stolen his marbles, which he refused to give up. The girl insisted, and then came the struggle. Arthur was about twelve years old, and his brother older; the girl about ten, and her brother two years younger: the battle now began between the girl and Arthur, who soon dropped his colors, handed over the marbles, and beat a hasty retreat, with tears in his eyes. Meanwhile Arthur's brother stood at a distance, inciting the fight, but taking care to keep out of it. Many years after, the Marquis, when in India, wrote to David Evans, and reminding him of their games in boyhood; and the Duke, in 1815, when passing through Denbigshire, inquired at Brynkinalt for David Evans, and recognized him as his old playfellow, but they never saw each other again.

Arthur Wellesley, by the death of his father in 1771, became dependent upon the care and prudence of his mother, a lady, as it fortunately happened, of talents not unequal to the task. Under this direction of his studies, he was sent to Eton, where very little seems to be recollected of him at the college. As he left before he was in the fifth form, his name was not cut in the Upper School when he went away. In the Lower School, however, it was cut upon a post, but afterward erased; and, about six-and-twenty years since, in some alterations, this post, with some other materials, was cleared away.

The tradition respecting Arthur in the school is that he was a spirited, active boy, but occasionally shy and meditative. Among his school-fellows was the facetious Bobus Smith (brother of the Rev. Sydney Smith), who, in after-life, when Arthur had conquered wherever he had fought, used to say: "I was the Duke of Wellington's first victory." "How?" "Why, one day at Eton, Arthur Wellesley and I had a fight, and he beat me soundly."

17

While at Eton, Arthur and his two brothers were invited to pass the holidays with Lady Dungannon, in Shropshire, and, being full of fun, asked each other what news they should tell when they arrived. One of them proposed that they should say—a pure invention—that their sister Anne had run off with the footman, thinking it was likely to produce some sensation. This they accordingly did, and greatly shocked Lady Dungannon; they entreated, however, that she would not mention the circumstance to any one, hoping, as they said, that their sister might come back again. Dady Dungannon now excused herself, having promised to pay a visit to her neighbor, Mrs. Mytton; and, unable to keep this secret, of course told it to her. On her return, she nearly killed them by saying, "Ah, my dear boys, ill news travels apace! Will you believe it? Mrs. Mytton knew all about poor Anne!" This story is worthy of Sheridan, and if he had heard it, he would certainly have introduced it in one of his plays.

Arthur, when at Eton, lived at Mrs. Ranganean's, one of the best boarding-houses in the place. There, when he had grown to be a father, he one day took his sons, Lord Douro and his brother: he looked over his bed-room, made several inquiries, and then descended into the kitchen, and pointed out to his sons where *he had cut his name on the kitchen door.* This interesting memento was soon after removed, during some repairs of the boarding-house; and the Duke, on one of his subsequent visits, expressed his annoyance at its disappearance.

Between Arthur and his elder brother, had any one speculated on the future career of both, how erroneous would have been his conclusions! At his first school, Wellesley gave certain promises of a distinguished manhood; Wellington did not; and yet how easily can this be reconciled! The taste and fancy that afterward produced the senator, were germane to the classic forms of Eton; while those mental properties which alone can constitute the soldier, like metal in a mine, lay dormant, until time betrayed the ore, and circumstances elicited its brilliancy.

From Eton, Arthur was transferred, first to private tuition at Brighton, and subsequently to the celebrated military seminary of Angers, in France.

For the deficiency of any early promise in the future hero we are not confined to negative evidence alone. His relative inferiority was the subject of some concern to his vigilant mother, and had its influence, as we are led to conclude, in the selection of the military profession for one who displayed so little of the family aptitude for elegant scholarship. At Angers, though the young student left no signal reputation behind him, it is clear that his time must have been productively employed. Pignerol, the director of the seminary, was an engineer of high repute, and the opportunities of acquiring not only professional knowledge, but a serviceable mastery of the French tongue, were not likely to have been lost on such a mind as that of his pupil. Altogether, six years were consumed in this course of education, which, though partial enough in itself, was so far in advance of the age, that we may conceive the young cadet to have carried with him to his corps a more than average store of professional acquirements.

We quote the above from a Memoir which appeared in the *Times* journal, in 1852, immediately after the Duke's death. It is somewhat at variance with the evidence of the late Dr. Benning, who, while traveling with Blayney, called to see the College at Angers, and inquired of the head of the establishment if he had any English boys of promise under his care, when he replied he had one Irish lad of great promise, of the name of Wesley, the son of Lord Mornington.

At the end of the stipulated term, he returned to England; and it would appear somewhat unexpectedly to Lady Mornington, whose first intimation that he had left France, was seeing him at the Haymarket Theatre, when her ladyship exclaimed, almost angrily, "I do believe there is my ugly boy, Arthur."

Meanwhile, his family had not been unmindful of his prospects; for we have the evidence of a letter in the possession of a gentleman at Trim, in which Lord Wellesley states that the Lord Lieutenant had been two years under promise to procure a commission for his brother Arthur, and had not been able to fulfill it. At length, in March, 1787, the Hon. Arthur Wellesley, being then in his eighteenth year, received his first commission as an ensign in the 73rd Regiment of Foot. The only point of interest in his position at this moment, was the fact that though the young officer commanded sufficient interest to bring his deserts into favorable notice, he was not circumstanced as to rely exclusively on such considerations for advancement. He possessed interest enough to make merit available, but not enough to dispense with it. On a remarkable occasion in aftertimes he spoke, in the House of Peers, of having "raised himself" by his own exertions to the position he then filled.

Here our sketch of the Duke's early life may be closed. His service of the Sovereigns and the public of this country for more than half a century—in diplomatic situations and in councils, as well as in the army—has scarcely a parallel in British history. His Dispatches are the best evidence of his well-regulated mind in education. No letters could ever be more temperately or more perspicuously expressed than those famous documents. Even as specimens of literary composition they are exceedingly good—plain, forcible, fluent, and occasionally even humorous. He once declared of the Dispatches, "Well, if these were to be written over again, I don't think I should alter a word." A single examination of these documents—the best record of his own achievements—will show what immense results in the aggregate were obtained by the Duke, solely in virtue of habits which he had sedulously cultivated from his boyhood—early rising, strict attention to details,—taking nothing ascertainable for granted—unflagging industry, and silence, except when speech was necessary, or certainly harmless. His early habit of punctuality is pleasingly illustrated in the following anecdote: "I will take care to be punctual at five to-morrow morning," said the engineer of New London Bridge, in acceptance of the Duke's request that he would meet him at that hour the following morning. "Say a quarter before five," replied the Duke, with a quiet smile; "I owe all I have achieved to being ready a quarter of an hour before it was deemed necessary to be so; and I learned that lesson when a boy."

But the paramount principle of the Duke's life was his respect for Truth, which he observed himself with earnestness akin to the admiration with which he recognized it in others: and we know that the best homage we can pay to virtue is its practice.

GEORGE CANNING AT ETON AND OXFORD.

This accomplished orator and statesman was born of Irish parents, in 1770, in the parish of Marylebone, London. His descent on the paternal side was from an ancient family, his ancestors having figured at different periods at Bristol, in Warwickshire, and in Ireland. His father died when the son was only a year old. The early education of Canning was superintended by his uncle, Mr. Stratford Canning, a merchant of London; and the expenses were in part defrayed from a small estate in Ireland bequeathed by his grandfather.* George Canning was first sent to Hyde Abbey School, near Winchester. In his thirteenth year he was entered as an Eton Oppidam, and placed in the Remove. He soon distinguished himself as a sedulous student, and of great quickness in mastering what he undertook to learn; keen and emulous in contest, yet mindful of steady discipline. At the same time, he was, says Mr. Creasy, "a boy of frank, generous, and conciliatory disposition, and of a bold manly, and unflinching spirit." His Latin versification obtained him great distinction, as attested by his compositions in the *Musæ*

---

* Mrs. Canning, through the influence of Queen Charlotte, was introduced by Garrick to the stage as her profession, and she subsequently married Reddish, the actor. Meanwhile, her son George had become the associate of actors of a low class, from which influence he was rescued by Moody, the Comedian, who stated the boy's case to Mr. Stratford Canning, and thus opened the road by which he advanced to power and fame. From an elegant work entitled *Poets and Statesmen: their Homes and Haunts in the Neighborhood of Eton and Windsor.* By William Dowlin, Esq. 1857.

Etonenses. He had written English verses from a very early age; and at Eton, in his sixteenth year, he planned with three school-fellows a periodical work called the *Microcosm*, which was published at Windsor weekly for nine months. Among Canning's contributions was a poem entitled "The Slavery of Greece," inspired by his zeal for the liberation of that country from the Turkish yoke, which one of the latest acts of his political life greatly contributed to accomplish. Another of his papers in the *Microcosm*, his last contribution, thus earnestly records his love of Eton: "From her to have sucked 'the milk of science,' to have contracted for her a pious fondness and veneration, which will bind me for ever to her interests, and perhaps to have improved by my earnest endeavors the younger part of the present generation, is to me a source of infinite pride and satisfaction."

At seventeen, Mr. Canning was entered as a student at Christ-church, Oxford, where he gained some academical honors by his Latin poetry, and cultivated that talent for oratory which he had begun to display at Eton. His splendid Latin poem on the Pilgrimage to Mecca, "*Iter ad Meccam*," gained him the highest honor in an University where such exercises are deemed the surest test of scholarship. At Oxford he formed an intimate friendship with Mr. Jenkinson, afterward Earl of Liverpool, who is supposed to have been of service to him in his political career. Canning's college vacations were occasionally passed in the house of Sheridan, who introduced him to Mr. Fox, and other leaders of the Whig party. On leaving Oxford, Canning entered at Lincoln's Inn; but he soon abandoned the study of the law for the political career that was promisingly opening to him.

Canning had a strong bias in favor of elegant literature, and would have been no mean poet and author had he not embarked so early on public life, and been incessantly occupied with its duties. Even amidst the cares of office, he found time for the indulgence of his brilliant wit; and, in conjunction with Mr. John Hookham Frere, Mr. Jenkinson, Mr. George Ellis, Lord Clare, Lord Mornington (afterward Marquis Wellesley), and other social and political friends, he started a paper called the *Anti-Jacobin*, some of its best poetry, burlesques, and *jeux-d'esprit*, being from Mr. Canning's pen. As party effusions, these pieces were highly popular and effective; and that they are still read with pleasure is attested by the fact that *the poetry of the Anti-Jacobin*, collected and published in a separate form, is still kept in print by the publisher.

Among the coincidences in Mr. Canning's career, it may be mentioned that he was the same age as his fellow-collegian, the Earl of Liverpool, and each became Premier, Canning succeeding Lord Liverpool, on the illness of the latter, on April 12, 1827: he died in the following August, in his 57th year, and was buried close to the grave of Pitt, his early patron. The next day after his burial, his widow was made a peeress.

Canning, as a statesman, we are reminded by his statue in Palace Yard, was "just alike to freedom and the throne;" and as an orator, eloquent, witty, and of consummate taste.

SIR WALTER SCOTT—HIS SCHOOLS AND READINGS.

This amiable poet and novelist, whose genius has gladdened many lands, and almost every country of the civilized world, was born at Edinburgh, in 1771, in a house at the head of the College Wynd. His father was a writer to the Signet; and his mother, the eldest daughter of Dr. Rutherford, was a well-educated gentlewoman, mixed in literary society, and from her superintendence of the early tuition of her son Walter, there is reason to infer that such advantages influenced his habits and taste. In an autobiographical fragment discovered in an old cabinet at Abbotsford, after Sir Walter's death, he says he was an uncommonly healthy child, but had nearly died in consequence of his first nurse being ill of a consumption. The woman was dismissed, and he was consigned to a healthy peasant, who used to boast of her *laddie* being what she called *a grand gentleman*.

When about eighteen months old, after a fever, he lost the power of his right leg, and was ever after lame. Yet, he was a remarkably active boy, dauntless, and full of fun and mischief, or, as he calls himself, in *Marmion*,

"A self-will'd imp; a grandame's child."

He was then sent to the farm-house of Sandy-Knowe, the residence of Scott's paternal grandfather. One Tibbie Hunter remembered the lame child coming to Sandy-Knowe—and that he was "a sweet-tempered bairn, a darling with all about the house." The young ewe-milkers delighted to carry him abroad on their backs among the crags; and he was very gleg (quick) at the uptake, and kenned every sheep and lamb by head-mark as well as any of them. But his great favorite was Auld Sandy Ormistoun, the cow-bailie; if the child saw him in the morning, he could not be satisfied unless the old man would set him astride on his shoulder, and take him to keep him company as he lay watching his charge:

"Here was poetic impulse given
By the green hill, and clear, blue heaven."

The cow-bailie blew a particular note on his whistle, which signified to the maid-servants in the house when the little boy wished to be carried home again. Scott told a friend, when spending a day in his old age among these well-remembered crags, that he delighted to roll about on the grass all day long in the midst of the flock, and that the sort of fellowship he thus formed with the sheep and lambs had impressed his mind with a degree of affectionate feeling toward them which had lasted through life. There is a story of his having been forgotten one day among the knolls when a thunder-storm came on; and his aunt, suddenly recollecting his situation, and running out to bring him home, is said to have found him lying on his back, clapping his hands at the lightning, and crying out, "Bonny! Bonny!" at every flash.

Scott thus relates his early impressions at Sandy-Knowe:

This was during the heat of the American war, and I remember being as anxious, on my uncle's weekly visits (for we heard news at no other time), to hear of the defeat of Washington, as if I had some deep and personal cause of antipathy to him. I know not how this was combined with a very strong prejudice in favor of the Stuart family, which I had originally imbibed from the songs and tales of the Jacobites. This latter political propensity was deeply confirmed by the stories told in my hearing of the cruelties exercised in the executions at Carlisle, and in the Highlands, after the battle of Culloden. One or two of our own distant relations had fallen on that occasion, and I remember detesting the name of Cumberland with more than infant hatred. Mr. Curle, farmer, at Yetbyre, had been present at their execution; and it was, probably, from him that I first heard these tragic tales, which made so great an impression on me. The local information which I conceive had some share in forming my future taste and pursuits, I derived from the old songs and tales which then formed the amusements of a retired country family. My grandmother, in whose youth the old Border depredations were matter of recent tradition, used to tell me many a tale of Watt of Harden, Wight Willie of Aikwood, Jamie Tellfer, of the fair Dodhead, and other heroes — merrymen all of the persuasion and calling of Robin Hood and Little John. . . . . Two or three old books which lay in the window-seat were explored for my amusement in the tedious winter days. Automathes and Ramsay's Tea-table Miscellany were my favorites; although, at a later period, an odd volume of Josephus's Wars of the Jews divided my partiality.

My kind and affectionate aunt, Miss Janet Scott, whose memory will ever be dear to me, used to read these works to'me with admirable patience, and I could repeat long passages by heart. The ballad of Hardyknute I was early master of, to the great annoyance of almost our only visitor, the worthy clergyman of the parish, Dr. Duncan, who had not patience to have a sober chat interrupted by my shouting forth this ditty. Methinks I see his tall, thin, emaciated figure, his legs cased in clasped gambadoes, and his face of a length that would have rivaled the Knight of La Mancha's, and hear him exclaiming, "One may as well speak in the mouth of a cannon as where that child is."

In his fourth year, Scott was taken by his aunt to Bath, in expectation that the waters might prove of some advantage to his lameness, but to little purpose. At Bath, he learned to read at a dame-school, and had an occasional lesson from his aunt. Afterward, when grown a big boy, he had a few lessons at Edinburgh, but never acquired a just pronunciation, nor could he read with much propriety. At Bath, Scott saw the venerable John Home, author of *Douglas;* and his uncle, Captain Robert Scott, introduced him to the little amusements which suited his age, and to the theatre. One evening, when the play was *As You Like It*, Scott was so scandalized at the quarrel between Orlando and his brother, that he screamed out, "A'n't they brothers?"

Scott now returned to Edinburgh.

"In 1779 (he says), I was sent to the second class of the Grammar School, or High School, of Edinburgh, then taught by Mr Luke Fraser, a good Latin scholar, and a worthy man Our class contained some very excellent scholars. The first *Dux* was James Buchan, who retained his honored place almost without a day's interval all the while we were at the High School. . . . . The next best scholar (*sed longo intervallo*) were my friend David Douglas, the heir and *eleve* of the celebrated Adam Smith, and James Hope, now a writer to the Signet. As for myself, I glanced like a meteor from one end of the class to the other, and commonly disgusted my kind master as much by my negligence and frivolity, as I occasionally pleased him by flashes of intellect and talent. Among my companions, my good nature and a flow of ready imagination rendered me very popular. Boys are uncommonly just in their feelings, and at least equally generous. My lameness, and the efforts which I made to supply that disadvantage, by making up in address what I wanted in activity, engaged the latter principle in my favor; and in the winter playhours, when hard exercise was impossible, my tales used to assemble an admiring audience like Luckie Brown's fireside, and happy was he that could sit next to the inexhaustible narrator. I was also, though often negligent at my own task, always ready to assist my friends; and hence I had a little party of staunch partisans and adherents, stout of hand and heart, though somewhat dull of head, the very tools for raising a hero to eminence. So on the whole, I made a brighter figure in the *yard* than in the *class*."

Mr. Lockhart notes upon these reminiscences, that a schoolfellow, Mr. Claud Russell, remembers Scott to have once made a great leap in his class, through the stupidity of some laggard on the dult's (dolt's) bench, who being asked, on boggling at *cum*, "what part of speech is *with*?" answered, "a substantive." The rector, after a moment's pause, thought it worth while to ask his *dux*—"Is *with* ever a substantive?" but all were silent till the query reached Scott, then near the bottom of the class, who instantly responded by quoting a verse from the book of Judges: "And Sampson said unto Delilah, if they bind me with seven green *withs* that were never dried, then shall I be weak, and as another man." Another upward movement, accomplished in a less laudable manner, Scott thus related to Mr. Rogers, the poet:

"There was a boy in my class at school, who stood always at the top, nor could I with all my efforts supplant him. Day came after day, and still he kept his place, do what I would; till at length I observed that when a question was asked him, he always fumbled with his fingers at a particular button on the lower part of his waistcoat To remove it, therefore, became expedient in my eyes; and in an evil moment it was removed with a knife. Great was my anxiety to know the success of my measure; it succeeded too well. When the boy was again questioned, his fingers sought again for the button, but it was not to be found In his distress he looked down for it; it was to be seen no more than to be felt. He stood confounded, and I took possession of his place: nor did he ever recover it, or ever, I believe, suspect who was the author of his wrong. Often in after-life has the sight of him smote me as I passed by him; and often have I resolved to make him some reparation; but it ended in good resolutions."

The autobiography tells us that Scott's translations in verse from Horace and Virgil were often approved by Dr. Adam. One of these little pieces, written in a weak, boyish scrawl, within pencil-marks still visible, had been carefully preserved by his mother; and was found folded up in a cover inscribed by the old lady—"*My Walter's first lines*, 1782."

At Kelso, at the age of thirteen, he first read Percy's *Reliques*, in an antique garden, under the shade of a huge plane-tree. This work had as great an effect in making him a poet as Spenser had on Cowley, but with Scott the seeds were long in germinating. Previous to this he had, indeed, tried his hand at verse. The following, among other lines, were discovered wrapped up in a cover inscribed by Dr. Adam, of the High School, "Walter Scott, July, 1783:"

> ON THE SETTING SUN.
>
> Those evening clouds, that setting ray,
> And beauteous tints serve to display
>   Their great Creator's praise;
> Then let the short-lived thing called man,
> Whose life's comprised within a span,
>   To him his homage raise.
> We often praise the evening clouds,
>   And tints so gay and bold,
> But seldom think upon our God,
>   Who tinged these clouds with gold.

In 1783, Scott was placed at the University of Edinburgh, where his studies were as irregular as at the High School.

Mr. Lockhart considers Scott to have underrated his own academical attainments. He had no pretensions to the claim of an extensive, far less of an accurate, Latin scholar; but he could read any Latin author, of any age, so as to catch without difficulty his meaning: and although his favorite Latin poet, as well as historian in later days, was Buchanan, he had preserved, or subsequently acquired, a strong relish for some others of more ancient date—particularly Lucian and Claudian. Of Greek he had forgotten even the alphabet; and, in 1830, having occasion to introduce from some authority on his table two Greek words into his *Introduction to Popular Poetry*, he sent for Mr. Lockhart, who was in the house, to insert the words in the MS. At an early period, Scott enjoyed the real Tasso and Ariosto; and read Gil Blas in the original: and not much later, he acquired as much Spanish as served for the Guerras Civiles de Granada, Lazarillo de Tormes, and above all, Don Quixote. He read all these languages in after-life with about the same facility. Somewhat later he acquired German. In these languages he sought for incidents and images; but for the treasures of diction he was content to dig on British soil.

At the age of seventeen, Scott saw Robert Burns. The poet, while at Professor Ferguson's one day, was struck by some lines attached to a print of a soldier digging in the snow, and inquired who was the author; none of the old or the learned spoke, when Scott answered, "They are by Langhorne." Burns, fixing his large bright eyes on the boy, and striding up to him, said, "it is no common course of reading taught you this." "This lad," said he to the company, "will be heard of yet."

Scott's early love of reading was, doubtless, fostered by the circumstance of his lameness. He had just given over the amusements of boyhood, when, to use his own words, "a long illness threw him back on the kingdom of fiction, as it were by a species of fatality." He had ruptured a blood-vessel, and motion and speech for a long time were pronounced to be dangerous. For several weeks he was confined to his bed, and almost his sole amusement was reading. He says:

"There was at this time a circulating library at Edinburgh, founded, I believe, by the celebrated Allan Ramsay, which, besides containing a most respectable collection of books of every description, was, as might have been expected, peculiarly rich in works of fiction. I was plunged into this great ocean of reading without compass or pilot; and unless when some one had the charity to play at chess with me, I was allowed to do nothing, save read, from morning to night. As my taste and appetite were gratified in nothing else, I indemnified myself by becoming a glutton of books. Accordingly, I believe I read almost all the old romances, old plays, and epic poetry, in that formidable collection, and no doubt was unconsciously amassing materials for the task in which it has been my lot to be so much employed."

Being somewhat satiated with fiction, Scott found in histories, memoirs, voyages and travels, events nearly as wonderful as those in the works of imagination, with the additional advantage, that they were at least in a great measure true. Thus Scott passed nearly two years, when he removed into the country, and would have felt very lonely but for the amusement which he derived from a good though old-fashioned library. He has well described these solitary and desultory studies in the first chapter of *Waverley*, where the hero is represented as "driving through the sea of books, like a vessel without pilot or rudder." "He had read, and stored in a memory of uncommon tenacity, much curious, though ill-arranged miscellaneous information. In English literature, he was master of Shakspeare and Milton, of our earlier dramatic authors, of many picturesque and interesting passages from our old historical chronicles, and was particularly well acquainted with Spenser, Drayton, and other poets, whose subjects have been on romantic fiction—of all themes the most fascinating to a youthful imagination, before the passions have roused themselves, and demand poetry of a more sentimental description." Other favorites were Pulci, the Decameron, and the chivalrous and romantic lore of Spain.

Upon his recovery, Scott returned to Edinburgh, and resumed his studies in the law, which had been interrupted by illness. In 1791, he was admitted a member of the Speculative Society for training in elocution and debate. On the first night he met there Mr. Jeffrey, who visited Scott next day, "in a small den on the sunk floor of his father's house, in George's-square, surrounded with dingy books;" and thus commenced a friendship between the two most distinguised men of letters which Edinburgh produced in their time. In the den, Scott had collected out-of-the-way things of all sorts. "He had more books than shelves; a small painted cabinet, with Scotch and Roman coins in it, and so forth. A claymore and Lochabar axe, given him by old Invernahyle, mounted guard on a little print of Prince Charlie; and *Broughton's Saucer* was hooked up against the wall below it." Such was the germ of the magnificent library and museum which Scott, in after-life, assembled in the castellated mansion which he built for himself at Abbotsford.*

Scott succeeded so far in his lucubrations as to be called to the bar as an advocate in 1792. He established himself in good style at Edinburgh, but had little practice. He rarely attempted literary composition; nor have any fugitive pieces of Scott's youth been found in any publication of the day. But in Dr. Anderson's *Bee* for May 9, 1792, the following notice is thought to refer to a contribution from Scott: "The Editor regrets that the verses of W. S. are *too defective for publication.*"

About this time Scott employed his leisure in collecting the ballad poetry of Scotland; and in this class of composition he made his first attempt at originality. Thus may be said to have commenced his literary life of six-and-thirty years. He breathed his last at Abbotsford in 1832; his mind never appearing to wander in its delirium toward those works which had filled all Europe with his fame. This fact is of interest in literary history; and it accords with the observation of honest Allan Cunningham, that "Scott, although the most accomplished author of his day, yet he had none of the airs of authorship."

Sir Walter Scott received his baronetcy from George IV. in 1820.

LORD HILL, THE WATERLOO HERO.

Rowland, Lord Viscount Hill, was born in Shropshire, in 1772. He was first placed at Ightfield, a neighboring village, and thence sent to Chester, where he won the affections of his

---

* The splendor in which Scott lived at Abbotsford was entirely obtained from the products of his pen : to this he owed his acres, his castle, and his means of hospitality. In 1826, through his losses in the publishing business, his debts amounted to 117,000*l*. He would listen to no overtures of composition with his creditors—his only demand was for time. He retrenched his expenses, took lodgings in Edinburgh, labored incessantly at his literary work, and in four years realized for his creditors no less than 70,000*l*.!

school-fellows from his gentle disposition, and the gallantry with which he was always ready to assist any comrade who had got into a scrape, at the same time that he was himself the least likely to be involved in one on his own account. He was of delicate constitution, and he was thrown more than usually upon the care of Mrs. Winfield, wife of one of the masters of the school. It is one of the delightful traits of Hill's character, that the grateful affection which he then felt for this amiable lady, continued an enduring sentiment in after-life, and was repeatedly exhibited after the delicate school-boy had grown up into one of the most renowned generals of his time. Thus, after the abdication of Napoleon in 1814, when Lord Hill accompanied his friend, Lord Combermere, on his entry into Chester, where he himself received a greeting all the more cordial from his having spent some of his earlier years at a Chester school, as he passed along the streets of the city in a triumphal procession, it was observed that his eye singled out among the applauding throng, one on whom he bestowed the kindest recognition. It was Mrs. Winfield whom he had thus distinguished: he had never forgotten her kindness to him when a boy.

The same love of horticulture, the same fondness for pet animals, which characterized Hill in after-life, had already been exhibited by him at school, where his little garden prospered, and his favorites throve, better than those of any of his companions. But there is another characteristic of his, which comes with something like surprise upon those who have been in the habit of associating the name of Hill so closely with the battle-field. "His sensibility," says Mrs. Winfield, "was almost feminine." One of the boys happened to cut his finger, and was brought by Rowland Hill to have it dressed; but her attention was soon drawn from the wound to Rowland, who had fainted.

And even after his military career had commenced, when it happened that a prize-fight was exhibited near the windows of his lodgings, such was the effect produced on him by the brutality of the scene, that he was carried fainting out of his room. So little does there require to be in common between the most heroic courage and the coarse and vulgar attribute of insensibility to the sight of blood and suffering. He explained afterward, in reference to the carnage which he had witnessed in war, that he had still the same feelings as at first, "but in the excitement of battle all individual sensation was lost sight of."

Young Hill entered the army in 1790, and upon leave of

absence went to a military academy at Strasburg, where he remained till 1791, when he obtained a lieutenancy. Lord Hill greatly distinguished himself at the battle of Waterloo, and was there exposed to the greatest personal danger: his horse was shot under him, and fell wounded in five places; he himself was rolled over and severely bruised, and for half an hour, in the mêlée, it was feared by his troops that he had been killed. But he rejoined them to their great delight, and was at their head to the close of the day.

COLERIDGE AT CHRIST'S HOSPITAL AND CAMBRIDGE.

Samuel Taylor Coleridge, "logician, metaphysician, bard," may be said to have commanded a larger number of zealous admirers than any other literary man in England since Dr. Johnson. Coleridge was a native of Devonshire, and was born in 1772, at St. Mary Ottery, of which parish his father was vicar. From 1775, he tells us in his *Biographia Literaria*, he continued at the reading-school, because he was too little to be trusted among his father's school-boys. He relates further, how, through the jealousy of a brother, he was in earliest childhood huffed away from the enjoyments of muscular activity by play, to take refuge by his mother's side, on his little stool, to read his little book, and listen to the talk of his elders. In 1782, he was sent to Christ's Hospital; and after passing six weeks in the branch school at Hertford, little Coleridge, already regarded by his relations as a talking prodigy, came up to the great school in London, where he continued for eight years, with Bowyer for his teacher, and Charles Lamb for his associate; Coleridge being "the poor friendless boy" in Elia's "Christ's Hospital Five-and-thirty Years Ago." Here Coleridge made very great progress in his classical studies; for he had before his fifteenth year translated the hymns of Synesius into English Anacreontics. His choice of these hymns for translation is explained by his having even at that early age, plunged deeply into metaphysics. He says: "At a very premature age, even before my fifteenth year, I had bewildered myself in metaphysics and theological controversy. Nothing else pleased me. History and particular facts lost all interest in my mind. Poetry itself, yea, novels and romances, became insipid to me." From such pursuits, Coleridge was, however, weaned for a time by the reading of Mr. Lisle Bowles's Sonnets, which had just then been published, and made a powerful influence upon his mind.

He describes himself as being, from eight to fourteen, "a playless dreamer, a *heluo librorum* (a glutton of books)." A stranger, whom he accidentally met one day in the streets of

London, and who was struck with his conversation, made him free of a circulating library, and he read through the collection, folios and all. At fourteen, he had, like Gibbon, a stock of erudition that might have puzzled a doctor, and a degree of ignorance of which a school-boy would have been ashamed. He had no ambition: his father was dead; and he would have apprenticed himself to a shoemaker who lived near the school, had not the head-master prevented him.

He has left some interesting recollections of Christ's Hospital in his time. "The discipline," he says, "was ultra-spartan: all domestic ties were to be put aside. 'Boy,' I remember Boyer saying to me once, when I was crying. the first day of my return after the holidays, 'Boy! the school is your mother! Boy! the school is your mother! Boy! the school is your brother! the school is your sister! the school is your first-cousin and your second-cousin, and all the rest of your relations! Let's have no more crying.'"

Coleridge became deputy-Grecian, or head-scholar, and obtained an exhibition or presentation from Christ's Hospital to Jesus College, Cambridge, in 1791. While at the University, he did not turn his attention at all to mathematics; but obtained a prize for a Greek ode on the Slave-trade, and distinguished himself in a contest for the Craven scholarship, in which Dr. Butler, afterward Bishop of Lichfield, was the successful candidate.

"Coleridge," says a school-fellow of his, who followed him to Cambridge in 1792, "was very studious, but his reading was desultory and capricious. He took little exercise; but he was ready at any time to unbend his mind to conversation; and for the sake of this, his room (the ground-floor room on the right hand of the staircase, facing the great gate) was a constant rendezvous of conversation—loving friends, I will not call them loungers, for they did not call to kill time, but to enjoy it. What evenings have I spent in tho-e rooms! What suppers, or *sizings*, as they were called, have I enjoyed, when Æschylus, and Plato, and Thucydides were pushed aside, with a pile of lexicons and the like, to discuss the pamphlets of the day! Ever and anon a pamphlet issued from the pen of Burke. There was no need of having the book before us:—Coleridge had read it in the morning, and in the evening he would repeat whole pages *verbatim*."

Coleridge did not take a degree. During the second year of his residence, he suddenly left the University in a fit of despondency; and after wandering for a while about the streets of London, in extreme pecuniary distress, terminated his adventure by enlisting in the 15th Dragoons, under the assumed name of Comberbach. He made but a poor dragoon, and never advanced beyond the awkward squad. He wrote letters, however, for all his comrades, and they attended to his horse and accoutrements. In four months his history and circumstances became known: he had written under his saddle, on the stable-wall, a Latin sentence, (Eheu! quam infortunii miserrimum est fuisse felicem!) which led to an inquiry by the captain of his troop; and Coleridge was discharged and restored to his family and friends. He returned to Cambridge; and shortly afterward went on a visit to an old school-fellow at Oxford, where an introduction to Southey, then an undergraduate at Balliol College, became

Anecdote Biographies. 271

the hinge on which a large part of his after-life was destined to turn.

Charles Lamb, in his "Christ's Hospital Five-And-Thirty Years Ago," has this delightful recollection of his fellow-Blue:

Come back into my memory, like as thou wert in the day-spring of my fancies, with hope like a fiery column before thee—the dark pillar not yet turned—Samuel Taylor Coleridge, Logician, Metaphysician, Bard! How have I seen the casual passer through the cloisters stand still, entranced with admiration (while he weighed the disproportion between the *speech* and the *garb* of the young Mirandola), to hear thee unfold, in thy deep and sweet intonations, the mysteries of Jamblichus, or Plotinus (for even in those years thou waxedst not pale at such philosophic draughts), or reciting Homer in his Greek, or Pindar—while the walls of the old Gray Friars re-echoed the accents of the *inspired charity-boy!*—Many were the "wit combats" (to dally awhile with the words of old Fuller) between him and ". V. Le G——, "which two I beheld like a Spanish great galleon, and an English man-of-war; Master Coleridge, like the former, was built far higher in learning, solid, but slow in his performances. C V., with the English man-of-war, lesser in bulk, but lighter in sailing, could turn with all tides, tack about, and take advantage of all winds by the quickness of his wit and invention."—*The Essays of Elia.*

ROBERT SOUTHEY AT HIS SCHOOLS, AND AT OXFORD.

Robert Southey, the business of whose life was the pursuit of literature, and the first and last joy of his heart, was born in the city of Bristol, in 1774, and was the son of a small tradesman.* His childhood, however, was not passed at home, but from the age of two to six, at the house of Miss Tyler, his aunt, in Bath. He had no playmates; he was never permitted to do anything in which by any possibility he might contract dirt; he was kept up late at night in dramatic society, and kept in bed late in the morning at the side of his aunt; and his chief pastime—for neither at this time nor at a later period had Southey any propensity for boyish sports—was pricking holes in playbills—an amusement, of course, suggested to him by Miss Tyler, and witnessed by her with infinite delight. As soon as the child could read, his aunt's friends furnished him with books. The son of Francis Newbery, of St. Paul's Churchyard, and the well-known publisher of *Goody Two Shoes*,† *Giles Gingerbread*, "and other such delectable histories in sixpenny books for children, splendidly bound in the flowered and gilt Dutch paper of former days," sent the child twenty such volumes.

"This," says Southey, in his autobiography, "was a rich present, and may have been more instrumental than I am aware in

---

* For the materials of this sketch the writer is greatly indebted to the first volume of the *Life and Letters of Robert Southey.* Edited by his Son, the Rev. Charles Cuthbert Southey, M.A. 1849. In this work, the narrative in the exquisite fragment of Autobiography ceases at Westminster School, when Southey had hardly attained his fifteenth year.

† "Godwin, the author of *Caleb Williams,* who had been a child's publisher himself, had always a strong persuasion that Goldsmith wrote *Goody Two Shoes;* and if so, the effort belongs to 1763; Mrs. Margery, radiant with gold and gingerbread, and rich in pictures as extravagantly ill-drawn as they are dear and well remembered, made her appearance at Christmas."—*Life and Adventures of Oliver Goldsmith.* By John Foster. 1848. Page 300.

giving me that love of books, and that decided determination to literature, as the one thing desirable, which manifested itself from my childhood, and which no circumstance in after-life ever slackened or abated."

Southey's first school was in the village of Corston, nine miles from Bristol: it is described in one of his earliest poems extant (the Retrospect), written after he had visited the house in 1793. It had been the mansion of some decayed family, and had its walled-gardens, summer-houses, gate-pillars, a large orchard, and fine old walnut-trees; the garden was the playground; and Southey recollected of the interior a black oaken staircase from the hall, and the school-room hung with faded tapestry, behind which the boys kept their hoards of crabs. The master was a remarkable man, but an unfit tutor: his whole delight was mathematics and astronomy, and he had constructed an orrery so large that it filled a room. Southey speaks of his ornamental penmanship*—such as flourishing an angel, a serpent, a fish, or a pen, and even historical pictures; and grand spelling-matches of puzzling words hunted from the dictionary. Here Southey read Cordery and Erasmus, and got into Phædrus.

Before the boy was seven years old, he had been at the theatre more frequently than he afterward went from the age of twenty till his death. The conversations to which he listened were invariably of actors, of authors, and of the triumphs of both; the familiar books of the household were tragedies and the "acting drama." Shakspeare was in his hands as soon as he could read: and it was long before he had any other knowledge of the history of England than what he gathered from Shakspeare's plays. "Indeed," he says, "when I first read the plain matter of fact, the difference which appeared then puzzled and did not please me; and for some time I preferred Shakspeare's authority to the historians." *Titus Andronicus* was at first Southey's favorite play. He went through Beaumont and Fletcher before he was eight years old, reading them merely for the interest which the stories afforded him, but acquiring imperceptibly familiarity with the diction, and ear for the blank verse of our great masters.

At the same tender age, the resolution was first formed to excel in the profession which the child heard extolled for its dignity from morning till night. At first the actors of plays were

---

* Southey wrote a stiff, cramp hand, but remarkably neat and regular. He states that he set the fashion for black-letter in title-pages and half-titles, from his admiration of German-text at school.

One of the earliest holiday letters which he wrote was a description of Stonehenge, from the Salisbury Guide, which surprised and delighted his master, and gained Southey great praise.

esteemed beyond all other men; these in their turn gave place to writers of plays, whom, almost as soon as he could hold a pen, the boy himself began to emulate. He was not quite nine when he set to work upon a tragedy, the subject being the continence of Scipio. In 1782 he went as a day-boarder to a school in Bristol, learning from his master, as invariably proved the case with him, much less than he contrived to teach himself. Before he had reached his twelfth year he had read with the keenest relish Hoole's translations of *Jerusalem Liberated* and the *Orlando Furioso*, and had been entranced with the *Faerie Queen* of Spenser.

At thirteen, Southey was not only master of Tasso, Ariosto, and Spenser, but well acquainted also, through translations, with Homer and Ovid. He was familiar with ancient history, and his acquaintance with the light literature of the day was bounded only by the supply. A more industrious infancy was never known; but it was surpassed by the ceaseless energy of youth, which, in its turn, was superseded by the unfaltering and unequaled labor of the man.

In his twelfth and thirteenth years he wrote three heroic epistles in rhyme; made some translations from Ovid, Virgil, and Horace; composed a satirical description of English manners, as delivered by Omai, the Tahitian, to his countrymen; and next began the story of the Trojan War in a dramatic form.

Southey was removed to Westminster School early in 1788, and had for his tutor Botch Hayes, so named from the manner in which he mended his pupils' verses; here Southey first appeared in print, in a weekly paper called the *Trifler*, in imitation of the *Microcosm* at Eton. He next set on foot the *Flagellant*, in which appeared a sarcastic attack upon corporal punishment, which so roused the wrath of Dr. Vincent, the head-master, that Southey acknowledged himself the writer and apologized, but he was compelled to leave the school. He returned to his aunt at Bristol. He next went to matriculate at Oxford; his name had been put down at Christchurch, but the Dean (Cyril Jackson) having heard of the *Flagellant*, refused to admit Southey. He, however, entered at Balliol College, where he went to reside in January, 1793;* one of his college friends declares that he was a perfect *heluo librorum* then as well as throughout his life; among his writings there is abundant evidence that he had drunk deeply both of the Greek and Latin

---

* He soon attacked the law against wearing boots at Balliol; and he refused to have his hair dressed and powdered by the college barber, which was customary with freshmen.

poets; and his letters at this time indicate a mind imbued with heathen philosophy and Grecian republicanism. He rose at five o'clock in the morning to study; yet he used to say that he learned two things only at Oxford—to row and to swim. He loved the place: in one of his delightful letters, he says:

> When I walk over these streets, what various recollections throng upon me! what scenes fancy delineates from the hour when Albert first marked it as the seat of learning! Bacon's study is demolished, so I shall never have the honor of being killed by its fall; before my window Latimer and Ridley were burnt, and there is not even a stone to mark the place where a monument should be erected to religious liberty.

No attempt was made to ground Southey in prosody; and, as this defect in his education was never remedied (when he went to Westminster he was too forward in other things to be placed low enough in the school for regular training in this), Southey remained to the last as liable to make a false quantity as any Scotchman.

In his nineteenth year Southey completed his *Joan of Arc*. Next year Mr. Coleridge came to Oxford, and was introduced to Southey, who describes him as "of most uncommon merit, of the strongest genius, the clearest judgment, the best heart." The two friends next planned the emigration scheme of "Pantisocracy," * which was soon given up. Southey left Oxford in the spring of 1795, and as a means of support, with Coleridge, gave public lectures, which were well attended. The poem of *Joan of Arc* was next printed and published by Mr. Cottle, of Bristol, which may be considered as the commencement of Southey's long and arduous career as an author; for it has been well observed that "no artisan in the workshop, no peasant in the field, no handicraftsman at his board, ever went so young to his apprenticeship, or wrought so unremittingly through life for a bare livelihood, as Robert Southey."

CHARLES LAMB AT CHRIST'S HOSPITAL.

This amiable poet and essayist, whose writings, serious and humorous, alike point to some healthy and benevolent moral, was born in the Inner Temple, in 1775. At the age of seven, he was received into the school of Christ's Hospital, and there remained till he had entered his fifteenth year. "Small of stature, delicate of frame, and constitutionally nervous and timid,"

---

* With this wild scheme of "Pantisocracy," Miss Tyler was so offended that she would never again see him. The expenses of his education, both at school and college, were defrayed by his uncle, the Rev Herbert Hill, at that time a chaplain to the British Factory at Lisbon, to whom he so gratefully addresses his dedication to his *Colloquies*:

"O friend! O more than father! whom I found
Forbearing always, always kind; to whom
No gratitude can speak the debt I owe."

says his biographer, Judge Talfourd, "he would seem unfitted to encounter the discipline of a school formed to restrain some hundreds of lads in the heart of the metropolis, or to fight his way among them. But the sweetness of his disposition won him favor from all; and although the antique peculiarities of the school tinged his opening imagination, they did not sadden his childhood." *

"Lamb," says his school-fellow Le Grice, " was an amiable, gentle boy, very sensible and keenly observing, indulged by his school-fellows and his master on account of his infirmity of speech. His countenance was mild; his complexion clear brown, with an expression which might lead you to think he was of Jewish descent. His eyes were not each of the same color: one was hazel, the other had specks of grey in the iris, mingled as we see red spots in the blood-stone. His step was plantigrade, which made his walk slow and peculiar, adding to the staid appearance of his figure."

He was unfitted for joining in any boisterous sport: while others were all fire and play, he stole along with all the self-concentration of a young monk. He passed from cloister to cloister — from the school to the Temple; and here in the gardens, on the terrace, or at the fountain, was his home and recreation. Here he had access to the library of Mr. Salt, one of the Benchers; and thus, to use Lamb's own words, he was "tumbled in a spacious closet of good old English reading, where he browsed at will upon that fair and wholesome pasturage."

When Lamb quitted school, he was "in Greek, but not Deputy Grecian." He had read Virgil, Sallust, Terence, selections from Lucian's Dialogues, and Xenophon; and evinced considerable skill in the niceties of Latin composition, both in prose and verse. But the impediment in his speech proved an insuperable obstacle to his striving for an exhibition, which was given under the condition of entering the church, for which he was unfitted by nature: to this apparently hard lot he submitted with cheerfulness. Toward the close of 1789, he quitted Christ's Hospital: thenceforth his employment lay in the South-Sea House, and in the accountant's office of the East India Company.

Lamb has left us many charming pictures of his school-days and school-fellows, which must have been as delightful to him as the accounts of them are to the reader. In his " Christ's Hospital Five-and-thirty Years Ago," he says:

* The letters of Charles Lamb, with a Sketch of his Life. By Thomas Noon Talfourd, one of his Executors. Vol. i. 1837.

"We had plenty of exercise *after* school hours; and, for myself, I must confess, that I was never happier than *in* them. The Upper and the Lower Grammar Schools were held in the same room; and an imaginary line only divided their bounds. Their character was as different as that of the inhabitants on the two sides of the Pyrenees. The Rev. James Boyer was the Upper-Master, but the Rev. Matthew Field presided over that portion of the department of which I had the good fortune to be a member. We lived a life as careless as birds. We talked and did just what we pleased, and nobody molested us. We carried an accidence, or a grammar, for form; but, for any trouble it gave us, we might take two years in getting through the verbs deponent, and another two in forgetting all that we had learned about them. There was now and then the formality of saying a lesson, but if you had not learned it, a brush across the shoulders (just enough to disturb a fly) was the sole remonstrance. Field never used the rod; and, in truth, he wielded the cane with no great good will—holding it 'like a dancer.' . . . . . . We had classics of our own, without being beholden to 'insolent Greece or haughty Rome,' that passed current amongst us—Peter Wilkins—the Adventures of the Hon. Captain Robert Boyle—the Fortunate Blue Coat Boy—and the like. Or we cultivated a turn for mechanic and scientific operations, making little sun-dials of paper, or wielding those ingenious parenthesis called *cat-cradles;* or making dry peas to dance upon the end of a tin pipe; or studying the art military over that laudable game 'French and English,' and a hundred other such devices to pass away the time—mixing the useful with the agreeable—as would have made the souls of Rousseau and John Locke chuckle to have seen us.

"Matthew Field had for many years the classical charge of a hundred children, during the four or five years of their education; and his very highest form seldom proceeded further than two or three of the introductory fables of Phædrus. How things were suffered to go on thus, I cannot guess. Boyer, who was the proper person to have remedied these abuses, always affected, perhaps felt, a delicacy in interfering in a province not strictly his own. I have not been without my suspicions, that he was not altogether displeased at the contrast we presented to his end of the school. We were a sort of helots to his young Spartans. He would sometimes, with ironic deference, send to borrow a rod of the Under-Master, and then, with sardonic grin, observe to one of his upper boys, 'how neat and fresh the twigs looked.' While his pale students were battering their brains over Xenophon and Plato, with a silence as deep as that enjoined by the Samite, we were enjoying ourselves at our ease, in our little Goshen. We saw a little into the secrets of the discipline, and the prospect did but the more reconcile us to our lot. His thunders rolled innocuous forces: his storms came near, but never touched us; contrary to Gideon's miracle, while all around were drenched, our fleece was dry.* His boys turned out the better scholars; we, I suspect, have the advantage in temper. His pupils cannot speak of him without something of terror alloying their gratitude: the remembrance of Field comes back with all the soothing images of indolence, and summer slumbers, and work like play, and innocent idleness, and Elysian exemptions, and life itself 'a Playing holiday.'

"Though sufficiently removed from the jurisdiction of Boyer, we were near enough (as I have said) to understand a little of his system. We occasionally heard sounds of the *Ululantes*, and caught glances of Tartarus. B. was a rabid pedant. His English style was crampt to barbarism. His Easter anthems (for his duty obliged him to these periodical flights) were grating as scrannel pipes. He would laugh, ay, and heartily, but then it must be at Flaccus's quibble about *Rex*—or at the *tristis severitas in vultu*, or *inspicere in patinas* of Terence—thin jests, which at their first broaching could hardly have had vis enough to move a Roman muscle.—He had two wigs, both pedantic, but of different omen. The one serene, smiling, fresh-powdered, betokening a mild day. The other, an old, discolored, unkempt, angry caxon, denoting frequent and bloody execution. Woe to the school when he made his morning appearance in his *passy*, or *passionate wig*. No comet expounded surer.—J B. had a heavy hand. I have known him double his knotty fist at a poor trembling child (the maternal milk hardly dry upon its lips) with a 'Sirrah, do you presume to set your wits at me?'

"Oh, it is pleasant, as it is rare, to find the same arm linked in yours at forty, which at thirteen helped it to turn over the Cicero *De Amicitia*, or some tale of Antique Friendship, which the young heart even then was burning to anticipate. Co-Grecian with S. was Th——, who has since executed with ability various diplomatic functions at the Northern courts. Th—— was a tall, dark, saturnine youth, sparing of speech, with raven locks. Thomas Fanshaw Middleton followed him (now Bishop of Calcutta), a scholar and a gentleman in his teens."†

---

* Cowley.

† A paper of interest akin to Lamb's "Recollections," was communicated by a quondam Blue, Mr. Peter Cunningham, F.S A., to the *Illustrated London News* for December 19, 1857. This genial and clever piece of picture-writing is entitled "Christ's Hospital and Christmas Eve."

SIR HUMPHRY DAVY AT PENZANCE: HIS SCHOOLS AND SELF-EDUCATION.

Humphry Davy, whose genius is unrivaled in the annals of modern chemistry, was born in 1778, at Penzance, in Cornwall, where his father was a carver. He was a healthy, strong, and active child; he "walked off" at nine months old, and before he was two years old he could speak fluently. Before he had learned his letters, he could recite little prayers and stories, which had been repeated to him till he got them by heart; and before he had learned to write, he amused himself with copying the figures in Æsop's Fables, and reading the *Pilgrim's Progress;* of the latter book he could repeat a great part, even before he could well read it. When scarcely five years old, he made rhymes and recited them in Christmas gambols, fancifully dressed for the occasion. His disposition as a child was remarkably sweet and affectionate. He had an extraordinary strong perception, which is attested by Dr. Paris, who, in his Life of Davy, tells us that " he would, at the age of five years, turn over the pages of a book as rapidly as if he were merely engaged in counting the leaves or in hunting after pictures, and yet on being questioned, he could generally give a very satisfactory account of the contents. The same facility was retained by him through life."

He first was sent to a school at which reading and writing only were taught. Thence he was removed to the grammar-school at Penzance, kept by the Rev. W. Coryton; and subsequently to Truro, under Dr. Cardew, whose school produced more men of distinguished ability than any other in the West of England. Young Davy took the lead in his class, and composed Latin and English verse with facility; but he was more remarkable out of school, and by his comrades, than for any great advance in learning. He excelled in story-telling, partly from books, especially the *Arabian Nights,* and partly from old people, particularly from his grandmother Davy, who had a rich store of traditions and marvels. These stories were narrated by Davy to his boyish companions under the balcony of the Star Inn; and here, with his play-fellow, Rowe, a printer, of Penzance, Davy also exhibited his earliest chemical experiments; and by means of those of an explosive nature, many a trick was played on the innkeeper, and some other testy folks in the neighborhood. This and another boyish pursuit followed him into manhood — namely, fishing; for when a child, with a crooked pin, tied to a stick by a bit of thread, he would go through the movements of the angler, and fish in the gutter of the street in which he lived; and, when he was able to wield a fishing-rod, or carry a gun, he roamed at large in quest of sport in the adjoining country. Under the same favorable circumstances, his taste for natural history was indulged in a little garden of his own, which he kept in order; and he was fond of collecting and painting birds and fishes.

Davy's early love of romantic scenery is shown in a poem composed by him, descriptive of St. Michael's Mount, and the traditionary history of its having been in the midst of a forest— in the following extract:

> "By the orient gleam
> Whitening the foam of the blue wave, that breaks
> Around his granite feet, but dimly seen,
> Majestic Michael rises! He whose brow
> Is crowned with castles, and whose rocky sides
> Are clad with dusky ivy : He whose base,
> Beat by the storms of ages, stands unmoved
> Amidst the wreck of things—the change of time.
> That base, encircled by the azure waves,
> Was once with verdure clad, the towering oaks,
> Whose awful shades among the Druids strayed
> To cut the hallowed mistletoe and hold
> High converse with their Gods."

"Davy was thought at the time (says his brother) a clever boy, but not a prodigy."* His last master, Dr. Cardew, speaks of his regularity in his school duties, but not of any extraordinary abilities; his best exercises were translations from the classics into English verse. At the age of fifteen, his school education was considered completed, and his self-education, to which he owed almost everything, was about to commence.

He spent the greater part of the next year in fishing, shooting, swimming, and solitary rambles; but, at length, he settled to study. Early in 1795, he was apprenticed to a surgeon and apothecary in Penzance; and about this time he commenced his note-books, the earliest of which contains a plan of study, and hints and essays, in which, says Dr. Davy, "with all the daring confidence of youth, he enters upon the most difficult problems in metaphysics and theology, and employing a syllogistic method of reasoning (which, as he observes in his *Consolations in Travel*, young men commonly follow, in entering upon such inquiries), he arrives, as might be expected, at a conclusion contrary to the good feelings and common sense of mankind."

In the following year, young Davy entered on the study of mathematics, and finished the elementary course; he was very systematic; the propositions are all entered very neatly, and the demonstrations given; the diagrams being done with a pen, without the aid of mathematical instruments, not even of a common

---
* Life of Sir Humphry Davy, by his brother, John Davy, M.D., F.R.S.

compass and ruler. But his favorite pursuit was metaphysics, and his rough notes show an acquaintance with the writings of Locke, Hartley, Bishop Berkeley, Hume, Helvetius, and Condorcet; Reid, and other Scotch metaphysicians. These studies he soon associated with physiology. In 1797, he commenced in earnest natural philosophy; and just as he was entering his nineteenth year, he began the study of chemistry with Lavoisier's *Elements* and Nicholson's *Dictionary*. He very soon entered on a course of experiments, his apparatus consisting mostly of phials, wine-glasses, and tea-cups, tobacco-pipes, and earthen crucibles; and his materials chiefly the mineral acids and the alkalies, and some other articles in common use in medicine. He began to experiment in his bed-room, in Mr. Tonkin's house at Penzance; and there being no fire in the room, when he required it he went down to the kitchen with his crucible. Such was Davy's rapidity in this new pursuit, that in four months he was in correspondence with Dr. Beddoes, relative to his researches on "Heat and Light," and a new hypothesis on their nature, to which Dr. Beddoes became a convert. The result was Davy's first publication, *Essays on Heat and Light,* in 1799, which had been in part written a few months before he had commenced the study of chemistry.

"Such," says Dr. Davy, "was the commencement of Humphry Davy's career of original research, which, in a few years, by a succession of discoveries, accomplished more in relation to change of theory and extension of science than, in the most ardent and ambitious moments of youth, he could either have hoped to effect or imagined possible."

Another of Humphry's early associates was Mr. Robert Dunkin, a saddler, and a member of the Society of Friends. He was an entirely self-taught man, and in addition to his making saddles, he built organs, constructed electrical machines, and wrote verses. He made experiments in company with young Davy, in which they were assisted by Mr. Tom Harvey, a druggist, at Penzance, who supplied Davy with chemicals for making detonating balls, etc. After a discussion on the notion of Heat, he was induced, one winter's day, to go to Larigan river, and try if he could develop heat by *rubbing two pieces of ice together*, an experiment which he repeated with much *éclat,* many years after, at the Royal Institution.

He had already become the friend of Mr. Gregory Watt (son of the celebrated James Watt), and with him visited the most remarkable mines near Penzance, collecting specimens of rocks and minerals. And here, working the Wherry Mine, underneath the sands, and its shaft in the sea, young Davy saw a steam-engine at work—this being one of the earliest of Watt's steam-engines that had been introduced into Cornwall. About this time he became acquainted with Mr. Davies Gilbert, afterward Davy's successor as President of the Royal Society.

Meanwhile, Davy's progress in medicine was considerable; so that in the fourth year of his studies, he was considered by Dr. Beddoes competent to take charge of the patients belonging to the Pneumatic Institution at Clifton, thus entering on his public career before he was twenty years old. Here he applied himself with great zeal to complete his experiments and essays on Light and Heat; and, above all, in investigating the effects of the gases in respiration. Of these, the nitrous oxide was one of the first he experimented upon; and his discovery of its wonderful agency was the origin of the researches which established his character as a chemical philosopher; though before it was published (in 1800), Davy had begun that series of galvanic experiments which ultimately led to some of his greatest discoveries. The materials for the *Researches* were rapidly collected: Davy says in a rough draft of the preface, "These experiments have been made since April, 1799, the period when I first breathed nitrous oxide. Ten months of incessant labor were employed in making them; three months in detailing them. The author was under twenty years of age, pupil to a surgeon-apothecary in the most remote town of Cornwall, with little access to philosophical books, and none at all to philosophical men."

So intense was his application, and so little his regard for health or even life, that he nearly lost it from the breathing of carburetted hydrogen, and was compelled for a time to leave the laboratory.

The following passage from a note-book shows the intellectual life he now led, as well as the variety of his pursuits:

"*Resolution*—To work two hours with pen before breakfast on 'The Lover of Nature;' and 'The Feelings of Eldon,' from six till eight; from nine till two, in experiments; from four to six, reading; seven till ten, metaphysical reading (*i. e.*, system of the universe)."

He now began to discontinue writing verses. In a letter of this time, he says: "Do not suppose I am turned poet. Philosophy, chemistry and medicine are my profession." Yet he meditated a poem in blank verse on the Deliverance of the Israelites from Egypt, the plan and characters of which he had sketched.

He had now during the short period of little more than two years, whilst he was at Clifton, published the *Essays on Heat and Light*, and contributed eight important papers to Nicholson's Journal. A higher distinction awaited him: the Royal Institution* had recently been founded in London; and in May, 1802, "Mr. Davy (late of Bristol) was appointed Professor of Chemistry." In April following, he gave his first lecture on galvanic phenomena, Sir Joseph Banks, Count Rumford, and other distinguished philosophers, being present. "His youth, his simplicity, his natural eloquence, his chemical knowledge, his happy illustrations and well-conducted experiments," and the auspicious state of science, insured Davy great and instant success. In the previous year, he had read before the Royal Society a paper upon " Galvanic Combinations ;" and from that period to 1829, almost every volume of the Transactions contains a communication by him.

At the Royal Institution, then, Davy began his brilliant scientific career, and he remained there until 1812. His greatest labors were his discovery of the decomposition of the fixed alkalies, and the reëstablishment of the simple nature of chlorine; his other researches were the investigation of astringent vegetables, in connection with the art of tanning; the analysis of rocks and minerals, in connection with geology; the comprehensive subject of agricultural chemistry; and galvanism and electro-chemical science. His lectures were often attended by 1000 persons. He was knighted in 1812, and subsequently created a baronet.

Davy's best known achievement was his invention of the miner's Safety Lamp in 1815. He became President of the Royal Society in 1820; he resigned the chair in 1827, and retired to the Continent. He died after a lingering illness, in 1829, at Geneva, where he is buried. A simple monument stands at the head of his grave: there is a tablet to his memory in Westminster Abbey, and a monument at Penzance, his birthplace. He retained his love of angling to the last: not long before his death, he resided in an hotel at Laybach, in Styria, where the success with which he transferred the trout to his basket procured him the title of "the English wizard." He spent the greater part of the day in angling, or in geologizing among the mountains.

GEORGE STEPHENSON, THE RAILWAY ENGINEER, AND HIS
SCHOOLMASTERS AND SELF-TUITION.

In the present age of great social changes, the application of steam to locomotive purposes, or, in other words, the invention

---

* The Royal Institution has been appropriately termed "the workshop of the Royal Society." Here Davy constructed his great voltaic battery of 2000 double plates of copper and zinc, four inches square, the whole surface being 128,000 square inches. The mineralogical collection in the Museum was also commenced by Davy. It must not be omitted, that he was one of the earliest experimenters in the Photographic Art.

of the railway, takes foremost rank, and confers upon its introducer the high merit of being a signal public benefactor. This honor is due to George Stephenson, who, from being a poor "cow-boy," raised himself to wealth and eminence, and without one solitary advantage except what he derived from his own genius, stamped his name upon the most wonderful achievement of our times. His early history is a surprising example of the triumph of singular and unerring sagacity over difficulties. His school instruction was little and late; but his education may be said to have begun almost from the moment he saw coal-wagons drawn upon the tramway before his father's cottage-door, and from his moulding clay-engines with his playmates.

George Stephenson was born in 1781, in the colliery village of Wylam, about eight miles west of Newcastle-on-Tyne, amid slag and cinders, in an ordinary laborer's cottage, with unplastered walls, bare rafters, and floor of clay. His father was the descendant of an ancient and honorable line of working men, and his mother, Mabel, was "a rale canny body;" but the wages of the former as a fireman amounting to no more than twelve shillings a week, schooling for George was out of the question, and he was taken by his father birdnesting, or told stories about Sinbad and Robinson Crusoe as a substitute. His interest in birds' nests never left him to his dying day, nor were other sights of his childhood less identified with the serious business of his life. In the rails of the wooden tram-road before his cottage, on which he saw the coal-wagons dragged by horses from the pit to the loading-quay, half the destiny of an age was latent, to be evolved hereafter by the very boy, who, after his own probation was over, had to keep his younger brothers and sisters out of the way of the horses. Thus eight years passed away, when the family removed to Dewley-burn, and George, to his great joy, was raised to the post of cow-boy to a neighboring farmer, at the wages of twopence a-day. He had plenty of spare time on his hands, which he spent in birdnesting, also in making whistles out of reeds and scrannel straws, and erecting Lilliputian mills in the little water streams that ran into the Dewley Bog. There can be no doubt that he indicated thus early that bent which is termed a mechanical genius. His favorite amusement, and this deserves to be noted, was the erection of *clay engines*, in conjunction with a certain Tom Tholoway. The boys found the clay for their engines in the adjoining bog, and the hemlock which grew about supplied them with abundance of imaginary steam-pipes. The place is still pointed out "just aboon the cut end," as the people of the hamlet describe it, where the future engineer made his first essays in modeling. As the boy grew older, and more able to work, he was set to lead the horses in plowing, and to hoe turnips, at the advanced wages of fourpence a-day. Then he was taken on at the colliery as a "picker," at sixpence a-day, whence he was advanced to be driver of the gin-horse at eightpence; and there are those who still remember him in that capacity as a "grit bare-legged laddie," whom they describe as "quick-witted and full of fun and tricks." He himself had some misgivings as to his physical dimensions, and was wont to hide himself when the owner of the colliery went round, lest he should be thought too little a boy to earn his small wages. His fixed ambition was to be an engineman; and great, therefore, was his exultation when, at about fourteen years of age, he was appointed fireman, at the wages of one shilling a-day.

Thenceforth his fortunes took him from one pit to another, and procured him rising wages with his rising stature. At Throckley-bridge, when advanced to twelve shillings a-week, "I am now," sad he, "a made man for life." At seventeen he shot ahead of his father, being made an engineman or plugman, while the latter remained a fireman. He soon studied and mastered the working of his engine, and it became a sort of pet with him. His greatest privilege was to find some one who could read to him by the engine-fire out of any book or stray newspaper which found its way into the colliery. Thus he heard that the Egyptians hatched birds' eggs by artificial heat, and endeavored to do the same in his engine-house. He learnt also, that the wonderful engines of Watt* and Boulton were to be found described

---

* James Watt, the great improver of the Steam-engine, born at Greenock, in 1736, received his early education mostly at home; although he attended for a time the public elementary schools in his native town. His ill-health, which often confined him to his chamber, appears to have led him to the cultivation, with unusual assiduity, of his intellectual powers. It is said that when only six years of age, he was discovered solving a geometrical problem upon the hearth with a piece of chalk; and other circumstances related of him justify the remark elicited from a friend on the above occasion, that he was "no common child." About 1.50, he amused himself by making an electrical machine; and it is related that his aunt upbraided him one evening at the tea-table for what seemed to her to be listless idleness: taking off the lid of the tea-kettle and putting it on again; holding sometimes a cup, and sometimes a silver spoon, over the steam; watching the exit of the steam from the spout; and counting the drops of water into which it became condensed. Hence, the boy pondering before the tea-kettle has been viewed as the embryo engineer prognosticating the discoveries which were to immortalize him. During his youth he indulged his love for botany on the banks of Loch Lomond, and his rambles among the mountain scenery of his native land aroused an attention to mineralogy and geology. Chemistry was a favorite subject when he was confined by ill-health to his father's dwelling. He read eagerly books on natural philosophy, surgery, and medicine. Leaving, however, all these studies, Watt applied himself to the profession of a mathematical instrument maker, and after a time settled in Glasgow, where, displaying much ingenuity and manual dexterity, his superior intelligence led to his sh p being a favorite resort for the most eminent scientific men in Glasgow. Watt needed only prompting to take up and conquer any subject; and Professor Robinson states that he learnt the German language in order to peruse Leupold's *Theatrum Machinarum*, because the solution of a problem on which he was engaged seemed to require it; and that similar reasons led him subse-

in books, and with the object of mastering these books, though a grown man, he went to a night-school at threepence a-week to learn his letters. He also practiced "pot-hooks," and at the age of nineteen was proud to be able to write his own name.

Stephenson may be said to have anticipated a Mechanics' Institute at the bottom of a coal-pit: for he, and others of the workmen less gifted, made their companions who could read give them some little instruction, and read any stray paper which might reach their remote village in the days of the Fist Napoleon's first efforts to conquer Europe.

In the winter of 1799, George removed to the night-school kept by a Scotch dominie, named Andrew Robertson, who was a skilled arithmetician. Here George learnt "figuring" much faster than his school-fellows—"he took to figures so wonderful." He worked out his sums in his bye-hours, improving every minute of his spare time by the engine-fire, solving the arithmetical problems set him upon his slate by his master, so that he soon became well advanced in arithmetic. At length, Robertson could carry Stephenson no further, the pupil having outstripped the master. He went on, however, with his writing lessons, and by the next year, 1802—when he signed his name on his marriage—he was able to write a good, legible round hand.

By improving his spare hours in the evening, he was silently and surely paving the way for being something more than a mere workman, by studying principles of mechanics, and the laws by which his engine worked. By steady conduct and saving habits, he not only sustained the pressure of the times, but procured the coveted means of educating his son. Soon afterward he signalized himself by curing a wheezy engine, at which "all the engineers of the neighborhood were tried, as well as Crowther of the Ouseburn, but they were clean bet." He got 10*l*. for this job, and from this day his services as an engineer came into request.

In 1814, he placed a locomotive on the Killingworth Railway; and this engine, improved in 1815, is the parent of the whole race of locomotives which has since sprung into existence. This was, indeed, a year of double triumph to Stephenson, for in it he produced his Safety Lamp for miners; though Sir Humphry Davy's lamp was reported to be something more per-

---

quently to study Italian. Without neglecting his business in the daytime, Watt devoted his nights to various and often profound studies ; and the mere difficulty of a subject, provided it was worthy of pursuit, seems to have recommended it to his indefatigable character. Thus was passed the early life of Watt, previous to his seriously directing his attention to the properties of steam.

feet than what was called "invention claimed by a person, an engine-wright, of the name of Stephenson."

In 1825, Stephenson's locomotive was worked on the Stockton and Darlington Railway; and in 1830, he drove his engine, "The Rocket," upon the Liverpool and Manchester line, across Chat Moss, at the rate of thirty miles an hour, and thereby gained the prize of 500*l*. Thirty years after he had been a worker in a pit at Newcastle, he traveled from that city to London, behind one of his own engines, in nine hours; and Liverpool and London have raised statues of George Stephenson, the Engineer, to whose intelligence and perseverance we owe the introduction of this mighty power.*

BOYHOOD AND EARLY DEATH OF HENRY KIRKE WHITE.

Few instances of early death from ardor in the pursuit of knowledge are so touching as that afforded in the brief span of the life of the amiable and gifted Henry Kirke White. He was born in 1785, at Nottingham, where his father followed the business of a butcher. He was sent to school at three years of age, and soon became so fond of reading that he could be scarcely got to lay down his book, that he might take his meals. At the age of seven, he attempted to express his ideas upon paper; his first composition being a tale, which, however, he only communicated to the servant, whom he had secretly taught to write. Before the age of eleven, in addition to reading and writing, he outstripped his school-fellows in arithmetic and French. Soon after this he began to write verse. He assisted at his father's business for some time, carrying the butcher's basket; but he so disliked this occupation, that at the age of fourteen, he was apprenticed to a stocking-weaver. But, to use his own words, he "wanted something to occupy his brain;" still, he scarcely dare complain, for he knew that his family could hardly afford to educate him for any higher employment. His mother, however, moved by his wretchedness, after he had been about a year at the loom, prevailed upon his father to place him in an attorney's office at Nottingham; where, notwithstanding he attended the office twelve hours a day, he applied his leisure to studying the Greek and Latin languages, and was able, in ten months, to read Horace. He also made considerable progress in Italian, Spanish, and Portuguese; in chemistry, electricity, and astronomy; while his less severe studies were drawing, music, and practical mechanics; and in extempore speaking, he

---

* The narration of these events has been principally condensed from Mr. Smiles's *Life of George Stephenson* (published in 1857); an admirable specimen of biographical writing, earnest and unaffected, and in every way worthy of its great subject.

distanced his competitors in a debating-society which was then held at Nottingham.

In his fifteenth year, he sent to a London periodical, the *Monthly Preceptor*, a translation from Horace, for which he received a silver medal. This success induced him to print, in 1803, a volume of verses, the longest of which, entitled *Clifton Grove*, is in the style of Goldsmith. This publication was harshly criticised in the *Monthly Review*, which distressed the young poet exceedingly; but it obtained for him the kindly notice and friendship of Mr. Southey, who considered the poems "to discover strong marks of genius." Meanwhile, Henry, by a course of religious reading, grew ardently devotional, so as to increase the desire which he had long felt for an University education. Despairing of this, he renewed his legal studies with such severe application, as rarely to allow himself more than two or three hours' sleep during the night, and often not going to bed at all. This excessive application brought on an alarming illness, from which his friends thought that he never entirely recovered. At length, in 1804, he quitted his employer at Nottingham, and after a year's preparatory study, entered St. John's College, Cambridge, where a sizarship had been obtained for him: but, says Mr. Southey, "the seeds of death were in him, and the place which he had so long looked on with hope, served unhappily as a hot-house to ripen them." His exertions at the University were very severe: he studied for a scholarship, but, through ill health, could not come forward. He then passed the general college examination, and at its close was declared the first man of his year. As an instance of how he used "to coin time, it is related that he committed to memory a whole tragedy of Euripides, during his walks." At the end of this term, he was again pronounced first man: a tutor in mathematics for the long vacation was now provided for him by the college; but this distinction was purchased at the sacrifice of health and life: he went to London to recruit his shattered nerves and spirits, but he got no better. He returned to the University worn out in body and mind, and died after an attack of delirium, October 19, 1806. Mr. Southey wrote a sketch of his life, and edited his *Remains*, the publication of which proved highly profitable to White's family. A tablet to his memory, with a medallion by Chantrey, was placed in All Saints' Church, Cambridge, at the expense of Mr. Boott, a young American gentleman. It bears the following inscription by Professor Smythe:

> Warm with the fond hope and learning's sacred flame,
> To Granta's bowers the youthful poet came;
> Unconquered powers the immortal mind displayed,
> But worn with anxious thought, the frame decayed.
> Pale o'er his lamp, and in his cell retired,
> The martyr student faded and expired.
> Oh! genius, taste, and piety sincere,
> Too early lost 'midst studies too severe!
> Foremost to mourn, was generous Southey seen,
> He told the tale, and showed what White had been;
> Nor told in vain. Far o'er the Atlantic wave
> A wanderer came, and sought the poet's grave:
> On yon low stone he saw his lonely name,
> And raised this fond memorial to his fame.

Lord Byron has consecrated some lines of pure pathos to the memory of White, who

> "View'd his own feather on the fatal dart,
> And wing'd the shaft that quiver'd in his heart."

Henry Kirke White's verse is fluent and correct, plaintive and reflective, and rich in fancy and description; and he affords a fine example of youthful ardor devoted to the purest and noblest objects. His case, has, however, been referred to as an alarming instance of the danger of mental pressure, and of the injury that extreme and misdirected application of the mind may do to the body. "The picture of a Kirke White," says a popular writer, "dying at the age of 21, of nocturnal study, wet towels round heated temples, want of sleep, want of air, want of everything which Nature intended for the body, is not only melancholy because it is connected with an early death; it is melancholy also on account of the certain effect which would have followed such a course unchecked if he had lived."

Dr. Forbes Winslow, however, considers this illustration unfortunate. "Kirke White," he adds, "from his earliest infancy, was of so delicate a constitution as to be unfit (as was supposed) for any active occupation. The question may naturally arise—would so active and irritable a mind, united to so feeble a frame, have lacked opportunity under any circumstances of rapidly wearing out both itself and its earthly tenement? The wasting fever of such a mind is not to be allayed by any restrictions as to hours of study, rest, or general hygiene."* Although difference of opinion exists as to the case of Kirke White, the effect of mental labor upon bodily health, in relation to age, temperament, and other circumstances, cannot be too closely watched; and wherever there is an insatiate craving after knowledge, so as to produce an overgrowth of mind, the extreme application cannot too soon be restrained.

* Journal of Psychological Medicine and Mental Pathology. New Series.—No. IX.

SIR ROBERT PEEL AT HARROW AND OXFORD.

This distinguished statesman, whose name is indissolubly associated with some of the most important events in the history of our time, was born in 1788, in a cottage adjoining Chamber Hall, his father's house, in the neighborhood of Bury, Lancashire, which happened at that time to be under repair. He descended from the ancient family of De Pele, established first in Yorkshire, and afterward in Lancashire. His grandfather commenced, and his father completed, the acquisition of a large fortune as a cotton-spinner; and, as if "to marshal him the way that he was going," Mr. Peel, the father, two years after the birth of his son Robert, entered the House of Commons as a member, and as a zealous supporter of Mr. Pitt: in 1800 he received a baronetcy.

The son was sent early to Hipperholme School, in Yorkshire, where he cut upon a block of stone (now preserved at Halifax) the following inscription:

R. PEEL.
No hostile hands can antedate my doom.

He was removed to Harrow School, and appears in the Speech Bill of 1803, as Peel, sen., Upper-Fifth Form, No. 58. Lord Byron, his school-fellow (and born in the same year), says of him:

"Peel, the orator and statesman (that was, or is, or is to be), was my form-fellow, and we were both at the top of our remove. We were on good terms, but his brother was my intimate friend. There were always great hopes of Peel amongst us all, masters and scholars—and he has not disappointed them. As a scholar, he was greatly my superior; as a declaimer and actor, I was reckoned at least his equal; as a school-boy out of school, I was always in scrapes, and *he never*, and *in school* he always knew his lesson, and I rarely,—but when I knew it, I knew it nearly as well. In general information, history, etc., I think I was his superior, as well as of most boys of my standing." *

He was (says his biographer, Doubleday) diligent, studious, and sagacious, if not quick, but never brilliant; preserving a high station among his school-mates by exertion and perseverance rather than genius; and being remarkable for prudent good sense rather than showy talent.† His memory is fondly cherished at Harrow, where the room which he occupied in a house in the town is kept in its original state, with a brick on which he cut his name, the genuineness of the inscription being verified by Peel's handwriting in a ciphering-book of the same date. His name is also cut in the panel of the old school-room, with those of his three sons, whom he placed in the school.

* For an anecdote of his friendship with Lord Byron, see page 291.
† Political Life of Sir Robert Peel, 1856, vol. i. p. 42.

In 1804, Peel left Harrow, and entered Christchurch, Oxford, as a gentleman commoner. At the University, he was a diligent and laborious student; and in 1808, on taking his degree, obtained a double first-class, the highest honors, both in classics and mathematics. Amongst his competitors were Mr. Gilbert, afterward Vice-Chancellor of the University; Mr. Hampden, Professor of Divinity; and Mr. Whately, the present Archbishop of Dublin.

A boy from Tunbridge School, writing to one of his former class-fellows an account of this examination, speaks with enthusiasm of the spirit of Peel's translations, especially of his beautiful rendering of the opening of the second book of Lucretius, beginning:

Suave mari magno turbantibus æquora ventis
E terra magnum alterius spectare laborem;

and ending with the picture of the philosopher gazing from his calm oriental rest on the disturbed, self-wearying, ignorant, erring world. "Often of late," said one of those to whom this letter at the time was read, "have I been struck with the fitness of this passage to Peel himself, who, having achieved so much amidst all the strife of party, could, free from its entanglements, see men of all parties gathering the ripening fruit of his measures."

Mr. Doubleday describes Peel's college acquirements as "of the solid kind, and such as a laborious student of good practical sagacity may always acquire. Of wit, or imagination, or of the inventive faculty in general, Mr. Peel had little; and to such men the absence of these more specious qualifications is a negative advantage. If they are unable to dazzle others, in the same ratio they are exempted from being dazzled by them; and hence it is that persons so qualified have a clearer view of the characters of those with whom they have to deal, and are better adapted to the ordinary business of life than their more accomplished competitors."

In the course of the year 1808, Mr. Peel completed his studies at Oxford. From his very cradle, it may be said, he was destined by his father for a politician; and in 1809, being of age, he entered Parliament for the borough of Cashel.

It is not our province to record the political life of this distinguished man, which extended beyond forty years. More germane is it in this place to glance at Sir Robert Peel as a patron of English Literature and men of letters. He tendered a baronetcy to Southey, and conferred on him a pension of 300*l.* a-year, and gave the same amount to Wordsworth; to James Montgomery, 150*l.* a-year; and to Tytler, to Tennyson, and M'Culloch, each 200*l.* a-year; and pensions to Frances Browne, and the widow of Thomas Hood. To him Mrs. Somerville and Professor Faraday are indebted for their pensions; nor should be forgotten his friendship with Lawrence, Wilkie, and Chantrey; his patronage of Collins, Roberts, and Stanfield; and his prompt relief of the sufferings of Haydon.*

LORD BYRON AT ABERDEEN, HARROW, AND CAMBRIDGE.

This celebrated man, who, as a poet of description and passion, will always occupy a high place, was born Jan. 22, 1788, at No. 24, in Holles-street, Cavendish-square, and was christened in the small parish church of St. Marylebone. He was the only son of Captain John Byron, of the Guards, and Catherine Gordon, of Gight, an Aberdeenshire heiress. Owing to an accident attending his birth, his feet were distorted, a defect which was the source of pain and mortification to him during the whole of his life. His mother's fortune was soon squandered by her profligate husband, and she retired to the city of Aberdeen, to bring up her son on a reduced income of about 130*l*. per annum. When about five years old, Byron was sent to a day-school at Aberdeen, kept by one Bowers, and remained there a twelvemonth, as appears by the following entry in the day-book of the school:

> "George Gordon Byron.
> 19th November, 792
> 19th November, 1793 —Paid one guinea."

Of the progress of his learning here, and at other places, we have the following record, in a sort of a journal which he once began, under the title of "My Dictionary," and which is preserved in one of his manuscript books:

> "I was sent at five years old, or earlier, to a school kept by a Mr Bowers, who was called *Bodsy Bowers*, by reason of his dapperness. It was a school for both sexes. I learned little there except to repeat by rote the first lesson, of monosyllables ('God made man.' 'Let us love him.'), by hearing it often repeated, without acquiring a letter. Whenever proof was made of my progress at home, I repeated these words with the most rapid fluency; but on turning over a new leaf, I continued to repeat them, so that the narrow boundaries of my first year's accomplishments were detected, my ears boxed (which they did not deserve, seeing that it was only by ear that I had acquired my letters), and my intellects consigned to a new preceptor. He was a very devout, clever little clergyman, named Ross, afterward minister of one of the Kirks (*East*, I think). Under him I made astonishing progress, and I recollect to this day his mild manners and good-natured painstaking. The moment I could read, my grand passion was *history*; and why, I know not, but I was particularly taken with the battle near the Lake Regillus in the Roman History; put into my hands the first. Four years ago, when standing on the heights of Tusculum, and looking down upon the little round lake that was once Regillus, and which dots the immense expanse below, I remembered my young enthusiasm and my old instructor. Afterward I had a very serious, saturnine, but kind young man, named Paterson, for a tutor. He was the son of my shoemaker, but a good scholar, as is common with the Scotch. He was a right Presbyterian also. With him I began Latin in Ruddiman's Grammar, and continued till I went to the grammar-school (*Scutice*, 'Schulo;' *Aberdonice*, 'Squeel'), where I threaded all the classes to the *fourth*, when I was recalled to England by the demise of my uncle."

In one of his Letters he says of his writing:

> "I acquired this handwriting, which I can hardly read myself, under the fair copies of

---

* Notes and Queries, No. 132.

Mr Duncan, of the same city : I don't think he could plume himself much upon my progress. However, I wrote much better than I have ev, r done since. Haste and agitation of one kind or another, have quite spoilt as pretty a scrawl as ever scratched over a frank."

Byron's early religious habits were fostered by his nurse, who taught him to repeat several of the Psalms; the 1st and 23d being among the earliest that he committed to memory; and through the care of this respectable woman, who was herself of a very religious disposition, he attained a far earlier and more intimate acquaintance with the Sacred Writings than falls to the lot of most young people. In a letter which he wrote to Mr. Murray from Italy, in 1821, after requesting of that gentleman to send him, by the first opportunity, a Bible, he adds : " Don't forget this, for I am a great reader and admirer of those books, and had read them through and through before I was eight years old. I speak, as a boy, from the recollected impression of that period at Aberdeen in 1796."

It was about 1798 that Byron is said to have composed his first rhymes upon an old friend of his mother's, to whom he had taken a dislike ; but he himself tells us that his " first dash into poetry" was in 1800, when he "made an attempt at elegy—a very dull one." On Byron succeeding to his uncle's title, his mother removed with him to the family seat, Newstead Abbey, in Nottinghamshire; and Mr. Rogers, a schoolmaster of Nottingham, improved him considerably by reading passages from Virgil and Cicero with him ; but, in less than a year, he was conveyed to a quiet boarding-school at Dulwich, where he remained two years under the tuition of Dr. Glennie. Within the next two years, his mother removed him to Harrow, where he remained till 1805, when he was sent to Trinity College, Cambridge. At Harrow, he was an irregular and turbulent scholar, though he eagerly devoured all sorts of learning except that which was prescribed for him: his talent for declamation was the only one by which he was particularly distinguished: he had no aptitude for merely verbal scholarship; and his patience seemed to have entirely failed him in the study of Greek. He frequently gave signs of a frank, noble, and generous spirit, which endeared him to his schoolmates, of which Moore, in his Life of the poet, relates the following instance :

" While Lord Byron and Mr. Peel were at Harrow together, a tyrant some few years older, whose name was * * * *, claimed a right to fag little Peel, which claim (whether rightly or wrongly, I know not) Peel resisted. His resistance, however, was in vain : * * * * not only subdued him, but determined also to punish the refractory slave, and proceeded forthwith to put his determination in practice, by inflicting a kind of bastinado on the inner fleshy side of the boy's arm, which during the operation, was twisted round with some degree of technical skill, to r nder the pain more acute. While the stripes were succeeding each other, and poor Peel was writhing under them, Byron saw and felt for the misery of his friend; and although he knew he was not strong enough to fight * * * * with any hope of success, and that it were dangerous even to approach him, he advanced to the scene of action, and with a blush of rage, tears in his eyes, and a voice trembling between terror and indignation, asked very humbly if * * * * would be pleased to tell him how many stripes he meant to inflict? 'Why?' returned the executioner, 'you little rascal, what is that to you?' 'Because, if you please,' said Byron, holding out his arm, 'I would take half.'"

Upon this, Mr. Moore judiciously remarks:

"There is a mixture of simplicity and magnanimity in this little trait which is truly heroic; and, however we may smile at the friendship of boys, it is but rarely that the friendship of manhood is capable of anything half so generous."

At Harrow, Byron was occasionally serious; and he would lie by the hour upon an altar-tomb in the churchyard, contemplating the glorious prospect from that elevated site, and viewing the distant metropolis in poetic contrast with the quiet beauty of the surrounding country: the monument is to this day called "Byron's Tomb."* His vacations were generally passed in Nottinghamshire: one of them was spent in the house of the Abbé Roufigny, in Took's-court, Chancery-lane, for the purpose of studying the French language, but most of his time was passed in boxing and fencing, to the no small disturbance of the old Abbé's establishment.

"Though Byron was lame," says one of his Harrow school-fellows, "he was a great lover of sports, and preferred hockey to Horace, relinquished even Helicon for Duck-puddle,† and gave up the best poet that ever wrote hard Latin for a game of cricket on the common. He was not remarkable (nor was he ever) for his learning; but he was always a clever, plain-spoken, and undaunted boy. I have seen him fight by the hour like a Trojan, and stand up against the disadvantage of his lameness with all the spirit of an ancient combatant. 'Don't you remember your battle with Pitt J—— (a brewer's son)?' said I to him in a letter (for I had witnessed it); but it seems he had forgotten it. 'You are mistaken, I think,' said he, in reply; 'it must have been with Rice-pudding Morgan, or Lord Jocelyn, or one of the Douglases, or George Raynsford, or Pryce (with whom I had two conflicts), or with Moses Moore ('the clod'), or with somebody else, and not with Pitt; for with all the above-named and other worthies of the fist had I an interchange of black eyes and bloody noses, at various and sundry periods; however, it may have happened for all that.'"

At Cambridge, by fits and starts, Byron devoted himself to pretty hard study, and continued to cultivate his taste for poetry.

* In a letter to Mr. Murray, of April, 1822, Byron says: "There is a spot in the churchyard, near the footpath, on the brow of the hill looking toward Windsor, and a tomb under a large tree (bearing the name of Peachie or Peachey), where I used to sit for hours and hours when a boy. This was my favorite spot."
† See Harrow School, described at page 93.

At the same time he indulged in many discreditable eccentricities, and caused great annoyance by keeping a bear and several bull-dogs. He frequently evinced the most generous and noble feelings, and chose his associates, with one or two exceptions, from among the young men of the greatest ability, wit, and character, to a few of whom he continued much attached in after-life. In 1806, while yet at college, he printed a thin quarto volume of poems for private circulation. Next year, he brought out his "Hours of Idleness," a collection of fugitive poems, which was treated with undue severity by the *Edinburgh Review;* upon which Byron retaliated in his biting satire of *English Bards and Scotch Reviewers,* published in 1809, a few days before he took his oath and seat in the House of Lords. In the same year he left England on a classical tour on the Continent, which enriched his mind with incidents and poetical imagery, and filled it with reflections of some of the finest and most melancholy scenery in the world. His travels finished his poetical education: its first-fruits was his splendid poem of *Childe Harold,* commencing a long trail of poetic fame; and he continued to write until the summer of 1823, when he joined with ardor and impetuosity in the cause of "Greek Independence:" and early in the following year, while in command of an expedition, he died, three months after he had reached the age of thirty-six. The bitter grief of his followers and attendants of all nations was a proof of his kindness of heart, and his goodness as a master.

THOMAS ARNOLD AT WINCHESTER AND OXFORD.

This devoted school reformer was born at West Cowes, in the Isle of Wight, in 1795. After being for some years at a private school in Wiltshire, he was sent, in 1897, to Winchester College, where, according to a Rugbeian writer in the *Quarterly Review,* who well remembers him, "however his dormant capabilities were recognized by his masters, he gave to his schoolfellows no great promise of a future excellence, which ripened slowly; but even then he showed his love for history rather than poetry, and for truth and facts in preference to fiction. Already in his school-boy correspondence did he inveigh against the incorrectness and exaggerations of the Roman historians; and thus early anticipate the views of Niebuhr." Another reviewer says:

" Along with the elements of classical learning, and a strong Wykehamist feeling, which he ever after continued to cherish, he probably acquired at Winchester an admiration, not without prejudice, for public education, and the system of English public schools. He afterward became distinguished, and sometimes dreaded, as a school reformer ; but his anxiety to improve, was only in proportion to the degree to which he was attached to the system, alike by the associations of his boyhood, and the convictions of his more mature experience."—*North British Review*, No. 4.

Arnold went to Oxford in 1811, and was elected as a scholar of Corpus Christi College. He did not bring with him any precocious amount of erudition; but he had soon so mastered the language and style of Herodotus and Thucydides, that he wrote narratives in the manner of either, to the admiration at least of his fellow-students. He devoted himself to the historians and philosophers of antiquity, rather than to the critical and verbal study of the poets, which has always been at Oxford the favorite field for philosophical training. Among his fellow-students were John Keble, author of the *Christian Year*, and John Taylor Coleridge, nephew of the poet, now a Judge of the Queen's Bench: with such minds, in the common room of Corpus, young Arnold "debated the classic and romantic question," and "discussed poetry and history, logic and philosophy." He took a high degree, gained the prose prizes, and in 1815 obtained a fellowship of Oriel, then reputed to be the blue ribbon of the University. Aristotle, Herodotus, and Thucydides formed the studies and relaxations of his maturing life; and on them, coupled with the Bible, he thought the knowledge of a Christian was the best based. There Arnold acted as tutor; and among his colleagues were Copleston, Whately, Keble, Pusey, Newman, and other celebrities of great earnestness and intellectual activity. He was naturally self-confident; and his independence of opinion and dogmatism offended and alarmed many members of other colleges; yet, though a true Christian reformer, what he most desired was to turn the capabilities of existing institutions to better results, to repair and not to overthrow. He was virulently misrepresented and opposed; but he pursued his course through good and evil report, and lived down calumny and opposition; and great and merited was his triumph when he appeared in the crowded theatre of the University as Professor of History. During his residence at the University, he availed himself largely of the Oxford libraries, entering upon an extensive course of reading, especially in modern history. Arnold was then, and continued till the day of his death, an enthusiast in his love of Oxford: he admired its system of tuition, its learned societies, and its magnificent libraries. A successful scholar from an English public school, he became a distinguished collegian: with his opinions and friendships formed at college, to him Oxford was a world in itself; he loved Oxford from first to last.

After a residence of nine years, he removed from Oxford to

Laleham, married, took private pupils, and passed another nine years peacefully in ripening his powers. Thence he removed, in 1827, to the head-mastership of Rugby, where his professional life began, as we have already illustrated.* (See ante, pages 92 and 93.)

Arnold threw himself into his great work of school reform.

> To do his duty to the utmost was the height of his ambition, those truly English sentiments by which Nelson and Wellington were inspired; and like them he was crowned with victory, for soon were verified the predictions of the Provost of Oriel, that *he would change the face of education through the public schools of England.* He was minded—*virtute officii*—to combine the care of souls to that of the intellects of the rising generation and to realize the Scripture in principle and in practice, without making an English school a college of Jesuits.
>
> A feeling of the failings and shortcomings of our public schools—pointed out by Cowper and others—had long been working among the thoughtful and serious, when Arnold led the way, giving shape and guidance to the movement.
>
> His principles were few: the fear of God was the beginning of his wisdom, and his object was not so much to teach knowledge as the means of acquiring it; to furnish, in a word, the key to the temple. He desired to awaken the intellect of each individual boy, and contended that the main movement must come from within, and not from without the pupil; and that all that could be, should be *done by* him, and not *for* him. In a word, his scheme was to call forth in the little world of school those capabilities which best befitted the boy for his career in the great one. He was not only possessed of strength, but had the art of imparting it to others; he had the power to grasp a subject himself, and then engraft it on the intellects of others.—*Quarterly Review*, No. 204.

Especially was Arnold an orthodox Oxonian in his belief of the indispensable usefulness of classical learning, not only as an important branch of knowledge, but as the substantial basis of education itself, the importance of which he has thus forcibly illustrated:

> "'The study of Greek and Latin, considered as mere languages, is of importance mainly as it enables us to understand and employ well that language in which we commonly think, and speak, and write. It does this because Greek and Latin are specimens of language at once highly perfect and capable of being understood without long and minute attention; the study of them, therefore, naturally involves that of the general principles of grammar; while their peculiar excellencies illustrate the points which render language clear, and forcible, and beautiful. But our *application* of this general knowledge must naturally be to our own language; to show us what are its peculiarities, what its beauties, what its defects; to teach us by the patterns, or the analogies offered by other languages, how the effect we admire in them may be produced with a somewhat different instrument. Every lesson in Greek or Latin may and ought to be made a lesson in English; the translation of every sentence in Demosthenes or Tacitus is properly an extemporaneous English composition; a problem, how to express with equal brevity, clearness, and force, in our own language, the thought which the original author has so admirably expressed in his." †

SIR HENRY HAVELOCK AT THE CHARTER-HOUSE.

To the notices of eminent Carthusians, at page 104 of the present volume, we must append some further record of Havelock, who took so noble a part in suppressing the Revolt in India in 1857, and who so heroically rescued the garrison of Cawnpore, but, within a few days of his victory, sank from the severe

---

* We reiterate our recommendation to the reader to turn to the recently published *Tom Brown's School-days* for many a delightful picture of daily life and discipline at Rugby during Arnold's mastership.

† Dr Arnold was the first English commentator who gave life to the study of the classics, by bringing the facts and manners which they disclose to the test of real life.

effects of the climate and the war. His life was throughout an eventful career; strong religious principle underlaid his whole character, and he was emphatically pronounced by Lord Hardinge to be "every inch a soldier, and every inch a Christian."

The late Henry Havelock was the son of William Havelock, the sicion of an old family originally seated at Great Grimsby, in Lincolnshire, where they are said to have settled in the time of King Alfred: local tradition derives their descent from Guthrum, the Danish chief*—the conquest of this part of the island by the Danes having been complete.

The deceased General was, however, content to know that his parents were English, and traced his lineage no higher than to an honest family which resided in Lincolnshire. William Havelock, his father, was born at Guisborough, in Yorkshire, made good his position at Sunderland, and then married Jane Carter, daughter of a conveyancer of that town. Henry, their illustrious son, was born at Ford Hall, near Sunderland, in 1795. When he was in his fifth year, his father immigrated to the south of England, and bought Ingress, at Swanscombe, in Kent. In his sixth year, Henry was sent with his elder brother, William (killed in the cavalry action at Ramnugger, 1843), as a parlor-boarder to a school at Dartford, kept by the Rev. J. Bradley, with whom he remained about three years. Courage and presence of mind are indicated in the incidents related of his childhood. He falls from a tree in Ingress Park, and is asked by his father whether he was not frightened? "No," is the reply; "I was thinking about the bird's eggs." He interferes in a fight, to secure fair play for a school-fellow, and gets a black eye. Called to give an account of the disfigurement to his master, he is silent, and takes his thrashing like a man. He was already an earnest reader of all papers which came in his way relating to military affairs, and made himself familiar with the movements of Napoleon. His tendencies toward the profession of a soldier were so strongly evinced, that his mother apprehended disappointment of her project of educating him for the law.

In 1804 he left Mr. Bradley's school for the Charter-house, and was placed in the boarding-house of the Rev. Dr. Matthew Raine, then head-master. In the memoranda which Havelock has left, he thus speaks of his school-fellows: "My most intimate friends at the Charter-house were Samuel Hinds, William Norris, and Julius Charles Hare. Hinds, a man of taste and a poet, spent his early years in traveling, married in France, distinguished himself in one of the colonial assemblies of his native

* Mr. John Marshman, in the Baptist Magazine, March, 1858.

island, Barbadoes, at the period of slave emancipation, and died at Bath about 1847.

"Norris, now Sir William Norris, was called to the bar, appointed successively Advocate Fiscal, or Queen's Advocate, Puisne Judge, and Chief-Justice at Ceylon, and subsequently Recorder of Penang. Hare went to Trinity College, Cambridge, in 1812, graduated B.A. 1815, and subsequently as M.A., became a Fellow and Tutor at Trinity. He is well known to the literary and religious world by his joint translation with Dr. Connop Thirlwall of part of the Roman history of Niebuhr; some volumes of sermons, and several polemical pamphlets.

"Nearly cotemporary with me and the boys just named, were Connop Thirlwall, now Bishop of St. David's; George Waddington, Dean of Durham, distinguished as a scholar and a man of letters; George Grote, the historian of Greece; Archdeacon Hale, now Master of the Charter-house; Alderman Thompson, the member for Westmoreland; Sir William MacNaghten, the talented but unfortunate envoy to Cabul; the Right Honorable Fox Maule, now Secretary-of-War; Eastlake, the painter; and Yates, the actor.

"In April, 1810, Henry Havelock had gone up into that fifth form, of which Walpole, grandson of Sir Robert, was first, Hare second, John Pindar third, and Havelock fourth. It consisted of some thirty boys, and lower down in it were Connop Thirlwall and Hinds."

The Rev. Mr. Brock* says: "Not merely thoughtful was the young Carthusian as a school-boy. He was religiously if not evangelically thoughtful. Thus, in his memoranda, he says: 'Of Henry Havelock it may be recorded, that there were early indications of the strivings of the good Spirit of God in his soul, though Satan and the world were permitted for many years to triumph.' Certainly, whilst at the Charter-house the evidence of those strivings was apparent. 'Methodist' was one current taunt; 'canting hypocrite' was another for any youngster who would dare to acknowledge God. However, he, with several others, as eminent in their several professions afterward as he was in his, outbraved the taunt. Without being ostentatious, they were faithful to their convictions, and regularly met in one of the sleeping-rooms of the Charter-house for religious purposes. Sermons were read by them with one another, and conversations ensued upon the reading, as to the bearing of the truth upon their own character and conduct; and 'Old Phlos' became more and more grounded and settled in his resolution to fear God."

* In his Biographical Sketch of Sir Henry Havelock, K.C.B. Third Edition. 1858.

Yet, Havelock's fear of God was neither doleful nor dismal: he could cultivate that, and read Greek and Latin with any of his associates: "he could search the Scriptures and pray to God, and yet do anything that it was manly or virtuous to do, either in the play-ground or elsewhere. And there was nothing manly or virtuous that he was not all the more ready to do because in simplicity and godly sincerity he walked with God. As with so many others, the religious impressions of Havelock were traceable to the influence and efforts of his mother when he was a little boy. It was her custom to assemble her children for reading the Scriptures and prayer in her own room. Henry was always of the party whenever he was at home, and in course of time he was expected to take the reading, which he generally did. It impressed him; and under these pleasant circumstances he knew, like Timothy, the Holy Scriptures from a child."

Under Dr. Raine, Havelock mastered the Greek and Latin classics, and throughout his after-life, as opportunity offered, he took great delight in keeping up his acquaintance with the great models of antiquity, the effect of which may be traced in the perspicuity and vigor of his own style. In 1811, Havelock reached the sixth form; in August, the learned and accomplished Dr. Raine died, and was succeeded by Dr. Russell; in December following, Havelock quitted the Charter-house.*

Havelock had now a profession to choose, and he was advised to enter as a student at one of the inns of court, with the view of preparing for the law. In 1814, accordingly, he became a pupil of the celebrated special pleader, Chitty, and there formed an intimacy with his fellow-student, afterward Sir Thomas Talfourd. Mr. Marshman relates, such was their congeniality of habits, that when they left the chambers of Chitty, they beguiled many an hour in walking on Westminster Bridge; "but their conversation was of other matters than the pleas of the Crown, and turned much oftener on the beauties of poetry than upon the contents of musty parchments. Havelock used to observe in after-life that the last time they took their stroll on the bridge, when he was about to embrace the military profession, Talfourd noticed the placid progress of the stream

---

* He was one of the most quiet boys in the school. At the recent meeting of the Liverpool Collegiate Institution, Mr. Gladstone remarked that Havelock's case disproved the vulgar notion that there is a natural antagonism between corporeal and mental excellence, and that those who are fond of manly sports are rarely good scholars. Thus, Havelock, when at the Charter-house, "used to stand looking on while others played, and his general meditative manner procured for him the name of 'Philosopher,' subsequently diminished to 'Old Philos'—"yet," added Mr. Gladstone, "he is now distinguishing himself by a temper, a courage, an activity, a zeal, a consistency, and a dogged and dauntless resolution, equal at least to any that England has produced this century."

under the arches, and repeated with ecstacy that line of Wordsworth—

"The river glideth at its own sweet will."

But the law was not the sphere for a man of Havelock's temperament. The tastes of his family were military: his brother William, described by Napier as "one of the most chivalrous officers in the service" during the Peninsular war, obtained for Henry a commission, in 1815.

"Under these circumstances," says the Rev. Mr. Brock, "Havelock's destination in life was changed and definitely fixed. He saw an opportunity of making his way honorably, of which, through the reverses in his family fortunes, he felt bound to take advantage; and having no scruples about the compatibility of war with Christianity, he became a soldier. He exchanged the pen for the sword. Instead of giving himself up to Blackstone, he took up Vattel for careful study. When he would have had to devote attention to 'cases,' he came to write 'dispatches.' For a Generalship rather than for a Judgeship was he henceforward a competitor. His fellow-student at special pleading rose to be Mr. Justice Talfourd, of the Common Pleas. He rose to be gazetted as Sir Henry Havelock, of Lucknow." *

He had resolved to go to India, whither he proceeded in 1823; here he was soon recognized as a man who would do what was right, and feared nothing. Havelock was accustomed to regard his transference to India as the most critical epoch of his existence; and the reason is thus recorded in his own memoranda—in which he is never mentioned but in the third person:

"A far more important event, as regarded the interests of the writer, ought to have been recorded whilst narrating the events of 1823, for it was while he was sailing across the wide Atlantic toward Bengal that the spirit of God came to him with its offers of peace and mandate of love, which, though for some time resisted, were received, and at length prevailed. There was wrought that great change in his soul which has been productive of unspeakable advantage to him in time, and he trusts has secured him happiness through eternity."

---

* "Not to be overlooked," says the Rev. Mr. Brock, "is the memorable death of the two men so many years afterward; the one on the bench at Stafford, whilst right eloquently pleading for greater sympathy between rich and poor; the other in camp at Lucknow, exhausted by his exertions for relieving helpless women and children from disgrace and death."—*Biographical Sketch*, page 17.

APPENDIX.

UNIVERSITY HONORS.

DURING the printing of this volume, the Author's attention was drawn to a very able and interesting inquiry, in the *Journal of Psychological and Mental Pathology*, New Series, No. IX.—January, 1858. This paper, entitled "Body and Mind," is from the pen of the Editor, Dr. Forbes Winslow, by whose permission is reprinted the following important Return, made in order to correct the very prevalent mistake in supposing that men who have attained great distinction and high honors at our two English Universities, do not, in after-life, occupy the most eminent positions at the Bar, on the Bench, and in the Senate. First, as to

OXFORD.—Earl of Eldon, English Prize Essay, 1771; Lord Tenterden (Lord Chief Justice of the King's Bench), English Essay, 1780, Latin verse, 1784; Sir W. E. Taunton (Judge in Court of King's Bench), English Essay, 1793; J. Phillimore (Professor of Civil Law), English Essay, 1798; Sir C. E Gray (Chief Justice of Bengal), English Essay, 1808; Sir J. T. Coleridge (Judge in Court of Queen's Bench), English Essay, 1813, Latin verse, 1810, Latin Essay, 1813, 1st class Classics, 1812; Herman Merivale (Professor of Political Economy), English Essay, 1830, 1st class Classics, 1827 ; Roundell Palmer (Deputy Steward of the University), Latin Essay, 1835, Latin verse, 1831, English verse, 1832, 1st class Classics, 1834; Lord Colchester, Latin verse, 1777 ; Sir J. Richardson (Judge in Common Pleas), Latin verse, 1792; Sir Christopher Puller (Chief Justice at Calcutta), Latin verse, 1794; G. K. Rickards (Professor of Political Economy), English verse, 1830, 2d class Classics, 1833; Nassau W. Senior (Professor of Political Economy), 1st class Classics, 1811; Sir Richard Bethell (Attorney-General, University Counsel), 1st class Classics, 1818 ; Honorable J. C. Talbot (Deputy High Steward), 1st class Classics, 1825 ; Travers Twiss (Regius Professor of Civil Law), 2d class Classics, 1830.

CAMBRIDGE.—Sir F. Maseres (Baron, Exchequer), 4th Wrangler, 1752, Senior Medalist; Sir Elijah Impey (Chief Justice, Fort William, Bengal), 2d Senior Optime, 1756, Senior Medalist; Sir J Wilson (Judge, Common Pleas), Senior Wrangler, 1761; Lord Alvanley (Chief Justice, Common Pleas), 12th Wrangler, 1766; the late Lord Ellenborough (Chief Justice, King's Bench), 3d Wrangler, 1771, Senior Medalist; Sir S. Lawrence (Judge, Common Pleas), 7th Wrangler, 1771; Sir H. Russell (Judge in India), 4th Senior Optime, 1772 ; the late Lord Manners (Chancellor of Ireland), 5th Wrangler, 1777; Chief Justice Warren, of Chester, 9th Wrangler, 1785; the late John Bell, Senior Wrangler, 1786, Senior Smith's Prizeman : Sir J Littledale (Judge in Court of Queen's Bench), Senior Wrangler, 1787, Senior Smith's Prizeman ; Lord Lyndhurst (late Lord Chancellor), 2d Wrangler, 1794, Junior Smith's Prizeman ; Sir John Beckett (Judge Advocate), 5th Wrangler, 1795; the late Sir John Williams (Judge, Queen's Bench), 18th Senior Optime, 1798 ; the late Sir N. C. Tindal (Chief Justice, Common Pleas), 8th Wrangler, 1799, Senior Medalist ; the late Sir L. Shadwell (Vice-Chancellor of England), 7th Wrangler, 1800, Junior Medalist ; Starkie (Downing Professor of Law, University Counsel), Senior Wrangler, 1803, Senior Smith's Prizeman ; Lord Wensleydale, 5th Wrangler, 1803, Senior Medalist; the late Sir

T. Coltman (Judge, Common Pleas), 13th Wrangler, 1803; Lord Chief Baron Pollock, Senior Wrangler, 1806, Senior Smith's Prizeman; Lord Langdale, Senior Wrangler, 1808, Senior Smith's Prizeman; the late Baron Alderson, Senior Wrangler, 1809, Senior Smith's Prizeman and Senior Medalist; Sir W. H. Maule (Judge, Common Pleas), Senior Wrangler, 810, Senior Smith's Prizeman; Baron Platt (Exchequer), 5th Junior Optime, 810; Chambers (Judge of Supreme Court, Bombay), 5th Wrangler, 1811; Lord Cranworth, 17th Wrangler, 1812; Mirehouse (Author of Law of Tithes, and Common Serjeant of City of London), 13th Senior Optime, 1812; Sir J. Romilly (Downing Professor of Law, and Professor of Law, University College, London), 4th Wrangler, 1813; Vice-Chancellor Kindersley, 4th Wrangler, 1814; Sir B. H. Malkin (Chief Justice of Prince of Wales's Island), 3d Wrangler, 1818; Lord Justice Turner, 9th Wrangler, 1819; the late R. C. Hildyard (Queen's Counsel), 12th Senior Optime, 1823; Mr. John Cowling, Q.C., M.P. (University Counsel, and Deputy High Steward), Senior Wrangler, 1824, Senior Smith's Prizeman; Vice-Chancellor Wood, 24th Wrangler, 1824; Vice-Chancellor Parker, 7th Wrangler, 1825; Mr. Loftus T. Wigram, Q.C. (M.P. for University), 8th Wrangler, 1825; Chief Justice Martin (New Zealand), 26th Wrangler, 1829, 3d in 1st class Classics, and Junior Medalist.

DUBLIN —'795, Sir T. Lefroy (Chief Justice of Queen's Bench), gold medal; '800, Sir J. L. Foster (Judge, Common Pleas), M.P. for University, 1807), gold medal; 1802, P C. Crampton (Queen's Counsel, Judge, Queen's Bench), gold medal; 1803. F. Blackburne (Lord Chancellor of Ireland), gold medal; 1811, R. H Greene (Baron of Exchequer), gold medal; 1823, J. H. Monahan (Chief Justice, Common Pleas), gold medal.

TRIPOS.

The original *Tripos*, from which the Cambridge class lists have derived their names, was a three legged stool, on which, on Ash-Wednesday, a bachelor of one or two years' standing (called therefrom the Bachelor of the Stool) used formerly to take his seat, and play the part of a public disputant in the quaint proceedings which accompanied admission to the degree of B.A. In course of time, the name was transferred from the stool to him that sat on it, and the disputant was called the *Tripos*; thence it passed to the *day* when the stool became a post of honor; then to the *lists* published on that day, containing the seniority of commencing B.A.'s arranged according to the pleasure of the Proctors; and, ultimately, it obtained the enlarged meaning now universally recognized, according to which it stands for the examination, whether in mathematics, classics, moral or physical science, as well as for the list by which the result of that examination is made known.—*Notes and Queries*, No. 117.

ST. PAUL'S SCHOOL FOUNDED. (Pages 48, 49.)

Among the *fasciculi* of Commemoration Addresses recited in praise of Dean Colet, the Founder of St. Paul's School, are entitled to special mention, "The number of the Fish," a lay, by the Rev. Dr. Kynaston, the High Master, illustrating Colet's prescribed number of scholars: "There shall be taught in the schole children of all nations indifferently, to the number of CLIII."—*Statutes*. Another of the learned High Master's Commemorations is entitled *Ipsum Audite*—"Hear ye Him;" Hymnus Gratulatorius super Fundatione D. Pauli Scholæ. In Latin and English Trochaic Verse, with Notes and Preface. Apposition, 1857.

The epigraph to this Hymn of Gratulation is as follows:
"Supra cathedram præceptoris sedet puer Jesus singulari opere, docentis gestu; quem totus grex, adiens scholam ac relinquens, hymno salutat. Et imm net Patris facies dicentis, *Ipsum audite:* nam hæc verba me auctore adscripsit."—*Erasmi Epistolæ.*

"Over the master's chair is set an image of the child Jesus, of admirable work, in the attitude of teaching; whom all the boys, on entering and leaving, salute with a hymn. And there is a representation of the Father, saying, *Hear ye Him:* these words he added by my advice."—*Letter of Erasmus on the Founding of St. Paul's School.*

Of St. Paul's, Knight, in his *Life of Colet,* states: "This noble impulse of Christian charity, in the founding of Grammar-schools, was one of the providential ways and means for bringing about the blessed Reformation; and it is therefore observable, that within thirty years before it, there were more Grammar-schools erected and endowed in England, than had been in three hundred years preceding."

Among the memorable things said of eminent Paulines is Archdeacon Tennison's tribute, in his Sermons preached before the scholars—to John, Duke of Marlborough, "who never besieged a town which he did not take, nor fought a battle which he did not win."

"But for St. Paul's School," said Lord John Russell, at the Apposition Banquet, 1846, "Milton's harp would have been mute and inglorious, and Marlborough's sword might have rusted in its scabbard."

GENERAL INDEX.

ABBOTT, G͟EORGE, Archbishop of Canterbury, 163.
Addison at Lichfield, Charter-house, and Oxford, 196; memories of, 196; Steele and Arbuthnot, 132, 133.
Aldgate Free Schools, 133
Alfred, birth of, 7; education of, 7; schools of, 8.
"Anatomy of Melancholy," the author of, 100.
Angers, Arthur Wellesley at, 258.
Anglo-Norman Schools, rise of, 21.
Anglo-Saxon Schools, rise of, 6.
Anne, literature in the reign of. 132.
Arbuthnot. his sound English, 133.
Archery, origin of, 9, 10.
Arnold, Dr. Thomas, his college associates, 294; head-master of Rugby, 92; at Oxford, 294; his love of Oxford, 294; his school reform, 295; at Winchester, 293.
Arrow, Silver, shooting for. at Harrow, 95.
Ascham, tutor to Lady Jane Grey, 78; his "Schoolmaster," 77; tutor to Queen Elizabeth, 77.,
Aubrey, John, schools in his times, 115; his schools in Wiltshire, 175
Augustan age of literature, 132.
Autobiographists, female, 126
Autograph of Dryden at Westminster School, 181.

Bacon, Lord, at Cambridge, 161; influence of his writings, 115 116.
Bacon, Roger, educational reformer, 26.
Baker's Chronicle, 110.
Balliol College, Oxford, boots forbidden to be worn at, 273.
Banks. Sir Joseph, at Harrow. Eton, and Oxford, 231; how he learnt botany, 232.
Barrow, Isaac, at Charter-house, 179.
Bartholomew, Saint, Schools, and the silver arrow, 59
Beaumont and Fletcher, educated, 89.
Bede, "the Wise Saxon," 6.
Bedford Free Grammar School, 74.
Bell and Lancaster, system of, 139.
Benefit of Clergy, 22.
Bible, the, and Edward VI., 67; translated by Wickliffe, 33; new translation of, by order of James I. 97.
Birmingham Free Grammar School, 73.
Blake, admiral, at Bridgwater and Oxford, 166
Blake, William, and the first Charity School, 127.
Bloomfield, Robert, his "Farmer's Boy," 253
Blues. eminent, 71.
Boating at Westminster and Eton, 86.
Bolingbroke, Lord, 134.

Books, the earliest. 11; early printed, 63; scarce at Oxford, 42
Boyer and Field, masters at Christ's Hospital, 276.
Boyle, the Hon. Robert, his education and love of science, 176.
Bradgate, Lady Jane Grey at, 78.
Brindley, how he taught himself mechanics, 217.
British games, early, 1.
British Museum established, 134, 135.
Britons, early education of, 1.
Brougham, Lord, education of, 246; on Public Education, 146.
Buchanan, tutor to James I., 96.
Bunyan, John, his school. boyhood, and favorite books. 177, 178, 179.
Burke, Edmund, at Baltimore and Dublin, 223, 224; his favorite authors, 225; and the Shackletons, 224.
Burleigh. Lord, at Cambridge, 153; his education, 69; his plan of study, 154.
Burns, Robert. "the Ayrshire plowman," 243; instructed by his father, 244; his love of reading, 243; his teacher, Murdoch. 245.
Burton, Robert, education of, 101.
Busby, Dr , his discipline at Westminster, 168; education at Westminster and Oxford, 167. 168; head-master of Westminster School, 84.
Butler Samuel, at Worcester and Cambridge, 171.
Bryon, Lord, his autobiography, 290; at Cambridge, 291; his early religious habits, 291; his first verse, 291; his lameness, 290; and Sir Robert Peel at Harrow, 291; "Byron's tomb," 292.

Cambridge, the sciences at, 119.
Cambridge University, fare in 1550, 156.
Cambridge University, rise of, 24.
Camden and Ben Jonson, 155.
Camden at Christ's Hospital and Westminster, 155.
Camden, Lord, at Eton and Cambridge. 213.
Canning, George, his literary tastes, 261; at Eton and Oxford, 260, 261.
Canterbury Schools, seventh century, 5.
Canute, King, a poet, 11.
Carew, Sir Peter, a truant, 80.
Carpenter, John, and the City of London School, 47.
Carthusians, influence, 104.
Caxton, the first English printer, education in his time, 150.
Charity Schools, rise of, 126.
Charles I., his accomplishments, 105; education of, 104; literature in his reign, 108.

20

Charles II incorporates the Royal Society, 122; Mathematical School, Christ's Hospital, 122; his patronage of letters, 121; visits Westminster School, 84
Charter of the Royal Society, 122.
Charter-house Poor Brethren, 104.
Charter-house School founded, 102.
Chatham, Lord, at Eton and Oxford, 207.
Chaucer, schools in the age of, 29.
Chelsea, Arthur Wellesley at, 256.
Chelsea, Sir Thomas More at, 62.
Chelsea College founded, 97.
Chivalrous education, system of, 55.
Christ's Hospital buildings, 70; founded by Edward VI., 68; Five-and-thirty years ago, by C Lamb, 275. 276.
Church schools, early, 22.
Churches, schools in, 39.
Clarendon, Lord, education of, 100; at Oxford and the Temple, 169. 170.
Clarendon Press, Oxford, established, 133.
Clerk, or "Clericus," 4.
Clergy, benefit of, 22.
Clergy, education of the, 4.
Clive, Lord, his daring boyhood, 220; at Madras, 220.
"Cocker's Arithmetic," 119.
Coke, Sir Edward, education of, 156; his legal studies, 159.
Coleridge, Samuel Taylor, at Cambridge, 270; at Christ's Hospital, 269; a glutton of books, 270.
Colet, Dean, founds St. Paul's School, 49.
Collins, William, poet, at Winchester and Oxford, 218, 219
Colleges, object of, 46.
Comines, Philip de, his character of Henry VII., 59.
Conveyancing, Anglo-Saxon, 4.
Cook, Sir Anthony, and his four learned daughters, 79.
Cook, Captain, education of on board ship, 221.
"Cotter's Saturday Night," the, by Burns, 246.
Cowley, "Of Myself," 173; at Westminster, 172.
Cowper at Market-street and Westminster, 226; his recollections of the play-ground, 227.
Cranmer, boyhood of, 65; godfather to Edward VI., 65.
Crichton, the Admirable, at Edinburgh, and his career, 89, 161. 162.
"Criss-cross Row, the," 143.
Crofts, Sir R., tutor of Edward VI., 51.
Cromwell, Oliver, boyhood and education, 120; at Cambridge, 120; at Huntingdon, 120.
Croyland Abbey, ruins, schools, etc., 17.
Curll castigated by the Westminster boys, 185.
Curtain tradition at Westminster School, 83.

Danes, the destroyers of learning, 11.
Davy, or Davie, Adam, 28.
Davy, Sir Humphry, his amusements, 277; his childhood, 277; obtains heat from ice, 279; at Penzance, 277; poetry, 278; safety-lamp, 281; studies, 287; in medicine and chemistry, 280; President of the Royal Society, 281; at the Royal Institution, 284.

Defoe at Stoke Newington, 123.
Disputations of the Anglo-Norman schools, 21.
Drayton, Michael, education of, 89.
Druids, schools of the, 2; their system, 2.
Dryden's cut autograph at Westminster, 84; his studies and works, 181; at Tichmarsh, Westminster, and Cambridge, 180.
"Dulce Domum" at Winchester, 32.
Dullness of Sir Dudley North, 188.
Dullness of Waller, 166.
Duns Scotus, 28.
Dunstan, St., the scholar of Glastonbury, 10.

Education, Central Society of, established, 146;. good in the seventeenth century, 108 : at home, 39 ; National Board of, 140 ; public, Sir T Moore, on, 63; grant by Parliament, 146.
Edward I., scholars in his reign, 28.
Edward II , education of, 27.
Edward III , his accomplishments, 28.
Edward IV., and his tutors. 50.
Edward V. in Ludlow Castle, 52.
Edward VI , boyhood and learning of, 65 ; founds Christ's Hospital, 68 ; his journal, 66; his tutors, 52.
Edward's, King, Schools, 72.
Edward the Black Prince, scholarship of, 30.
"Eikon Basilike," authorship of, 106
Eldon, Lord, and Dr. Johnson, at Oxford, 238.
Eldon, Lord, at Newcastle and Oxford, 236, 238.
Eldon School, at Vauxhall, 238.
Elizabeth, Queen, education of, 76; founds Westminster School, 82; statesmen, poets, and dramatists of her reign, 88.
English language, formation of the, 12; settlement of, 26.
English, sound writing in the 17th century, 126.
Essays, Lord Bacon's, 110.
Eton College, building of, 44; founded by Henry VI., 42; completed by Henry VII., 44; expenses, early, at, 45.
Eton Montem, 45.
Etonians, eminent, 46.
Evelyn, John, at Wotton, Eton, and Oxford, 173; memoirs and diary, 174.
Evelyn, Mrs., 128.

Falkland, Lord, his character, 170.
Female education in 1871, 40; school of More, 62.
Fergusou, James, teaches himself the classics and astronomy, 212.
Ferguson, Robert, at Newington, 124.
Flogging in schools, 81.
Foot-ball at Rugby, 92.
Free schools, rise of, 126.
French in the age of Chaucer, 30.
Fuller, Thomas, his memory, 102; his "Schoolmaster," 102.

Games at Harrow School, 94.
Gay, John, at Barnstaple, 202.
Gay, Swift, and Pope, their friendship, 202
George I. and George II., reigns of, 184.
George III., education of, 35.
George IV., education of, 144; his patronage of literature, 145.

General Index.

Gibbon at Kingston, Westminster, and Oxford, 229, 230.
Gifford, William, scholar and critic, 239.
Glastonbury scholars 10
Gloucester, Sunday Schools first founded at, 138.
Goodman, Dean, and Dr. Andrews, Westminster masters, 82.
"Goody Two Shoes," authorship of, 271.
Gower, the poet, and Richard II, 35.
Grammar School, the first, 48; of the 17th century, 115.
Grammarian and poet laureate, an eminent one, 59.
Gray at Eton and Cambridge, 215; ode on Eton College, 2 6,
Gray and West's letters, 215, 216.
Gresham College founded, 88.
Grey, Lady Jane, and her schoolmaster, Roger Ascham, 78.
Gunter's Scale, 1 8.

Hale, Sir Matthew, at Oxford and Lincoln's-inn, 170; his plan of instruction, 109.
Halstead, Miss, her lives of Richard III. and Margaret Beaufort, 58, 59
Hastings, Warren, at Westminster, 228, 229.
Harrovians, eminent, 95.
Harrow school buildings, 94, 95; foundation of, 93.
Harper, Sir W, and the Bedford Grammar School, 75.
Harvey, Dr. William, education of, 90.
Havelock, Sir Henry, at the Charter-house School, 104
Henry I., education of, 18.
Henry II., his love of letters, 19.
Henry III., education of, 26.
Henry IV., his accomplishments, 36.
Henry V. at Queen's College, Oxford, 36; his college associates, 38.
Henry VI., childhood and youth of, 41; his education, 42.
Henry VII., troubled boyhood of, 56; was he an Etonian? 58
Henry VIII, early life and character of, 60; education and accomplishments of, 61.
Henry, Prince, education of, 87; house of, in Fleet-street, 98; his patronage of learned men, 99.
Henry, Philip, at Westminster, 182.
Herbert, Lord, in Shropshire, 105; his plan of education, 1 8
Highgate Grammar School, 127.
Hill, Lord, his affectionate disposition, 267; at Chester, 268; at Waterloo, 269.
Holbein's Charter Picture at Christ's Hospital, 69
Hooker, Richard, at Heavitree and Oxford, 157, 158.
Hornbook of the 18th century, 143; history of the, 140.
Horrocks, the astronomer, 119.
Hunter, John, want of education, 222.
Hutchinson, Mrs., 126.
Hymns, Morning and Evening, by Bishop Ken, 187; Dr. Watts's, 198.

Ingulphus at Westminster, 17.

James I., education of, 95, literature of his reign, 99.

James I. of Scotland, musical education of, 39.
James II., boyhood and education of, 124; his governor, 124.
John of Salisbury, 19.
John, troubled reign of, 25.
Johnson, Dr., and George III., 138; at Lichfield, Stourbridge, and Oxford, 207, 208, 209, 210; memorials of Johnson at Lichfield, 211.
Jones, Sir William, at Harrow and Oxford, 232, 233; his plan of study, 234.
Jonson, Ben, education of, 90
Judd, Sir A., at Tunbridge School, 74.

Ken, Bishop, at Winchester, 185; at Oxford, 186; his Morning and Evening Hymns, 187.
King's College, Cambridge, founded by Henry VI. 46.
King's College and School, London, founded, 145.

Ladies, learned English, 79; in the reign of Charles I., 108.
Lamb, Charles, at Christ's Hospital, 274.
Lanfranc, his schools, 16.
Latimer, boyhood of, 64.
Latin idiom in the reign of James I., 99.
Latinity in the 2th century, 20.
Lawrence, Sir Thomas's precocity, 254.
"Learning is better than house and land," 9.
Lectures at Gresham College, 88.
Letters, early English, 38.
Library, the King's, in the British Museum, 137.
Library of Richard of Bury, 37.
Lichfield Free Grammar-school, 78.
Literary Fund, the, founded, 145.
Literature of the 7th century, 125.
Locke at Westminster and Oxford, 114; education of, 114; his system of education, 113; his "Thoughts on Education," 115; on the Understanding, 114.
Logarithms, invention of, 117.
London University College and School founded, 145.
Lovell, Lord, and Richard III., 56.
Ludlow Castle, Edward IV. and V. in, 50, 50; Milton and Butler at, 50
Lyon, John, the founder of Harrow School, 93.

Macaulay, Lord, his account of Warren Hastings, 228, 229
"Manners makyth Man," 149.
Mansfield, Lord, at Westminster, 206.
Manuscript books, costliness of, 51.
Marlborough, the Great Duke of, at St. Paul's School, 194.
Marvell at Hull and Cambridge. 175.
Mary, Queen, her infancy and childhood, 75.
Mary, wife of William III., 131.
Mary, Queen of Scots, education of, 76.
Mathematical boys at Christ's Hospital, 71, 122.
Merchant Taylors' School founded, 86; scholars, eminent, 87.
Milner, the brothers Joseph and Isaac, 238.
Milton, education of, 111; his love of letters, 112; his system of education, 112, 113.
Monastic schools, 7th century, 5.

Monitorial system of Bell and Lancaster, 139.
Monks, the transcribers and illuminators of MSS., 12.
More, Sir Thomas, boyhood and rise of, 151; at Oxford, 152; school of, 62.
Morning'on, Lord, his musical taste, 250.
Morton, Cardinal, and Sir T. More, 151.
Musical education, early, 40.

Napier's Bones, or Rods, 118.
Nelson, Lord, his schools in Norfolk, 240; he first goes to sea, 242.
Newcastle, the Duchess of, 126.
News, letter of, 1701-10, 111.
Newspapers, their educational aid, 111; introduced, 110.
Newton's birthplace, 190; at Grantham and Cambridge, 91, 192.
Nobility, ill-educated, 61.
Nonconformist schools at Islington and Newington Green, 123
Norman French, 26.
"Novum Organum" of Lord Bacon, 117.
North, Sir Dudley, his adventures, 189.

"Old Phlos" at the Charter-house, 104, 293.
"Opus Majus" of Roger Bacon, 27.
Owen, Dame, her free schools, 127.
Oxford discipline, rigid, 81; poet laureate at, 69; the sciences at, 118; University, rise of, 23.

Paley, Archdeacon, at Giggleswick and Cambridge, 230; on teaching, 231.
Pancake custom on Shrove Tuesday, at Westminster School, 83.
Parr, Dr., at Harrow and Cambridge, 234, 235; on Tenderness to Animals, 235
Paston, Sir John, books for, 57; and Edward IV., 55; William, at Eton, 44.
Paul's, St., School, founded, 48.
Paulines, eminent, 50.
Peacham's "Complete Gentleman," 107.
Peel, Sir Robert, at Harrow, 288; at Oxford, 289; in Yorkshire, 288.
Penn, William, at Chigwell and Oxford, 192.
Peter of Blois, 19.
"Pilgrim's Progress," the, 177-179.
Pitt, Mr., boyhood of, 252.
Plays at Westminster School, 86.
"Pons Asinorum," 27.
Pope, childhood of, 199; paraphrase, by, 201; and Prior, 133; schools and self-tuition, 198, 199, 200; in Windsor Forest, 200.
Porson at Happesburgh, Eton, and Cambridge, 246, 247, 248; his classical annotations and emendations, 245; in Essex-court, Temple, 249; his habits and character, 249.
Primer and Hornbook, the, 140.
Printing, introduction of, 53.
Prior, Matthew, at Westminster and Cambridge, 195.
Psalms of David, paraphrased by Lord Bacon, 117.

Raikes, Robert, founder of Sunday Schools, 138.
Raleigh, Sir Walter, education of, 89.
Recorde, Robert, 117.
Reformation, schools before the, 73.

Revolution, the, schools at the time of, 127.
Richard I., the poet king, 22
Richard II., education of, 35; and Gower, 36.
Richard III, childhood and education of, 64; at Middleham Castle, 66
Ridley, Bishop, and Edward VI., 68.
Roman-British Schools, 3
Roman Education in England, 3.
Roper, Margaret, More's daughter, 63.
Royal Society Incorporated, 122.
Royal Society of Literature, 145.
Rugby gold medal, 93; school, 90.
Rugbeians, eminent, 93.

Saxon language, the, 12.
School, the Blue Coat, 70; Charter-house, founded, 102; City of London, 47; St. Clement's Charity, 130; Eldon, at Vauxhall, 289; Eton founded, 43; Grammar, the first, 48; Harrow, founded, 93; Highgate Grammar, 127; King's College, London, 145; Ladies' Charity, 130; Lanfranc's, 16; London University, 145; Mercers', 48; Merchant Taylors', founded, 86, 87; Milton's, 112; Sir Thomas More's, 62; Rugby founded. 90; Tennison's, 131; Westminster, founded, 81; Winchester, founded. 31.
Schools in the age of Chaucer, 29; Alfred's, 7; Anglo-Norman, 21; Anglo-Saxon, 6; Canterbury, 5; Church, 22; in churches, 38; Croyland Abbey, 17; Druid, 2; Early British, 1; Free or Charity, rise of, 126, 127; Glastonbury, 10; Kensington Grammar, 129; King Edward's, at Birmingham, Lichfield, Tunbridge, and Bedford, 72; Monastic, 6; Nonconformist, 123; Owen's Free, 127; Parochial, early, 38; Roman British, 3; in the 17th century, 115; Sunday, founded, 138; Westminster, 129.
"Schoolmaster, the Good," by Fuller, 101.
"Schoolmaster, the, by Ascham, 77, 78.
Schoolmasters of the 7th century, 175.
Scientific Treatises first in English, 117.
Scott, Sir Walter, his academical attainments 265; at Bath and Edinburgh, 263; his first verses, 265; sees Robert Burns, 265; and Mr. Jeffrey, 267; his lameness, 262; his love of reading, 266; his poetry, 267; at Sandy-knowe, 262, 263.
Scriptorium of the abbeys, 12.
Scriveners in Chaucer's time, 29.
Selden, John, education of, 101.
Shakspeare, education of, 164; at Stratford Grammar-school, 164; a militiaman, 165.
Shenstone at Hales-Owen and Oxford, 213, 214; his "Schoolmistress," 213.
Sherborne, King's School at, 73.
Sheriff, Lawr, founds Rugby School, 91.
Sidney, Sir Philip, at Shrewsbury and Oxford, 89, 158; portrait of, 159, 160.
Society for the Propagation of the Gospel established, 132.
Society for Promoting Christian Knowledge established, 131, 132.
South, Dr., at Westminster, 184, 185.
Southey, Robert, his autobiography, 271; his first books, 272; at Bristol School, 272; and Coleridge, 274; at Corston, 272; his handwriting, 272; his love of Shakspeare, 272; his translations, 273; at Westminster and Oxford, 273.

Spenser at Cambridge, 90, 157.
Sports of the old London scholars, 19.
Steam-engine, Marquis of Worcester's, 123; James Watt's childhood, 283.
Stephen, education of, 9.
Stephenson, George, his clay engines, 282; a poor "cow-boy," 282; at his engine, 283; his first lesson, 283; his locomotives, 284; at a night school, 284; his safety-lamp, 284.
Stone, Edmund, how he taught himself mathematics, 202.
Stowell, Lord, 236; at Oxford, 237.
Sunday Schools established, 133.
Suppings in public during Lent at Christ's Hospital, 70.
Surrey, Lord, his boyhood and accomplishments, 153.
Sutton, Thomas, founds the Charter-house, 103.
Swimming in the Thames, Sir Dudley North's, 189.

Taylor, Jeremy, at Cambridge, 172.
Tennison's Library and School, 131.
Tenterden, Lord, Chief Justice, at Canterbury and Oxford, 252.
Testament, Lady Jane Grey's, 73.
Thomas a Becket, 19.
Trim, Wellington's school at, 256.
Truant punished, 16th century, 80.
Tunbridge Free Grammar School, 74.
Tusser, Thomas, at Eton, 173.

University education in Shakspeare's time, 165; expenses in the 13th century, 25.
Universities, rise of, 23.

Vegetius, the Duke of Marlborough's copy of, 194.
Vinny Bourne at Westminster, 227.

Waller at Market Wickham and Cambridge, 166, 167; his dullness, 166; in Parliament, 167.
Wantage, Alfred born at, 7; Jubilee, 7.
Warwick, Earl of, and Henry VI., 41.

Watt, James, sketch of, 283.
Watts, Dr. Isaac, his schools and educational works, 198, 199.
Wellesley, the Marquis, at Eton and Oxford, 250; his classical taste, and love of Eton, 251.
Wellington, Duke of, his "Dispatches," 259; his schools, 256
Wesley, John, his books and diary, 205; at the Charter-house and Oxford, 203; founds Methodism, 205; his management of time, 206.
Wesleys and Wellesleys, the, 203.
Westminster Abbey School, 83.
Westminster College founded, 81; Hall and Library, 85.
Westminster Scholar, a poor one. 85.
Westminster School, South ou, 184.
Westminsters, eminent, 84, 85.
Westminster Green, Blue, Grey, and Black Coat Schools, 129.
White, Henry Kirke, at Cambridge, 286; his early death, 286; at Nottingham, 285.
"Whole Duty of Man, the," 121.
Wickliffe translates the Bible, 33.
William the Conqueror, educated, 15.
William II., education of, 18.
William III., education of, 130.
William IV., education of, 145.
William of Wykeham, early fortunes of, 149; founds Winchester College, 31.
Winchester College, 31; school in Bishop Ken's time, 185.
Wolsey, Cardinal, his boyhood, 64.
Wooll, Dr., head-master at Rugby, 92.
Woolsthorpe manor-house, the birthplace of Newton, 191.
Wren, Sir Christopher, his scientific attainments, 183; at Westminster and Oxford, 182.
Wright, Thomas, M. A., on the English language, 14.
Writing, introduction of, 3; a test of education, 108.
Wyatt, Sir Thomas, his education and youth, 152.
Wykehamists, distinguished, 32, 33.

www.ingramcontent.com/pod-product-compliance
Lightning Source LLC
Chambersburg PA
CBHW030018240426
43672CB00007B/997